# THE IDENTITY PROJECT

# THE IDENTITY PROJECT

## THE UNMAKING OF A DEMOCRACY

Rahul Bhatia

Context

cntxt

Published by Context, an imprint of Westland Books, a division of Nasadiya Technologies Private Limited, in 2024

No. 269/2B, First Floor, 'Irai Arul', Vimalraj Street, Nethaji Nagar, Alapakkam Main Road, Maduravoyal, Chennai 600095

Westland, the Westland logo, Context and the Context logo are the trademarks of Nasadiya Technologies Private Limited, or its affiliates.



ISBN: 9789360458195

10 9 8 7 6 5 4 3 2 1



Typeset by Jojy Philip

Printed at Manipal Technologies Limited, Manipal

*To Richa, Rhea, Aanya and Dad:*
*Because it matters.*

# Contents

# Introduction

A decade or so ago, people I loved began to go mad.

There was a man I adored, a relative, who was funny even when he stood still. He emerged from his bathroom every morning in a banian and towel, his large face coated in shaving lather. Sometimes he wore sunglasses while he shaved, an act that made his brothers chuckle and his wife groan. Never could a straight reply be extracted from him, not about lunch, or where his children were, or what time he would return from the shop, or where the keys to the scooter were. I watched his stamina for turning everything into comic material in awe, and tried to match him, joke for joke, to establish our connection. So it was strange when he began to speak passionately about Muslims, arguing that they were less than human, and that India had to become a Hindu nation to save itself. Muslims had been absent from his conversations before, but now they were everywhere. He had decided he was oppressed, that he had been in hiding with his thoughts, and nothing could shake his conviction. Now he was full of dark notions whose paths led to danger, but he did not see it that way. The future he envisaged burgeoned with opportunity, and there was a jaunty optimism in his bearing that I recognised as triumphalism. He had aligned himself with the fortunes of a political party as if it was a sports team. His team was about to win the 2014 elections.

Before or after his man won—I cannot remember when—

his smiley-faced jokes acquired a touch of arsenic. He sent me edited video clips and invented headlines that depicted the country in twisted ways I did not recognise at all. It was clear that secularism represented a past he wanted to break with; one that included generations of flawed and corrupting leadership by the Congress party; the traitorous behaviour of liberals; and a compromised media. Not just politics, he wanted the nation-state rebuilt.

He picked up disparaging words that had become acceptable by dint of their unthinking repetition, and took pleasure in the discomfort they caused. Bristling at one, presstitute, I brought to his notice that the phrase and its implications included me. I wondered if reminders of our bond would bring him back, but those were early days, before it became clear that the condition was autoimmune, emerging from within. He made sure not to speak the word in my presence from then on, but there were other words ready to channel the feelings he had kept to himself. The vocabulary seemed to have one purpose: to strip people, ideas and expectations of their language and join new meaning to them. And as he unveiled this unsettling lexicon in waves, it came to feel like a project of deconstruction. Week after week, as the extent of his transformation became clearer, I felt him pulling away from my memory of his previous self. It was not so much a descent into paranoia as much as his having found peace.

Then another person I was fond of, who had not yet found success in business, became obsessed with Ayodhya, the site of the Babri masjid. He could not be shaken out of the belief that a temple for the god Ram had to be built on that very spot. It had nothing to do with him, but he insisted it was important. Then a relative took to calling Rahul Gandhi 'Pappu', a putdown that revealed an abdication of independent thought. An aunt's partner, a genial man who treated me to milkshakes and onion rings when I was small, told me one day to be wary of Muslims. 'They don't see themselves as Indians. Jaat hi alag hai.' They are made of something different, he said. My aunt would join in: 'You don't know. They're savages. I've seen what they're capable of.' Two thoughtful friends with kind hearts felt comfortable enough to talk about the howling from the 'mozzies' minarets near our home.

Eventually, this dispossession came closer. A relative who measured his life in the obligations he had fulfilled, who believed in carrying people along, who had never held any political opinions, much less strong ones, would tell me, when we met and talked sometimes, that the country needed a benevolent dictator, a strong leader. The phrases were interchangeable. Modi, then the chief minister of Gujarat, was the man he had in mind. I expressed reservations. 'But India is a big country,' he responded. 'It's not his fiefdom. Do you think he will be allowed to do what he wants if he becomes prime minister? It will not happen.' His confidence came not from a faith in India's institutions but from the belief that the country's systemic slowness would restrain a leader's worst impulses. We began to argue; I thought he was unwise, and he thought I was 'extra-smart'—a fool who thought himself wise. Once, during an argument, he became exasperated and said, 'Why don't you convert to Islam?' We kept our distance from each other for some time.

This played out in other families, with other sets of friends. Acquaintances reported, in confusion, that they too had lost family members, including parents, to the condition. No one really knew what they believed in. Our elders had raised us with values that they had themselves abandoned.

Like moisture that warps paper, something unseen was changing us. Reasonable people said worrying things about democracy and minorities, and began to amplify the triumphant messages of Modi's party. Trying to change their mind was pointless. For the Bharatiya Janata Party, to which Modi belonged, history was as much a priority as the present and future. It needed old injustices to remind its Hindu constituents of Muslim conquerors and the dangers they posed. That was where its power lay: in the narrative of eternal danger and vigilance. Our families heard these messages and made these concerns their own. Arguments would time-travel, hopping back centuries until a suitable villain, usually a Muslim, was found. It weathered my defiance. The people I loved were emboldened to reveal this new side of themselves all at once, armed with facts plucked from here and there, which they thrust like daggers in a fog. They had become true believers.

If it wasn't for these transformations, this book would probably not exist. There would be nothing to unravel, no language and ideology to interpret. But a new kind of India was emerging, and the old norms of secularism and equality—however flawed their execution—were being cast off. This unfamiliar country had begun to justify even murder if the occasion demanded it. I did not understand it, and so I tried to.

This book is a reported elegy, an investigative memoir, an attempt to see the roots of Hindutva, the unbending ideology of Hindu extremism. It follows riot victims, perpetrators and police (some names have been changed to protect sources). It examines structural weaknesses that allow governance to be hijacked by religious and commercial interests. It pieces together fragments of history to bring the present into focus. It looks into the surprising origins of India's identification project. It tries to find, as the book's main character asks, where the poison is coming from.

ONE

# AFTERMATH

# 1

# They Get No Respect

The man responsible for keeping India safe rose from his seat at 6.20 in the evening, holding a sheaf of papers that contained everything he wanted his adversaries to hear. It was only fair, seeing that he had listened to them go on for over six hours. Forty-four of them had spoken, each rising when the speaker called out their name from the well. Some of them began with the words—or a slight variation of—'I rise to oppose this Bill.' They used their allocated time to warn him of the profound mistake he was about to make.

One of them had said that the legislation he was introducing was ill-considered, and that it was destined to be struck down in court. He urged the man, the minister of home affairs, to reconsider what he was doing. 'Knowing this is unconstitutional, you're ramming through this Bill. This is a sad day. A small part of the Constitution is being wrecked by this Bill.' He demanded to know who would take responsibility for it, and dared the government to summon the Attorney General to explain the Bill's rationale.

Another opposition lawmaker disputed the basis of the Bill, and questioned the minister's understanding of India's past. He glared at the minister with contempt. 'I don't understand which history books the learned home minister has read, which authors he has consulted. What are you doing to the Constitution? You're blowing it to bits. What are your intentions? We've known what your intentions have been since 2014,' he shouted. With the lawmakers in the upper house of parliament he pleaded that the Bill would harm India's Muslims. 'It weakens the foundation of our culture, our beliefs, our ethos. It has consequences that you cannot even imagine. Those who have no idea of India cannot protect the idea of India.' Hands thumped tabletops in appreciation.

All along, the home minister, Amit Shah, sat slouching, with an arm extended along the back of his seat. He was impassive as he listened. He was rumoured to be so good at it that a newspaper attributed the Bharatiya Janata Party's victory in the general elections of 2014 partly to Shah's listening.

Now and then, Shah leaned forward and jotted down a few words on a sheet. Then, shortly after 6 p.m., he stood up while a turbaned steward hurried down the aisle with a glass of water for him. Shah looked around at his party members and opponents in parliament, and explained why he was introducing a refugee law. The ministers who sat behind him watched him closely, their arms raised to applaud the words they knew were coming from their leader, the one man who had Narendra Modi's ear.

Shah took his time, and spoke gently, with great patience. He explained to them, and to the country, what his Citizenship Amendment Bill would do for persecuted minorities from nations beside India. 'Right now, whether in Pakistan, Afghanistan, or Bangladesh, they have no rights,' he reasoned. 'They get no respect.' His amendment to citizenship laws would grant the oppressed a place 'to practise their religion and traditions with respect'. Not everyone could apply, he clarified. The sufferers had to be of Hindu, Jain, Buddhist, Sikh, Christian or Parsi faith. If they met the religious standard, and had arrived before 2015, refugees from the three countries could seek Indian citizenship. No justification was provided for the date; none was felt necessary.

He reminded his opponents from the Congress Party that the amendment would not have been necessary had India not been partitioned along religious lines in 1947. But Partition had happened, leaving minorities who had crossed the new border into Pakistan at the mercy of a frightened and vengeful majority. It was for the refugees among them that he had introduced the bill, he said; Indian Muslims had nothing to fear.

He did not assuage the politicians' concerns, but instead attributed gamesmanship to them. 'Do your politics,' he told the lawmakers across the aisle, 'but I appeal to you that these are highly sensitive matters, and these sorts of fires tend to burn our own house down.'

Shortly after he expounded on his legislation, the Citizenship Amendment Bill became the Citizenship Amendment Act. It was passed, as it was expected to, on the basis of the Bharatiya Janata Party's comfortable majority in parliament.

The legislation's meaning was not left to chance. Before long, online groups, forums, social media and the news at night were discussing its merits, and Shah announced that 1.3 billion Indians had supported his endeavour, implying that there was no opposition, and no reason for anybody to oppose a law whose only purpose was to comfort the afflicted.

# 2

# Tin Roof Refuge

The present did nothing for Ali, for he was a student of history. He had kept away from politics in life generally but also specifically on campus at Delhi University and then Jamia Millia Islamia University, he said, as explanation for how he had failed to register the events of 11 December 2019. In class and on the streets, however, he began to hear about it from his friends and his university teachers, and an unsettling feeling was transmitted to him through these interactions, namely that the refugee Act was only one part of the story, and that if he understood the full thing, he would see its menace. He heard that it was not designed for refugees but for Muslims within the country, and that its true intent was to leave them without a country.

Students were preparing for their exams, or in the middle of taking them, but minds were wandering; as world-ending as their assessments were, something even more apocalyptic was occurring. Across Jamia, people read the Constitution's preamble to remind each other of what they had been assured under the terms of the contract. Ali began to listen to what was being said around him, and what was being read. He paid attention particularly to Shah's words and understood from them that the legislation was discrimination cloaked in benefaction: for all the talk of granting refuge to persecuted minorities, the offer was contingent on faith—it did not apply to Muslims. He did not believe Shah's explanation that the law was evidence of India's generosity, and that Muslims were excluded only because there was no way they could possibly be minorities in Muslim countries. The small-heartedness of the distinction struck Ali as petty. Religion had played little role in the granting and refusal of citizenship until then. But now it had become state policy to choose who to help based on religious choice.

As Ali spoke to friends and teachers who had begun to think through the CAA's implications, he understood that the refugee law was not all that Shah had planned. Some months before, Shah had described how matters would unfold. 'Understand the chronology,' he was filmed saying—first would come the CAA, then something called the National Register of Citizens. They went together.

The CAA gave refuge, while the NRC took it away.

The register was a database of citizens that had been introduced in the eastern state of Assam, which shared a porous border with Bangladesh. It was an accounting of who belonged, and who wanted to belong. In theory, paperwork demonstrating that their parents had been citizens of India since at least 1971 was enough to merit inclusion on the list. That was the year of Bangladesh's liberation, the year of the last great migration into India, when ten million or so crossed the eastern border into West Bengal and Assam. But inclusion was dependent on locating and producing decades-old identification documents that often preceded the searcher's birth. The requirements were stringent: names and addresses had to match the official record. If there were errors, either by oversight or the form-filler's hand, their citizenship was deemed suspect. If a neighbour challenged a person's inclusion on the list, proof of citizenship was required once more. This was not simply a bureaucracy's routine suspicion, the kind of nit-picking one could expect at the motor vehicles department, but an immigration officer's exclusionary eye turned on citizens.

As a consequence of the exercise, four million of Assam's thirty-two million residents were left stateless (the number was later halved to 1.9 million). Residents scrambled to find papers that would prove they belonged to the land, travelling hundreds of kilometres to foreigners' tribunals inclined to mark most people as suspect. Watching all this, and seeing that over a million Hindus were excluded from the list, the chief minister of Assam, a man from Shah's own party, pleaded for the exercise to be cancelled.

Ali took some time to arrive at enlightenment, but eventually he did: Shah had said the NRC would happen across India. At first, every citizen would face the same inconveniences as the residents of Assam. They would scramble to find unimpeachable documents, rush to prove they were of the country, even if their parents and grandparents had been citizens, even if they had the right of the soil. A government officer would then decide on what was supposed to have been a settled matter. And even if safeguards were put in place, the relationship between the country and the citizen would hinge on the officer's decision to be benevolent or unkind. It would turn people stateless, in effect transforming them into refugees.

The chronology had to be understood, Shah had said. His Citizenship Amendment Act would become a safety net for Hindus, Jains, Buddhists, Sikhs, Christians and Parsis excluded from the NRC, showing them a path to citizenship once more. The only people not offered the CAA's protections were India's two hundred million Muslims. And so, no matter for how long they had paid their taxes, and travelled on an Indian passport, and voted—and even if they hadn't done so, but had been secure in the knowledge that they belonged—the register and the law would combine to introduce insecurity, reminding them that, if a Muslim's citizenship became doubtful, their future in India would be very different from their past. There was talk of seizing property and revoking the right to vote.

On 13 December 2019, two days after Shah had stood up in parliament, the teachers' association at Jamia—'It's like Oxford University for a Muslim kid from Bihar,' a student told me—sent out a call for participation in a protest after the Friday afternoon prayers. They summoned students and teachers to Gate 7 of the university's campus, near a statue of the Urdu poet Ghalib, where the faculty of social sciences was located. 'We react to anything that impinges on Muslim identity,' a teacher said.

After the afternoon prayers, hundreds came. The teachers were sensitive to appearances, and they emphasised that this meeting was not about the government, only about the Act, the effects of which could be seen in Assam. The social science teachers were joined by professors from the university's Centre for North East Studies. The teachers shared how their Assamese students had left for home and sold their belongings to raise the money they needed to be put on the citizenship list. They talked about the panic in the state, the detention centres where not-citizens were placed, the long distances and treacherous terrain people travelled to reach citizenship hearings, the sudden summons that provided a day's notice. They talked about the heartlessness behind it, and said that it would affect the poorest most of all.

Outside Jamia, the police stood in the cold and braced for trouble. At some point they fired tear gas at students, and students and faculty members threw the canisters right back at them. The Delhi police answered to Shah. The police batons stung harder than at any protest the students had seen before, and the blows were not always below the knee, as a court had ordered. The students, in turn, picked up stones. Ali joined the crowds. 'It was either this or the detention centres,' he said.

The police had blocked Jamia's gates with yellow metal barriers about five feet high, hemming in the students and the teachers. To the evident surprise of the police, the protestors jumped over them.

'People called it a protest to break India. But there were Hindu ceremonies, and people read from the Guru Granth Sahib,' the student said. After tussling for four or five hours on the road outside, a senior policeman at the Jamia outpost arrived with a message for the university proctor, 'Your children are animals. Take them back in.' Ali had not heard the words, but his friends had; he felt encouraged when he realised that the police could not tame the students. 'They weren't able to dislodge these two to three thousand students. How are they going to remove two hundred million of us?' he said.

That night, a charismatic student leader from Jawaharlal Nehru University, the capital's pre-eminent institution, stood at Jamia in a sleeveless down jacket, his hair falling over his face, his hands buried deep in his pockets. 'For years they have sent hundreds of thousands of Muslims away. They say things like, "your father's brother stays there, so go there",' Sharjeel Imam said. 'There', in this case, was Pakistan, or Bangladesh. Anywhere but India. 'Is the worth of any human being less than any other?' Imam shouted at the crowd of men gathered around.

Imam wanted them to bring India to a halt by means of a 'chakka jam' wherever they could, an immobilisation so complete that it could not go ignored. 'Isn't it in the Quran that if someone tries to remove you from your home, you should fight and remove them from their home? Is it not?' People nodded, and someone shouted that god was great. Imam's voice strained.

'How do we organise?' someone asked.

'It's simple. Who will jam the system? Who will not jam the system? Yes, or no? It's that simple,' he said. It dawned on Imam that they were looking for a leader. But civil disobedience could not be organised centrally. It would be more effective if a million people devised a million different ways to mess things up. He told them to look within, and not follow political leaders or student associations: 'They're all pimps,' he said. 'Remove from your mind any inferiority complex. Do not look to them for approval,' he said, referring to Hindus. 'Are you seeing the consequences of seeking approval? Look at what has happened in the last seventy years! Can you see any approval?' Imam was describing the lived experience of India's Muslims since independence. The government's own surveys showed that even the most oppressed class of Hindus was more prosperous than Muslims.

Ali went home feeling wiser and emboldened. But parents are parents, and his mother said, 'Are you mad? Why do you have to go? Let others protest.' But children are also children, and so he went back the next day. Nothing much happened.

By the time Ali and his friends reached Jamia by train late on the afternoon of 15 December, he noticed that the road outside the university was nearly deserted. The police had removed the barricades outside. Something had occurred there, he thought, noticing debris on the street, the smoke in various places, and the injuries on the homeless man who usually slept below the metro station. Ali walked on with his friends, and at some point he saw armed forces in a crouch. 'Do you know the movie *300*? It was like that,' he said. He remembered the way they clustered around each other in a defensive position. Further on, he saw the students. He thought there were eight or nine thousand students marching down the long road outside the university. They kept walking and chanting until they encountered new barricades and riot police, who appeared behind them. It was there, where the road had narrowed, that the police let them have it from two sides.

Those at the front of the protest received a beating and turned back. The rear continued to press forward, unaware of the barricades and the assault. The footage from the protest was shaky. Broken and fragmented calls for help were posted on every platform. The ferocity of the violence surprised the students. 'I don't know what changed,' a student told me, trying to understand the police reaction. 'Nothing about the protests had changed.'

A soft-spoken student named Minhajuddin was in the section for postgraduates in the Ibn Sina block, an old library in Jamia, that evening. He had heard about the violence outside, but kept working. It had nothing to do with him. He did not do politics. The room was usually full, but there was plenty of room due to the protests. At around six-thirty in the evening, he heard a commotion downstairs from inside the building. Windows were being shattered, and students were screaming. The students told each other that the police had entered the building. They bolted the library door and hid in corners, covering their faces. 'Fifteen or twenty' police in riot gear broke in anyway, he said. He couldn't tell who they were, except that they wore 'army colours, helmets, pads, and carried plastic sticks'. None of them wore a badge. 'They began to beat the students. The rest you have seen on that viral clip—how they entered, and how they started beating us.'

Everybody saw it. The police lined them up against a wall, and the women were made to leave the room. Then they crowded the men and went at them with batons and rods. Beatings happened at the back, at the front, in the middle. A dazed student wandered about holding his head, and received another blow to the skull. Under attack, the students shielded their heads and left. One of the men noticed the camera, and hit it a few times. Shortly after, the video ended.

When I mentioned the clip to Minhajuddin, he told me the clip I had seen was less violent. On the first floor where he was, students were not allowed to leave the room.

Squeezed in the crowd, Minhajuddin made for the exit. One by one, as the students left, the police struck them on their hands and legs with their weapons. As Minhajuddin went by, he felt a whip and a burning pain across his left cheek that almost made him faint. Although he did not know it then, his eye was rendered useless by the attack. It may have been his beard, he said later, that got the police's attention. He wore it long then. He staggered to a toilet and slumped there, dabbing his face with a white kerchief, unaware of the damage, while around him more students took shelter beside the commodes and between the urinals. College guards in blue uniforms joined them there, equally frightened. But the police were everywhere, and they soon arrived in the bathroom to beat them all, whether they were on the floor or in the stalls. Minhajuddin remembered seeing the face of a policeman who entered the toilet with a mind to beat anyone he found. The man saw his eye and left the toilet.

That night Minhajuddin travelled across Delhi looking first for an ambulance and then for a hospital with an eye surgeon. He eventually reached the country's largest hospital, the All India Institute of Medical Sciences, which ran a series of tests for hours before telling him that nothing could be done about his sight. He walked over to a police outpost to file a complaint. They transferred him to a nearby station, and asked him to wait on a wooden bench. The station was filling up with other students. 'They wanted to frame the injured students by calling them protestors and detaining them. They wanted to put me in the same category and frame me too, but they couldn't. I had called them on my own.' The police let him go eventually after writing down his complaint, but they refused to write a First Information Report, an official acknowledgement of a witness account. Without an FIR, there would be nothing to investigate. He took the police to court, but found them armed with a doctor's opinion that his eye had been struck by a stone. The doctor's opinion was based on documents submitted by the police. 'It always happens that the police gets favourable reports. The doctors are theirs. Influence works.' When his father arrived from Bihar, he begged Minhajuddin to return. 'What are you going to do here now?' he said, wanting nothing more than safety. 'Leave it all and come home.'

'They wanted to teach us a lesson,' Minhajuddin said to me nearly two years after the incident. He was still a postgrad, but had left the student residence and now lived with his sister on the third floor of a cramped apartment block for university staff. When I met him there and asked about his injury, he put on slippers and took me downstairs to a small park. We sat on a scuffed bench below a street lamp. His sister, who was at home, became anxious when reporters asked questions, he said. 'They just kept beating us so that we would never protest again.' He could no longer cross the road without help. His beard was now cut close to his skin, more a statement of style than faith. He was unsure if anything would come of his complaint. 'The police has to investigate itself. How will this happen?' he wondered, rocking on the wooden bench, staring into the darkness.

# 3

# The Graveyard

While the police attacked the library, Ali and his friends took the route behind the Christian graveyard, not through it—Ali believed in ghosts—to a colony behind the college. They knew of a narrow gate they could slip through to rejoin the protests. Then they heard the sounds of panic: it all grew louder, and bodies clattered into the locked gate. Arms pushed at the grille and legs kicked at the frame, as the students begged to be let out. Residents nearby ran down with ladders and tossed them over the wall. Women apparated and made the boys swear they would not venture into the university. A man with a wound on his face managed to drag his bike up a ladder and over the wall. A tear-gas canister was fired into Ali's left leg, felling him. The police were swinging hard. The gas made him cry and 'froze' his nose and throat. While he suffocated, someone handed him a small sachet of salt to rub into his eyes. The streetlights had been switched off. From a terrace a few kilometres away, Ali's parents watched the flashes and heard the bangs.

The police seemed to know every path, Ali thought. A friend called to say they would find safety in the university's central mosque. 'I told him to get out. That's where they would come first,' Ali said. Later, when he saw how the mosque's windows were shattered, how the police had ransacked it, he concluded that religion was the reason. Nobody attacks places of worship that way, he said.

Ali stayed the night with a friend near the university, barely sleeping, remembering old stories of police arriving at odd hours to take away every Muslim man they could find in that area. 'We hadn't eaten, and we were all beaten.'

To take the edge off, they watched YouTube tutorials on joint-rolling. All the while, messages brought rumours that Shah had ordered the Delhi police to pick up every Muslim man in the area. They waited for something to happen. They said prayers for a boy who they heard had died. They mourned him, and asked for mercy and forgiveness for him for a long while, but they eventually learned that he was still alive. 'We killed him,' Ali laughed.

Then Ali heard a man call out in the silence, his voice a reminder that others were also alive. He may have been in the university, but Ali couldn't be sure. It was more than a voice, it was a connection, for he shouted a verse from the Quran over and over, a repetition done in desperation: 'Nara hoo taqbir, Allahu Akbar.' It was a call to not give up hope. The words were whispered by fathers into the ears of newborns, a reminder of a power greater than a human's despair, Ali said.

Ali remembered it as a howl that gave him strength. 'When I heard it in this situation, in front of the police, the armed forces, the guns, I finally understood. I understood that there is something bigger than a tyrant.' The next morning he left for home.

That evening I caught a cab to Mumbai University. A large crowd had gathered by the front in two distinct groups. One was of students. They kept away from the other, a raucous group of spindly and sweaty men practised in delivering slogans. The Mumbai police kept watch nearby, telling them all where to stand and sit. The political group was obedient, the students were reluctant. Their slogans about the Citizenship Act were more cutting. They had words for Shah and Modi that sent a shiver of laughter through the people around them. There was some relief that a fragile coalition unfriendly to the BJP was in charge of the state. They could smile and say things freely in front of a police that would let them.

The press were provocateurs. A journalist from TV9 thrust a microphone at a protestor and asked her for a statement about the violence students were responsible for in Delhi. Women in burkhas climbed up the gates beside others, but constables ordered only them down. After a while, at dusk, the police informed everyone that the protest was over, and elderly women, students and politicians all started leaving reluctantly, for they had found people like themselves. The professional protestors were compliant too, and they tried to harness the general disappointment productively by issuing reassurances that they would all meet again, soon, for a much larger protest. The revolution would be conducted in an agreeable manner.

Outside, I hailed a rickshaw. The driver was amused by the protest, and struck up a conversation. He defended Shah's Act. 'It only gives refuge to Hindus from elsewhere,' he said. He was a proud member of the Rashtriya Swayamsevak Sangh, he said, glancing at me in his mirror as he spoke. I hoped my expression gave nothing away. The RSS's chief traits were its freedom from doubt and a fiercely Hindu imagination that found succour in the past. Its members seemed to know more about obscure passages in the Quran than about bomb-making, which explained why so many of them kept blowing themselves up. The driver said the protests were a plot to break up India, and that liberals cared more about protecting Muslims than Hindus. We argued a while without going anywhere, swinging from one injustice to another, one slight to another.

'[Muslims] should be cut up,' he said at one point, startling me. He wanted a nation not just for Hindus, but one in which Muslims were killed or driven out. After that there was nothing more to say.

# 4

# Everyone Is a Suspect

It was a brown-wet day in January, a month after the protests, and the gates to Ambedkar University in North East Delhi were shut tight. People on the outside grasped the bars and pleaded with inflexible guards who spoke anxiously to the bosses on their walkie-talkies. More people were arriving. Disaffection had spread beyond Jamia to other university campuses, including other cities like Mumbai. Even the students of the elite Indian Institutes of Technology, normally distant from India's everyday concerns, were pricked by conscience. A collective called Pinjra Tod—Break the Prison—had organised a discussion on the Citizenship Amendment Act for that day at Ambedkar University. The group had begun as a movement against strict timekeeping in girls' hostels, but it did not limit itself to just one injustice. Its members now campaigned against wrongful imprisonment, the privatisation of education and abuses by university administrators. Their demands for equality and free mobility worried the intelligence bureau, whose agents phoned now and then to ask if their protests would be peaceful, a Pinjra Tod member told me, laughing.

I rang up a student organiser about the guards, and she told me to meet her at the back gate. Within minutes she appeared from somewhere, stern and impatient. I was taken aback by how serious she looked. She nodded once and began walking away. There were no introductions, no words exchanged. Her name was Prashastika. She led me through a maze of lanes between university buildings. In some places Urdu verse had been painted on the walls, and in others were three stark words: 'Destroy the RSS.'

Declarations to destroy the RSS at Ambedkar University came as naturally as breathing. The university was named after Bhimrao Ramji Ambedkar, who was born into a caste considered untouchable. Ambedkar, a social reformer who drove himself to illness as he drafted India's Constitution, famously rebelled against Hinduism's oppressive caste strictures and the religion itself, whose codes he argued had set back social progress. Hinduism as it was understood, he wrote, was 'really Law, or at best legalised class ethics'. He advocated for its destruction, because for as 'long as people look upon it as Religion they will not be ready for a change, because the idea of Religion is generally speaking not associated with the idea of change. But the idea of law is associated with the idea of change, and when people come to know that what is called Religion is really Law, old and archaic, they will be ready for a change, for people know and accept that law can be changed.' He eventually converted to Buddhism in 1956, along with half a million followers among the lower castes.

The organisers at Ambedkar University had booked a room for a discussion on Shah's new law, but plans had changed. The only place available was on a large blue tarp spread in a corridor near the main gate. It felt hurried, but determined. The previous year, members of the youth wing of the RSS had swarmed the campus to shut down a showing of *Ram Ke Naam* (*In the Name of God*), a documentary about Hindu right-wing violence. They threw chairs against a door, cut off the electricity, and shouted 'slogans citing that their Hindu sentiments were being hurt', according to a news report. In response, the university administration denied all outsiders entry to the campus, Prashastika said. This explained the meeting's illicit tang. She hadn't told the administration that human rights activists, the most undesirable of all outsiders, were the chief guests.

'If you want to protest state power and the surveillance nation, come to the protests,' one of the organisers shouted at random.

There were more than fifty people sitting on the floor because there were no chairs. Lawyers, activists, protestors and technologists took turns to speak. 'In normal times,' said Tanima Kishore, a slightly built advocate who worked on human trafficking cases, 'India always had procedures for refugees. They would be given a long-term visa. What these people are bringing in now, they say it's for inclusion, but that's not the case. It's not inclusionary. It's exclusionary. It's discriminatory, because it's specific to certain religions, it's specific to the country of origin, specific to religious persecution. It doesn't even cover cases of political persecution. It doesn't cover the Rohingyas, it doesn't cover people from Sri Lanka. They've told the whole nation that they're criminals and that they will have to show their papers. Right now, everybody is a suspect.' The students considered this. A cold drizzle fell. Slowly the crowd grew bigger, with more people turning up with steaming cups of tea.

'These people want a Hindu nation. They should ask Hindus if this is what they want, because we know you are with us,' said Zainab, a young woman in a hijab. She sat on the floor, her back to a wall, her eyes hard. 'What's happening will be trouble for us, but it'll mean trouble for you too. Soon they'll tell you how to live, how to eat, how to behave. Right now Muslims are threatened, but this is bad for Dalits and women too, because we know that anything can happen in this country.'

Zainab invoked religious riots of decades past that had

gone unpunished. She had just left a protest at Shaheen Bagh, a busy thoroughfare that a group of old women had occupied for over a month. The government's supporters complained that the protestors were causing traffic jams, although reporters found that, at the same time, 'security reasons' had compelled the police to barricade other roads. 'Women have been sitting there through the rain and the coldest winter in a hundred and eighteen years,' Zainab said. 'This government says it cares about Muslim women. Where's their care now? Instead, they send their own women disguised in burkhas and then send their own news channels to interview them.' There was more applause, more shaking of heads. (Reporters and editors from channels aligned with the government had turned up at protests not to cover the crowd's grievances, but to portray women and children on television as misguided and violent.)

Meanwhile, Prashastika had turned her attention to the guards at the gate. She stomped over, tore through them and yanked open the barriers to let in the people outside. They scurried in as a soft rain fell. The guards put up no resistance. They had been told only to keep the gate shut, not what to do if they were pulled open. One of them had enough of this drama, and he left his post to hear a speaker from Assam describe detention camps filled with Indians whose documents could not confirm that they were Indians. He was moved by what he was hearing. 'The people talking are doing all this for the country,' the guard said. His own time was past, he said, but perhaps the young would save us. Such were the times that even a single sentence acknowledging trouble was enough to feel kinship with complete strangers.

Zainab concluded her talk. Prashastika introduced the next speaker, a security researcher wearing a leather jacket. Srinivas Kodali, a chronicler of technology legislation in India, was troubled by the dearth of scrutiny powerful technologies and their inventors faced. He had a reputation for accurately divining political intent from obscure official documents, thousands of which he had hoarded through official information requests. 'The dangers to democracy are endless,' he said to the sitting crowd, and gave them a brief history of how politics, national security and technological progression had brought them all together on a rainy day at the site of a protest. His voice was meditative and even, as if he was reading a manual aloud, and his body, usually vibrating with unexpended energy, was still as he explained. He calmly listed government programmes that grew more invasive in the aftermath of wars, terrorist attacks and failures of intelligence. There were now so many repositories of information that 'we are becoming a database nation', he said. There would soon be a data protection bill, but it would not protect their data, he explained. 'That is the world we are living in.'

His listeners' eyes wandered when he spoke, frantically looking for something to hold on to. But dystopia was fertile ground for fearful liberal students. They knew that the police were using new technologies to identify dissenters. They had seen unidentified drones flying over protests, taking pictures, picking out dissenters, and saw police point cameras at crowds. Their data was being transmitted to an unknown location, for unknown purposes. There was an imbalance in what they knew and what the police knew. Furthermore, word had it that police were looking at mobile phone location records to identify protestors. At the same time, electronic evidence of police beatings disappeared. There would soon be murmurs that a car registration database identified Muslim addresses. Such developments were considered inevitable because anything was plausible. A sheet pinned to a corkboard fluttered beside Kodali. Someone had scribbled on it, 'HINDUTVA GESTAPO EVERYWHERE!'

When it ended, Prashastika stood up and raised a fist high. 'We don't accept the CAA!' she yelled.

'We don't accept, we don't accept,' the stragglers chanted.

'Take back the data protection bill,' she yelled.

'Take it back, take it back.'

One by one the audience peeled away until only Prashastika was left.

In the first months of 2020, Prashastika felt afraid. No matter where the protests were held, she was accosted by roving groups of Hindu men on edge who demanded, 'Are you Mussalman or Hindu?' Stating her religion was not enough, for they wanted evidence, and ordered her to recite holy texts. 'People would be leaving protests for the metro and they would be stopped and asked to show their ID card. And if somebody was visibly a Muslim, they would be stopped by any random person.'

In her apartment building she had put up a poster announcing 'No CAA, no NRC'. Soon, furious members of the building's managing committee called the police to investigate its appearance. She hid her pamphlets and told her mother to claim ignorance if the police asked questions. 'There's a micro witch-hunt,' she said of the way the law was looking for protestors. Delhi police had accused members of Pinjra Tod of organising violence, and buried them under a heap of crippling offences. Its founders faced charges for 'sedition, attempt to murder, criminal conspiracy and promoting enmity between two groups', and were detained under the Unlawful Activities Prevention Act, a harsh law that ensured detention for years. 'There was a total breakdown of institutions, and all the while we were going to the same institutions for justice.' She would protest outside the headquarters of the Delhi police at ITO, declaiming in one breath 'Delhi police, hai hai!' and then 'Delhi police, stand with us!' the next. 'It's funny, but so unfortunate. You're being beaten by the same police. The same police hates you.' The task of shaming the police for abandoning protestors, and pleading with them to remember their commitment, had exhausted her. After a while, she stopped attending the protests altogether. Her paranoia that the state would become more violent superseded the guilt she felt for abandoning her friends. She sensed menace. Resistance was exhausting. The police beatings in Jamia and other universities were exhausting. The lack of public opposition tired her.

All around, individuals chose self-preservation. Some chose not to protest, some chose not to visit protest sites, some decided not to speak about sensitive matters online, and someone, Prashastika said, even took off the nameplate outside the house he and his boyfriend lived in. I asked if this was really true, and Prashastika explained that the man, her friend, was gay and Muslim. 'He's from a working-class family.'

That anecdote stayed with me, and I asked her if I could speak with him. At this she hesitated. He did not wish to be known, she said, and it went without saying that he did not want to be found. He desired no association with people he did not know personally. The only path to him was through listening patiently to his friends, who had drawn themselves tight around him in loyalty, and by pleading with them to advocate for my cause. I made promises that I hoped would persuade him, promises of the kind reporters make and hope to keep, dangling earnestness and openness in a show of vulnerability. I knew, though, that while I would keep my word, India was reassessing the promises it had made to its people, including those that its founders had set in stone. Now it was in the mood for reclaiming all sorts of things—histories, territories, languages, words, thousand-rupee notes, information—and it extracted anything it desired from activists, lawyers and journalists. Its employees visited troublemakers at dawn with warrants in languages they did not understand, arrested them on charges designed to keep them in prison, took away their computers, letters and documents, and saw conspiracies in the classics they possessed, knowing fully that its account of events would be believed, because it was a time when people read into everything but books. The state, overarching and omniscient in matters of touch and thought, had no scruples about planting evidence remotely on an activist's computer, and letting infirm human rights activists die in jail. So how secure, then, could any entrusted secrets truly be? As a reporter, I was concerned by the powers of confiscation the state apparatus could exercise. Its lawyers had once argued before a court that Indians had no fundamental right to privacy if one went by a strict reading of laws. If private knowledge could be assigned no respect, what was property?

I should have been more explicit about the dangers when Prashastika's friend sent word that he would talk. I, his interlocutor, would not betray his confidence, but such were the times that his words could end up on the government's preferred news channels, framed in ways designed to damage him. He listened, and considered my request. Finally, he said that he would tell me about the nameplate.

His name was J— (it was longer, but J— was our agreement). J— grew up on a coffee plantation in Mangalore and he was a Muslim. His father had a job that paid little, but he somehow put together enough for his son to attend a private school, J— said. He could only pay some portion of the fee, and so J—, for whom he wanted a happier life, became the 'scholarship kid' to Brahmin children whose parents could pay the fees in full. His school was filled with boys with enough money, who tended to their work with foreheads smeared with ash without any need to think of their place in the world; their rank in life's hierarchy was pre-ordained. J— wanted their approval then, he said. He worked at his Sanskrit in the belief that mastering the language would grant him entry into the hearts and minds of Brahmins, and therefore everyone else in Hindu society. He could not place the exact time, he said, when he began to offload the ballast of his faith and lived life as a Hindu.

J— created a Hindu name for himself. It was armour, and opened new possibilities. Better than dreams, it made his days bearable. The name he took on, Avinash, protected him from the things people would have otherwise said. 'I put in an effort to keep friends,' he said. That J—, whose actions he now looked at through time's lens, was desperate. If that J— slipped up and was caught in the act of prayer, or if his Muslimness became more than background noise, or if he mentioned a Muslim festival in passing, or ate meat, he would have to scramble to close the distance it created. But between them was something he could not bridge.

'The gaze,' he said, 'I can't describe it, but it was there in the way they looked at you. And there was this feeling that they talked. You just know.' It resonated over the phone, the way he said it. He felt its weight, and wanted me to feel it too.

His name sometimes spared him the gaze and any other judgement, for his name was not simply Hindu, it was almost Brahminical. It meant indestructible. The name suspended him from the unspoken rules against renting houses to Muslims, or people who preferred not to do business with his kind—the typical shapeshifting required of people who must live where they are unwelcome.

He was twenty when he fell hopelessly for a Hindu man, and they decided to live together. He had enrolled at Ambedkar University in Delhi, whose students brooked no authority and painted their thoughts on the walls. It felt as if he had found a home. For the first time, friendships occurred without demand. His people drew close and tight, and they would feel protective of who he was. But even his closest friends did not know how perilous his life was. When they made him a special nameplate with his real name for his front door, he put it away. The neighbours could not know there was a Muslim in their midst. Neither did he want the men who delivered milk, eggs, bread and the newspaper to identify him. Every single person was a danger. 'I didn't know if I was overreacting,' he said.

In 2014, before Narendra Modi became prime minister, his offerings to the electorate were prosperity and development with a healthy side of ruefulness. The past six decades were full of misrule and political greed, he insisted, full of wasted potential, of greatness not touched, of personal bank accounts starved of wealth. No matter what people had accumulated, Modi made them believe they had nothing. His messages were relayed and amplified by supporters and leaders of corporations and newspapers, and the lights on history and fact were rearranged ever so slightly to show that Modi would not only fix modern India, he would right ancient wrongs. 'You gave them six decades,' he said. 'Give me just six years.' He went about the country making promises as if he was a free credit card. When he said that illicit wealth stashed abroad amounted to fifteen lakh rupees for each family, and that he would bring back black money, J—'s family 'fell in love with him'; like many others, their minds bridged the gap between the two statements, and they became convinced he would personally deposit fifteen lakh rupees in each family's bank account. J— said that 'sixty or seventy per cent' of his family voted for Modi.

But where people had hoped for accounting, they received instead a thorough auditing, and, by the time the protests were underway, J—'s mother 'thought Modi was Iblis, the shaitan at the end of days'. J— joined the early protests at first, but stopped when it all started to feel like an earnest facsimile of civic duty. His professors, caught up at the edge of the agitation with ideas about solidarity and participatory democracy, would 'invite students to go to the protests and have chai'. J— bristled at the symbolism of this. His professors did not see the matter the way he did, as a development that targeted him in particular. They opposed it out of some fealty to high-minded ideals; he opposed it for survival. This distinction angered him.

I asked if he had written about his feelings. 'I felt the urge to write about the Citizenship Amendment Act,' he told me, but he did not. More than that, he thought about what it all meant. Was discrimination recent, the main product of Modi's emergence, as some people thought? His experiences told him otherwise. 'People were blaming Modi's party, but no one, in my twenty-five years on earth, had given me comfort.' He reasoned that 'the poison was always there. It just wasn't always visible.'

The season of protests also coincided with the local elections in Delhi. As polling in the city-state approached, lawmakers from Modi's party raised the temperature with every utterance. One member of a state legislative assembly warned Muslims, 'We are eighty per cent and you are just seventeen per cent. Imagine what will happen if we take charge. Beware of the majority when you live in this country. This is our country.' It was reported that at another campaign event, Anurag Thakur, a lawmaker and cricket administrator, encouraged a crowd to sing a violent anthem against an unseen enemy: 'Shoot the bastards who betray the nation.' (Within two years he would become India's junior finance minister, and then its minister of sport.) Another made a campaign promise to demolish every mosque in his constituency if he won.

As soon as the first calls for violence were made, J— knew that someone would answer sooner rather than later. The hate he was seeing had two parts. One was visible: it was expressed in the public utterances of elected representatives. The other was private, received by people in their own homes, in messages of mysterious origin. He wrote to his friends at night on WhatsApp, pleading with them to talk sense into their families. He had seen the anti-Muslim videos they shared privately, in which right-wing types declared that 'these people spit in other people's food'. He wanted them to counter the misinformation they received every day, the little videos, jokes, unnamed open letters, all the digital detritus that lit up the darker parts of their minds. He wanted his friends to fight on his behalf the things they said about Muslims. He had surmised that this was the best way to reach people who were far gone; they would not listen to reason, but perhaps someone they had grown up with, someone they loved, could get through to them.

J— walked about Delhi during pockets of quiet. In the evenings, when people gathered in parks to sing anthems of unity, he looked away. It was romantic, but he only saw farce. Nothing had changed for him for decades. Who was convinced by their songs? What value did they have? Who were they for? He thought of Barack Obama, a man who had become a symbol. But a symbol of what, exactly? He had promised hope and change, but there, right behind him, was Trump. What good were years of hope if they ended in horror, he wondered. Experience had taught him that the problem ran deeper. He saw it coming, and told a friend, 'There's a lot of hatred being spewed against Muslims. Anything can happen now. Mass killings can happen.'

J— told me that he would touch the wrought-iron rods outside his bedroom window each night, and give thanks for the solid iron door that stood immovable outside his home. He promised me he would stay in touch. Then he disappeared, no longer answering when I called, no longer allowing himself to be found.

# 5

# A Call for Freedom

The protestors occupied Shaheen Bagh, a thoroughfare along a walled stretch of the Yamuna River in New Delhi. They were primarily women. They sat in near-freezing temperatures and when rain turned the ground muddy. Men lined up at the edges in protection. There were cameras and camera phones covering this moment; more women arrived to strengthen the protest, and then tents went up, and a stage was erected, and voices shrieked out of speakers at all hours of the night. The police in Delhi were capable of extreme cruelty, that much was now clear, and people wondered if they would strike the women protestors there. Days passed, but there was no evidence to show how the protest would be handled by officials; it was as if their imagination could not compute novel modes of protest. And so the machinery of government was pressed into accusing them of disrupting Delhi's traffic, and lawyers appointed by the Supreme Court pleaded with them to move, but they would not move. Some would refer to it as an occupation, a place where Indians could not go; the subtext was religious and territorial, the emotions evoked those of Partition and separation. The women sat on tarp, facing the speaker on stage, who wailed at the demands the citizenship law made of them. His voice was strained and hoarse, and the broken speakers above the crowds removed his softer notes and made him sharp and indecipherable. What remained was a high-pitched speech that was, even if you did not understand the words, an aural indication of distress.

After him there were activists who would talk about matters from a variety of legal and technical perspectives from their areas of expertise, and all of this would serve to fill the main concern with additional meaning. They flocked to protest because they felt less alone amidst all the anger and disappointment and struggles for some kind of recourse, and because, for a brief moment, the world they imagined aligned with the interests of the crowd. But the people were already roused, and they needed no further prodding; the threat of displacement was motivation enough.

At the edges of the protest area, men held up banners for photographers: 'No CAA, no NRC'. The tea stall that served sugary tea in clay pots had a sign outside that said the same thing. Business was good. I bought a cup, and the judgemental child behind the counter asked, 'That's all?'

There were posters on the walls and slogans drawn on the roads, and protestors everywhere who sang songs and did their own dances in groups. When small gatherings of men bellowed 'Azaadi!' the shout for freedom came out loud and raw from several places, as if that was all they had ever desired. The collective feeling was of rebellion. I wrote in my notebook at that moment: 'It is what they want when they find the words. And they have found the words.' Three years later I read the words again, grimacing at the mawkishness. In proximity to it, the moment possessed significance, but with distance I could see that only the witnessing of the moment gave it power. There was nothing more to be extracted, because the one thing that would have given it resolution was not granted: freedom.

*

My mind goes blank when I try to remember what happened next. There is only shame and embarrassment. I watched the pandemic's commencement anxiously, and read the first cases reported as if the sick were responsible. By March 2020, three months after the protests began, the contagion of hate found a new host in Covid. News channels focused on a large and lawful congregation of Muslims in Delhi as the origin of the pathogen's acceleration. Each day, a senior official from the health ministry announced in a televised press conference the number of cases the ministry had connected to the meeting, and the percentage of all cases the Muslims were responsible for. The information did nothing except serve as a reminder of where to place blame.

I bolted from Delhi for home, hoping that I was transporting only my clothes and notebooks. At home in Mumbai, in absolute safety, I strained against the leash of familial responsibility, desperate to return to the capital, but unwilling to leave. An editor I admired would sometimes say, 'It's only a story', to douse the blind passions of reporters in his charge. At times I agreed, but the justification was weak. It was a crutch to employ when work became truly inconvenient. And while I washed my hands and sanitised every surface about me, smalltime Delhi politicians began to issue threats that made violence inevitable. They likened the citizenship Act protestors to traitors, and invited crowds to shoot them. All this occurred as the pandemic grew monstrous—a consequence, the nightly news implied, of poor hygiene and civic apathy by a people who recognised no law of man.

These concerns coalesced in the public mind. It was established that the troublemakers who caused traffic jams and occupied public land also contributed to a public health emergency.

Then the killings began. I absorbed it all on screens, scrolling up and down to catch every angle, clicking on tweets to read replies and opinions, composing furious rebuttals I did not send, watching clips from three days of violence. This was India's first major riot in the camera age, and there would be no dearth of evidence when the time came. Meanwhile, artists and journalists put together resources for orphans and the homeless: these many milk cartons, those many matchboxes, that much sugar. A friend who had volunteered with aid groups in East Delhi called with news that men were dumping bodies in sewage canals. But this too slipped away as the virus lingered, and more died of breathlessness in a single day than in Delhi during the week the violence occurred. The task was no longer about documenting events as they occurred, but about putting together an account of what remained.

# 6

## On Their Own

Md Meharban was never without his cameras, for he had friends across East Delhi, and they called him when unusual things happened around them. He was young, a little over twenty to my eye when we first met in 2021 and walked along Jamia's external wall. Then he had pointed out slogans and art painted on the wall that had since been censored with a diluted coat of paint. The underlying slogans and cartoons were still visible, and we stood in silence, feeling good about the metaphor.

Now, at the metro station at Gokulpuri one morning, Meharban looked over the station's boundary wall at a canal below. It was thin and angled, and ran along Delhi's border with the state of Uttar Pradesh; houses in both territories used it for refuse. What moved between its banks was no longer water, but an unreflective grey sludge that corroded its surroundings. I wanted to see what had happened after the protests, and he said he would show me. 'There were Caterpillar machines bringing out bodies right below us from the naala,' he said. I imagined a metal paw trawling the sludge for bodies. But the act of imagining felt forced, for the people who lived there were now working. From above, there was no sign of violence, only urban neglect. A group of men stood on a mound of garbage beside the canal, feeding their white horses. Two boys squatted on the very edge of a roof to look at the animals. Whatever foliage had once existed here was now overrun by rectangular residences made of exposed brick that stretched to the grey horizon. The two indulgences that households afforded were a large plastic water tank and a small dish antenna pointed to the eastern sky. This was a Muslim neighbourhood, I thought, for while the national flag fluttered above some houses, not a single house held aloft the triangular bhagwa.

I noticed a large police station right below the metro and mentioned this to Meharban. 'Do me a favour,' he said. 'Count the steps from here to where I'm taking you.' I counted ninety-one steps before we arrived. He had brought me to the Gokulpuri spare-parts market for automobiles. Headlights and fan belts hung off the walls in industrial garlands, and metal sprockets and other dull parts were piled in mixed lumps. It was a chaotic market, meant for a car mechanic's discerning eye. A large white banner below an awning announced Malik Tyre, an establishment that sold tyres of various dimensions. Beside it was Raees Body Parts and Arsalan Tyre Shop. Inside and outside, men wore white caps. The words, the headdress, the language of the political posters all indicated a market dominated by Muslims. The place had been set on fire by Hindu gangs in February 2020, Meharban said. It had been a slow burning, with men returning in waves to set fire to one more shop, one more vehicle, one more tyre. Despite the calls, no police had traversed the ninety-one steps. The bazaar had been rebuilt, and was bustling once more, even though working hours had just begun.

I searched for signs of damage, but it was futile. Time had passed, and skin had grown over the burns. The bazaar was not simply active, but vibrant. I caught a whiff of shampoo, oil and food, all signs of daily life. I looked harder. Was the blackened exterior of a shop from a fire, or was the stain from a downpour?

Was the market's feeling of newness, of fresh paint and unblemished cloth awnings, a consequence of the violence that had singed it all at once?

I approached an elderly man sitting on a car seat on a plank balanced on a stack of tyres in his scrap shop. A fan extracted from an elevator cooled him. I mistook his equanimity for grandfatherly reserve, a countenance that was moved by neither peace nor riot, but it was just his face. 'The arsonists were all from here,' he said, referring to the neighbourhood behind the market. 'They arrived on bikes, and knew the names of the people who owned the shops. This is the murder of humanity. It's all politics. Ever since Modi came, the trouble began.'

His son, a young man, watched me warily. 'I lost sixty or seventy lakhs, but I have no proof to offer because what proof does a scrap dealer have?' the man said. The figure surprised me. I did not know how to assess the value of scrap. I sat beside him, waiting for him to say more. He was slow to speak, and said only what was necessary. He flicked through the pictures on his phone until he came to one of aluminium wheels fused in a fire's heat. It was so hot that the paint burned off the building, he said. Would I like some tea, he then asked, remembering his tehzeeb.

'Nil battey nil,' a man named Anees bhai said. The indivisible was divided by itself, leaving nothing behind. 'They finished us. They want us to leave this market.' Like others, he recalled gunshots and men shouting Jai Shri Ram. 'They had guns, swords and tridents. They stood by the tree and screamed.' They came in waves—one bunch then, another a few hours later, another some hours after that, as if there was no one to stop them. There were twenty-five or thirty men at one time. He could not be precise, but he remembered they wore scarves on their faces, and he remembered how long it took for the fire engines to arrive. In the meantime, 'because the shops weren't burning properly, they went next door to the petrol station to buy some petrol'. Anees's rubber-tyre store was on the market's front line, and it needed no fuel to burn. He ran away and watched the fire on his television later, and prayed that god would have mercy. A friend of Anees bhai's pulled up a paint can to sit on beside him, and as he heard his friend's story he relived what had happened and tearfully ordered a cold drink for me.

Meharban pointed to the underside of the metro at one corner of the market. The blue paint on the exterior was black underneath. It resembled the black grease one finds above the stove in grimy kitchens. 'That's the heat from the fire,' he said. The heat had roasted the paint. On one of the pillars that held up the station was a poster advertising the prime minister's loan guarantee scheme for small businesses. 'A loan worth one lakh to twenty-five lakhs will be approved in one day without any guarantee,' it announced. Modi's face covered a quarter of the poster, wearing a smile that could not be interpreted. His name was nowhere on the poster, but he existed beside the words as a reminder that the three-quarters remaining on the page were made possible only because of the space he occupied.

The visit to the market was an impulsive detour on the way to Al-Hind Hospital, which sat among the low, unfinished buildings of Mustafabad in North East Delhi. I had asked Meharban to introduce me to the doctor in charge, and he had agreed straightaway. Along the way he kept up a dialogue about Mustafabad's alleys that I did not hear, for my attention was on the uneven ground. Sewage overflowed from the drains in each alley, and flies flitted with fear and hungry purpose. A child with dried mucus under her nose wailed in one alley, and motorcycles roared down the narrow lanes, attacking us with their horns as they went. The brightly painted doors were made of metal; perhaps they could withstand fire. We went deeper and deeper into it, and just when all hope was lost, we turned a corner. 'We have reached,' he said. The only indications of its existence were the many banners and posters sprawled across the street outside, all concealing one another in their enthusiasm to announce the hospital's director, Dr M.A. Anwar, MBBS, who was pleasantly surprised to receive visitors who were still intact. Built like a gym instructor and dressed in a black tracksuit, the doctor started up from his chair, embraced Meharban and bounded up the stairs. Patients on either side of the staircase lay in their beds and watched this man curiously as he leapt about enthusiastically. Upstairs, Anwar pulled aside a curtain and ushered us into a private visiting room, away from his customers coughing outside. 'It's a hospital only in name,' he said, chuckling. 'It's really a clinic.'

Meharban interrupted him in protest. 'What hospitals couldn't do, this clinic did. Those big hospitals were of no use to anyone.' Dr Anwar smiled at him. They knew each other from the riots. The hospital was four floors tall, and every floor, as well as the roof, was filled with gunshot-wounds and stabbing cases when the riots occurred. Apart from the brief corrective, Meharban checked his messages while Anwar talked; they resembled people who knew each other's routine. 'I started this place in 2017 with the idea that it would serve people who live around here. They are of an illiterate type, somewhat oppressed,' Anwar said.

'Tell him where you got the idea from,' Meharban said, looking up from his phone.

When Anwar was in college, he lived for a time in Maliana, a village in Uttar Pradesh where a massacre of Muslims had occurred in May 1987. Muslim parents had stopped their children from attending school, he said. He tried persuading them to give their children an opportunity in life, and learned that while parents were willing to take their chance with violence, they feared its aftermath. 'Many people died, but also because they didn't receive medical treatment. People would tell us that hospitals would not see them. Doctors would keep their doors closed. Since then I thought, when times are bad, there should be doctors who see everybody,' Anwar said.

Al-Hind Hospital was two years old in December 2019 when the citizenship Act was introduced in parliament. Anwar watched the news on his mobile constantly. 'The country we have expended our energy in wants to put us in detention centres, and we will spend years trying to prove our citizenship. It makes you want to look for a country where these problems don't exist.'

For a few days in February 2020, while the BJP's leaders instigated violence, Anwar left the city to attend a funeral. On the way back, he called the police officer in charge of his jurisdiction to say he was picking up a box of sweets for him. He mentioned this as a demonstration of their closeness. When the hate speeches began, he complained to his friend in the police and asked him to take note of the threats. 'When men say such things from a stage, matters get serious,' Anwar said.

On the evening of 23 February 2020, a political leader named Kapil Mishra gathered a crowd less than a kilometre from Shaheen Bagh, the North East Delhi site where the women sat protesting the new law. Mishra accused the women of creating a 'riot-like situation'. He demanded that the roads be cleared in three days, or else 'we will not listen to the police . . . After that, we will have to come on the roads. Long live Mother India!' The police beside him wore cricket helmets and bulletproof vests and listened unmoved to his threats of violence.

Mishra was from the petrol-and-match section of the BJP, a group whose utterances were so extreme that they were often written off as the lunatic fringe. But their inflammations were calibrated for electoral gain, and when they went unpunished, the words expanded the boundaries of socially acceptable behaviour. Mishra's ideology was expedience, and so he was at once a willing receptacle and an originator of outlandish party messaging. When he was a member of the Aam Aadmi

Party, a once scrappy populist outfit that won sixty-seven out of seventy seats in Delhi's assembly elections three years after it was founded, Mishra accused Modi of being a Pakistani spy. But when he joined the BJP in 2019, he became a model party worker, wearing a saffron shawl, covering his head when someone smeared vermilion on his forehead and responding to any criticism of the party by shooting the messenger. Now he accused the leader of the Aam Aadmi Party of corruption. He was a modern arsonist, whose main weapons were suggestion and misinformation on social media and among crowds. Months after the speech at Shaheen Bagh, he invited 'writers, thinkers, professors, experts, artists, and people interested in faith' to join a new project he called the 'Hindu Ecosystem'. The ecosystem's members put their minds to churning out a range of poems, memes, jokes and factoids to give communal hatred a cloak of levity and scholarship. A message could be as simple as a picture of a bearded man wearing a skullcap, crying that he hadn't eaten meat that day. It could be a joke about no Muslim child being too young to make a wife. A series of pejoratives—circumcised, or mullah, or puncturewaala (people who patch punctures)—were deployed in a call to boycott a Muslim superstar's film. Even old structures were open to attack; anonymous Hindu scholars announced on social media that they had found evidence of an older Hindu presence on Muslim monuments like the Qutub Minar. The messages were bereft of any moral, social, or legal restraint. The basis of these pictures and words was not history but an emotion so strong it could displace fact. With enough time, this disinformation would corrode histories and identities, and crystallise new memories in the minds of those who received them. But all of it was built on violence. Within minutes of searching Mishra's Instagram, I was deep in pages threatening people who called the RSS a terror organisation. A beloved cartoon character, Doraemon, a blue Japanese robot who produced gadgets for every situation, had been repurposed too. Holding up a sword, he was made to say, Look, a device for killing mullahs.

When Anwar heard Mishra's speech, he visited the police to file an official complaint, but found the police reluctant to act. He lectured his friend in the police, 'There's no point in our occupying these posts if we cannot stop crimes like these. File a complaint according to the provisions of the law.' His friend replied weakly that he couldn't file the complaint because the speech was not in his jurisdiction.

At the hospital, visitors brought Anwar troubling rumours. Someone said Muslims were being killed in graveyards, someone said murderers were stalking Mustafabad's streets. His friend in the police had heard the rumours too, and called him. 'Dr Anwar, tell people around you, especially the elders, that these are just rumours. Tell them to stay at home.' Anwar scratched his foot as he remembered the day. Just then, a bespectacled man in a white salwar suit walked in, and he looked up.

'Waleikum asalaam,' Anwar said as he rose from his seat. He hugged his visitor, who smiled uncertainly at the strangers in the room. 'This is Nisar bhai,' Anwar said. He had been summoned to speak with us. The man's hair was neatly cut, and black up top and white on the sides. In his shirt pocket was a pen. He considered the room and sat down on the hospital bed quietly, his legs folded. Anwar said that terrible things had happened to Nisar, and while he elaborated on the man's travails, I noticed that his visitor's attention was on something else. His lips were closed and his eyes were concentrated on the wall across from him, as if nothing said or done in the room could help him, and he was only there because the doctor had called him. Nisar was a witness to the riots, and was fighting to have his case heard by the courts. He was under pressure to recant his account, but had resisted so far. Lately, though, we learned, Nisar had admitted to Anwar that his resolve had wavered. The pressure was too great, and his visits to the court were exacting. His business was suffering and his finances were dwindling. The doctor had summoned him to meet people so that they would tell him encouraging things. His hope was that words would be enough to give Nisar strength. With the introduction done, Anwar returned to his story.

On 24 February, patients arrived at the hospital from Farooqia Masjid and Shiv Vihar. There were only four or five of them, Anwar recalled, but several others who carried them. They came with news of stone-throwing. His police friend called to say it was all a misunderstanding, but requested him to reassure the neighbourhood. 'Then at about two thirty or three in the afternoon, I received word that thirty or forty people were active bleeds in an alley in Chand Bagh, and someone was trying to murder them. There was no one to rescue them, and something bad could happen. I didn't know whether it was safe, whether I could dress their injuries, whether people were throwing stones.' Eventually he put on a white dress and a helmet, and left for the alley with his surgical bag.

The men were resting in the alley when Anwar arrived. Notwithstanding the blood and the relief on the survivors' faces, the lane itself was otherwise peaceful, an indication that they had been injured elsewhere. Their injuries were not yet serious, but they needed staunching. He worked quickly, suturing their wounds without anaesthetic, and returned to Al-Hind. The ride was only twelve minutes long, but he remembered his staff phoning him several times, their voices raised in concern. Patients with stab wounds and blunt force injuries were arriving from across North East Delhi, they said, and the hospital was overwhelmed. Anwar summoned his brothers for help. When he stepped inside the hospital, 'it was like a movie. I don't remember what happened. Events just went out of control. We were doing everything. It went on this way till nine or ten that night.'

Some blocks away, on the main road that divided the Hindus of Shahdara from the Muslims of Mustafabad, Meharban watched the stones come down in the distance. 'Who is going to tell them to stop?' he asked someone, anyone. Some forty or fifty men wearing backpacks stood on the roof of Mohan Nursing Home, behind a giant 'H' on the hospital's rooftop. Their identities were concealed by motorcycle helmets, and they pulled bricks and rocks out of cartons they had hauled upstairs, past worried nurses. The hospital was a few steps away from Mishra's official residence. They flung stones at Muslim men standing below, across the street, who hurled them back hopelessly. Bricks and stones looped up, reaching their apex gently, and accelerated to the ground. The men above raised their hands in victory, thrust their groins out rhythmically, and vigorously shook one hand. There was bedlam, the sound of public disturbance, with men shouting, groups amassing on either edge of the road, and people breaking away to hurl something across the dividers. Vehicles were ablaze, the sky was darkened by smoke, and projectiles travelled in high and low parabolas. There were blasts.

Meharban filmed the men on the roof from the top of a building across the street. A crowd had gathered around for the spectacle—old and young, men and women, even a rickshaw driver in his uniform. They argued that a hospital should not have treated Hindu patients, and Meharban rebuked them. He fixed his lens on a man wearing black on the hospital roof, and grumbled about his equipment's limitations. The man stood behind the 'H' sign, loaded a rifle, and fired at men below. The crack echoed down the street. Other helmeted men brought out more guns, and first fired at Muslims below, and then at the group Meharban stood with. A bullet pierced a slim rickshaw driver. He was lowered down a ladder. A man held each arm, and one held his legs. But they felt the pull of gravity on his limbs, and when his head struck a rung on the way down, his eyes did not blink. 'I think he was already dead then,' Meharban told me a year later.

The driver's corpse was taken to Al-Hind, where Anwar called for an ambulance to Guru Teg Bahadur Hospital. Government doctors there would issue a death certificate. Anwar sat beside the body as the driver tried to find a safe route to the larger hospital. The roads were empty, but the police had erected barricades, and would let no one, not even an ambulance, pass. They turned to the arterial roads, eventually landing on a narrow path that ran along a canal. Anwar noticed a car full of men carrying swords trailing them. He ducked below their line of sight. When they arrived at the hospital, the police would not let them in. Anwar called a senior doctor for help. The doctor replied, 'I will not be able to help you.'

'We did what we could,' Anwar told me. 'We thought, no matter what happens, we have to save ourselves and save others. We would call hundreds of police at the same time, asking if they could spare a man to travel in ambulances. We would call them for help. We would call the helpline and they wouldn't answer, and when they did, all they said was, "Let's see. We'll try and do something."'

'They weren't doing a thing,' Meharban added.

'You know, there was a sweet shop here . . . ' Anwar said.

'Let me tell that story,' Meharban said, laughing. 'When things got really bad here, when there were fires everywhere, these Muslim boys got mad. They wanted to attack a sweet shop run by a Hindu and burn it down. Doctor saab told them that if anything happened to the shop, he would shut the hospital down. Nothing happened. They left it alone.'

'I told them I would jump into the fire,' Anwar said, annoyed now.

'In Chand Bagh, Muslims formed a human chain around Hindu journalists,' Meharban said. 'In Hindu areas, no journalist was safe.'

'Journalists would come to my hospital and say, doctor saab, we survived somehow,' he said, amused. 'The biggest thing here is, there are several Hindu houses and temples in this area. There is not a scratch on these places. Rioters attack places that are soft, that are weak. But here nothing happened. People were not harassed.'

That night, a police official friendly with Anwar called to say that matters were getting worse. He said he would send a car to transport Anwar and his family to safety. 'I said I had patients, but that my family would go. But my wife and children didn't want to leave me, and they stayed.'

'On top of that, she cooked food for me,' Meharban said.

'I didn't know what was going on outside those days because I was inside the hospital,' Anwar said. 'But when I think about it now, many things start to make sense.'

All the while, Nisar sat still, his bearing tight as he heard the doctor's expansive descriptions. But my curiosity about him grew when his posture relaxed and he looked past us, as if the conversations had sparked a private memory. This coming and going of his attention happened silently and frequently, and I had a sense he wanted to say more. Before he left, I asked him for his number.

# 7

# Tearing

Some days later I met a man who had been unwise, and as a result had his insides photographed by Dr Anwar.

There had been skirmishes at the edge of Mustafabad for a few days, some serious enough to portend much worse. All along the alley, the steel gates of houses were shut from inside or padlocked, and the usual rush of machine, man and beast was nowhere to be seen. Shamsuddin, the patriarch, had commanded his family to stay inside until the danger outside had passed. But his son, Imran, somehow got it into his head that he could quickly fetch supplies from a ration store nearby. It was evening, he remembered, around five thirty or so on the second day of the riots. Imran waited till Shamsuddin went to another room, and then he slipped away. His reasoning was that they lived so far inside Mustafabad that no one would come this way. The fighting was at the mosque a few minutes away from where he wanted to go: the shop was at gate number twenty-five. Geographically, it was not far from home; a minute or so was all he needed to be home. What was he thinking? Was he thinking? What do twenty-six-year-olds think?

Outside, it was as it had always been. Open drains, and lanes for cars leading to lanes for motorbikes leading to lanes that could only be crossed on foot. The only difference, Imran noticed, was the silence and the darkness. On other days motorcycles juddered up and down the uneven concrete-tile-mud paths, honking, unwatched children running barefoot outside. Now the streetlights were cut.

Then he was outside the shop at the corner. Its shutter was half closed, primed to be shut quickly. It was the only shop half open for dal and sugar, ingredients he wanted for a hungry relative. He was standing around, waiting, when he saw a puff of dust rise into the air beside him. He registered a sharp sound, and then panic. Someone shouted, Run, Run! It happened very quickly, he said. Then he saw them, and although it was only a glimpse, he knew who they were from the motorcycle helmets on their heads, and the guns, swords and daggers in their hands. There were men in police uniform among them.

'I ran,' he said.

The alley was straight for a stretch before it curved to the right. He had to get beyond that curve, away from the projectiles, out of their line of sight. Then he could turn into smaller alleys on either side and hide himself in some hollow. He heard the gunshots, he heard them shout, 'Jai Shri Ram', and he kept running until he got home. Only then did he put his hands on his thighs to catch his breath. His palms felt sticky, and when he looked at them they were red, and when he looked down he saw that his groin was torn from back to front.

'There and then I fell down,' he said.

We were in his living room, half of which was occupied by the largest bed I had ever seen. It was made for three generations of a family to rest on, and must have been ten feet wide. Imran brought out tea, biscuits, samosas, snacks, sweets, and sat beside his father. A friend came over, kicked off his shoes and fell asleep at a respectful distance on the bed.

Shamsuddin, an old carpenter who made furniture for palatial Hindu homes, was the bed's creator. He told me he didn't know where to take Imran. The hospital was an obvious place, but 'bullets were flying outside hospitals', he said. He had heard that in other parts of the city, the police were preventing ambulances transporting injured Muslims from reaching hospitals. Shamsuddin carried Imran to the home of his local legislator. 'I thought, he is a big man. Something or the other will work,' he said. But the legislator declined to help, and told him to take his son away. He found his way, eventually, to Al-Hind, Dr Anwar's hospital. The building was unfinished. It was as if a construction site had been taken over by medical personnel, which added to the sense of emergency. Every bed was occupied, and patients and bodies were sent up to the roof. Anwar had shown me a picture of Imran on the operating table. I pressed my legs tightly together when I saw the ruin. The gash from his front to his back was five inches long, and everything had spilled out of his groin. The doctor separated the fragments inside him from the tissue and muscle, stitched him up, and referred him to Lok Nayak, a government hospital.

The woman at the admissions desk at Lok Nayak told Shamsuddin she wouldn't admit Imran. 'Didn't you think before firing bullets and throwing stones?' she said. 'Do you have no shame?'

'You,' Shamsuddin recognised, was not him. It was *you people*. Shamsuddin asked her, 'Does this mean you were there? You're sitting in a hospital and accusing him of doing those things. So you were there too?'

The approach was unwise, for it only angered her further. 'You don't know how to talk,' she said, referring to his manners. 'I'm not admitting him here. Get him out of here,' she told an attendant. The hospital staff shoved him out of the hospital.

With nowhere to go and his son lying at his feet, Shamsuddin wept outside the hospital, he said.

'I thought, better if Imran had died and I had died too,' he said.

He called his sons to tell them what had happened, and they, in turn, phoned Anwar, the doctor at Al-Hind, to tell him. By then a support network had sprung up around Delhi, and soon a volunteer ambulance took Imran away for medical attention. They would look after him for two months.

But it was in the nature of the moment that injury followed injury, and in no time the police questioned the volunteers about Shamsuddin and Imran. 'They asked weird questions about us. "Who are they? Why have you kept them here? Don't you know they could be troublemakers?" They asked us why we were a part of the riots, accused us of causing trouble, accused us of firing bullets. The volunteers told us to leave,' Shamsuddin said.

As Imran recovered, the crime branch of the Delhi police called him to the station and threatened him. 'They accused me of being a rioter, and threatened to jail me unless I named five other people. They told me to think about it. They say anything they want to,' Imran said. The son was argumentative, but the father was weary. The pandemic had made life difficult enough. Jobs had dried up, and without money there was less of everything. 'There's no work, and no food,' Shamsuddin said. 'How are people going to fight?'

The police were not alone in this. Looking at Imran's case files, one of his doctors asked Shamsuddin, 'Are you sure you didn't tear up your son with a knife by yourself?' Shamsuddin would not let this slight go. 'Would you injure your son with a knife?' he asked the doctor. 'Who would tear their son with a knife?' At government hospitals the doctors asked strange questions and made strange assertions. They could not believe that his son had stumbled into a riot. They had not been there, but they thought it was all fairly obvious.

Dr Anwar showed up for duty at Guru Teg Bahadur Hospital during the violence. He overheard colleagues use a cricketing analogy to discuss Muslims dying on the operating table. 'They would say, "one more wicket down".' I couldn't tell if his smile was a grimace. Imran was two months from being married when the bullet entered him. Eighteen months later he was still unmarried; the injury would be a lifelong companion. Its effects surprised him. Winter made his right leg swell up, and the pain went from his toe to his head, stopping to radiate in his chest. He could not sit still, and quietly went to the bathroom three or four or times an hour. He couldn't travel far from home, or walk regular distances, or climb up more than a flight of stairs, or carry anything that required the slightest effort. The medicines were bankrupting his father. The Delhi government had allocated twenty thousand rupees for his suffering.

Shamsuddin remembered how the village he grew up in, near Meerut, in northern India, had known peace for years. The recollection may not have been entirely accurate, for Meerut had in fact experienced terrible communal violence, but he smiled at the memory and I let it slide. 'If there was a fight, the village Hindus would say, "You sleep well. I'll sleep outside your house. They'll have to kill me first".' Eventually, the casual hatred that had swept across India found his village. He noticed how differently the younger boys talked. 'They say, "There are only two-three of you in the village. We can flatten you anytime." When times like these come, people go mad. Nobody looks at what they're doing,' Shamsuddin told me. 'I don't know what is inside people's head.'

He thought the news was to blame. He said it hesitantly, but was met with immediate agreement. Shamsuddin's friend woke up and said, 'The biggest pestilence is the media.' They all shared their thoughts on the news at once. The friend kept going. 'They are our biggest enemy. If they speak poisonous things every night on the news, what will happen? It's entering our veins.' He was shouting now. 'Hindu-Muslim, Hindu-Muslim. That's all they do. Is there any news they show us?'

Shamsuddin grinned at the hopelessness of it. 'Somebody

shouts, "say Jai Shri Ram", someone shouts, "say Allahu Akbar". Sister-fuckers, all of them.'

'But the difference is,' his friend said, 'watch what happens when the Muslim says anything. They're in jail in one minute. What is a man to do?'

This reminded Shamsuddin of the police. 'The law doesn't help like it used to. Now they get into Muslims, threatening them. They see a Muslim,' he said, stroking an imaginary beard, 'and there's the threat of arrest. I was going on my bike the other day, and one of them stopped me. It happened that I didn't have any money in my pocket. I told him so and told him to let me go. And one of them says, "Oye, sister-fucker mullah, come here. You're lying." This is the truth: oye, mullah, you're lying. This is reality.'

Finally, Shamsuddin rose up from his enormous bed, where we had sat all the while, and said he would drive me to the main road on his bike. The main entrance to Old Mustafabad was a long walk from his home. He stopped at the corner shop where Imran had stood. 'This was the place,' he said. The shop's orange shutters were slathered with political ads.

Mustafabad was officially a town right on the eastern edge of Delhi. A hundred and thirteen thousand people lived within its borders, and their days were spent looking for a way out. Each house looked wildly different from the one beside it, and each new floor looked different from the one below it. Women stayed out of sight. The men watched everyone who came and went, and their heads turned to follow unfamiliar faces, or anything out of place. The area possessed the same sense of neglect I had seen in other Muslim neighbourhoods, where the expectation of basic civic services had long since evaporated.

The shop was deep inside. A crowd of Hindu men hundreds large had walked ten or fifteen minutes into the conurbation, down an open road, carrying guns and swords and sticks and little bombs, shouting slogans all the while, Shamsuddin said. I responded, naively, that I was surprised no one had stopped them.

'Some of them were wearing what the police wear,' he said. 'They had everything. They had things the police have.'

A few minutes later he stopped outside a mosque with an exterior of glistening wine-red tiles. It was sheathed in bamboo scaffolding and tattered green tarp. The men had entered the mosque before heading down the road to where they would find Imran, he told me. Inside was the mosque's imam, and they did such things to him that Imran and Shamsuddin would forget their own miseries. 'They broke his eyes,' Imran had said. 'If you had seen his face . . .'

Where was the imam now, I asked, half knowing the answer.

He left, Shamsuddin said. Much later, when I asked someone else, the man replied, 'Oh, he died.'

# 8

# Testimony

It was late in April, and the onset of a series of days that were each hotter than the last. It took a while to find a rickshaw driver willing to travel from Nizamuddin's quiet lanes to Mustafabad, the border town where Nisar, the witness I had met at Anwar's hospital, lived with his family. Finally a driver grudgingly charged a distance premium of half the regular fare. He was quiet most of the way, but when we crossed the Signature Bridge over the Yamuna River, and the Muslim neighbourhood became apparent, he revealed that he rarely ventured this way.

'It's too crowded. If I was the prime minister, I would pass a population control bill. There's no place left,' he said.

The streets were crowded with cyclists, pedestrians and juddering tempos pumping out dark fumes, but it was no busier than a South Delhi market. The small houses squeezed together doubled as small industries that produced small things. The only difference was the area's predominant religion. Reining in Muslim demographics had been a popular talking point among Hindu leaders since at least the 1920s. The fear of a Muslim population that would eventually surpass Hindus had been debunked endlessly, but few people seemed to want to register that population growth rates fall with greater education. It had happened to Hindus, and it would happen to Muslims well before they overtook Hindus centuries in the future. And so this restless demand for a vague kind of control, so convinced of its logic, had lost none of its menace in the past century. The driver grumbled a while about the area being 'no fun'. He taught yoga in the mornings to boys and young men, he said. His shirt buttons were wide open, and so were his eyes; he insisted on knowing what I was doing in Mustafabad. I told him a friend was at a hospital. After he left, I wondered if the extra charge wasn't for distance, but for dragging him to a Muslim neighbourhood.

I walked through Mustafabad in search of Nisar's home. He had sent me his address, but the buildings were pressed so tight, and so bereft of any difference, that even an exact location felt like an approximation. The flies and heat and uneven path and the high summer's summoning of chemical odours from the drains made me want to turn away immediately. As I turned into Nisar's street, an immaculately coiffed fabric salesman with an enormous but desperate smile wailed, 'Ya Allah, someone save me.'

Nisar met me outside his home and we walked to his shop. Nearly half a year had gone by since we had last met. In between, we spoke with each other late at night, usually after he had been to the courts for his hearings. It was surprising how many times he went to court, and he tried to explain that he was named a witness in some of the government's cases. I tried to understand the importance of the case numbers, but he spoke quickly, and had a thick accent from some place in western Uttar Pradesh. There was no chance of understanding everything. I could only put together little fragments of information: he had been attacked, he escaped, his house was set on fire, his wife survived, they ran away, there were threats, he abandoned his old home and now lived here, and he was considering installing CCTV cameras outside, but wondered whether it would attract unwanted attention.

He was leaner than I remembered from Dr Anwar's hospital, and his face was more gaunt, as if the delayed stress had finally found him. He walked slowly, with a limp, and wore a brace around his stomach. The sign above his new shop a street away featured a child wearing sunglasses and a T-shirt emblazoned with a skull. It advertised Nisar as a specialist in the designing and manufacturing of trousers and jackets. He was particularly proud of the grey check drawstring denims with a neon yellow lining and metal chains lashed along each leg over a red Batman logo and an invitation to come play PUBG at a palace. He knew his market. Young mothers swarmed to it when the shutters went up. Nisar stood outside it for a few minutes each day, checking on merchandise that had to be delivered. But while his ear was to the phone, his eyes scanned the lanes to ensure that his enemies were not watching him.

Later, we returned to his home, and he offered me the headrest on his bed, and he lay down at its foot and complained about the cruelty that followed the riots. He knew of Muslim landowners who received phone calls from Hindu real estate agents who asked, politely, if they were selling below the market, and then, impolitely, suggested that holdouts would eventually run out of luck. 'You survived once. You won't survive next time. Take the money and go,' an agent told a friend of Nisar's.

The new house was no match for the house he had been driven from, he said. The earlier house had air and sky. This front door opened to a litany of urban failures, failures he reflected onto himself. It was temporary, he said to himself.

The house he lived in was unfinished, even months after they had rented the place. Underfed cats wandered in from the terrace upstairs and hid behind bags of cement kept on the stairs. A curtain billowed through a wall opening where a window should have been. Half the house was painted in unintended impressionistic daubs, the other half was cement, for money was tight. 'It takes time to make a house. It takes time to create new systems. We've come from zero,' he said. The fire had eviscerated his finances. Approximately forty-five lakhs in assets he had put together over thirty years were no longer his to use. He was on the floor now, he said, but what else could he do except what god had put him on earth for: to work.

I had heard him speak this way many times, but now that we were meeting in person, I asked him to slow down and tell me what had happened. He smiled and sat up, but just as he began to speak, the door to the room crashed open and Afseen, his granddaughter, marched in to assess us.

'Take her away,' he shouted to Asma, his wife, while the toddler watched. 'She's interrupting my work.'

On 24 February 2020, at about three in the afternoon, an uproar outside Nisar's house brought him to his window. A large crowd of men was passing by on a narrow road beside a canal through Bhagirathi Vihar, his neighbourhood in North East Delhi, chanting 'Victory to Lord Ram!' and 'Wake up Hindus, wake up!' Nisar had lived there for nearly twenty years, and had never heard a crowd like this before. He conferred with Asma. They decided, somewhat uncertainly, that the procession was probably harmless.

'It felt like the usual political sloganeering,' he said to me. In this neighbourhood, nothing came in the way of fraternity. Muslims and Hindus called each other over for chai, and sat outside together late at night. That brotherhood was usually protection enough. If there was any disturbance, elders came out to settle matters before they grew unmanageable. For Nisar, hope was a way of life. His house overlooked a sewage canal, but when he looked out of his window he chose to see instead the unbroken sky. Small things like this brought him inordinate pleasure.

Nisar had moved alone from the countryside to North East Delhi when he was eleven. Soon after he arrived, he found a job at a garment factory and he had lived in the city ever since, working his way up the industry and eventually starting a small business of his own. At forty-seven, he felt that financial security was finally near. From the ground floor of his home, he designed denim garments and sold them across Delhi. There was enough demand for him to acquire the house, purchase three motorcycles and travel to prospective buyers in other cities. But he could not think of business while the men were outside. Peering through their window, Nisar and Asma saw the procession move down the street. They were unsettled by the many unfamiliar faces they saw in the crowd, but Nisar was just as surprised by some of the faces that he did recognise. Some of them he had known from when he was much younger—they were his neighbours' children. They would not have dared even open their mouth in front of him back then. But here they were now, announcing their dedication to the god Ram outside his house, saying the gentle greeting like it was a taunt, a war cry. The moment felt ridiculous to him because the boys were not pious at all. 'One of them used to lie intoxicated in the sewage canal,' he told me.

After a few minutes, the chants intensified. Asma told Ilma, their daughter, and Sumaiya, their pregnant daughter-in-law, to leave before real trouble began. 'We thought that they wouldn't be able to run,' Nisar said. Asma had other fears—the women were in their early twenties. Suhail, Nisar's younger son, was ordered to drive them to a relative's house in a nearby neighbourhood. Nisar stayed behind with Asma and their other son, their nerves frayed, until Suhail returned twenty minutes later. Then Nisar slipped out behind the crowd to see what was happening, keeping his distance so that he would go unnoticed.

The men stopped a few minutes from Nisar's house, at a low bridge over the sewage canal where four roads met. They put up barricades and brought out large loudspeakers that Nisar recognised as the property of a neighbour who ran an audio equipment rental business. He saw a local leader from the BJP on the bridge. He was rousing the crowd. Soon, worrying slogans rang out from them, and the crowd responded to each of them. He heard them say 'kill the mullahs', and then 'make the circumcised run away', and 'set their houses on fire'. Someone screamed, 'Bring out whatever weapons you have at home.' When they shouted their support for the Citizenship Amendment Act, Nisar listened in disbelief, before he had a moment of clarity. He saw in that moment that the things around him were a kind of set, and the people around him were actors repeating lines they had rehearsed, because it was not normal, and not possible, for these men whose parents he knew to be so passionate about a legislation for refugees. He thought in that moment about what it took for people to fall in line with a government's logic so fully that they would attack other citizens.

While the chants continued, Nisar looked around and noticed a neighbour, a teacher who tutored children after school. Nisar was on friendly terms with him, and he told the teacher to step forward and stop the men from goading each other on. 'What is happening here? Let's stop this from happening,' he said. 'They're raising hell. We're elders. Let's stop these boys from doing this.' He did not forget the way the teacher nodded without a word and turned away from him, as if something had already been decided. It was at this point that Nisar took off from the bridge and ran home, where he, like so many others in those hours, lowered the shutters and reinforced every entry point with locks and prayed that it was enough.

Then the music began. On the bridge, the crowd was hundreds strong, and the atmosphere was oddly festive, as if it was Holi, with its loud sounds and raucous men. In between,

Nisar heard them shout 'Jai Shri Ram' and other religious slogans with urgency. He felt the mood's pulse quicken, and rang the police. 'Come quickly,' he told them, 'there's going to be a riot.' The police assured him that his worries had been registered. But the only sign of them, and that too for a limited time, was at the end of the emergency hotline, Nisar said. Otherwise, they were invisible.

The onset of darkness was the final signal. That evening, at five or six, while the music played, the men on the bridge began breaking into the empty homes and shops of Muslims who had left until the trouble passed. Notably, they didn't touch homes with Muslims still inside. Meanwhile, unaware Muslim men on their motorcycles turned corners in blissful ignorance and ran smack into the mob. They left their vehicles where they were and jumped into the sewage canals. Nisar looked out from his window and saw some of these pursuits. The feeling of being under siege grew. While his view allowed him to see only a narrow section of Bhagirathi Vihar, he could hear screams, and people sent him videos of atrocities filmed just moments before. In one clip, a motorcycle burned while people strolled past. In another, a man lay on the ground with his entrails clearly visible. Nisar noticed his neighbour, the tuition teacher, close to the body. He was on his phone. Nisar thought he was taking instructions.

As it grew darker, and the beat thumped outside, he closed the curtains and kept watch on the growing crowds outside his home from a gap between them. There were young men wearing masks and orange clothes—the colour of Hindu political parties—young men up and down the lane he lived on, young men all the way to the bridge. They were passing each other swords and sticks from a concrete-brick storehouse. There seemed no limit to the weapons they carried. Some boys carried a metal rod with a curved end sharpened to a point. Some removed the bolt on shears to create a pair of daggers. All of it was set to music.

The crowd dissolved into smaller groups. Some of them stalked Bhagirathi Vihar's alleys, others patrolled its intersections. The men demanded the identification papers of anyone who appeared to be Muslim, judging crudely by skin colour, nose, beard and skullcap. If there was any doubt, they ordered men to expose their genitals for confirmation. Nisar stood beside his first-floor window, the only vantage point that concealed him. He was torn between recording the men outside and watching them with his own eyes. Sometimes he crouched below the window base, raising the phone just enough for its camera to film indistinct figures and a halted truck carrying gas cylinders. One video was maddeningly unsteady, but it captured young men stopping vehicles and talking to each other in the darkness. Not a face could be discerned. When I asked Ahmed about this, he said, 'My whole body was shaking.' Behind him, Asma begged him to be careful and make sure they did not see him.

He witnessed freshly beaten men staggering down the road, and he witnessed men clutching their skull; it was clear to him that the beatings were administered by young Hindu men, and that the recipients were Muslim. His sons hissed at him to get back, but Nisar stayed where he was, caught, like all witnesses, in the land between bravery and foolishness. Then, late at night, he heard a number of loud bangs around the men on the bridge: they sounded like fireworks, or metal striking metal, or gunshots. Then a voice rang out, echoing between the low houses on either side of the canal. 'I cannot believe how many of our Hindu brothers are here,' the voice of a delighted man on the bridge was amplified by the loudspeakers. The volume had been turned up enough for Nisar to hear, even though he was some distance away. 'It looks like they have all come here. Save your energy,' he advised the crowd. 'Save your energy levels! We have all night.' The music played.

A neighbour filmed the scene and sent Nisar the video. The

lights of a police car flashed, illuminating the crowd, the bridge, and the buildings. It slowed near the men, but then kept going, leaving them to do their work. 'The police car came, roamed around a bit, and went away,' Nisar's neighbour narrated. The men roared, 'Long live the Delhi Police!' and 'Jai Shri Ram!' The car continued to drive away from the bridge, along a narrow road beside the canal.

'All night it was madness,' Nisar said. 'Everywhere, madness. In the colony, on the bridge, by the canal.' In the darkness the pogrom came to him through sounds. He heard shouting, people running, and screams. He dared not sleep.

The hours that would uproot his notions of the country began soon after sunrise, when Nisar heard a commotion below his window. Some of the rioters were breaking into his neighbour's house. They stripped the residence bare, even pulling off the ceiling fans. It occurred to Nisar then that hiding was pointless, for they knew the location of each Muslim home. And so he called out to them from his window to reason with them. Stones and iron rods flew through his window. One of the rods even struck Asma, he said. And then about forty of them were focused on his door, the shutter and the locks, and within moments they were inside.

And here, as he explained how he went from witness to participant, his story acquired a manic edge. Nisar, Asma and the children fled to the rooftop, locking a gate behind them. Downstairs, the mob dragged out the motorcycles Nisar kept inside the house, doused them with fuel and set them on fire, along with sacks of clothes meant for distribution, and money and jewellery for his daughter's wedding. 'Do whatever you want to,' he said angrily, and then, 'Why are you doing this? Who has told you to do this? What is the matter? Go to your homes.' Then the men swarmed up the stairs and tried to pry open the gate on the roof.

Nisar panicked. He was dimly aware that people on nearby

rooftops, some of whom he probably knew, were watching the show and pelting them with stones. He took Asma by her hand, helped her over the roof wall and lowered her with one hand to the top of an adjoining house. But the roof of that house was too low for her to jump safely, and she dangled above it. The owner of the house happened to see them, and he quickly brought a ladder and helped Asma down. Nisar and his sons followed. The neighbour did not dare try to shelter them, and Nisar did not ask for his protection. They hurried across more roofs, scrambled down to the street and ran into the home of a close friend, a Hindu. The friend ushered them deep inside, away from the windows, and gave them chai. There they caught their breath and finally wept.

The family waited for hours for the hunt to end. Then, sometime that afternoon, there was silence. Nisar looked out and noticed two policemen. It was an opening. But by the time they stepped out, the police had gone. Thirty or forty men had returned, and they rushed over from both sides to the Muslim family they had somehow missed. Cornered in the alley, Nisar pleaded, 'Let us go.'

To his surprise, a man he knew well and considered a friend came forward from the crowd. Nisar recalled that the man 'shouted that nobody would touch us. That if anybody did, he would kill them.' Hindu neighbours watching from their homes came out and gathered around the family, forming a protective barrier between them and the rioters. The neighbours helped the family hurry out of Bhagirathi Vihar, and left them near a solitary cop some distance away.

'What did we do after that? We ran,' Nisar told me. 'I didn't even turn around to look at my home.' He couldn't explain why the man he knew had chosen to save him. Nothing about that day made sense.

He was told of a camp that had been made for survivors like him. It was in the courtyard of Eidgah mosque, a few streets over from Bhagirathi Vihar. It was a cold, wet night, and he was restless. Refugees huddled under giant tents for warmth. He estimated that thousands had arrived from all over Delhi. He could hear attackers outside trying to find a way in. There were hundreds of other refugees from North East Delhi, and they had similar stories of unfamiliar crowds that knew exactly where the Muslims lived among the Hindus. 'There's a saying,' Nisar said, 'Ghar ka bhedi, Lanka dhaye. Only someone inside your house knows you.'

What he meant by this was that locals had called the outsiders. Locals had pointed out the houses in which Muslims lived, the shops they owned, and outsiders got to work. He pulled out photographs of the rioters from a folder he had kept in a packet. He touched it as if it was precious, I noticed. His memories he would share happily, even going over them repeatedly to make sure I understood, but his papers he was reluctant to reveal. Nisar was a talkative man, but he shuffled the papers and passed them to me in silence, frowning now and then as I took pictures of his photographs of the rioters. The photographs had been taken at close range, as if the crowds were comfortable enough with the photographer to ignore his presence. It was a betrayal, and every act, from the supply of loudspeakers to the photographs themselves, was loaded with unfairness, with the knowledge that he could not live there, and could not have taken those pictures because he was the wrong kind of man, yet Nisar could not bring himself to see it that way. To him, his persecutors were puppets. The men who showed them this way, the actual conductors of violence and hate—where were those people, he asked. Why did no one demand their uncovering? Why did no one ask who they were?

The photographs were enlargements of footage he had received on his phone from Hindu neighbours who had recorded the roving gangs. Groups of men blocked the thoroughfare outside his house, a man held half of a large pair of shears like a gun, and paper and ash was everywhere. These blurry elements of a riot and his own testimony were all he seemed to have. It was his recognition of this fact that had narrowed his ambitions considerably, to the point that all he wanted, to the detriment of other aspects of his life, was for his experience to be preserved where it truly mattered: in a police station, in a court of law. He was determined to see his attackers jailed. At the same time, the image of their imprisonment bothered him. 'This was a fight between citizens and the government. Why did your sons need to get involved? Why did you not stop them? Why did it have to come to this?' He said that one of his alleged attackers, a man named Vikas, had been jailed. 'His family is ruined. Who will look after his baby? This awful thing did not have to happen. What is his mother going to do? Why was he fighting for a party? Imagine fighting for a political party.' He was in tears again.

Four days after Nisar's escape, the Delhi government announced a compensation package for any physical and financial damage the state's residents had suffered. The rupee rates were published in a document with the chief minister's smiling visage at the bottom. Ten lakh rupees for an adult's death in the family, half that for the death of a child, five lakh for uninsured shops, twenty-five thousand rupees for a lost rickshaw. When Nisar tried to claim his due, he was told to have his complaint acknowledged by the police first. He visited the Gokulpuri station near the charred car spares market. 'The station was filled with people registering their complaints,' Nisar said. When it was his turn, Nisar relayed events as he had witnessed them, and reported the names of his attackers. But the officer writing his complaint told him that his testimony had to be saada—without the embellishment of names. 'I would have to say that the rioters were unknown persons,' Nisar remembered. The officer told him that a generic complaint would receive police approval faster, and therefore his relief money would be released to him that much sooner. The details could always be added later.

For a while, Nisar said, he was tempted by the possibility. But eventually he refused the offer. 'I didn't want the money,' he said. 'Whether it's twenty-five thousand, two-and-a-half lakh or five lakh, I don't want it. I wanted the report written the way I saw it. I wanted him to write that I had evidence, that I had videos.' The videos were on his phone, which was in his pocket then, but he didn't mention this to the officer. 'I had a feeling they weren't doing what they were supposed to,' Nisar said. He feared they would confiscate his phone and destroy the evidence. He returned home, made copies of his evidence and returned to the police to register a case.

That was when a new ordeal began. The police interrogated Nisar. Sometimes there were two of them, sometimes a few more. If a senior officer had decided the questioning was going nowhere and took charge, seven or eight police came along and stood around him, probing his memory and integrity. They asked him the same questions again and again, to which he had the same replies: he knew the boys, they were from his colony, and he had seen them murder nine men.

This went on for ten or fifteen days every month for a year. Come here, one branch of police would say. Go there, someone else would say. He came, he went.

They asked if he was sure of the men he had named.

Yes.

Absolutely sure?

Yes.

One hundred per cent sure?

Arey bhai, haan.

They would write down the names after listening to him carefully, but forget a few in their official report. Noticing the discrepancy, he would repeat the names of the murderers they had missed, and they would listen carefully again, but would miss the same names on their second try. This dance between recollection and record would continue until they were in step. Then the investigators would ask him the same questions again, and Nisar wondered if they were really interested in his testimony, and if it wasn't all actually being done to grind him down. 'I told them, "Sir, the only solution for you now is my death. There is no other choice."'

Eventually, they wrote down what he told them: that two hundred to two hundred and fifty people had assembled and these people were shouting slogans such as 'Jai Shri Ram', 'long live Hindu unity', 'arise Hindus arise'. He recognised eighteen boys. He noticed iron rods and wooden sticks in their hands, and saw them gathering Hindus to evict Muslims. 'On hearing loud noises he got frightened and came down in his room. He further stated that due to fear he made a number of [calls to the police] but no one came to help him and on the same day in the evening the riot started,' the police recorded in his statement. The next day the same people were part of the crowd that robbed him. He told the police that the mob checked people's IDs. If they found a Muslim, they would 'beat him to death and dump his body into the [canal]'. This went on for three days, Nisar said.

As Nisar made the rounds of police stations and repeated everything he knew, a local legislator involved in the violence called him on his phone and asked in an extra-friendly way, 'Why don't you come over and we'll have a chat?' Someone offered him enough money to cover everything he had lost, and to live a good life. He had expected this to happen, and told his wife that the money wasn't worth it. On the street, when the two policemen with him had picked up their pace and the lawyers he was with had fallen behind, a man had caught hold of him and hissed, 'Heard you're giving evidence?' In the courtroom, one of the men he had named enquired of the witnesses as politely as he could, 'Who is Nisar Ahmad?' Then a mother of one of the men accused of murder screamed,

'Nisar Ahmad! Where are you? I'm going to kill you!' She said she would hound him in this life and the next.

The pressure was relentless. A month after his complaint, a Delhi police constable rang Nisar and put a BJP councillor on the phone. Nisar knew him all too well as the man who had stood on the bridge near his home and urged the crowd to kill Muslims. He had been photographed with Union ministers—not in the photo's centre, but always just to the side, giving him the whiff of a small-time satrap. The councillor had questions about the accused Nisar had named.

The following month, when Nisar went home to salvage what was left, five of his attackers visited his home. The next month, a suspect named by Nisar called him in a threatening tone. Then the police constable called again to demand that he not name a particular suspect. Another accused called to plead for a meeting and was refused; the following day he called again, this time from inside Nisar's sister's home. He told Nisar to speak with her, for she had something to tell him, but he refused. Nisar's sister had continued to stay in Bhagirathi Vihar, a few homes down from Nisar's former residence. She was a small woman with a jumpy manner and a stricken face, as if horrors recalled and anticipated were etched into her appearance. It was understood by everyone that she was Nisar's weakness. She was motivated to persuade him. She had a family, and soon visited him to request that he withdraw his complaint. She returned without success. The family that had given Nisar's family refuge during the riots was visited by a local who threatened them for their actions. The head of the household, a decent man Nisar had known for a decade, called him. He was inconsolable, and said he didn't know what to do.

The police dithered on security when he asked for it. The judge, though, ordered them to protect him immediately, and bring him to the courts themselves. He told Nisar to be careful on hearing days.

This meant being careful all the time. After we met at the hospital in late November 2021, he was summoned at least three times that month to tell the story again. 'The whole day goes in this when they call,' he said. In April 2022, the month we met in Mustafabad, he received court summonses on six separate days. 'I'm unable to do any work,' he said, defeated. One investigator wanted Nisar to accompany him to Bhagirathi Vihar to point out where the CCTV cameras were. A policeman asked him to return to Bhagirathi Vihar to point out the houses of the accused.

It all felt like testing, probing the limits of his tolerance. They rubbed him against every surface of the justice system: long hours, repetition, days spent sitting in a police station, identifying people, the same questions asked again. He knew this, and kept going back, sometimes losing his temper with them, mostly just answering the questions. 'It feels like they don't want to find the people who did this, because those people are still outside and free. Where are the people who organised this? I told the judge that I knew these boys. They don't have it in them to kill. Who made them do this?'

I came to see Nisar as special because he was unyielding to convenience and pragmatism. His insistence on naming his neighbours, and on visiting the police and court on every date that he was called, however many times each month, had a financial price, and this exacted a toll on his mind. He had lost almost half a crore in merchandise and equipment in the violence. It was a sum whose meaning I could imagine; it had taken me eighteen years of work, of learning the ways of money, to put together as much. Nisar's loss was compounded by each summons, which demanded his attendance with the threat that if he did not turn up, 'a warrant will be issued to compel your attendance'. His punctuality would not assure him a hearing that day, or the ear of an investigator. His interrogators had lives to lead, they had vacations, they had to be elsewhere on urgent business that day. Meanwhile, he would have to wait.

This is not to say he did not waver. I rang him late one night, when he had returned after a whole day of waiting for an inspector to turn up. 'Too much is happening. I can't bear it any more.' He was angry, but calmed down within minutes. He mentioned conversations with police investigators who privately expressed their helplessness: 'Nisar bhai, I don't know what I am supposed to do.' He had several stories like this, of policemen unable to disobey illegal orders. Depending on who told him how helpless they were, or who was stern in court that day, they would have Nisar's sympathy. On days when a policeman shook his head and smiled ruefully at how lawless the country was, Nisar would say that the police were working hard. On days when the judge criticised the police, Nisar would say, 'the police isn't working properly'. I saw him not as easily swayed, but as so overwhelmed by the frailties and dysfunctions of the colossal justice system that he did not know where to affix blame. Judges hearing his cases were transferred. The process of hearing his case would begin all over again. The burden he shouldered was that justice was his responsibility alone, because no other part of it seemed to work. His enthusiasm was forced, and he felt a need to express it to me. He had somehow survived the great reservations of his family, the threats of his neighbours, and had corrected the police on several occasions. But it was taking too long, he said. He wanted not just the foot soldiers, but their leaders in jail.

'I don't know what's happening. This is Delhi. All the powers of this country are here. And even then the courts don't function properly. How must it be in smaller courts?' he wondered. 'The breeze that flows from the seat of power should be clean. That's how good messages reach the country's furthest places.'

He had his village in mind when he said that the mahaul—a word that encompassed the air, the earth and the taste of a place—had changed. 'We used to plough the fields together. People of both communities used to live among each other. Now they don't. People have changed. The way they talk has changed.

It's not that fighting happens only when we're fighting. The grounds for anything happening are being created. Men want to live among their own. But India will grow when people live among each other. New laws have to be made because people are changing. Why is China advancing? They don't focus on these things. Make roads, make dispensaries. When brothers hate each other, the house doesn't move forward. I have washed idols in temples. I have touched their feet. Anyone shares knowledge, I respect him. I don't know why people focus on one book, one knowledge.'

# 9

# Traitors

'My mood's been off since last night,' Nisar said one day, handing me his phone.

He was nearly asleep when his nephew, who ran a shop distributing rations, sent him a video he had accidentally received. Or perhaps it was done on purpose to spread disquiet, and show a Muslim man his place.

A young man's face appeared, round and crisply bearded. His baseball cap was worn back to front, and his white shirt had shoulder pads. Birds chirped and leaves rustled while he told Hindus to defend themselves. The video had been posted to an online group in support of a Hindu nation. 'Brothers, be ready for the third. Something big can happen on the third. You should be ready for what can happen. Keep your weapons ready, keep acid ready. For your safety,' he said. 'Don't riot, but if there is a riot, don't spare them. Remember this. Jai Shri Ram.'

Nisar said, 'Eid is on the third.'

'I have one more thing to say,' the man continued. 'There are traitors in our midst. We have to remove them from our groups, however many groups there are. If we get in trouble, it's because they're rats. Remember, our own people are a bigger danger than them. Everybody should be ready. Jai Shri Ram.'

We located the young man in minutes after finding his name in the clip. The video had been posted on a platform built to resemble Instagram, and then we found him in photographs and videos taken at The Iron University, a gym in Uttar Pradesh that was less than half an hour away. Going by his frequent updates, he was not hiding. In one picture he lifted dumbbells, in others he posed beside muscular men he admired. Nishant Thakur was a wrestler who saw himself as an enforcer. 'Do your duty, leave the chaos to us,' Thakur wrote. He was a 'criminal mind' and 'proud to be a paagal [mad] Hindu', a declaration he bookended with orange flags, an iconographic marker of nationalist Hindus. Hate groups filled with provocative news stories amplified Thakur's call to Hindus. Noticing that the name of one group ended with the number '94', Nisar remarked that it was the postal code for Old Mustafabad. The conclusion easiest to reach was that the group was responsible for the area.

Nisar looked at the floor in silence for a while. He finally said, 'Thakur's talking about collecting and using weapons. What a big thing to do.' In moments like these, Nisar seemed like a man from another time. A more jaded person would have merely been perturbed by the implications of Thakur's call. Nisar, however, could not begin to imagine that a mind would seek such violence. In fleeting moments like these, Nisar felt to me like a lighthouse.

In the meantime he summoned the nephew who had received the video. The young man had shuttered his ration shop in the afternoon and hurried over to meet Nisar. He was dressed in black, and his shirt had long sleeves, despite the temperature. The video had come to him from a person he did not know. Plenty of people had his number, he said.

'But why did it come to you?' Nisar demanded an answer. 'Did your friends send it to you?'

The nephew was baffled by the insinuation. He loudly protested his innocence. Nisar did not believe him, but said nothing further. The mistrust dissipated by itself.

'Two nights ago they came on motorbikes twice and shouted Jai Shri Ram,' he said to Nisar after a while.

'Who did?' Nisar asked.

'Bajrang Dal boys. They came on bikes at three in the morning, and then at six. Everybody got scared,' he said. The militant affiliate of the RSS had chosen the time well. It was the month of Ramzan, and Muslims were awake in their homes, preparing food before the dawn fast began. 'People started calling me to ask what they should do. I told them to sell their houses and go away. What else will they do? Anytime two-three boys get together, Jai Shri Ram starts.'

Later Nisar told me that the words Jai Shri Ram filled him with dread, as if terrorists had come. 'These people will beat police tomorrow, and judges the next,' he said.

When Nisar was contemplative, he went quiet and touched his fingertips with his thumb, the way people touching prayer beads do. He sat back against a wall and looked across the room with a smile. 'I don't know. It feels like we're living in such a strange place. It feels like anything can happen in this atmosphere.' He mumbled, 'This coming and going. These difficulties. The difficulty in work. Breathing. I'm not able to breathe. What to do, what not to do? I'm unable to make sense of it. There's no freedom to live.'

The third of May came and went, and there was no incident barring the bulldozers that demolished Muslim homes across the country. Weeks passed. One day, Nisar wrote from Delhi to tell me about a cluster of new summonses he had received. He would present his testimony and stand as a witness four times in one week before a new judge. He was optimistic, because a spurt of summonses meant that gears somewhere were turning. I wrote back to him from Mumbai: Nisar bhai, I'll meet you in court.

# 10

# His Day in Court

In the last days of May 2022, Nisar headed to Court No. 71 on the fifth floor of the Karkardooma court complex in East Delhi. It was an officious series of buildings, and the walls were coated with stickers advertising candidates for the upcoming elections. Long queues headed inside for civil and family matters to be adjudicated disintegrated when the gates opened at nine thirty, with Nisar somewhere inside. He popped out the other side of the security funnel eventually and took a moment to smooth his linen shirt and dab his brow with a kerchief. An unfit and unarmed constable, sweating excessively, trailed him closely for protection. The sign above Court 71 described it as a sessions court, and the judge in it went by the name of Pulastya Pramachala, a twister that even lawyers who knew him mangled. Nisar's appointment was for ten that morning, and he had arrived early, but now the justice was late, so he waited on a chair covered in plastic, and chatted with the policemen off to one side of the room doing paperwork. It was quiet, but for the sound of pages turning and files being shuffled. At the head of the room, on a raised ledge beyond a glass or acrylic screen, clerks would type out what was said. Behind them, on a higher stage, was Pramachala's chair. What elevated the chair, more than its raised vantage point, more than the emblem of the Emperor Ashoka directly behind it, the words 'Satyameva Jayate'—Truth Will Prevail—beside it, was the presence of a white towel draped over its back. It felt absurd that one of the perks of power in a humid country was the expectation of a dry back.

The policemen were bored. A muscular cop flexed his back muscles. 'This judge comes late,' one cop told a clerk. Nisar leaned over to say that this was the third judge hearing this particular case. 'I couldn't tell the previous judge my evidence. Couldn't tell him the full thing,' he said. 'Then the judge changed and I couldn't tell them the whole thing. Now I have to do this again,' he said. 'It keeps stopping halfway.' And yet he was hopeful, as evinced by a smile that nearly faded before he reinforced it. For support he had come with Sagar, a small and trim man who described himself as an artist, but later corrected me. Not artist, artiste; he worked in Bollywood, where a new project was just getting started. When Nisar was out of earshot, he said to me, 'You won't find a braver man.'

Within minutes the room filled equally with police and lawyers. It grew stuffier, and Nisar fiddled with his handkerchief. Four overhead fans were on, but the heat was intense. At eleven minutes past ten, the judge arrived, and Nisar straightened in his seat. He was ready to be called there and then by this man who looked like a principal about to set chaos straight. He was bald, and wore glasses, but it was his unpitying look when he summoned the police that really brought a smile to Nisar's face. He said it with complete authority, with no deference to rank. And the hearings hadn't even begun. This was why Nisar thought it would be his day. While the judge read case papers, the lawyers stood against the glass screen and searched for signs in the face of the judge, who ignored them and showed them nothing.

Then the day began properly. A man in the witness box had been taken into custody, but lawyers were filing for anticipatory bail. The judge raised his voice, shook his head and told them it was wrong. He ordered the cops to do something. One slouchy cop scratching his crotch called the man over politely and parked him in the corner of the room furthest from the door. A cluster of male lawyers argued that the man's wife needed to be inseminated. There was talk of cysts and ovulation. The judge was not impressed, and turned down a bail extension. 'I give you a temporary bail, you'll make it permanent.' He ordered the police to take him into custody and told his lawyer to go to the high court.

The second case was about a man who owed a small sum of money. He was unkempt, and perplexed to find himself in court for the matter. The judge spoke with him gently but sternly, like a parent not yet exercising authority, and told him to pay by 1 July. In the next case, ten defendants were summoned to the witness box. Eight were young men, two were older. It was the state versus them. They crowded inside the compartment, holding rags to their faces. The clerk handed the judge a file five or six inches thick, and he began reading it. The lawyers waited at the head of the room. The men in the witness box waited, wearing a look I came to recognise among detainees brought to court: a featureless landscape. Circumstance had beaten them into detachment. The police stared at the floor and did administrative work. The clerks brought out other files. The constable there for Nisar's protection dozed in the last row, his chins lapping on his chest. Nisar watched it all and held onto the evidence he had brought the judge in a packet. Then the prosecutor for the state, a man I recognised but could not place, asked the judge if he could leave. He had to attend a hearing in a high-profile case involving a student leader who had been jailed for a speech two years before. The judge was not pleased.

Men walked in, men walked out, hours passed, and at some point a string of policemen came in, each with his fingers intertwined with those of a defendant in judicial custody. They did so unselfconsciously, and looked to the judge as if they were marrying. They both knew not to let go even when they entered the witness box. At one point there were eighteen people inside and outside the witness box, each with an arm outstretched, linked in body and mind. An advocate announced he would make an oral submission, at which the judge's face clouded. He stopped the lawyer there and then with a withering order: 'I'm not a god, and I'm not Akbar. I have to go by the law, and so do you.' The lawyer was chastised, and given ten minutes to print his submission.

'How can you stand this?' I asked Nisar. He had been present in court for dozens of hearings where nothing happened.

'It becomes a habit,' he said.

At 2.15 p.m., two public prosecutors told Nisar to be ready. He was an eyewitness for the government's case, and his testimony would hold special significance. He nodded and continued waiting. The boys he had seen grow up without incident, who he now claimed had damaged and killed, were brought to the witness stand. One of them, Dinesh, was dressed all in white, and his oiled hair shone under the lights. Another, Rinku, stood beside him unsteadily. An advocate asked Nisar to come to the front.

But before he could begin, Pramachala asked the government's lawyers for evidence on a compact disc.

'Is it necessary for this case?'

The prosecution said it was. A senior cop said that it was.

'Then why isn't it here? On what basis are you carrying on this case?' He asked why they hadn't made copies of the CD. The prosecution settled on misdirection; they had added a document to the file. The answer was mystifying to the gallery, and even the judge, who had probably seen plenty, was surprised.

'I'm asking you one thing and you're giving me another answer,' he said. His fingers pressed together on his lips, and he watched the policeman and the prosecution.

'Tell me,' he said, finally, worryingly politely, 'how should we proceed? Tell me.'

The room went quiet. The prosecution said nothing, and neither did the police. The judge turned to Nisar and spoke softly. For how long had Nisar been waiting to give his testimony? Two years, he replied. The judge apologised for keeping him waiting, and assured him that he would have a chance to present his testimony soon. Pramachala gave the prosecution ten days to put their evidence together.

Nisar smiled weakly, pressed his palms together in respect to the judge, and took his packet outside. He was satisfied with the outcome.

'He made them tight. Now they'll be good. They'll have to do as he says.'

'Yes, but you essentially have another delay,' I said.

'Yes. It's a delay.'

I asked M. Raja, who represented Nisar, if the government's prosecutors were interested in seeing the boys in jail. His answer was in effect: not really.

Then, four days later, on a Saturday morning, Nisar had to return to the same court. While I waited outside for him, the corridor filled up with Muslim men who said they had been picked up for rioting without evidence.

'I was just standing there,' a laundryman said. He had eight cases registered to his name. 'There's nothing, no photo, no evidence.' He too had visited the court over and over. A boy nearby, who plastered walls for a living, had thirteen cases against him.

A senior police officer, his tight slacks riding up his clenched butt, saluted the judge. Nisar leaned over to me and expressed his admiration for the officer, who he said was accomplished at extrajudicial killings. 'He's an encounter specialist. Thirty-five encounters,' he said. Decades of red-tapism had reconfigured Indian minds into viewing all delays, including hold-ups in justice, as bureaucratic inflexibility. Encounter specialists hurried things along, freeing up taxpayer money, jail space and the court's time. It was the sort of efficiency defeated minds longed for, overlooking the gossamer-thin pretext the police provided: how a dangerous delinquent broke free, or how a hardened criminal lunged for a gun.

When he was called shortly after ten, Nisar stood up from his chair, took his plastic bag and went to the front of the room, where the investigating officers and lawyers were. The judge looked at Nisar and told the prosecution not to waste Nisar's time. He ordered them to organise themselves so that Nisar wasn't called repeatedly. Then he apologised to Nisar and said that it wouldn't happen that day. Nisar was assured, once again, that he could give his testimony once matters were organised better.

Once more, Nisar pressed his palms to the judge and smiled wanly, and sighed when his back was turned. Outside, he caught up with the lawyer and asked about his payment as a witness. 'You'll get paid next time,' the lawyer said.

Nisar was unhappy, and he tried to complain to his lawyer. 'I keep coming here again and again. I haven't been able to give my testimony.'

The lawyer was irked by Nisar's persistence, and told him sharply to let it go. 'You shouldn't take tension about this. You just come to the court when he calls you. Let the other guy take tension. You go now.' He dismissed Nisar as an inconvenience. Outside the court complex, as he waited for his taxi to arrive, Nisar said, 'I don't know what's going on. I want to give my testimony, but they don't seem to want it. If you don't take testimony, it'll be like the riots never happened.'

He felt, in these moments, somehow reduced by his experiences, as if there was an unwritten set of rules instead of written laws. In these moments, I felt, he needed commiseration and reassurance. I stopped writing and told him reflexively, 'It'll be okay, Nisar bhai.' I did not believe it—there were too many forces and calculations at work—but perhaps it was what he required.

But he ignored it, unlike before, when he gave consoling words his consideration. 'This is why witnesses die without giving testimony,' he said. 'They're killing time.'

I stood beside him, bristling on his behalf. Pramachala came with the possibility of a fresh start, an honest attempt to reach the truth. But the delays and adjournments, for whatever reason, turned recent crimes into distant ones, turned memories brittle, turned the resolution of a witness soft.

His taxi arrived, and the driver announced immediately that he would not take Nisar inside the Muslim neighbourhood. Mustafabad was too large, and its streets were too narrow for a car. In a tone that signalled he would not budge, the driver explained that the journey would end at the bridge on the main road. That was where Nisar had seen the crowds and the loudspeakers. From there he would have to find his own way. For a second Nisar was roused to protest, but the emotion left him just as quickly. He gave me an awkward hug, sat behind the driver, and left.

# 11

# Bleak House

When Nisar was next summoned to Pramachala's court, months had passed. Lawyers sensed a quickening in the hearings, even if they were only to see if the evidence was admissible. He reached there in the morning, this time accompanied by an Islamic scholar who had come from the Jamaat. He was there to give Nisar heart. Some years before, Nisar had invited him home to do the Tarawi during Ramzan—a slow, meditative reading of a section of the Quran. It was like namaz, but more detailed, he explained: 'The Tarawi reminds people how to live and how to behave. It takes two hours to read, not ten minutes.'

In the intervening months, Pramachala's grey beard had grown out, as had his mullet. His pate was shiny, and reflected clearly a fluorescent light above. As I entered the full room, he was, as usual, displeased by someone. He spent most of the morning frowning as he read case documents, arching his eyebrows at lawyers, and schooling them on the finer points of the laws they freely and dramatically invoked in their arguments. It was stifling and led to unpleasantness. He gave them no room to breathe, catching hold of words as they left their mouth, asking questions before a thought had been fully articulated. If half the thought was substandard, why wait for the full thing?

To one lawyer struggling to make his case, he said, 'It's better that I read the case file instead of you arguing it.'

Lawyers entered the room confident, but by mid-morning they had surrendered. This was how time passed in this judge's arena: in endless demands for basic competence from people waiting out time, and in his bottomless disappointment. If anything brought him happiness, it was when someone hapless stumbled into his range with a weak argument, a presumption, or a pointless question. Then his demeanour altered slightly—just enough for the lawyers to sense that bloodless violence was imminent.

That morning, a special public prosecutor opened his piece with the usual pretence that his evidence was solid. He showed Pramachala a frame from a video shot during the violence. The judge interrupted him to ask where the complete video was, and then again to ask if he knew its source. The prosecutor's explanation did not satisfy Pramachala, and he continued to interrupt the lawyer in a search for authenticity, but the lawyer only wanted to move on. The breaks made him argumentatively immobile, and the point he hoped to make soon became a chimera. The public prosecutor was the Union government's representative in court, but he also considered himself a respected prosecutor. At the latest of the judge's questions, his irritation, his sense of self, his importance, all rose to the surface, and he screamed at the judge.

'I am a respected advocate! You cannot treat me like this!' the lawyer, a man named Gaur, shouted. Pramachala made him miserable, he said. 'I'm very agitated.'

In Pramachala's court, fear ran only one way. All authority and respect was focused on him. That was the natural order. But the lawyer had spun off whatever axis he had been assigned, and the anticipation of violence silenced people. Pramachala did not take disrespect well. 'What do you want from me?' he said, also shouting.

'I have no expectations,' he said. Of you, people heard. 'Are you a headmaster? You've turned this court into a school.' He stomped away and found an empty chair that was furthest from the judge, but one from where he could show the judge his anger. He looked all around the judge, but not at him. He would not give him that. Pramachala could see him, and he considered what to do about this indiscipline.

'I've turned it into a school?' he said. It felt like he was goading him towards contempt or disbarment.

'All of us public prosecutors are going to boycott the court!' Gaur kept going. 'You've got into the habit of giving lectures.' Sensing that he was now in uncharted territory, Gaur's voice carried a softer edge to show that his rebellion was in the court's interest. 'The juniors will not tell you this.'

'Look, you have to answer my questions,' Pramachala said.

'If you're unhappy with me, throw out my case.' He stared down the judge.

'It's my job. I'm not throwing out or transferring your case,' Pramachala said. It was as if he knew that the case would be heard all over again.

'Let us tell you things step by step. Hear us out. It'll make the working atmosphere better.'

Pramachala smiled. 'May I speak?'

Gaur permitted him.

'I need to understand your case. I have to ask you questions. And when I ask you questions, your reply is unconnected. It leaves my question behind. If you and your investigating officer can't give me a set point and I ask you where a video or picture was taken, am I asking you something out of the scope of your charge sheet?'

As reasonableness returned to the proceedings, Gaur made a peace offering. 'We want to work to your satisfaction.' He told Pramachala that he would submit a site plan that explained where the riot's major events had happened.

'The viral footage. Where is it from? What is its provenance? Is it from a mobile? A CCTV? Where is it from? That's the kind of detail I want,' Pramachala explained, forcing a smile. He announced a break for water so that everybody could cool off. He rose slowly, with the look of a man who had imagined a fight turning out differently.

Three lawyers sitting in the back row waited until he was gone before laughing at what had transpired. One of them, a young man with neat hair and shirt tucked in tidily, had filmed Gaur, and he laughed at his surreptitious video. It was risky, recording in a courtroom where it was strictly prohibited, in which police were everywhere. Later someone explained that his father, K.K. Tyagi, was a legal counsel for the BJP.

Nishant Tyagi, the son, turned to talk to me. I had watched the proceedings standing behind the last row, out of everyone's way, and he gestured to me to come closer so that he could say something. I obeyed, and he said—in a low voice that conveyed he was sharing confidences—that Nisar's testimony could not be trusted because he had been paid 'fifteen lakhs by the Delhi government and the Jamaat to implicate my client'. He claimed that the hearings were 'a conspiracy' to frame a BJP councillor, a man named Kanhaiya Lal. Nisar had accused Lal of first coordinating the riots in Bhagirathi Vihar, and then of questioning Nisar's memories of who he had seen. Lal had wanted to know if Nisar had mentioned a man named Mowgli, one of the fourteen men on trial, Nisar recorded in a police complaint. I listened to Tyagi, waiting for him to finish being clever. Perhaps he saw himself as some legal mastermind, slipping in an insinuation that he imagined the journo would print, leading to Nisar's testimony being seen as motivated or engineered by a religious body. 'Kid,' I wanted to say, throwing my weight, 'try harder.' Instead, I asked him how he knew about the payments, and his reply was unconvincing: 'You hear things.' He claimed he had evidence of the payments. I waited for the evidence, and if it was brought up in court, I did not hear it.

The lawyers with him were eager to cross-examine Nisar. 'I told my client that I'm going to skin his hide,' Tyagi told a ponytailed advocate with a smudge of vermilion on his forehead. The lawyer, named Rakshpal Singh, was in charge of the Delhi legal cell of the Vishwa Hindu Parishad, which worked closely with the RSS. He said to Tyagi, 'I'm going to turn him into a rag doll.' What his confidence was based on I couldn't tell. When I searched for his name on the Delhi courts website, every bail application he had filed for nearly five years appeared before me; all of them had been dismissed. But they slapped palms and laughed, sure they had found a chink in the testimony Nisar had given to the police.

The water break Pramachala had called for was prolonged. After half an hour had passed, we learned that he was in his chambers behind the courtroom with the government's lawyers. We realised he was about to return only when a line of constables entered the courtroom holding onto a line of accused. Their fingers were intertwined, and their faces revealed nothing of how they felt. One by one, the suspects, who were all young men, some of whom were in their teens during the riots, entered the dock while holding onto their constable's fingers.

Forty minutes after he had called for a quick break, Pramachala returned. It was just before lunch. Nisar was ordered to a chair at the front, where he would face the judge. From there he would give his testimony, and the judge would provide him his full attention from his raised platform. Eight hundred and eighty-seven days had passed since Nisar's escape, and now his memory would be tested.

Pramachala immediately asked Nisar's address, and Nisar said it out loud. I was alarmed by this, and looked at the wooden enclosure where the suspects stood. They had blank faces. Then he told Nisar to give his testimony.

Held back for so long, Nisar took off with his story, as if the judge would be transferred mid-sentence. He believed that his words, once uttered in court, would be set in stone. He began with the procession, the slogans and chanting on the bridge, and told them the story, everything, and under the judge's questioning he admitted there were things he did not know. Nisar said, for instance, that there had been chaos all night long. He said there was looting in the darkness. 'How did you know there was looting if it was dark? Be specific,' the judge said. 'You have to tell me what you saw with your eyes, heard with your ears, smelled with your nose, tasted with your tongue, or felt on your body. Hold this truth in your fist and answer.'

Nine advocates for the defence and three public prosecutors stood over Nisar at the front of the room, crowding him, making smaller the space around him. There had been no preparation, no attempt to tell their witness what to expect. (A criminal lawyer told me that preparing a witness was considered interference with testimony.)

Nisar was a frustrating witness. He struggled to be precise. He forgot the judge's advice, forgot how he was expected to speak, and rambled on at the judge. The lawyer who boasted he would turn Nisar into a rag doll stood so close to Nisar that his foot constantly nudged the witness, distracting him. 'I knew that if I complained it would break my concentration,' Nisar told me later. At times, the judge would be short with him, and throw up his hands and say that he didn't understand. When the judge asked about what the crowd did, he replied that they took all his motorcycles, including one he had given his son as a wedding present. At the mention of the present, the judge reminded him to 'stick to the question', but he said it softly, with a smile. The lawyers, defence and prosecution both, looked at each other over Nisar's head and grinned.

Beside Nisar, not four feet away, the fourteen accused stood in the dock, a rickety wooden construction waist-high and shaped like a square bracket. All of them were men, but a few of them had not let go of boyhood; some of them had been nineteen when the violence occurred in North East Delhi, and their manner was in contrast to the worried faces around them. They whispered in each other's ears and smiled. One of them was rail-thin and dressed in a white shirt meant for an evening out. He had the loose limbs of a dancer, and laughed as if his presence there was the result of a misunderstanding.

But as the day went on they grew tired of standing and became restless. Someone yawned, someone twirled his moustache, someone picked his nose. Every few minutes someone or the other stared at the clock right above my head, and then at me for a few minutes. Their phone chats allegedly revealed that on the nights of 25 and 26 February 2020, they formed a WhatsApp group with as many as one hundred and twenty-five members. One spoke of his 'team' killing two 'mullas'. Another asked if anyone had bullets for a '315', an Indian pistol. One said, 'Brothers . . . if anyone has any problems, or if you find yourself short of men, tell me. I will bring my entire team. We have everything you need. Bullets, guns, everything.'

Nisar tried to tell his story within the strict parameters of the judge's questions. Nor was that the only constraint. Each question demanded crisp storytelling, but brevity did not come easily to him. When he stopped, a long pause followed while the judge looked at the ceiling and softly translated Nisar's replies from Hindi to the transcriber beside him in English. The exercise served two purposes. Repeating the answer allowed Pramachala to cast its logic about in his mind, and it was often at this stage that he would stop midway and ask Nisar for clarification. It also gave him control over what was recorded at that moment. As the transcriber typed his words, the lawyers watched her screen on a monitor to make sure the details were correct. All of this gave the whole day a jarring motion, like being caught in a traffic jam.

Stripped of distraction and extraneous detail by the judge, Nisar's testimony came alive. As he spoke, the witnesses in the room could finally imagine. They fell silent when he described his wife's escape, and even then he could barely be heard over the silence. Instead, he was overtaken by the deference of the silence, a deference he had rarely experienced, and a mournful sound rose out of him. I could not see Nisar's face, but the judge could, and his stern countenance softened momentarily. The judge said to him, 'Ahmad, brother, be brave and be hopeful. There are ups and downs. You are down now, but there are ladders in life too.' He reminded everyone that the testimony would continue after the weekend. All this left Nisar shrunken by the day's end, withered by the effort.

The next day of hearings began like all the others—in protracted exhibitions of incompleteness and embarrassment. The public prosecutor, Ahmad, had submitted a CD with screen grabs, but no video. 'Who will verify where the screen grabs come from?' Pramachala asked. Then the ponytailed defence lawyer enthusiastically took control of the prosecution mic to tell the judge that nothing in Nisar's testimony had incriminated his clients; Nisar had witnessed each of the accused in the crowds, but sloganeering and being present did not mean they were guilty. The judge replied with a laugh, 'Give it time, give it time.'

That afternoon, after the accused were brought in once more, Pramachala asked Nisar about the men he saw. 'Can you identify them in this courtroom?'

With that, the room's occupants fell silent, and the processes that hummed on—the policemen ordering files in the corner, the lawyers reading case documents, the judge's assistants conferring with one another behind the glass screen—stopped. They looked to Nisar, who was alone. The lawyers who were crowding him minutes ago had moved aside, and a policeman came forward to stand beside him. Nisar stood up from the plastic chair slowly and took uncertain steps towards the men in the dock. The room was not large, and now they were close enough to touch him. He looked at the judge pleadingly, unsure of how close to go. 'Don't worry,' the judge and the lawyers said, both his own and from the defence. More uniformed men, some of whom greeted him every day in the court, edged forward as if to say, we're here.

'Step back from the witness box,' Pramachala told the policemen, 'or he might point to you as a suspect.' The men had only ever felt the judge's whip, not his taste in humour, and they backed away towards the exit in alarm. 'Wait! Where are you going?' the judge said, grinning. 'Don't be afraid!'

Nisar stood no more than three feet away from the accused. Their talking and laughing had ceased, and they watched him blankly. Nisar named the first man. The judge asked him to point to the accused when he named them. Nisar raised his arm and pointed to the man closest to the judge. He looked at the man's face and spoke his name. The judge asked the man if that was his name. He replied that it was. The judge ordered him to move to the crowd's rear. Nisar pointed to each man and named him. The judge asked each man if that was his name. 'Yes,' the men replied, except for one, who gave another name. Then Nisar stopped, and told the judge he recognised some of them only by their faces.

The moment was procedural and necessary, but his proximity to the fourteen men now amplified the bravery in his decision to become a witness. It was during this dramatic passage in the proceedings that his testimony on the page, records of which shuffled from the police to the court, breathed life. These men, standing here, were those men, he said. They went from being 'the accused' to being present in the room. A new light was cast on them and their standing was changed, for the witness had taken their name before a judge.

It was near the day's end, and the judge announced that the

defence would cross-examine Nisar the following morning. Nisar sat down and wiped his forehead. Later that night he wrote to me, 'I spoke ruk-ruk ke [haltingly] for so long that I forgot some things. I'm also a little worried about being shot.' The next morning, when it was almost 11.30, the defence attempted to take Nisar's testimony apart. Nine lawyers stood around him, each one awaiting his turn. The first of them asked Nisar how long he had lived in Bhagirathi Vihar, if his shop was open or closed, if he had workers, what their names were, and what their fathers' names were. The judge, who had restrained himself so far, divined the lawyer's line of questioning and asked his own questions. Nisar responded that the shop was closed due to a nephew's wedding. The defence lawyer asked if he had given a wedding card to the police. The judge raised his eyebrows, and the lawyer dropped the question.

Another lawyer stepped up to ask if the crowd Nisar had seen 'was peaceful or violent'.

'Violent,' Nisar said.

The lawyer began another question, but the judge stopped him. 'Do you want to know why they were violent?'

'No,' the lawyer said.

'I do. Why do you feel it was violent?' the judge asked Nisar.

'They called out people in defence of the Citizenship Amendment Act, there was sloganeering, they carried sticks, and they shouted victory to Lord Ram.'

The defence accused Nisar of lying, and not being present at the bridge. 'You didn't hear the slogans, nor was there a mob in the first place.'

Someone asked how wide the road outside his house was. Someone asked how far the bridge was from his home. Someone insisted Nisar was nearsighted. Someone asked how many cameras Nisar's phone had. Every line of questioning, when it was initiated, felt like an inspired approach; perhaps some new method of attack was being established. You could imagine the argument's evolution: that he was not present, that he could not see the bridge from his home, that his eyesight limited what he could see, that he was put up to all this. It was in the follow-up questions, though, that the defence revealed they had nothing. They would repeat their questions and ask about irrelevancies triumphantly, and the judge would say, 'disallowed' and 'matter of record'. They were waiting for Nisar to make a mistake that would hurt his credibility as a witness.

The lawyer with the ponytail had questions about the time Nisar escaped. That was all. There was no rag doll at the end of it, only a legal drama with a laugh track.

One of the accused, Ankit Chaudhary, was a 'high-value prisoner', a nervous security coordinator in a blue safari suit told me. He was accused of leading a murderous gang during the riots, and his arrival in court was usually preceded by several policemen. He wore a cap, and had vermilion on his ears, a religious marking. He was short but muscled, and everybody, including the police, joked with him and treated him with a certain deference. His topmost shirt button was open. He was comfortable enough to start walking out of the courtroom without his minder. Chaudhary called attention to himself by the way he stood, seeming to swagger without moving. Even in the courtroom, he stood where he wanted to, and asked a constable to vacate a chair. He persuaded them to let his friends sit beside him. The police were amused by his demands, but did what he said. When the judge was not in court, he would leave his cap on. He did not look like a prisoner, a man on trial. If anything, he looked temporarily restrained. The policemen around him acted as if they knew it too. 'They're behaving like they've done something great,' Nisar said.

At 4.11 p.m., the judge closed matters for that day. Nisar's testimony would continue on a future date that was still undecided. He stepped out and ran his fingers through his hair.

Relief was all over his face, and his protective escort was relaxed too, for the accused were no longer on the premises. Nisar often complained that the men in the dock were dangerous, but they were only foot soldiers. He did not think them capable of organising violence, only inflicting it. But the really dangerous men, the ones who hid behind the actions of foot soldiers, were still free. We began to discuss this when the policeman spoke up.

'And who's going to catch them?' he asked.

# 12

## Seeking Reassurance

When will you finish the book? Nisar asked me; a question to bring everything to a halt. It was in early 2022. We were on his motorbike, which was covered in pigeon droppings, and contained only as much petrol as he needed for his immediate purpose. We had just returned from the Bhagirathi Vihar street he had lived on. Whatever had energised him to revisit his old home now disappeared. He lowered the kerchief he had worn as a mask, and parked his bike in an alley. He was thinking. 'Can you do it soon?' he said.

'Probably two more years,' I said. I had assured him that I would have it translated into Urdu for him.

'You could keep working on the big book, but also do a small one that people can read right now. Write a book that children read in school. It should teach them to love. It will be better than their studies.'

I smiled, and he responded with a forced smile. The country was spinning away from him, and its connections to him were fraying.

'I don't know what's happening,' he said. 'There's no justice.' Something was on his mind, and after a while he told me what it was. 'Three more people were arrested. The main guy has been caught—the man on the microphone.' The man had praised the Delhi police the night the killings happened. Nisar was miserable. 'I wanted to cry when I heard. He has young children, and a wife. His family went to see him in court.'

Our conversations were sometimes uneven, ricocheting from a throwaway line on unemployment to a metaphor about uprooted trees, before landing on an assertion that politicians hampered police work. Before I could contemplate one utterance, Nisar's mind would float elsewhere. Over time, our conversations changed from daily events to his thoughts about life. The words would gallop out of his mouth, parables and philosophies ready for every present moment that disturbed him. He thought about subjects afflicting the country, and concluded that people had strayed from a righteous path. The burden of his unheard evidence made him more certain that the problem was not religion, but his morality; he was a humanist grappling with the disappearance of public propriety. He argued for more people like himself even as he suspected he was not essential to the country's new direction. He wanted accountability, and for the law to work, and for people to not call for killings. A man like him seemed to come in the way. His constant prayers for better sense and rule of law had gone unanswered. Although he could have let go of these desires and been at peace, he held on. He was rewarded with a rattled mind, and his conversations had a touch of manic energy.

'There's no work for anyone. People's attention is on the news. I'm going mad with the news, so I stopped watching it,' he said. 'It's like something has come and uprooted a tree. It takes years for a tree to grow again. The police want to work, but the politicians stop them from working. But the local police aren't working. It breaks people when courts take a long time. It encourages dishonesty. Why is there this carelessness? Why is it taking the police over two years to submit a video to court?'

# 13

# Private Memories

'I was everywhere,' Meharban said to me one night outside Jamia. When the protests ended on account of the virus, activists held an exhibition of his photographs. Protestors who saw themselves in his pictures cried. The rest of the photographs, he planned to publish in a book of photographs with other photographers. Seeing his work on Instagram and Twitter, Western magazines gave him special assignments, but in the current political environment no Indian publisher wanted to take responsibility for a coffee table book on agitators and police beatings, he told me.

He had not worked alone. During those months he partnered with other photographers. They stayed in touch over the phone constantly, telling each other where they were, the direction people were running from and the sources of the gunshots. They followed victims, and pointed to where the armed and helmeted foot soldiers of Hindu organisations had mobilised.

Meharban had a private Instagram account filled with pictures he wanted no one to see without his permission. It was a catalogue of his rage. One image was of a severed finger. In another, a man held onto what was left of his eye. He showed me a bruised woman on a hospital bed; she was weeks from giving birth. Then, without a word, he showed me one more.

I didn't know what to say. It was a close-up of a slim man's torso. There was no point in asking his name. The long cut down the middle was for the autopsy, but all the other incisions had been made in anger. It was as if the body was representative of a larger idea. It made sense when Meharban said, 'I feel safe when I'm in the ghetto. Here I can say anything. Nobody cares when you talk about the government. They know it's true. Anywhere else I would have to make sure someone isn't listening.' We walked on in the ghetto outside Jamia. The ghetto was a shield, even if it was of limited utility, for unlike the rest of the city, only the most extraordinary disruptions led to religious killings in a ghetto. The rest of the time it was just fine.

# 14

# Dangerous Hours

On a cold night in November 2021, at a tea stall outside one of Jamia's gates, Ali sipped a cup of tea in the light of a single bulb and told me where he came from. His was the only Muslim family on lane six in Mahipalpur, a dense neighbourhood near Delhi airport. Otherwise, there were only Hindus.

You could not imagine what that meant, Ali said. The best you could manage was empathy. His family did everything that was asked of them, he said. They lived watchfully. They dressed like everyone else. They were not particularly religious, and as far back as he remembered they concealed even the smallest accoutrements of faith. They celebrated Eid quietly. They did not visit mosques because they didn't pray very often, and the nearest one was seven kilometres away. They were surrounded by temples, orange flags and watching eyes. The family downstairs, otherwise good people, were firm supporters of the prime minister, which meant they sometimes said things. Cruel things, little pinpricks, spoken casually, easily. In the circumstances, a religious Muslim would be considered a challenge. One had to be careful. Words were a precursor to terrible things, so why give anyone the opportunity to speak?

Caution had sharpened Ali's father in the ways of others, and blunted his own expectations. Thirty years before, in

1992, thousands of Hindus tore past barricades and the police to break down the Babri Masjid, a four-hundred-and-seventy-five-year-old Mughal-era mosque which they imagined was built on the birthplace of the god Ram. Fury followed the celebrations. In Bombay, there were riots first (at least nine hundred were killed, most of them Muslims) and then twelve bombs went off at landmark buildings, in a cinema, hotels, in busy markets, in which a further two hundred and fifty died and over a thousand were hurt. When he talked about it, in the safety of his home, where he could be as religious as he wished, and express whatever was in his heart, Ali's father chose to say, 'No one prayed at the mosque anyway.'

All of this giving in and letting go only took them so far, Ali said. He stopped and turned to friends behind him, smiling shyly. 'This is where the more politically aware students hang out,' he told me. He watched a policeman pass by and kept an eye on him until he had left the area. He did not trust them.

Ali's world was mostly peaceful, except for the dangerous times. He had seen them so often that he could recognise their onset. He had seen it in Hindu classmates who were liberal friends one year at Delhi University, but who spoke of 'traitors' the next. He had watched his worried mother call their landlord the day the court was to deliver its judgement about the unused mosque's destruction. He remembered the landlord's assurances to her that nothing would happen to them, and remembered how the man stood sentry between their grief and the joyous bedlam outside. 'Dangerous hours,' Ali said. Dangerous hours were times when the rules of life and man were suddenly lifted. For how long would their safety be contingent on the protection of a Hindu person? It was no way to live, so his family left for the ghetto near Jamia.

They decided to settle in the Old Kanal Housing and Land Authority—although people just called it Okhla—a predominantly Muslim neighbourhood beside the Yamuna river in East Delhi. Here, at least at the very beginning, they found unhappiness. Loose wires electrocuted people, and anyone could put up posters anywhere and not take them down. Nobody collected waste. The buildings were squat and black power cables sliced the sky. There were advertisements for flats with 'two sides open view' of other buildings. All of it looked illegal, like a place that had sprouted without the requisite permissions, and which could no longer be moved. We arrived at the edge of the settlement nearest to the river, and walked along an open drain packed with sludge.

'These houses have the best view,' he said, indicating the buildings above the drain. I had kept my distance from the drain, but went closer for a better angle on my camera. The smell.

'What's good about it?' I said.

'If you don't look at the gutter, it's wide open,' he replied, pointing to the sky.

Ali strode through the ghetto in his slippers, with his arms held behind his erect back and angled shoulders, his bearing regal and ponderous; he was a young man with a problem the size of a country. 'I've realised the benefits of community,' he said about the ghetto and its inhabitants. Community gave him that rarest of sensations: a feeling of privilege.

One night, in a smoky restaurant, perhaps softened up by the plate of kebabs after a platter of biryani that was already too much, he wondered what it was like to be afforded the privilege of stupidity. The foolishness he had in mind was a freedom that Hindus took for granted—the freedom to say dumb things. A Hindu student he knew at Jamia declared with confidence that of course Muslim men were waging holy war by marrying Hindu women. They called it 'love jihad'. She didn't get beaten up for saying this, he said, smiling. The phrase was now widely parroted. It was the kind of stupidity Ali wished he was permitted. 'Of course, we're second-class citizens,' so it wasn't possible.

'I want to lash out, but I'm not able to speak my mind,' he said. He wondered what it was like to have the whole Hindu experience, every last bit of it, which seemed to include 'shooting a Muslim, and maybe going to jail a while, but then you come out a hero'.

# TWO

# A NEW COUNTRY

# 1

# In Defence of Faith

By moonlight and lamplight across north India, far from the eyes and ears of the colonial power that had put down an uprising in 1857, just two decades before, tireless preachers of a new sect of Hinduism spoke of a distant epoch of breathtaking glory, an age full of astonishments.

They asked their listeners to imagine power that was once theirs. Imagine, there were guns, and advanced philosophies of war and defence—such as weapons of water to counter weapons of fire—and unsurpassed scientific prowess that made India a teacher to the world. Imagine, visitors longed for the country the way they hankered after Europe now. Imagine, above all, how it was a time of one holy book, the Vedas.

And if they could imagine this, all this that had the ring of truth to it, then why did they live in superstition and fear? How did it come to be that villages prayed to a deity representing revenge, that they forged sacred metal seals that elevated local policemen to idols, that they begged the goddess of cholera for mercy? The preachers were itinerant representatives of the Arya Samaj—a reformist Hindu sect—and they illuminated this path taken to poverty and ignorance: the learnings of that advanced civilisation were lost in the great war depicted in the Mahabharata, they said. Everything ever gained was lost in the war, and the greatest of men who ever lived were also lost. But redemption and a return to glory was possible. They would need to return to the old books, for everything that was ever revealed was within them, and anything that anyone ever needed was within them.

The traumas of the 1857 cry for independence and its quelling were still fresh in parts of north India, as was what came after: the killing of rebels by cannon and public hanging, the faraway discussions about the effectiveness of flogging or loading with irons instead of death, the reorganisation of India's army, the territory's handover from the East India Company to the Queen—like a gift between relatives—and the taxes imposed on it to recover the costs of war. The loss was felt so strongly, the author Alok Rai wrote in *Hindi Nationalism*, that decades would pass before the event was recalled. The pain was so deep that it wrapped itself around all of life unnoticed.

The preachers arrived dressed in homespun clothes as a statement of self-reliance and quiet defiance, their stories of ancient might and superiority a salve for powerlessness, their contempt for Western influence a distraction from humiliation. What had the West given them that they had not once already created? they said. They asked questions meant to chastise and encourage, like an army of knowing teachers determined to help the forlorn rise above themselves. 'Why do you feel inferior to others? What is it that makes you ashamed of calling yourselves Indians? Why have you parted with your national pride and prestige? Why cannot you walk with your heads erect and high?' Their words echoed those of their leader.

The sect was founded by an ascetic tall and fat and smooth all over, who travelled, for a time, with nothing between him and the world but a loincloth. His birth name was Mula Shankar, but Dayanand Saraswati was the name he would adopt later in life. His fame would last, etching his name into infrastructure across India: Dayanand Saraswati bridge in Gujarat, Dayanand Saraswati junction in South Mumbai, a bus station, schools and colleges all over. Dayanand was born in 1824 in the state of Kathiawar, now Gujarat, into a traditional family of Brahmins—the highest of high castes. His father wished a religious life for him, and set him on a path to learning Sanskrit and memorising the Vedas. The education was in keeping with the times in a Hindu household where idol worship and the word of priests was taken above all else. It was tradition, how things had always been done. Tradition was comfort, tradition was cultural gravity.

There was a story told often to establish the moment of Dayanand's inflection from normal life towards immortality. When Dayanand was fourteen, his father led him to a temple on the evening of a sacred day. They would sit in abstinence in the inner sanctum for a vigil till sunrise, awaiting the rewards of divine attention for their persistence and suffering. The prayers began, and they focused their minds. As evening turned to night, one by one, devotees staggered out of the temple in a daze. The temple priests could no longer stay awake, and departed. The temple servants fell asleep outside as well. Dayanand watched them go, fighting the temptation to give up. When hunger came, he ignored the feeling. When his eyes closed, he splashed them with cold water. His father had prohibited him from eating, and warned him that his devotion would be irrelevant if sleep overcame him; before long, his father fell asleep. Dayanand watched the ceremony, near delirious with a cascade of questions and 'thought upon thought' about the recipient of his concentration, when he had a revelation. How was it possible, he wondered, for the unflinching trident-wielding temple idol before him to be a deity if even a mouse, its feet filthy, could tread on it? He shook awake his father, who explained that while god could not be perceived by men in this kal-yug, the age of darkness, he was pleased when the idol representing him was worshipped. Dayanand looked askance at the reasoning. He would later hold this moment responsible for his discontent with Hinduism's idol worship, and his followers would accept this explanation. (The truth was probably more complicated: a chronicler of India's religions in the early 1900s wrote that Dayanand was raised in a state influenced by a powerful sect of Jains who had given up idol worship in the fifteenth century, and he must have imbibed some of their practices.)

In his early twenties, determined to thwart his father's plans for his marriage, Dayanand fled his home. Almost immediately, he was relieved of his possessions, a development history records him as welcoming. Dayanand longed for knowledge and understanding of the roots of Hinduism, and reportedly read the books unmediated. He wanted to see for himself. He roamed across the plains and found other ascetics, and entered their orders in search of a truth that could receive no reply, a truth that would subjugate all argument. As he wandered, he shed parts of himself in order to better receive that truth, and he renounced his attachments when he was twenty-four. There was nothing more to be gained from money, family and caste. He was itinerant this way for more than a decade, learning from one teacher or another, about the human body's nerve circles and nerve centres, and the idea that 'God is personal, that the human soul is distinct from God, and that the world is real'.

Dayanand was thirty-six when he found what he was looking for in a blind Brahmin in Mathura; the year was 1850. The teacher ordered him to throw his books into the Yamuna River as a condition for receiving his teachings. He could not bear the influences of modern literature in the presence of the holy. He would beat and berate Dayanand and teach him the Vedas and the works of the Sanskrit grammarian Panini. The three years Dayanand spent there were formative, he wrote. He learned the Vedas, the hymns that formed the basis of Hinduism, and he took from his lessons the learning that Hinduism had once been pure, but it was now filled with robed middlemen and rogue superstitions. Before his departure, his teacher gave him one last instruction: to disregard the teachings of men and reach, instead, for the wisdom of ancient teachers, and go forth and teach the Hindu scriptures to a land that had forgotten them.

Dayanand wandered once more, taking these teachings to pandits, missionaries and pilgrims in the holy town of Haridwar on the banks of the Ganges. At first, though, he was unsuccessful in winning converts. Dayanand was a scold and, worse, a scold in Sanskrit, insisting in runic grammar that the holy men's practices and traditions had no value. On the advice of a well-wisher, he began to scold people in Hindi instead. There were other influences. Inspired by the habits of Christian missionaries, he opened schools that taught only Sanskrit—hopeful that students would one day proselytise for him—published books and pamphlets and gave endless lectures.

By the time he was fifty, Dayanand's following was substantial, especially in northern and western India. In packed halls and homes he railed against Hinduism's bloated and false worship; a correspondent wrote that pandits feared Dayanand as 'the champions of Rama dreaded the monster who is so conspicuous in the Ramayana'. He spoke in a sonorous voice, each word articulated slowly and loudly for the people standing at the back and outside. Dayanand steered them towards the education of girls, and away from child marriage and the banishment of widows; a girl should be at least twelve by the time she was married, and a widow was good for at least two children, he said. He argued for a reformation within the institution of caste, and railed against untouchability, a Brahminical construct. He argued that other religions were facsimiles of facsimiles of the books he preached. They nodded along. But then, he reminded them frequently, so was his own.

Witnesses recorded that Dayanand's arguments were passionate and backed by first principles. 'He may be regarded as the Lord Bishop of the Reformed Vedic Church,' an observer wrote. Dayanand took his knowledge and oratorial might up and down the Ganges, debating and holding forth. He called Hindu priests 'popes' in Hindi, and his listeners laughed at his wit. Some venues said he would no longer be welcome in the future, others threw him out then and there. At religious debates in front of large crowds, Dayanand demanded that priests explain where their authority came from, asking for the exact passage in their Book, and if they located the words, he extracted their meaning. At one meeting he asked a row of priests to show him where in the authoritative texts of Hinduism it was written that idols had to be worshipped. A priest replied that it was not in those texts, but in later writings and interpretations. Those interpretations, Dayanand told the priests, were self-serving, and their supposed importance was a benediction to themselves.

His supporters saw his theological debates as cosmic grudge matches, and they took pleasure in the spectator sport of Dayanand picking apart his opponents. But although his methods were entertaining, some witnesses found them maddening. At a discussion in Ajmer, Dayanand heard the locality's Hindus and Muslims debate the weaknesses of their religions. Finally he said to the Muslim, 'You grow a beard,' and to the Hindu priest he said, 'You grow a choti (ponytail): I would catch you by the beard, and you by the choti. I have neither; you cannot catch me.' The *Christian Intelligencer* reported that he allowed his opponents to speak, but he was 'extremely authoritative in all his positions', for Dayanand had already made up his mind. When he listened, it was 'with a kind of contemptuous courtesy'. His confidence infuriated the recipients of his attacks, and they declared it unnecessary to respond to an 'irresponsible wandering sanyasi'.

Still, listeners came out apparently transformed, their minds opened to new possibilities. His ideas offered to many a liberation from the holy men's interpretations of Hinduism, from their mediation in the affairs of a man and his god, in the matters of life and the afterlife. To many others, Dayanand's ideas were so troubling that they thought him 'a paid missionary of the British government', an allegation he would work hard to refute all his life. The respect afforded to him seemed matched, at times, with fear and derision. A procession celebrating him began with a decorated elephant, several musicians, and police for his protection. Behind them was another procession, less celebratory, featuring a donkey. The district magistrate of Benares, a British man, worried that Dayanand's discussion would cause trouble in his jurisdiction, and simply banned him from the city. From time to time, when there were no men to save them, his preachers received beatings. This was because Dayanand's acerbic criticisms of other religions were repeated by his followers. 'Wherever they went,' one observer wrote, 'one hears of slander, passion, and unfair methods; and disturbances in the streets and squares have been pitiably common.' But the sect spread and grew, from Bombay to the United Provinces a thousand miles away, with people hearing and understanding Dayanand's calls for purity in piety.

The undiluted Hinduism Dayanand preached may have been advanced five thousand years ago, but its punitive instincts were five millennia old; solid Old Testament Hinduism. There were eighteen kinds of disputes in the jurisdiction of courts, Dayanand wrote: 'debt, deposit, sale, partnership, wages, gifts, agreements, transactions, ownership, boundaries, assault, defamation, theft, transgression, adultery, altercation, inheritance and gambling'. He provided the appropriate punishment for the severity of the crime: 'Punishment should be inflicted on the genitals, belly, tongue, hands, legs, eyes, nose, ears, body, and property . . . Adultery is punished with death, a woman to be torn in pieces by dogs and a man to be burnt to ashes on a hot iron bed.' Dayanand believed the punishments would dissuade further crime. A British member of the Samaj described it as 'a reformatory agitation which inculcates a morality of almost unattainable severity'.

Missionaries were struck by how familiar the movement's methods were. The *Congregationalist*, a Boston newspaper, wrote of its paradox—the Arya Samaj was reflexive in its opposition to Christianity, but also influenced by its nemesis. 'Its ethics are Christian and not Hindu. It has turned its back on Brahminism, although it professes to derive its tenets solely from the Vedas. It condemns child marriage and widow burning, forbids the worship of ancestors, encourages education, and in general the spirit of its creed is very high. It assigns benevolence to the supreme Creator; heaven and hell it considers conditions or character, not places; obedience to God is one of its requirements.' The London Missionary Society was more certain: the teachings preached by the Arya Samaj were 'stolen from Christianity'.

Literature published by various missions active in India marvelled at the Arya Samaj's methods of disseminating its theology, especially its instinct for outreach through the press. In its decennial review of missions, the London Missionary Society attributed the Samaj's popularity to its use of vernacular media, where it was 'editing, publishing, and expounding the veds in the current Hindee language, and issuing a monthly magazine in Hindee and Urdu'. In short order, the Samaj's views were represented by more than twenty-five journals. The British Samaji who was daunted by the sect's moral education was convinced that it was propagating 'the most active and public propaganda . . . in India, or perhaps in the world, not excepting the Christian missionary enterprises'.

Dayanand's teachings were a potent threat. 'In estimating the forces which operate to either hinder or promote the spread of Gospel truth in Northern India, the Arya Samaj must be recognised as among the chief,' the president of the American Presbyterian College in Lahore wrote. The sect's preachers stood on streets, reiterating to passersby that the West had nothing new to offer the East. Its official journal argued that Christians had worked so hard to translate a book into hundreds of languages, so should Hindus not do the same for a book that held secret knowledge? The Arya Samaj told its readers about mass conversions by missionaries, and urged them to stop their countrymen from walking towards 'spiritual death'. Dayanand went further, converting two Christians in 1877. These first ceremonies were isolated events, but soon his followers formalised the practice by having Brahmin priests administer conversions by dipping the misled in the Ganges. For large masses they created a ceremony involving a sacred fire, a lecture and the tonsuring of heads: 'the ceremony began to be applied to whole communities of Sikh untouchables, who were thereby "purified" and admitted to full Sikh status. This was done to forestall possible Christian conversion of such groups', a historian wrote.

The conversions that added numbers to the faith, the presentation of a civilisational tussle between a native spiritualism and materialistic foreign influences, and the propagation of a theory of history in which the deeply oppressed were once the world's marvels—all of this read like responses to deep insecurity. The confidence they engendered was fragile, but it grew stronger with the repetition of fantasies. 'An immense quantity of literature pours from the press' at considerable cost to reiterate ideas of Hindu primacy, a chronicler of India's religions wrote. It was inevitable that minds began to turn.

'Hundreds of men of the student class, under Dayananda's influence, believe that the ancient Hindus were as far advanced in the natural sciences as modern Europeans are, and that they had invented not only firearms and locomotives but telegraphs and aeroplanes as well.'

In February 1881, six years after the creation of Arya Samaj, with his renown spreading fast, Dayanand, whose stomach turned at the sight of meat, produced a slim treatise in defence of cows. *Gokarunanidhi—Ocean of Mercy for the Cow* put forward economic and moral justifications for the protection of cows. Dayanand framed his arguments as a conversation between a nature-loving 'protectionist' (a Hindu) and a carnivorous 'slayer' (Muslim). The characters tussled philosophically, one enthusiastic about turning the living into food, the other gently making the case for life, except with mild name-calling:

> [Protectionist:] Just mark that carnivorous persons are destitute of mercy and similar other godly qualities which characterise humanity. They are ever prepared to accomplish their selfish designs by injuring others. Whenever a flesh eater sees a fat and robust animal he says, as it were, to himself, what a nice thing it will be to kill and eat it. While on the contrary if a vegetarian sees it he feels delighted at its healthy and happy life.

The arguments spanned seventy-six pages in the book, speaking to the converted and the ready to believe. For the rest, Dayanand put forward a novel concept at the end: the creation of cow-protection societies. Members of the societies would be called cow protectors, their job to uphold the rules and laws of nature. They would contribute a hundredth of their income to the cause of purchasing and protecting cows, and buy and cultivate land for cattle to graze on. On closer inspection, the society's remit was not simply cow protection, but society itself. It would work for the common good, respect those who helped its aims, and exclude anyone who disagreed with its politics.

Dayanand wasn't the first to defend the sanctity of the cow, a tenet originally put forth in the Vedas, but he was among its most prominent adherents. In 1882, a year after his tract, Dayanand petitioned the Queen to demand that cows be protected; they were more sacred than gods. A newspaper sympathetic to Dayanand's arguments encouraged the government to achieve 'everlasting fame' by banning their slaughter. Cow-protection societies bursting with eager young men and wealthy old financiers sprouted, alert to violations of the rules and laws of nature as written in the Vedas. They were on the lookout for acts 'in defiance of Hindu feelings'. Dayanand wrote that 'the professed object of [his cow protection society] was humane and politically unimportant', and that its sole purpose was to provide shelters for weary cattle. The expenses, he explained, would be met through charitable payments by the neighbourhood.

There was a straining, a quiet anger, among people as the cow-protection movement gathered. The organisations behind it were driven by a notion of Hindu unity, revivalism, traditional values and a rejection of alien cultural elements that spanned food, language, habit and education. But no platform attracted reformers, traditionalists and everyone in between the way the cow-protection movement did. Even as urbane religious gurus made the economic case for cows with dubious numbers in western India, ascetics were dispatched by societies to villages for a quiet word. Between 1880 and 1890, 'organising efforts swept the urban centres of [the United Provinces] . . . collective activities on behalf of the cow were reported in cities such as Cawnpore, Lucknow, Ghazipur, Benares, Aligarh, Pratapgarh and, pre-eminently, Allahabad'.

The economic utility of a cow was among the most popular

lines of argument in its defence. Preachers calculated the output of such a creature, and spread their calculations across the country. The importance 'of preserving, protecting, and improving the bovine species could hardly be overestimated,' Sriman Swamy, a widely followed preacher renowned for his completely believable and patently false calculations, said. He estimated that a healthy cow could feed forty-five thousand mouths during its most productive years. At the other end of his calculation was cow dung, produced at the rate of two hundred and seventy pounds every month. Over twenty-four years a cow produced enough dung to fertilise an acre of rice-growing land. Dung also had healing properties, and stopped the spread of cholera. Swami said he had, by his own hand, treated half a dozen cases of enlarged spleen with cow's urine. He believed that the high cost of grain, milk and butter were evidence of cattle's scarcity, and feared for the cow's survival. The bottomless appetite of the English and foreign cultures were to blame. He did not mean Muslims, Swami made sure to tell crowds. Muslims were exempt from his calculations because, he said, they did not eat cows. The beef-eating that was ascribed to them was only a slur cast by the colonialists, who wanted to see strife between Hindus and Muslims. It was common to hear of Muslims spoken of as being in line with the feelings of the religious majority, so that any such behaviour was seen as deviancy.

Cow-protection meetings could be frequented by as many as five thousand people. In *Sacred Symbol as Mobilizing Ideology*, a study of the period, Sandria Freitag wrote that at one such meeting, in Azmatgarh, 'a picture of a cow, representing the residence of all the Hindu gods, was placed on a stool before the platform, and copies of it were circulated. The speaker urged his listeners to only milk "the cow" after its calf had been satisfied and told them that the cow was a "universal mother" since every man drank cow's milk. It was therefore matricide to kill a cow.' But the picture of the cow also included a man with a sword drawn—the representation of a Muslim. 'The lesson was obvious,' she wrote. 'To prevent such matricide, the participants would agree to establish a [society], adopt rules, and choose officers. The local sponsors would often speak as well, and the most prestigious supporter, usually presiding at the meeting, would indicate his support and enthusiasm.'

The discussions over cows were a shroud for incitements that threaded grievance and nationalism. 'While dwelling on the sanctity of the cow, they taught how this sanctity was daily violated under British rule, and how, in consequence, the soil was becoming infertile, and the people impoverished,' an observer wrote in the *Calcutta Review*. Signs of restlessness were evident. A convoy of cattle meant for soldiers in Bihar was followed by a silent mob for days on end. They were not deterred by warnings to keep their distance. Eventually they attacked the police station where the cattle were kept for safety.

Administrators noticed that communal riots frequently occurred where the protection societies and their volunteers went. The *Pioneer* of Allahabad, a newspaper whose sympathies were in line with those of its British stewards, was in no doubt that cow-protection societies were at the heart of growing religious animosity. By May 1894, it noticed, the operations of cow-protection societies had 'spread to the country districts, where for generations the rival sects'—meaning Hindus and Muslims—'had lived in harmony'. The bigotry the newspaper's correspondents had observed was so extreme that they recognised the limitations of law. The rule of the land was no match for the hidden rules in men's hearts. The reporters attributed this bigotry, which existed in the absence of open lines between influential Hindus and their Muslim friends, to the 'secret influence' the societies bore. The prognosis was not good, the *Pioneer* concluded: 'many years must pass before the bulk of the Hindu population are cured of the rabid fanaticism with which they have been inoculated.'

In the North-Western Provinces, a patch of old country where Uttar Pradesh stands today, Hindu leaders first tried persuasion to wean Muslims, Christians and groups seen as 'untouchable' off cows—demanding in some cases signed guarantees that they would no longer kill cattle. If disagreement followed, so did violence. Large numbers of Hindus armed with sticks and knives attacked smaller groups of Muslims with guns. They would fight, retreat to assess their losses and return to settle matters the same day. The bursts of violence were not spontaneous, administrators suspected. They believed that the riots were planned.

Undercurrents of unsettling feelings had been noticed for years. They emerged not only in riots, but in the brutality of exterminations, and in what was fought over.

In library archives in New Delhi, London, Boston and New York, I tried to grasp at history, hoping that it would help me answer Nisar's one question: where is the poison coming from? At first I was excited by the possibilities that existed in various databases. Typing a search term and waiting a few seconds for the process to complete, I would will the results to go as far back in time as they could. 'Oldest first,' I would adjust the search filter, and the past appeared in cyclostyled black and white—not only the report I sought, but other events alongside it, conjuring the world that day. Every result had potential, because each person or event came with their own timeline of life and afterlife. Their life was usually documented, but it was the afterlife that had room for exploration: here, from my vantage point in the present, I could look back to see how their ideas travelled, and what they became. I read newspapers and papers and books and chapters and tracts and pamphlets, and for a time lost myself to the notion that these words, written down, were exactly what had occurred over a century ago.

Eventually it dawned on me that the newspapers I was reading were English-owned or missionary-run, and even if they were not, I could not vouch for whose eye had witnessed events and whose hand had described them. I would remind myself that untangling modern events alone had qualified verifiers for the Nobel Prize. And so, as I read these accounts, and began to learn but not quite understand, there arose a sensation of looking in from outside, and feeling as if the records before me were a flattening of complex desires and interactions by the recorder. Pictures would emerge and retreat, lost and found in flawed accounts, and after a while I did what came naturally and let myself be carried along.

In 1882, upon learning that a rare kind of communal riot had occurred, and hearing that it had the markings of a massacre, and understanding that its magnitude was greater than anything witnessed in the region for half a century, a correspondent for the *Pioneer* hitched a ride with a missionary to the town of Salem, in what is now the southern state of Tamil Nadu. I imagined both were British. They went by horse, the fastest transportation available over unrailed country. Fires were still burning in Selam (as the locals called it) when they arrived, and men still had that look in their eyes, that unreadiness to cede control of the streets. They stopped the correspondent at the border; the town was not ready for observers to be allowed inside, and for witnesses to be let outside. Their rule ended only when soldiers marched into town later that day to remove the writ of emotion and establish once more the restraints of law. And then the correspondent finally saw what had been done. Those scattered columns of smoke, indicative of violence from a distance, now rose, on coming closer, above Muslim homes. The bodies the correspondent saw would eventually be given burials, not cremations. At the centre of all the troubles was a razed mosque, its furniture demolished, its chandeliers shattered. Children and swine had been dragged to the mosque's wells and thrown inside. The driving force of the calamity was not merely eradication, but soil ruined with blasphemy.

The correspondent wandered through the town investigating the recent past, and stumbled upon the reason for the killings. Residents said that when this place belonged to the Mughals, the nawabs in charge had decreed that no Hindu music would be played in processions outside the town's mosques. Anywhere else, Hindu festival music, with its loud drums and wild drummers, its dancing and pausing, its unceasing singing and announcing, its calls to god and its calling to the streets, was raucous and alive and a public affair. But outside mosques, where prayers occurred at dawn, noon, a little later, and then a little later again, and then at night, Hindu expressions of devotion were indistinguishable from nuisance. Peace was maintained through pockets of silence. Residents told the reporter that the understanding had been kept alive until the approval and construction of a new mosque.

The local magistrate, a British nawab in his own right, decreed that the old rule would apply outside the new mosque. But the organisers of processions found the edict too broad, and a court with real authority soon agreed: the nawabs were no longer kings, this was an enlightened time, the magistrate had overstepped. Music was to be avoided only during prayer time, the court said. From then on, magistrates—who were most familiar with the troubles and sensitivities of the districts they oversaw—had little say in the matter of music outside mosques. Despite the judgement, the magistrate once more imposed his authority in public meetings about the matter of music outside mosques. It was only then that the town's Hindus, who could no longer carry the weight of this religious restriction, began to kill.

But that was at the first pass of information. A clearer

picture emerged in the correspondent's second draft of history, when more witnesses were found. The town's Hindus asked the magistrate for permission to organise a procession for the annual Mariamman festival, a joyous procession with animals, drums on wheels, dancing drummers, fire dancers and breathers and twirlers, and hundreds if not thousands following the music and the idols. The magistrate turned them away. He could not guarantee their protection, he said, letting them know that their procession was unwise, that it would lead to a breach of the peace. But that very day he allowed Muslims to celebrate the Kutba festival.

Further drafts brought more evidence of officials struggling to draw lines between genuine worship and an intention to be a nuisance. At last count, over a hundred and sixty Hindus were arrested for their role in the riots. Many of them, it was observed, had arrived from outside Salem to join in the mayhem.

Two hundred miles to the east of Salem, late one night in 1889, a procession from an ancient temple tried to pass by a new mosque. There was again music and again shouting, and it was soon a serious situation. The military arrived quickly, surrounded the mosque and took away the Muslims inside and a few Hindus outside. The Muslims were arrested for attacking Hindus, but the Hindus were fined more for banging 'tom-toms' outside the mosque during prayer time. The police—whose senior posts in south India were filled with Europeans and lower posts with locals—agreed that Hindus had the right to play music outside that mosque because it did not meet their conditions for a place of worship. The magistrate heard everyone and threw up his hands, exasperated by the uncharitable behaviour. On all sides were people looking for a problem. A newspaper called the rioters 'inmates', a term unchallenged for its accurate connotations of madness.

Elsewhere in the country other moments of irritation and

defiance flared into destruction, an outcome guaranteed if festivals of the two religions coincided. Drums that sounded to one set of ears like an unwillingness to yield were heard like battle cries by another. Newspapers recorded these disruptions, asking on occasion why the decades-long peace between Hinduism and Islam, India's two major religions, had abruptly ended. The gist of their mourning was, what had happened? What had changed?

The large disturbance that came after happened in Bombay, when the sound of tom-toms led to a riot that spread through bazaars and cloth markets, in Poona, where Muslims were boycotted economically, in Yeola, where more of the same occurred, and in other places. The anger was so stark that blame for it was pinned on the cow-protection movement.

There were enough accounts to render events indecipherable. But a new reality was emerging, an observer from the *Calcutta Review* noticed—one detached from reality itself. One of several rumours about the English was that they had conducted massacres in India. It spread widely, and although it contained no substance, the anonymous author wrote, its existence alone was a portent, for rumours 'have a certain injurious effect, since they prepare the mind of a native for more actively poisonous seed, while their very absurdity promotes a disregard among [people] of more serious symptoms'. The rumours were a sign of a people willing to suspend all judgement.

And all the while, the outlets for the Arya Samaj's influence continued to grow. In its seminaries, children spent sixteen years of their lives protectively swaddled, hidden away from the influences of family, friends and the world outside, their lives moulded into Dayanand's ideal of god's emissaries. It had meeting houses where people congregated to discuss politics. Its numbers were found to be recruited into army regiments where, it was noticed, the sect had 'tampered with the loyalty of certain regiments'. And, last of all, was the unceasing propaganda of its representatives, who seemed to be everywhere in general but nowhere in particular, whose output worried the British for 'the growing antagonism which it has bred between Hindus and Mahomedans, for the Mahomedans are convinced that the Arya Samaj is animated with no less bitter hostility towards Islam than towards British rule'. The concern, then as in the future, was about groups who operated out of sight, like the corroding influence of a persistent rumour.

# 2

# The Book and the Rifle

Towards the end of the nineteenth century, and then for a time after, the Arya Samaj stepped aside in history. This is not to say that its effect was diminished, but that Dayanand's ideas and preaching were no longer a novelty. He had wanted listeners, and had found them, as well as their children. His words were absorbed by stronger currents: the struggle to be free, and to create a particular kind of country.

In the 1920s, a body that considered itself a custodian of Hindu values rose to prominence: the Hindu Mahasabha—the All-India Hindu Grand Assembly, a political organisation for whom every matter pertaining to Hinduism required careful consideration. The Mahasabha's chief concern was with the 'self-preservation and religious safety of the Hindu community'. Its birth in 1915 was itself a response to Muslims being granted separate electorates, and it rapidly became the pole to which every anxious Hindu's compass needle pointed. (Its correspondence revealed it as a support group for regional parties and people invested in the politics of Hinduism.) Going through the letters of its leaders, I imagined the dinner-party tones these upper-caste men wearing dhotis and waistcoats spoke in when they said, as if it was completely reasonable, that 'fundamental differences' between 'Hindu culture and Muslim culture and politics' meant that the two religions could not survive in harmony. 'You see,' one of its leaders told an interviewer, 'when Muslims conquered any country, if they did not have the upper hand, if they were not in a majority, they considered it Darul Harb, the land of conflict. Where they were in a majority, it was Darul Aman. And it was part of their faith to convert Darul Harb into Darul Aman.' In his view, Muslims were 'second class citizens'. He wanted for them freedom of movement, and the ability to participate in trade and commerce, but he drew the line at political participation.

In the 1920s and 1930s, one Mahasabha official was in particular demand. From distant parts of the country, embattled men wrote to Balakrishna Sheoram Moonje with stories of Muslim aggression, of how men and boys seemed to come together and beat up peaceful Hindus. They wrote to him for advice and support, for his dedication to Hindu society was renowned. These letters were sent across time: in 1938, a letter from an Arya Samaj outpost in Bengal, complaining of Muslim attacks on a peaceful procession; in 1922 or '23, instructions from the head of a major Hindu monastery to investigate reports of forced conversions in the Malabar region. There were others.

His surviving correspondence and private diaries revealed a man fixated by a vision of Hindus evolving from a peace-loving race to a martial one. Moonje was a cataract surgeon with a scholar's beard and a seriousness about himself, but his days were filled with politics, religion and military strength. His ideas of peace and security were distilled into a single expression: 'The universe is sustained and maintained by sword.' At other times, he suggested Hindus should be guided by a cryptic Vedic image that echoed words by Benito Mussolini: 'The Book and the Rifle'.

Moonje had graduated with second-class honours from the University of Bombay in February 1899. He was twenty-seven, and free to practise medicine and surgery. But Moonje was drawn to blood. He was soon on a ship to South Africa with four civil surgeons of the Bombay Command Regiment, and by 1 October 1901 he was awarded a Queen's South Africa clasp for his service in treating soldiers injured by the Boers in Natal. On returning to India, Moonje established a charitable eye dispensary in Nagpur. He was a striking man, with broad shoulders and wavy hair swept back, a wild beard, and usually dressed in a long, formal kurta. A columnist visiting his infirmary described Moonje as 'somewhat showy' and made a point of mentioning his spectacles. This simple observation mystifyingly caused Moonje grave offence.

Moonje, for a time the acting president of the Mahasabha, considered himself a Hindu man driven by Hinduism's truths, and therefore by Hinduism's logic. He said he was 'a scientist working in a laboratory with balanced judgement'. But just as Hindu truth was buttressed by Hindu logic, he concluded that Hindu logic was built on something far sturdier. 'There is one imperishable point on which the system is based . . . faith in one God, the Almighty which pervades the entire universe and which is revealed in the Vedas, the Scriptures or the revealed Book of the Hindus. This is the only one element of faith which is accepted without question as a self-evident and self-existing Truth.' His words could have been Dayanand's from fifty years before.

Moonje's depiction of Hindus was as blameless and well-meaning. At a youth conference in Madras in January 1934, in a presidential address that was over half an hour long, Moonje said to the youth gathered to hear him, 'If we analyse the history of communal differences that have taken place in India during, say, the last ten or fifteen years, it will be no exaggeration to say that aggression or initiation to start such disturbances has never come from the Hindus. In fact, the Hindus have always suffered badly during the first stages of such disturbances simply because they have been taken unawares . . .'

He would proactively rush to restive parts of the country and either conduct investigations of riots that found Muslims at fault, or find other ways to throw himself into disturbances. He claimed to have personally overseen thousands of reconversions from Islam to Hinduism personally. His life was in service of a concern that appeared overblown then, as now: Hindus were in danger.

Moonje travelled from province to province preaching imminent demographic disaster, leaving forwarding addresses as he went. Muslim and Catholic populations were rising rapidly, 'at the cost of Hindus entirely', he said. This was a suspicion he had held for some time. In 1891, Moonje began attending Hislop College, a Christian missionary institution in the central Indian city of Nagpur. Moonje, who would later say he always stood first in Bible class, asked a teacher, 'Is it a fact that the Christian missionary professors teaching in the college receive some commission from the Christian Missionary Society if they convert Hindu boys to Christianity?' The teacher was riled by the question, and said, 'My boy, don't be foolish and misguided. Don't be carried away by misunderstandings. There is no such thing as paying commission. Only when boys feel the urge to Christianity, [can they] be converted. Such conversions are regarded by us as our sacred duty. But it must be purely voluntary and there should not be the slightest tinge of coercion.'

Even though Muslim and Catholic populations were rising at a faster rate than Hindus, the future Moonje was concerned about was unimaginably distant. Their absolute numbers were far smaller. Undivided India contained over two hundred million Hindus, fewer than seventy million Muslims and about five million Christians. It took Muslims three decades to add the numbers that Hindus had accumulated in one. Yet Moonje was fearful of this imagined future, and he wanted other Hindus to be alarmed by the percentages.

The idea of Hinduism itself was nebulous, even though it had hardened in Moonje's mind. The census of 1921 made special note that 'Hinduism has no one central distinguishing concept'. It was an elastic term, vague enough to encompass diffuse races, traditions and beliefs. Enumerators travelling from hovel to hovel, ink and paper in hand, had found cosmopolitan Bengalis and 'untouchable' Punjabis who identified as Hindus, forest dwellers whose beliefs loosely fitted with the religion, and tribes who, 'by long association with Hinduism, have acquired an indefinite position on its outskirts'. But the census was as much about the beliefs of the people it catalogued as the cataloguers themselves. To exaggerate their numbers, Hindu enumerators were likely to admit to their own column the thousands of peripheral groups who existed on the edges of the religion's sprawl. But Brahmin enumerators, who sat atop the caste pile, were just as likely to deny such primitive clans entry to the faith. The Hindu column, then, was as much an accumulation of disparate belief systems as a product of them. Who a Hindu was depended on who was asked, and who was asking.

Moonje mourned the lack of a 'Hindu Church' and blamed the religion's caste divisions for its absence. 'The Mahomedans,' he wrote, 'form one organic community, religiously well-organised and disciplined, so that any injury done to any part of the community anywhere, is felt as keenly all through out. In a word there is a living communal feeling [that] is so high and overpowering that they can hardly think of any public movement unless in terms of their communal interests.' The unity of Muslims was due to 'there being no caste system among Mahomedans'. Every young Muslim was a potential soldier, 'fired by the fanaticism of acquiring heavenly glory if killed in the defence and propagation of his faith'.

Moonje felt past assaults and slights on Hindus, real or imagined, as strongly as recent insult. 'I am not a historian,'

Moonje said at a conference in Kolhapur, 'but I have read books on history.' One of the history books he read, *Indian Islam,* from which he borrowed liberally, was written by Murray Titus, an American missionary in India. The book was challenged soon after its publication for depending on outdated sources, but Moonje trusted it enough to conclude that Hindu society had 'gone through terrible ordeals during the last one thousand years, the like of which no other nation had the misfortune to face'. He thought Islam had assimilated such a large part of the population that Hinduism's survival was miraculous. 'The wonder really is that we have not been wiped out of existence as Hindus, like the persons of Persia, and the Afghans of Afghanistan.' His reading of history had led him to other assumptions that had congealed into fact. In an act of breathtaking confidence, he placed the map of Islamic conquest over his understanding of Buddhism's geographic spread, and concluded that people around Delhi 'resisted Islamic aggression so stubbornly that they suffered hardly 14 per cent of casualties', while people on the frontiers gave up and were absorbed into Islam easily due to their belief in Buddhism in its 'decadence and degenerate forms'.

Moonje was certainly no historian, and his concepts about Muslims needed work too. To the north of Delhi, circumcised Muslim agriculturalists professed to the faith, but they prayed to their old village gods. To the city's south-west were sects who attached Muslim last names to Hindu names, and celebrated Hindu festivals. Another Muslim tribe worshipped the Hindu god Shiva. Some worshipped rivers and trees. In one northern town, Muslim homes had a dedicated 'God's house' in which Allah and the deity Kali were sent prayers.

Among the things Moonje believed was that peace had atrophied the Hindu instinct for war—his people were barely able to defend themselves. Mahatma Gandhi, whose 'preaching of non-violence is perverting the minds of the Hindu youth', frustrated him. He longed for a Hindu force to match the ferociousness Muslims seemed to summon instantly. Moonje concluded that that task was difficult, but possible. Hindus could become a martial race, he said, but they would need the muscle of the lower castes that Brahmins had discriminated against for centuries. If Hindus were to organise and protect themselves, Moonje wrote, they would have to abolish caste and build 'communal feeling' among lower castes: 'the higher caste are deprived of the very material help these lower caste can render them in times of emergency of Hindu Muslim riots,' he wrote in a letter in 1923.

In their correspondence, Moonje and other Hindu leaders often referred to Muslims as part of an unpatriotic monolith allied only to the cause of Islam. It was a view that led them to see the religion as an existential threat to a Hindu India. Islam's philosophy drove its 'votaries and warriors' towards jihad, 'for bringing the whole world under the rule of Islam'. He believed that differences between Hindus and Muslims could not be resolved, and that war was inevitable. Moonje applied what he believed was scientific rigour to understanding why Muslims, whom he viewed as former Hindus, took to killing so easily; he did not see any flaw in his assumptions, and therefore he was convinced by the results. But it was not scientific rigour at work, only the rationale of bigotry when he concluded early marriage—implying intercourse—'saps all manhood and energy from the Hindu race', and that the practice of spilling animal blood and meat-eating produced a 'violence of temper' among Muslims.

There was so little the communities could agree on, he said, that even the act of playing music in the wrong place set them off. At a cow-protection conference in the 1920s or 1930s, Moonje discussed the inevitable stone-throwing and rioting that followed Hindu processions passing by mosques. He was a clever man, alert to the effect of his words upon an audience, and here he chose to plant a seed. Hindus had to be mindful of the music they played in processions as they passed mosques, he said, but were Muslims not to blame for building mosques on main roads? Where else could a Hindu procession go, he asked the attendees.

In Moonje's longing for Hindus to be less intellectual and more martial was a barely concealed admiration for the warlike attributes he assigned Muslims. He and other religious leaders disregarded recent history and accused Hindus of being a race of peace-lovers who were unequal to their myths; colossal disappointments who did not live up to the rousing stories they told about kings who were tactical geniuses, and warrior queens who leapt onto horses. But it was not in Moonje's nature to simply complain. He believed in taking action.

On 22 June 1918, in the dying days of the Great War, Moonje addressed a letter to the chief commissioner of the province he resided in. To combat the German threat to India, Moonje proposed that the authorities introduce army conscription and rely on a corps of volunteers. Moonje claimed that, for over a decade before the war, Germany had moulded its education system to infuse an intellectual and military awareness into every child. 'In a word, Germany worked on so quietly and systematically that before it actually showed its hand by declaring this war, not even its nearest neighbour nations knew that the whole nation was literally an extensive military encampment, well-trained, armed to the teeth, and prepared for war at the shortest possible notice. Having to deal with such a scientific and determined foe, we have to proceed in the same way.' He assured the chief commissioner that if the colonial administration chose such a path, they could easily raise a standing reserve of fifty thousand or a hundred thousand 'well trained, able-bodied, young, intelligent, partially educated men'.

Moonje suggested a few ways to build such a force: the creation of a Boy Scouts movement, preliminary military training for children who were eight years old, establishing a military college for officer training, removing all restrictions on the ownership of firearms 'to revive the liking for military profession and for warlike sports', encouraging rifle-shooting clubs, as well as creating local militia to protect Indians from 'internal disorders and breaches of peace'.

In time, this articulation of Moonje's vision would be applied, but with a different enemy in mind. Between the wars, Moonje grew convinced that a Hindu army and private militias could resolve the Muslim problem. He forged pacts between Sikhs, Christians and Hindus to combat any possible Muslim aggression. He would look to Germany, once again, for inspiration. The district magistrate of Belgaum wrote about Moonje's plans for Muslims in a confidential report. 'Dr. Munje stated that Hindus should not be afraid of Mahomedans as they were originally Hindus of India and gave an example of the treatment of the Jews at the hands of the Nazis in Germany.'

Supporters from across the dominion wrote to inform Moonje that they were enlisting soldiers for the Mahasabha's Ram Sena. All the while, his military ideas continued to grow and evolve. He envisaged a military school that would supply to the armed forces a steady stream of officers whose understanding was rooted in Hinduism's precepts. If not there, they would work as police constables and serve society in other ways. He would train them so that, 'along with the training of the mind and development of the intellect, the body also should be equally developed'. The training that students received would be based on religiously ordained duties. Moonje dreamed of unifying young Hindu men by filling them with ideas of brotherhood, removing thoughts of caste from their minds, and cultivating patriotism and duty towards the motherland. He wrote to princes and British officials to raise funds for the school, and campaigned for permissions allowing his students to use arms. It was all to rejuvenate a martial spirit within Hindus, he said.

The aims and structure of the school were deeply influenced by Balilla, a fascist youth organisation that had impressed Moonje during a visit to Italy in March 1931. He didn't care for the children's drills, but their spirit was evident. The Italian historian Marzia Casolari told me that Moonje's interest in fascism was likely stoked by the propaganda efforts of the Italian consul of Calcutta and Bombay, a man named Gino Scarpa. It was Scarpa who arranged Moonje's meeting with Mussolini, she said. Casolari wrote the first detailed account of Moonje's fascination with Mussolini, and of his visit to Italy. 'Others knew about the story, but no one had written it' when she began visiting archives across India in the early 1990s, she said.

Moonje had longed to meet Mussolini, a fascination he shared with other Hindu leaders. To them, Mussolini embodied the virtues of development, discipline and order put into practice. They had surely read newspapers and books praising him in Marathi. In Rome, on 19 March in 1931, his wish was granted. In his cursive style, Moonje recorded the meeting in his diary.

The sun had begun its descent that day, a Thursday, when the immense wooden doors that led to the Globe Room on the middle floor of the Palazzo Venezia were opened for Moonje. The room was half a millennium old, and to enter it, a writer described, was to experience a landscape so vast that it required a field glass to see the silhouette of Mussolini at the room's far corner. Moonje stepped inside, seeing not the ornate gold-leaf ceiling high above him, not the lion of Saint Mark and the she-wolf of Rome in relief, not the towering granite pillars sunk into the walls, not the exquisite carved frieze that ran along the room, not the coats of arms of the popes responsible for the palace, not the chandelier wider than an emperor's doorway. He wrote nothing about them, for his eyes were set on Mussolini, a large man on a wide chair behind a desk twelve feet long in the room's furthest corner.

The desk was created for permanence, with swirls carved into its edges, and on it was a bronze lion placed at one corner, a tall lamp with an umbrella shade, and several telephones, their wires running wild on the carpet beneath Mussolini's feet. The room was filled with a dim light, the chandelier reflected in a dull gold by the coffered ceiling, but illumination was not the intention. In the age-old practice of the strong leader, Mussolini desired his subjects to look up from the streets below and see the lit room as evidence of how hard he worked, and how little he slept. Moonje walked past the balcony where Mussolini liked to wave to the crowds below—the balcony from which he would declare war on Britain and France nine years later. Did Moonje notice at all, upon entering the room, its absence of a seat for him? The chamber, the hall, the landscape contained nothing but a resting place for the eye. That point of focus rose from his chair to greet Moonje, who could not help but study Mussolini's bearing.

Moonje recorded him as a 'tall man with broad face and double chin and broad chest. His face shows him to be a man of strong will and powerful personality.' They discussed India's freedom movement, and the possibility of India and England making peace. Then Mussolini asked Moonje what he thought of the military schools in Italy. 'Every aspiring and growing nation needs such organisations,' Moonje said. 'India needs them most for her military regeneration . . . I am working for it. I have already started an organisation of my own, conceived independently with similar objectives.'

Moonje would be remembered in time for his propulsion of the Hindu Right, and he advocated tirelessly for Hindu physical might as if it was a calling. And yet the organisation 'conceived independently with similar objectives' that he referred to was not his military school. It couldn't have been, because the school did not exist until 1937, six years after the meeting with Mussolini. However, when the paperwork that defined the purpose of his school was complete, it contained a clause: an organisation begun in 1925 would receive the assets of his school if it was ever dissolved. All the school's properties, both moveable and immoveable, 'including cash money', would be transferred to the Rashtriya Swayamsevak Sangh, which was led by a Marathi-speaking Brahmin named Doctor Keshav Baliram Hedgewar, or Doctor ji. Moonje had known Hedgewar for at least two decades, and was convinced he was a force in organising and training young Indians. Under Hedgewar's guidance, the RSS nurtured and shaped malleable minds to believe in Hindu purity. 'There's something about the idea of youth,' Casolari told me. 'They are interested in the youth because it is the creation of a new man. You manipulate minds, and create a particular kind of nation.'

By the end of that decade, with Britain distracted by war, and calls for a Muslim nation carved out of India growing louder, Moonje was more certain that Hindus would need to defend themselves against the forces of the Muslim League. 'The Moslems are making themselves a nuisance,' he wrote in a letter dated 18 October 1939. 'We shall have to fight both the government and the Moslems . . . The Hindu Mahasabha will give its support to such fights as the Muslim League is supporting [their militia]. You must prepare the volunteers in your towns. The Rashtriya Swayamsevak Sangh may be useful and handy.'

# 3

# Unreliable Patriots

Hedgewar was born in 1889, and the world he grew up in was filled with conflict, with stories of Hindus who could not play music, of Muslims who stopped religious processions on the streets. It was a time of simmering grievances, a time when communal discontent was commonly expressed without restraint in the press. This was the environment Hedgewar encountered as he came of age: of Hindus unable to exercise free will.

When he was thirteen the plague took his parents, and the six siblings left behind were 'rudderless on the ocean of life', a biography would recall. The children went looking for food and work, and grew apart under the pressure of survival. His eldest brother 'took to a loose and indisciplined life', and his other brother left for another city. But Hedgewar himself, according to the writer, veered towards a life of discipline and pride. 'Even when he was tormented by extreme hunger, he never accepted food from his friends,' his biographer wrote. 'He never begged for money.' If there were human failings or frailties, evidence was unprovided; the book was a collection of virtues. Hedgewar ran five miles a day, swam, indulged in rebellious capers against the British, performed feats of insubordination to show administrators he bowed to no one, and impressed his teachers at Neil City High School, a school he was eventually expelled from for leading agitations against the British.

On the advice of Hindu nationalist leaders, including Moonje, Hedgewar travelled to Calcutta in 1910. He gained admission to the National Medical College of Calcutta University, where he received a degree in medicine. But his real education was political, an observer wrote. In Calcutta, 'Hedgewar purposefully made contacts with proponents of many different political groups', namely underground groups inspired by Italy's secret societies.

The city was already well-acquainted with secret societies; they littered the landscape like boyish enthusiasms, present everywhere, but ultimately pointless. In 1902, though, a member of a secret society in Baroda, on the country's western coast, approached a nascent Calcutta organisation named Anushilan Samiti with a plan to create a raft of revolutionary societies whose young recruits would be trained in 'activities which might be helpful for ultimate military action'. An official report by the Bengal police said that Anushilan Samiti was 'in its outward appearance, a harmless, and one might say commendable institution, which professed to train boys to nurse the sick, to collect funds for famine relief, and to start gymnasia for physical training. Secretly, it was a depot for the collection of firearms, for training boys to deeds of violence and desperation, for instructing them in shooting and sword play.'

While the young focused on physical work, older men financed their operations. When new recruits arrived at Anushilan Samiti's offices, they were told inspiring stories of purity, valour and uprising, about the French Revolution and men who were considered god's own soldiers, and of the ways of guerrilla warfare. The volunteers were put through drills to toughen them, and the value of discipline was constantly emphasised. But even as the organisation 'spread like wildfire', with a network of five hundred closely bound chapters that served as fertile recruiting ground, Anushilan's founders, who were paranoid about secrecy, would tell volunteers only its purpose—to end the British Raj—while keeping its methods from them. There was good reason for this. The society's growing influence, its messages and violent tendencies ensured it was under watch. Some of its factions believed in 'the sword alone', and they grew close to other societies that spread propaganda, funded revolutionaries in the guise of charity and distributed arms and ammunition. Additionally, Anushilan Samiti published a radical weekly newspaper, *Jugantar*, that advocated for total independence, not a measured path to freedom. It thought little of the careful speeches and political conferences where extreme and moderate political factions negotiated the proper way to boycott foreign goods and encourage domestic production. (Anushilan's factions used a mix of economic boycotts and intimidation to hasten the use of local goods.) *Jugantar* advocated for a flood of propaganda that would 'excite in [people] a desire for freedom'.

The propaganda it wanted had already been published. The administration had noticed four emerging methods of writing in Calcutta that stopped ' just short' of outright sedition. One method denounced British officials, and in the same breath mentioned 'defending the chastity of mothers and sisters'. Another was poetry that spoke of the personal hardship that true freedom would require. Then there were invented histories of aggrieved revolutionaries, whose fabricated actions were conveyed without opinion; the stories were meant to provide historical background in the mind of the reader. Finally, most crucially, was the free publication of bomb-making recipes. Taken together, the propaganda aroused emotions, provided historic inspiration, gave them reasons to act and showed people what they could do.

*Jugantar* wanted to move Bengalis to action, to unshackle them from their mental bonds to moral strength. It wanted an uprising. To that end, it published a roadmap to revolution. One morning, its readers came by a startling articulation of insurrection on *Jugantar*'s pages. An article titled 'The Formation of Bands' called for a thousand Bengalis of the eighty million to 'form themselves into a band'. The writer imagined them forming 'district bands' that would expand, 'capitalising on contemporary events and local disturbances'. Discipline, order and secrecy were valued characteristics, and applicants were admitted on evidence of 'loyalty, energy, selflessness, perseverance, reliability and obedience'. If bands needed help, *Jugantar* said, it was happy to introduce them to other bands. It asked readers to exercise good judgement on the matter, though, and not trust the post with any secret communications.

By the time Hedgewar arrived in Calcutta in 1910, revolutionaries were everywhere; holding a Gita in their left hand and a sword in their right while they swore secrecy by firelight; practising marksmanship in abandoned forts; robbing shops for funds; making plans to murder, and murdering; constructing bombs and filling cartridges with gunpowder; memorising complicated codes that concealed the names and addresses of their members; organising themselves into territories, and creating lists of their neighbours, their jobs, their moral failings, and maps of roads and routes of escape. The members of one society swore an oath to bring a schoolchild over to its cause every year. Anushilan Samiti required its district organisers to focus on disseminating its central idea at schools and colleges, for 'unmarried youth are the receptacles of enthusiasm, self-sacrifice, and energy for work'. Secrecy and punishment were in the air.

Hedgewar's followers would say that he impressed the leaders of Anushilan Samiti with his questions about their concerns, and grew so close to them that he was put under watch. The authorities' surveillance of Hedgewar became RSS lore. The excitement was in near-discovery, in narrow escape. In one story, Hedgewar finds a man in Calcutta suspiciously friendly, and, while his friends are fooled, he is not. His suspicions are confirmed eventually, for the man is a British spy. Soon the spy realises that Hedgewar knows his identity, and he leaves quickly in fear and embarrassment, but with regard for his adversary: 'Years later, his respect for [Hedgewar] had not diminished. He always called him "My worthiest enemy". Indeed!'

Awarded a 'Licentiate in Medicine and Surgery' from Calcutta National Medical College in late January 1914, Hedgewar returned to Nagpur to begin a medical practice, but India was lurching towards a complicated freedom, and medicine seemed inconsequential. He joined the Mahasabha and wrote pamphlets, and 'considered seriously' more violent methods to help India win independence. Unlike his heroes, who had advocated for a limited independence, Hedgewar desired a completely free India. He believed that Gandhi's non-cooperation movement would provide that outcome, but he was soon dismayed by the movement's betrayal of people's trust when its leaders linked India's freedom struggle with a global Muslim solidarity movement that sought to strengthen the Turkish Caliph. His views of the solidarity movement implied that there could be no working together. To Hedgewar, India's Muslims were more concerned with religion than the fate of their country. They were 'unreliable patriots'.

Depictions of Hedgewar during those days of national tumult are dramatic, emphasising a searching mind asking big questions. A contemporary children's comic book on his life by Gyan Ganga Prakashan, a publisher of mythological books, shows him lying awake at night in a crisp white shirt. 'From morning to night he worked hard,' a caption says. 'In the night when on bed he used to think about his nation. Many questions troubled him.' The questions were:

1. 'Ours was a golden land! Why has it become so poor?'
2. 'We have a glorious past. Why we are enslaved?'
3. 'The outsiders from north or west were small in number. How did they outhunt us?'
4. 'What lessons should we learn from our history?'
5. 'Who is responsible for our present plight? Britishers? Or Mohamedans?'
6. 'Will these bad days of our country go away?'

The next panel shows him sitting upright in bed, his arms folded, his lips pursed, his thought bubble now large, fully formed, shaded an urgent yellow:

'The slavery brought us drudgery. Our vices made us slaves. We had lost our social sense and had no discipline. Therefore this vast country could be won by the enemy. We are responsible for our downfall. If Hindus are well organised, if they become unselfish, this dull picture can be changed into a bright one. It is most essential. I will do it.' Although the sentences in the thought bubble were tilted, unbalanced, unhinged, taken with other panels displaying his strength, it was a comic portrait of a deep-thinking warrior.

The comic was for unformed minds. 'Mohamadens took pleasure in acting against Hindus,' it tells them. 'Even a sound of drums disturbed them in mosques. They attacked processions. Hindus were meek and frightened. Many times Doctor ji himself took the base drum and led processions.'

The violence outside mosques and temples, along the routes of religious processions, had not subsided. People still played music to annoy, and the response was still a riot.

Upon reaching Nagpur on the morning of 20 September 1926, Moonje met with Hedgewar. The town was decorated for Ganesh Chaturthi. Moonje was delighted by the many processions he saw, and by their magnificence. He took satisfaction in seeing the grand assemblages blare music when they passed mosques, and that Muslims did not object, 'whether they liked it or not', he wrote in his diary.

But this pleasure was ruined by two young men whose procession fell silent as they passed a mosque. Moonje watched Hedgewar walk up to them to urge them to not stop, and let the music go on. But they ignored his encouragements and instead snapped at him. Moonje was dismayed by their contempt for Hedgewar, the way they said they needed no enlightenment from him. The men had been damaged by Gandhi's suicidal ideas of communal unity, Moonje thought. Peace was not for him. He looked for unrest, and ways to amplify it. He stood by, giving people encouragement to act on their emotions. Later that day, when people brought him a broken idol whose damage they blamed Muslims for, Moonje proposed taking out a procession on the streets of Nagpur with the broken idol. The event would have roused communal feeling, which was probably the point of such a parade. But the idol's keepers were reluctant, and Moonje decided to visit them with Hedgewar to prove that the procession was a worthy cause. Ultimately, both men were unsuccessful, and there was peace.

From February 1926 to August 1927, there were fifty-two riots in colonial India. Seventeen of them were provoked by music and processions outside places of worship, and they left about two hundred dead and seventeen hundred injured. The deadliest of them took place over two phases in Calcutta from April to May in 1926: a hundred and thirteen dead, one thousand seventy injured. A report from the time noted that rioters wielding daggers stabbed passersby and disappeared into labyrinthine commercial buildings. The secretary of state said that 'the playing of music before a mosque by a Hindu procession' had begun the violence.

Moonje and other stalwarts of the movement to unite Hindus travelled to Calcutta shortly after the unrest had subsided. The injured had barely healed, and tempers barely cooled, when

Moonje delivered an incendiary speech about the ongoing 'civil war' between Hindus and Muslims. Hindus were politically dominated by the English, and dominated otherwise by Muslims and their 'aggressive mentality', he said. A reporter for the Associated Press wrote that Moonje 'warned Mohamedans of consequences of such reckless oppression of helpless Hindus in places where they happened to be in the minority, and said if the spirit of retaliation was roused among Hindus he shuddered to think of the consequences which would befall his Muslim brethren'. Elsewhere in Calcutta, another major Hindu leader, Pandit Madan Mohan Malviya, urged gatherings of jamadars—men who performed menial tasks, such as carrying 'cheques of large amount for their masters'—and watchmen to get in shape, protect themselves and their temples, and read the 'religious and noble books'. Malviya played up their duties, telling them there was no humiliation in the work of servants, that their work was to protect humanity and preserve peace. Some of them, he said obliquely, had done well during the Calcutta riots—they now understood the value of physical strength. They needed to build gyms in every locality, and grow stronger. 'A man without physical culture ought to be deemed a woman,' he said.

Peace and violence were intertwined in these speeches, as well as peace through violence. So plain was the purpose of these speeches that a newspaper asked 'whether the . . . words were not a direct incitement to the riotous passions of an ignorant and turbulent section of the Calcutta masses'. Malviya and Moonje were careful not to endorse individual acts of 'self-defence', but in what they praised and what they derided as feminine they led their uneducated audience to the precipice of dangerous realisations, and left them to take the final step on their own.

Hedgewar believed that Hindus, who made 'a weak and disorganised showing' during riots, could do with protection by a group of Hindus working towards a common goal.

In 1925, on a day that marked the mythological victory of the god Ram over Raavan, in some tellings a story of good over evil, Hedgewar had announced the creation of the Rashtriya Swayamsevak Sangh. He had been troubled that in colonial India 'the enthusiasm [for nationalism] in the country was cooling down'. Everywhere he looked was disorder and disunity. The British grip on their colony was weakening, and little fires were flaring. People were arguing over language, religion and caste. Muslims and Hindus were fighting constantly, and rumour and conspiracy only furthered mistrust. In the northeastern provinces, Hindus told stories of Muslims abducting their women to force them into marriage. Elsewhere, Hindus, who outnumbered by far the adherents of every other religion in British India, believed they had grown weak. Hedgewar was careful to state that his organisation bore no ill-feeling towards others, 'but its object was that the Hindus should have the strength to resist attacks made on their community by others'.

He had Muslims in mind. Hedgewar thought the community spread riots 'with their poisonous hissing'. And like Moonje before him, he said that riots were really 'Muslim riots because in every single case it is they who start them and go on the offensive'. Hedgewar was convinced that India's saviours would be of a specific faith: 'Only Hindus would free Hindustan and they alone could save Hindu culture.' Ideas this extreme required a suspension of disbelief, a willingness to see every word that emanated from leaders as true. Children, with their wet-plaster minds, were the ideal receptacle for such notions. Moonje would articulate this idealised vision of legions of youth when he described them as possessing 'broad chests, muscular shoulders, big limbs, and tall stature', with 'massive intellect capable of grasping any system of science and knowledge and with capacity to wield a rifle'.

Now, when young boys arrived at camps run by the RSS, they stood erect and placed their right arm sideways across their chest, and chanted a secret oath in unison:

> Before the All-Powerful God and my ancestors, I most solemnly take this oath, that I become a member of the Rashtriya Swayam Sewak Sangh in order to gain freedom for the Hindu nation by keeping intact my sacred Hindu religion, Hindu society and Hindu culture. I shall perform the work of the Sangh honestly, disinterestedly, with my heart and soul and I shall adhere to this oath all my life.

As I read about the gatherings and the teachings they imparted, it seemed as if the ideals of the Arya Samaj, Anushilan Samiti and the Mahasabha had reached their final form: RSS guerrilla camps where trainees and officers across India were taught to reject doubt and be certain about Hindu greatness. They were trained to use daggers, swords and wooden staffs. Their teachers were preparing them for 'organised violence', to play 'the game of killing masses of men with the ambition of winning victory'. On their days off, the boys went out for picnics, where leaders repeated stories of legendary Hindu valour, and reminded them that 'Hindus were suffering because they had become unorganised, liberal, generous and peaceable'.

The ideology caught on, and the RSS soon became the fastest-growing group in an expanding galaxy of extreme Hindu outfits. In 1930s Karachi, the RSS promised locals a glass of milk with a layer of thick cream in exchange for pledging support to their cause. All they had to do was turn up, take an oath and salute the RSS's flag. In other places volunteers went door to door to ask for a few paise to help defend Hinduism. Some gave them time and money; one supporter gave them an aeroplane. The organisation purchased printing presses, fired Muslim workers and published pamphlets advertising its ideas. The RSS claimed that all this evangelism helped it build sympathy for the cause.

Although accounts of its popularity varied wildly, in 1938 it had forty thousand members. Two years later, it had one lakh.

'The RSS method of recruitment was practically identical to that of the Balilla youth organisation in Italy,' Casolari, the historian, wrote in her book *In the Shadow of the Swastika*. Members of the RSS 'for instance, were grouped according to their age (6–7 to 10; 10 to 14; 14 to 28; 28 and older). This is strikingly close to the age bands used by fascist youth organisations, with its subdivision of boys and young men in Figli della Lupa, Balilla, Avanguardisti, and Camicie Nere (Sons of the She-Wolf, Balilla, Avant-gardists and Blackshirts).'

A secret home ministry note written by an informant in 1942 described the organisation as a 'pan-Hindu Boy Scout Movement with physical training, discipline and public service as its objectives'. The informant documented the RSS's indoctrination of its students. For several days, from before dawn till past dusk, young volunteers at its camps would hear one speaker after another talk of keeping guard over Muslims, the 'thief in their midst'. Hedgewar's successor, the chief organiser of the RSS at the time, a man named M.S. Golwalkar, beseeched them to create feelings of hatred 'toward men of other religions', and argued that the perils of individuality could be seen in the fate of occupied France. He urged them to spill blood for their country, even if the blood was their own brother's, 'because only he who follows and sticks to their principles would be regarded as their real brother'.

The organisation's leaders grew more frank about the superiority of the Hindu race. Golwalkar, the RSS head, saw valuable lessons in Hitler's treatment of Jews. It was 'well-nigh impossible' for different people to be 'assimilated into one united whole, a good lesson for us in Hindustan to learn and profit by'. Golwalkar asked for nothing less than total submission from Muslims. He accused them of identifying 'with the enemies of this land. They still think they have come here to conquer and establish their kingdoms.' When the end of the British Raj came, the decision to carve a Muslim nation out of India sent the organisation into grief. Its leaders decided to take on the very task it had been created for: to defend the country and the ideas it was based on.

# 4

# The Mound of Dead Men

My father's father was born in 1911 in Larkana, and he lived for ninety-one years. His childhood home was not far from Mohenjo Daro, the largest habitation during the Indus Valley civilisation. I was fascinated by the name when I first heard it as a child, for its twisted pronunciation in Sindhi evoked *muan jo daro,* a gateway for the dead, a portal for spirits evicted from their earthly abode. *Muan* (corpses), or *muo maro* (die, you corpse), were curses addressed to someone irredeemable, like a son. But it wasn't that. Time and technology revealed not a portal, but a burial site: it was a mound of dead men and dead memories. Its name suggested a calamity, a place of significance, without saying why it was so.

There is not much I remember about my grandfather except for the way he sat in his single-seat sofa, his elbows on its arms, his body leaning forward, his legs crossed at the ankles, as if prepared to answer the doorbell. He comes back in fragments. There he was, at Wilson College, a grand institution beside the sea in South Bombay when the city was a collection of islands. He was once given a leather whip by his neighbour and friend, a member of the Bhutto clan whose rule was profitable and deaths spectacular. Then he is suddenly older, playing tennis somewhere in his shorts. Time passes. He is even older now, and settled in Indore with restless children in various stages of migration. He is dressed in a white kurta-pyjama, on the sofa people would vacate for him, giving my newly married mother a spelling test. What is missing in these memories is his life's big moment, the tightrope he walked from misery to survival: India's Partition, Pakistan's creation, in August 1947. He came from somewhere when it occurred, he crossed some border to be here, with millions alongside him. But he did not speak of the path he took, nor what he did to arrive. Perhaps he did so once, but not later in life, and not around grandchildren visiting him briefly over the summer.

Did he arrive on a train in 1947? Or on a cart? Did he walk? His wife and two of his children were almost certainly with him. What did they see through the endless rain of that summer? What did they survive when this country held on for dear life after its division by a British official who knew little about it? Did they resist the madness that was in the gutters, in the wells, in the water, on the tip of swords and kirpans, on bullets fired at passing trains, on notices plastered with malicious intent? Or did they plunge into it? Neighbours and milkmen and farmers turned into not-themselves for a time. A person temporarily someone else, doing things they would never have otherwise done. What did the family do? Did they pass by the fields where men with weapons waited in tall grass? Even children were granted no expectations. People left their homes empty, and returned to houses that had been annexed by the aggrieved; if they had been chased from their homes in one country, why couldn't they have the houses of their religious adversaries? The talk everywhere was of impending attacks, and preparations for holy war.

On 6 September 1947, barely three weeks after India's independence, Jawaharlal Nehru, the prime minister, his senior colleague Vallabhbhai Patel and the governor-general of India, Viscount Mountbatten of Burma, and the ministers of defence, railways and refugees set up an emergency committee for the purpose of rapid action. It was based on an approach taken by the United Kingdom during the emergency of the war, when events developed at a scarcely believable pace. They were charged with at once reconstituting the army, filling police forces hollowed by departures, running an administration without enough administrators, ensuring electricity and running water and working telephone lines, keeping food supply lines stable, dealing with excessive rain and watching out for, above all, the possibility of a famine if fields full of the winter's harvest of rice and corn were abandoned. All this, while marshalling cholera tablets, ordering loudhailers and floodlights for refugee camps, sourcing spare parts for jeeps, providing security at hospitals and watching soldiers, police and regular citizens decide, at once and en masse, to partake in criminal behaviour.

As the migrations continued between India and Pakistan, observers recorded the extent of the disorder. Within a week of India's independence, refugees had already run into hundreds of thousands, and properties abandoned by people forced out of their homes on one side of the border were occupied by refugees arriving from the other side. Villages armed themselves and shot strangers dead. There were reports of stabbings in a hospital, shootings at the railway station, threats made to the employers of Muslim house staff. Every day: these many stabbings, those many shootings, these many injured, those many gone. These many hungry, those many robbed. The committee met at the Viceroy's residence once a day in the weeks after Partition, sometimes twice. They received hourly reports of the strife, and heard rumours of its magnitude. Sometimes they flew over the country and brought back stories of what they had seen: trails of refugees many miles long headed in both directions. Did my grandfather see the planes above his head? Did he sense the wildness seeping upward, into the minds of leaders expected to stay calm? No one was immune to it. After a spate of mass killings on trains carrying refugees between India and Pakistan, the Viceroy suggested that if soldiers charged with guarding passengers were found unharmed on trains afflicted by massacres, they were probably complicit; he recommended shooting the soldiers within half an hour. Another leader asked if it was fine to whip rioters in public. The deputy prime minister considered blowing up houses where shots were fired from windows. People complained that police fired over the heads of rioters as a warning, instead of at their bodies as a statement. Soldiers were authorised to shoot any civilian found with a gun near a railway line. The penalty for stabbing someone was death. Permanent suppression of one kind or another was on everyone's mind. The committee wondered if their actions to bring peace would instead lead to violence. Could they encourage Sikhs to sheathe their daggers, or would it provoke them to murder?

At the centre of these displacements was Nehru, the new leader of a brand-new country. His long-awaited destiny had arrived with India's independence; with great power came painful chores. (In time he would spend his waking hours exhausted, and fall asleep during daytime meetings. The chief of his intelligence apparatus would watch him work, take meetings, give speeches—the regular work of leaders—and conclude that it was Nehru's unusual intensity and involvement that would eventually kill him.) Nehru's concerns at the time were those of a first-time rider on a panicked horse, about creating systems and rules in the midst of chaos and bewilderment. He would kick at crowds when they became unruly, or clamber over a dense crush of people who did not clear a path for him quickly enough. He took physical liberties without thought, impulsive expressions of annoyance his victims mystifyingly approved of—one looter confronted by Nehru on a Delhi street declared that it would be an honour to die at his hands. Nehru left him alone with his haul, feeling more and more that he was out of step with his time. Left to himself, he sent out tender notes written on the bark of Kashmiri willow trees, and longed for Kashmir's mountains.

Nehru was distressed by the partitions that followed Partition. He wrote a letter to India's president expressing his helplessness about the divisions. He noticed that Muslims, in particular, were being hunted and killed, regardless of who they were. Every foreign ambassador had been visited by a mob looking to kill any Muslim staff they had. Over three quarters of Delhi's Muslims were now in camps. He understood that violence followed violence, but had conscience and the fear of consequence abandoned the land entirely? The massacres in Delhi, which began in the first days of September 1947, were inexplicable to him. It was unimaginable, the existence of such anger, so long-drawn-out and so specific, with special attention given to how a person was dispatched from life. The marks left on the dead, he said, felt like personal vengeance. 'There is a limit to killing and brutality and that limit has been passed during these days in North India. A people who indulge in this kind of thing not only brutalise themselves but poison the environment . . . individual attacks continue in odd places by the kind of persons who are normally quiet and peaceful. Little children are butchered in the streets. The houses in many parts of Delhi are still full of corpses. These corpses are being discovered as people go inside and find dead bodies which have been lying there for many days.' He was losing faith in his countrymen. 'The future appears to be dark not so much because 50,000 or 100,000 people have been murdered, but because of the mentality that has accompanied this and that perhaps might continue.' He gave himself to the moment, and wrote that he did not want to lead a nation so callous about life.

Ordinary citizens had been violent, but Nehru was certain that the killings were too organised to have been emotional acts. There were too many people writing to him, telling him that influential neighbours and small groups were going from door to door to cause ferment in the name of protecting Hinduism. When the inspector-general of the Delhi police wondered if the riots and massacres were indeed organised, Nehru replied that there was no doubt in his mind. A week before the troubles in Delhi began, he said, inflammatory notices and leaflets had been spread in the city by a certain organisation. He believed that 'well-organised' bands of Sikhs and Hindus with an allegiance to the RSS had committed murders in Delhi. 'It seems to me clear that the RSS have had a great deal to do with the present disturbances not only in Delhi but elsewhere,' he wrote to Vallabhbhai Patel in September 1947. He complained that the Delhi police had not handled the matter professionally, and was unhappy with the workings of the intelligence apparatus; the mischief makers seemed to have better intelligence than the government, Nehru said.

The intelligence reports he received were a troubling view into the sprawl of the RSS—not simply a landscape of governance dotted with people sympathetic to its cause, but of decisions and actions incompatible with a just society. Nehru heard that arms meant for the home guard in Kashmir were instead distributed to the organisation by sympathisers. He received word that members of the RSS had been given positions as special magistrates and special police officers by the deputy commissioner of New Delhi. Nehru wondered if the deputy commissioner's 'sympathies lay in a certain direction', preventing the city's law enforcement from taking preventive action against rioters. 'As far as I can make out, we have had to face a very definite and well-organised attempt of certain Sikh and Hindu fascist elements to overturn the Government, or at least to break up its present character. It has been something much more than a communal disturbance,' Nehru wrote. 'Many of these people have been brutal and callous in the extreme. They have functioned as pure terrorists. They could only do so, of course, with success in a favourable atmosphere so far as public opinion was concerned. They had that atmosphere. These gangs have not been broken up yet although something had been done to them, and they are still capable of great mischief.' He wrote of a recent incident at Safdarjung Hospital in Delhi. A Hindu gang a few dozen strong hunted down Muslims in a segregated ward, 'a horrible reminder of the type of persons we have to deal with'. Worse still, the hospital was staffed with twenty police, all of whom were unarmed and did not seem to protect the ward. All around there was violence, and Nehru was hampered by district officials who openly gave speeches in opposition to government policy. He struggled to understand where people's sympathies lay, and if they would listen to reason.

Across undivided India, through complaints and investigations and good fortune, police and intelligence officials made discoveries about the RSS's capabilities and its store of arms. In January 1947, its offices in Punjab were searched by police. Across Sialkot, Rawalpindi and Hoshiarpur, fifty bamboo sticks, seventy-seven spearheads and thirty-eight axe handles were found during the searches. In Multan, nearly fifty of its members met, many of whom were armed with hockey sticks. They met secretly at night, and in temples and fairs, preparing for a war they were convinced was coming. Their exercises were military in nature, and their tools were swords and acid; anything that could be weaponised. Their numbers continued to grow. By March that year, the RSS had nearly fifty thousand members in the province. But they weren't simply preparing for a war, they were eager to make it happen. Walking through Muslim quarters, they shouted slogans against Pakistan as a provocation, and instructed newspaper editors to cover the organisation's activities sympathetically. All the while, the organisation's appetite for mayhem in the name of self-defence expanded, and these new capabilities came as news. The RSS created a stabbing squad that would assault lone Muslims. In April that year, one member blew himself up, and the police realised they were now making bombs. In one branch, the police found nineteen bombs. In another city, it collected empty water bottles and fused bulbs as raw materials for explosives. It set up a 'revenge' squad and a small army trained to use explosives. Meanwhile, Hindu firearms suppliers gave the RSS's members guns. Other police raids unearthed detailed preparations. When a house that belonged to the chief of the Jullundur RSS branch was searched, police found explosives and literature on the construction of landmines, daggers, acid, a bow and arrows, maps of Hindu and Muslim habitations and lists of house tenants and owners where Hindus and Muslims coexisted. Police sent back urgent reports: the RSS was organising, and partnering with other militant groups, and rousing passions and intimidating Muslims without fear.

They stumbled upon plans that showed how the organisation's members had divided cities into zones. 'For each zone a leader had been appointed. Sufficient arms were supplied to each zone, so that upon a given signal, the whole city could be taken by surprise and the massacre of Muslims started,' police reports from 1948 noted. The plans ranged from detailed and specific to outlandish; one involved dropping bombs on a mosque from an aeroplane.

But so much more was concealed, revealed only in the RSS's own publications well in the future. Along parts of the Ravi River, which ran through Punjab, RSS volunteers gathered to learn the proper way to handle bombs and pistols. There was no shortage of explosives. The RSS had bomb-makers willing to produce for its cause, and it had men and women who would transport them at personal risk. The locations of their training camps were changed regularly, and only a few people knew of the arrangements, for 'widespread information could pose an unnecessary danger'. They possessed high-powered torches that could shine red, green and white beams for over a mile, and fire brigade horns that could send signals and relay coded messages over vast distances. All of this, the organisation convinced itself, was defensive in preparation; they did not want a fight, but the way Muslims were going, a battle was inevitable.

Nehru fretted about the ineffectiveness of his intelligence services, seeing them as inadequate in matters of identifying both the perpetrators of violence and the spreaders of deadly rumours. 'The prime minister pointed out that at present the Intelligence organisation of those who were creating mischief in Delhi was better than that of the Government,' minutes of a cabinet meeting on 25 September 1947 recorded. Lord Ismay, chief of the governor-general's staff, suggested the creation of a small Central Intelligence Bureau to sort intelligence reports. Meanwhile, the RSS had some of its volunteers live their lives as Muslims, and these members would allegedly report on the machinations of the Muslim League, which had called for the creation of a separate Muslim nation. The volunteers would bring back news of fantastic conspiracies, such as a plan to kill senior members of the RSS before slaughtering the unprotected Hindu community at large. This news would not be shared with the police for action, but be used by its volunteers as justification for murder. In one instance, three groups of RSS men simultaneously flung grenades at Muslim tenements and detonated bombs at the instructions of senior leaders. The attacks were justified as pre-emptive action. In Kangra Valley, the administration and the police ignored urgent orders to investigate an attack by armed RSS workers on Muslims. Instead, RSS stories recall, the administration sent word through a policeman that the volunteers should quickly cremate the bodies; logs from a local worker's timber shop were used to cover the bodies and then set on fire.

The attacks on Muslims, the usurping of property, the hurried cremation of Muslim bodies and the disposal of evidence, would be recorded in RSS mythology as a sign of its usefulness, its reach and its cunning.

# 5

# A Most Unnatural Way

In 2002, two members of the RSS, Manik Chandra Vajpayee and Sridhar Paradkar, produced a 'history written in blood' of their organisation's work during Partition. 'RSS emerged as the herald of hope to the people forcibly thrown out from Pakistan,' they began, explaining how their acts of murder and conspiracy across the new republics were led by duty. The epic seven hundred-page tale was a model RSS production featuring killer Muslims and grateful Hindus. According to the book, RSS volunteers worked closely with the Indian army, spreading across east and west Punjab, providing food, money and accommodation, posting armed sentries at the gates of Hindu settlements, and accompanying Hindu refugees on trains from Pakistan to India.

The book, *Partition-Days: The fiery saga of RSS*, was a typical artefact of RSS institutional memory, a collection of stories meant to be viewed with none of the scepticism its members had for more factual histories. It was a link to the stories, ideas and versions of history its members carried in their minds, an inextricable weaving of larger undeniable events and smaller fictitious anecdotes, a limited lie or a qualified truth, a rendering of history that, in the absence of unimpeachable documentation, resided in the hearts and words of those who wanted to believe. And so a Hindu policeman who arrested an RSS volunteer and confiscated three trunks filled with bombs in Lahore was labelled a 'great Hindu loyalist of Pakistan', and the bombs the organisation made were for 'protecting the people as well as for self-defence'. Its volunteers did not break down under interrogation, neither under threat of chilli inserted into their behinds nor when Pakistani police beat the soles of their feet and plucked out their pubic hair. Heroism, cleverness and subterranean support marked this history of the organisation's role during Partition. That was why, they wrote, the RSS 'had a long reach. There was hardly a section of the society where they did not have trustworthy collaborators. [They had] their contacts everywhere. Their communication network was so efficient that information of a planned police raid would reach them before the raiding party.'

Besides sending its foot soldiers into the streets and overseeing violent campaigns, the RSS worked in other ways to cultivate Hindu minds. Their approach was to discredit sources of authority by tainting them as immoral, and creating an atmosphere of suspicion through the publication and repetition of rumours and suggestions. A volunteer who would leave the organisation and write a remarkable critique of its workings in the 1960s described how it used character assassination as a weapon. 'They would attribute the worst kind of criminal motives to a person who dares to differ from them or criticise their theories and practices,' the worker D.R. Goyal wrote in his book *Rashtriya Swayamsewak Sangh*. 'I recall an incident of 1946. In a newspaper a photograph of Jawaharlal Nehru had appeared which showed somebody lighting his cigarette. That photograph was cut out and kept by a number of Sangh workers in that area of Hoshiarpur (where I was also a minor functionary of the RSS) to be shown to simple-minded, credulous small-town folk as an evidence of the personal degradation of the man. It was presented as a kind of obscenity. While showing it to people the RSS men would comment: "Look, if this man is not ashamed of being photographed with a cigarette between his lips what would he not be doing in private?" . . . Other photographs in this repertoire were those of Nehru shaking hands with Lady Mountbatten and his sister Vijayalaxmi Pandit wearing a sleeveless blouse and sitting, bare-headed, around a table in the all-male company of Indians and foreigners.

'This incident is only the tip of the iceberg that is their arsenal of character assassination; the morbid details which they give are such that no civilised person would like to repeat,' Goyal wrote. 'For obvious reasons these things do not appear in the press, except as innuendos and insinuations and that too only in the house journals of the RSS like the *Organiser*. But that is heard every day in the streets so that the uncommitted and the uninitiated feel exasperated and, on hearing such charges, only say: "Damn it, don't they say all kinds of things about other people." This atmosphere, in a way, helps the RSS because the contention becomes pro- and anti- and nobody bothers about going into the facts of the case and understand the validity of the charge or the lack of it.'

There had been other indications of a discreet campaign to prod citizens into religious violence. In November 1946, ten months before India's independence, a leader from the Congress party in Lahore wrote a letter to Vallabhbhai Patel, who would soon become the deputy prime minister and home minister of India. He complained that a local newspaper, *Dawn*, was producing communal news, and he wanted the Congress's leaders to do something about it. But he was vastly more concerned about circulars shared by large numbers of Hindus that urged the community to organise and arm itself. 'The Rashtriya Sangh is especially creating panic and disaffection, and they excite others to take the offensive,' he wrote. His complaint included a copy of the circular, a document with a list of infuriating instructions supposedly issued by the leader Mohammad Ali Jinnah, who had fought for an independent homeland carved out of India for Muslims. The document was unbelievable in its blatant motives, from the first sentence—which claimed that it was recorded by a member of Jinnah's party—to the unmistakably Muslim name at the bottom: 'Yours faithfully, Habibur Rahman'.

The whole thing felt tailored to the specific insecurities of unquestioning minds. The instructions were that 'all Muslims of India shall die for Pakistan', that India should be conquered and its citizens converted to Islam, that 'one Muslim must get rights of 5 Hindus, i.e. each Muslim is equal to five Hindus', that Hindu shops, factories and temples should be looted and destroyed, that Muslim spies would infiltrate every village and district in India, that Muslims would distribute weapons in major cities and keep on themselves all kinds of weapons that would help drive Hindus out of India, and that 'Hindu women and girls should be raped, kidnapped and converted to Muslims'.

It was all a lie—meant to find and widen divisions and insecurities, to make believers and soldiers out of the credulous. The lawmaker wanted leaders to denounce the fake list on the floor of the House to 'counteract the effects of this circular'. Patel replied that there was no proof of its authenticity, and that many such documents were in circulation. 'The best course, therefore, would be to take notice of none.' In any case, he wrote, the press had come to some kind of agreement about their approach to covering communal news. He was not happy about it, but would act only if it required his intervention.

Whether leaders took notice or not, citizens certainly did, and they responded to the divisive rhetoric from the RSS's propaganda arm. In September 1947, a month after Partition, the RSS journal, *Organiser*, published a Gallup poll with four questions. It asked readers if Muslims on India's side of the border in Punjab should be exchanged for Hindus on the other side, or if the Muslims of Delhi should also go; whether the Muslims of Delhi could be 'loyal and patriotic citizens'; and whether it was advisable to 'keep Muslims in high and reasonable government posts of trust and confidence'. It published the poll in English and Hindi.

About 85,000 people replied. Around 84,600 thought that even the Muslims in Delhi should be sent away, that they would be disloyal, and agreed that they should not be in a position of power. The hostility was unsurprising, given the respondents were RSS supporters. But that a large number of respondents expressed such feelings apparently surprised the Criminal Investigation Department. Senior officers wondered how to put a stop to such straw polls.

In the months after India's Partition, unrest continued to fester. A small stone thrown at a mosque would bring a mass of Muslims on to the streets. A joke by a Muslim brought the RSS to their doorstep. The organisation told its volunteers to prepare themselves for the civil war to come. Outside Delhi, in villages across the northern countryside, RSS instructors came from as far as Kerala and Punjab to train and organise boys. They stood in the fields and practised with sticks, attacking and defending themselves against an enemy they had to imagine. The group's loose organisational structure meant that its members acted in 'their individual capacity' and undertook 'a sort of guerrilla warfare'. RSS members warned Hindu households not to give shelter to Muslim scavengers during periods of mayhem. The volunteers wanted nothing less than the complete disappearance of Muslims from public life. One volunteer reportedly said that 'Muslims would quit India only when [a] movement for their total extermination . . . would take place'.

Mohandas Karamchand Gandhi was wary of the RSS's organisational abilities and its rapid growth—particularly in Punjab—and described it as a 'communal body with a totalitarian outlook'. The RSS's leaders said its only interest was in social welfare, but dispatches by the country's police and investigative agencies described a violent organisation attempting to enlist police in acts of violence. RSS workers told policemen that they were preparing to attack Muslims in Delhi, and gently requested them not to open fire on the organisation's members. They were just as brazen in other jurisdictions, informing the police that riots would break out, and that their people would wear a white kerchief around their wrist as a mark of identification. 'It is learned that such contacts have been made with other policemen and officers in charge of police stations,' the superintendent of police wrote in a confidential note. 'It is a part of the programme of the RSS to contact men in the services, especially the police and the military, and win them over. This fact was reported by me long ago,' a frustrated inspector wrote.

Through the last months of 1947, secret reports about the group grew more urgent. RSS volunteers were raising large sums. They were strategising what they would do if they were banned, and were planning to contest the next election. The Criminal Investigation Department suspected that the RSS's workers had conspired to bomb Muslim neighbourhoods. On 6 December 1947 came another dispatch. Fifty RSS workers had gathered a hundred and fifty kilometres south of New Delhi to discuss 'ways and means of capturing the seats in the government'. At a gathering of approximately fifty thousand members, the group's leaders told old stories, hoisted the organisation's flag and told attendees that they were doing holy work. 'The flow of the Ganges cannot be stopped by any obstruction,' one said.

Two days later, a police informant attended a meeting at an RSS camp closed to outsiders. He reported that Golwalkar roused the crowd with encouragements to enrol new volunteers in every house and 'instil in them the essence of Hinduism'. The informant, whose identity was a secret, wrote: 'Referring to the government, [Golwalkar] said that law cannot meet force. We should be prepared for guerilla warfare . . .'

The RSS leader said he would not be content until the organisation finished Pakistan, and that anyone who stood in their way would be finished, whether 'it was the Nehru government or any other government'. Muslims had to leave India, he said. 'Mahatma Gandhi could not mislead them any longer. We have the means whereby such men can be immediately silenced, but it is our tradition not to be inimical to Hindus. If we are compelled, we will have to resort to that course too.'

One of the dispatches contained an aside. 'It is also alleged that one of its programmes would be to assassinate the leading persons of the Congress in order to terrorise the public and to get their hold over them.'

From across India, Nehru was receiving information about the RSS's reach, and through December he wrote letters to the maharaja of Jammu and Kashmir, to his deputy, to the prime minister of the United Provinces, and to others, urging leaders to shut down the RSS and investigate how rifles and sten guns were being diverted to them. 'The RSS in various parts of the country is at present engaged in active opposition to our government and has created any amount of trouble for us,' he wrote. He held them responsible for the desecration of mosques and attacks on Muslims in Jammu, and the abduction of Muslim women. 'A greater folly I cannot imagine. But this is typical of the RSS mentality which is incapable of understanding what is good for the country.'

From another leader he demanded answers about what actions had been taken against the RSS. 'You told me that you were going to take action against the RSS. When is this going to happen?' he wrote on 29 December 1947. He learned that a sixth of Ajmer's Muslim population had left the town, and more were departing. 'The RSS there and elsewhere is in aggressive mood and issues threats which frighten many people,' he told his deputy in a letter.

In January 1948, RSS workers circulated pamphlets blaming Gandhi 'for amalgamating the two races of India in a most unnatural way'. (What a natural amalgamation looked like—*that* they wouldn't say.) Every river and mountain was sacred to Hindus in some way, they said, and every town and temple held ideas of Hinduism. 'Even the soil of this land shows the signs of Hindu race.' Gandhi's way, they wrote, had 'proved suicidal', and they declared him a 'traitor to the race'. The splitting of India had traumatised communal Hindu organisations, and they swung between talk of rejoining India and of a 'population exchange'—the transfer of millions of unwelcome Hindus and Muslims—between the two countries. These reactions, and the organisations' expertise in matters of rumour and mayhem, would become the subject of secret official correspondence, with Pakistan insisting Nehru restrict the RSS and Hindu Mahasabha if he expected 'to achieve permanent results'.

Between these forces, Nehru would despair, 'The position today is that while Pakistan has followed and is following an intensely communal policy, we are tending to do the same and thus completely playing into the hands of Pakistan. Hindus in Pakistan are terrified and want to come away. There is no doubt that Muslims in India are also full of fear.'

All through January, increasingly hasty dispatches and telegrams brought Nehru news of damaging ideas pouring out of the mouths of communalists, and visitors brought him news of what the government did not know. The communalists' intentions and pace demanded his urgent attention, for tumult and insecurity were finding favour among the public. They represented a pulling away from his government's policies, a wilful hastening into impulse and reaction, whose end result would only be war, further unhappiness and newer complications.

'I have to face today exceedingly reactionary and bigoted Hindus who object to my way of life,' he would write to a friend, 'because they think I am not sufficiently Hindu in regard to it. My language is objected to because it is Hindustani and not pure Hindi. My clothes are objected to, and generally my way of life. If these people had their way, neither you nor I would have a tolerable existence.' He heard stories of their popularity, of the unchallenged marches in Bengal, Punjab and the princely states, of the large crowds that came to their processions and speeches, and he wondered if the country, still not a year old, had already chosen blood over peace. Each day brought something from the communalists that concerned him, some nudging of acceptable behaviour, some testing of boundaries, some defiance of the law. Nehru found these happenings extraordinary, and asked his chief of police what he planned to do when, in a business district in central Delhi, not far from parliament, members of the Hindu Mahasabha openly shouted slogans calling for the death of leaders.

And whether the words were spoken or whether they were written, they had the same effect of quickening the hearts of men and overcoming their senses. They were all unbalanced, and even he, Nehru admitted, did not know how to remain neutral towards the troublemakers. He wrote to an aide that he had seen enough evidence to hold the RSS responsible for recent violence. Some members of the RSS were even training in sympathetic territories and returning with arms and ammunition, he wrote on 28 January.

And then, three days later, on 31 January, having noticed it and discussed it, having felt its proximity and its dangers,

Nehru stood on a weapons carrier pulled by roped soldiers, waving away the crowd of crying citizens who came as close as they could, palms pressed in prayer, to be near Mohandas Karamchand Gandhi, who lay still behind him while petals floated down from bombers flying low. Nathuram Godse, his murderer, was identified as a member of the Hindu Mahasabha. (Dhirendra Jha, an untiring historian of the RSS, would make the case that Godse was still a member of the RSS when he murdered Gandhi.)

Within days, police across India went door to door to find every RSS member they could. Crowds searched for RSS members to beat, and RSS offices and enterprises to incinerate. The government searched itself to find members in the civil service. By the end of 1948, thirty-one thousand two hundred and sixty-eight arrests had been made across India. Files were filled with the names and departments of government employees who were arrested. They were everywhere, in the railways, the military engineering service, the national government, the press, the ministry of communications, the ministry of defence, the ministry of finance, civil aviation, the central ordnance depot, the army. The man in charge of Amritsar's police and military departments was caught organising RSS cells in the armed services. The police found members in army canteens, and sympathisers among the upper ranks of law enforcement. There was evidence that public finances were used to train RSS workers. Even the interrogators of RSS members were suspected of being RSS.

The neighbourhood searches were mixed. Sometimes they resulted in lists of the organisation's members or a wireless radio, but most times there was neither trace of man nor evidence. One intelligence report lamented that the RSS seemed to know about police actions before they happened. Information leaked, and incriminating material was disposed of; the police once hurried to seize an RSS printing press but arrived to find that it had been moved elsewhere. It was a while before someone realised that operators at telephone exchanges were suspect; it was there that confidential orders were intercepted. A law enforcement officer reported the existence of a 'clique among telephone operators . . . It can only be detected if we put in our own men to keep an unobstructed watch during the night shift.'

It was in this moment, a month after Gandhi's murder, a month after the beating and near shooting of his killer, that Nehru reckoned with the entrenched bureaucracy of communalism, a state-like apparatus that was incompatible with his ideas for India. 'While the investigation about Bapu's assassination by Godse is proceeding here and Bombay and elsewhere, there appears to be certain lack of real effort in tracing the larger conspiracy. More and more I have come to the conclusion that Bapu's murder was not an isolated business but part of a much wider campaign organised chiefly by the RSS. A large number of RSS men have been arrested, probably many of them more or less innocent,' he wrote in a letter to Vallabhbhai Patel. 'But a considerable number of their key men are still abroad or underground or even sometimes flourishing in the open. Many of these people are in our offices and in the police. It is hardly possible to keep anything secret from their group. I was told the other day by a responsible police officer that no search could be conducted in secret because previous intimation always reached the parties concerned.'

He wondered how to deal with the many sympathisers within the Delhi police. 'It may not be easy to deal with all of them. But I think something more than has been done can be undertaken.' More than just arrests were needed. 'I have little doubt that the RSS organisation is still fairly active in many ways and will hit back when it can. To be complacent about it might lead to fresh disaster. I am told that they have taken to a number of apparently innocent activities and are utilising them to keep their organisation in proper trim.'

The parts of law enforcement that still worked pieced together the shape of the organisation. The home ministry reported that it was run along 'Nazi' lines, and that the top leaders were not disclosed to the rank and file. Teachers were go-betweens. 'Their main slogan and rallying cry for propaganda is "Hinduism is in Danger".' Recruits were trained in six-month batches, and 'from each batch a suicidal squad is picked'. The squad consisted of educated boys who were chosen to be sacrificed in case an operation went wrong. After they were trained, they met the organisation's directors in temples and dilapidated houses. They had a special salute and a code. A right hand raised to the chest, then lowered, and a code word mumbled. The code word for the RSS (then known as the RSSS) was '18.193'. R was the eighteenth letter of the alphabet, and S, which was the nineteenth, was mentioned three times. This squad was sworn to secrecy. It was prohibited from moving on foot. At its disposal were, instead, cars and the RSS's 'inter-provincial courier system' for sending messages.

The slogans and posters the RSS had pasted all over Delhi had been scrubbed and painted over, as if papering over its name would erase its existence. But the RSS's members had gone underground, from where they kept up their activities. The group organised protests across Delhi to have the restrictions on it removed. At public demonstrations in support of itself, members sent cyclists to observe police across the city, and recruited children to drop off banned pamphlets at busy shops. Its volunteers would decades later recall this time as extremely traumatic; the institutional memory of it was so strong that their eyes would tear up in remembrance of a happening before they were even born.

As its members planned and courted mass arrest, old police files recorded a complaint: someone wrote that the search for justice took seven young RSS workers to Delhi's Assembly Hall sometime during lunch. Like the batches of protestors before them, they received farewells given to heroes. The garlands were a sign of their importance, the sweets were an anaesthetic for pain still to be inflicted. The workers would congregate and shout slogans in public. This would be followed by beatings and jail for the young men.

The ride to the police station at Parliament Street was rough, but it was all going to plan. The aim was to be inside, to fill the stomach of the penal system until it could take no more.

Only when they were within the law's holding cell, the infinite possibilities of freedom closed to them, were metaphor and theory replaced by the reality that they were now in the empire of policemen. Men in uniform gathered around the boys and said things that hurt their ears. Dinner was so vile it could not be classified as food. But that, too, was interrupted because the police arrived with orders to transfer them elsewhere. They were hurried up and taken away. The new station was to the north, in the city's older parts. It stood in the shadow of the Jama Masjid, whose resonant azaan also hurt their ears. The workers began to sit, but were told to stand in the open, where the January wind cut them like knives from several directions.

Before midnight, twenty-five men with bayoneted rifles surrounded them. There were four men for each boy. Without a please or thank you, the boys were told to get into a truck idling nearby. They imagined the empty seats were for their use, a brief illusion, because they were pushed to the floor. The men, who took pleasure in demonstrating where power lay, took the seats instead. Whoever the boys had once been, whatever family they came from, this was who they would be from then on. The truck transmitted the road to their behinds, the men's mouths transmitted the gutter to their ears, and they left for a nameless place in the dark.

Hurtling through small hills and sacred forests, the boys watched Delhi, its city life, its laws, all disappear. Where are we going, one of them asked. To wash your leader's face, one of the men replied. Whatever they asked, the response was abuse. Did they understand that although they were ready for jail, they were unprepared for what lay outside it? Did they realise then that the jail they wanted to fill was joined to a nameless landscape of punishment?

The truck went on for hours, for or a hundred kilometres or so, arriving at a canal. The driver stepped out to confer with officers following in another car. Their voices carried in murmurs, containing nothing discernible but trouble. With new instructions, the driver turned off the road and drove along the canal, away from civilisation, deep into territory unfamiliar to the boys. At a place where the foliage was thick enough to hide bodies, the truck engine was turned off. The men marched out the boys.

There were no geographic markers that indicated where they were, and no witness whose dialect could be placed. Water burbled as it passed, the cold wind pricked them as it went by. Stand up straight, one of the men said, but the boys could not manage the military poise the men demanded. This led to a beating. The stripping of money, clothing and mistaken notions commenced. Then two men approached each boy. One took hold of his head, the other of his feet, and they swung him into the canal. Seven splashes in all. The boys panicked, their nostrils burning and ears brimming with cold water. They tried to swim to the edge, but the men standing at the banks pushed them back with more beatings. Stay in, they said. When the police were certain that the protestors had learned a lesson for the crime of being associated with the RSS, they returned to the truck and left. The boys swam to land and stood shivering on the edge.

Eventually they found a watchman on the road to Delhi, and he gave them matches for warmth. He recalled earlier batches of their colleagues who had been tossed into the canal where they now stood. He gave them directions to Delhi. Along the way they came to a village and begged for food and protection. From there they found a train home that was lorded over by a ticket collector with no sympathy for the ticketless. They were ejected from the train, and walked in the general direction of the city, found another train and walked some more. This way they arrived at Delhi station, where the police saw them on the platform and detained two of them once more. The rest, tired and hungry, offered resistance once more. Then they, too, were taken away, and no one, at least until the writing of the complaint this interlude is based on, was heard from again.

This was the sort of story the organisation told about its ordeal, the sort of story its members would tell their grandchildren at home decades in the future.

In public, the RSS's leaders wrote letters explaining that they stood for a democratic and secular India, and did not advocate a Hindu nation. They claimed that it did not work in the shadows, and wasn't a private army. That was all a work of imagination, Golwalkar wrote. But in private the RSS told its members that on being arrested they should promise to leave the organisation, and then join a 'National Democratic Body', a political party that would soon be formed to keep the RSS's mission alive.

The party took shape slowly, with the unmistakable influence of the organisation it sprang from. At a meeting that led to the formation of this party, ideologues discussed ways in which Muslims could be accommodated in the India the party hoped to form. 'It is morally incumbent on them to celebrate' major RSS festivals, a member said. They were also free to offer prayers to Mecca, but could they not offer their prayers in Hindi or Sanskrit, a more acceptable language to a country of Hindu faith? But there were divisions between them on how much tolerance was too much. At another meeting to discuss the new party, a speaker wondered if Muslim citizenship could be revoked altogether.

THREE

# FAMILY MATTERS

# 1

# The Family

Running a finger over a row of books in a Delhi library one afternoon, I stopped at a title that promised danger. The stacks were abundant in books like *True Story of the RSS*, and *RSS Misunderstood*, and *Is RSS the Enemy?*, which often turned out to be self-published polemics that were too long, however short they were. This one was different. On its front was the full title: *In the Belly of the Beast: The Hindu Supremacist RSS and the BJP of India, An Insider's Story.* I read the first page, and then the next, slowly, with rising giddiness. Not long after, I was beside a Sikh gentleman at his photocopying machine. What pages, he asked. Everything, I said. In the long hour that followed, I wondered if the book's presence on these shelves was an oversight. This was the closest that any writer had come to describing the organisation from within. That night I swallowed its contents whole, scanned a copy for myself to store in several places for safekeeping, and wrote to its author. We mailed, and then scheduled a video call, and then arranged to meet in Kolkata, where he planned to be in July 2022, two months later.

On the day we were to meet, I waited for him in a wide lane outside a mall in eastern Kolkata, watching rickshaw drivers wash their vehicles late in the morning. Above, heavy monsoon clouds moved slowly, holding themselves together. I noticed him in the distance: a small man in a blue ikat-print kurta clutching a shopping bag bulging with vegetables. He had kind eyes behind his glasses, and his hair was short and grey. He explained that his wife was away and that his cook needed ingredients for lunch. I followed him down one street and then another to his building. We walked through the unmanned gate, which was hinged to a boundary wall crowned with nail tips. His living room contained three daybeds of various sizes, and I imagined that his visitors stayed longer than they anticipated. It was a small flat, made for one or two people. A maid brought out mangoes and sweets and placed them on a small table between us.

Partha Banerjee told me he had left the RSS behind almost forty years ago, and he said it as if he had firmly closed the door to that chapter of his life. But RSS people like to say that an RSS man will always be an RSS man, and there is a reason for this—it seduces through community and family, exerting a gravitational force on individuals. That was why, even though he had left the RSS, he thought about it often, and about what he could have been. Instead he was transformed from being an insider marked for future greatness to a complete outcast. His book was largely responsible for this outcome. It was a shy confessional, but its critique of the organisation was so clear-eyed that even his father, whose devotion to the RSS tolerated no questioning, distanced himself from him. 'He was completely heartbroken,' Partha said. 'We stopped talking to each other for a very long time.'

The space between them had lasted years, giving him clarity, and he now saw his father not just fondly, but also as a man with distasteful views. The look on his face, when he spoke about his father, showed his acceptance of both impressions. There were no new discoveries to make, only accretions of insights from recollections. As a parent, Jitendra Banerjee was an honest man who raised his children without compromise on their values and their education. He made time for Partha's cricket and football matches, and took him to watch *The Bridge on the River Kwai.* He wanted his son to be shaped by good cinema, and partake in the culture of the time. That part of him could not be removed from who he was.

But he was also RSS through and through, and the things he did and said were also in his nature. When his son looked past the love, he saw his father's 'completely racist, Islamophobic and fascist' nature. Partha said his racism was expressed 'in a moderate way'. These aspects of him were plain to see, in what he read, what he said, in the values he brought home to the family. 'I would hear from my father that communists and communism are evil, Islam was evil, and Christianity was evil. I was reading RSS magazines and newspapers that were completely full of hatred. I did not know it was hatred because I thought it was true. I was made to believe that what I was reading and hearing was the ultimate reality.'

Partha was born in 1956. After he told me about his father, he said he wanted to show me who his father was within the RSS. He walked over slowly from the chair in his living room to a book cabinet by the wall, lowered himself on a daybed placed against it and extended an arm to catch a shallow groove in one of the cabinet's sliding glass panes. He used his free arm for balance. Behind the panes were colourised pictures of his parents, some of which were covered in plastic to preserve their memory. In one family photo, Mr and Mrs Banerjee kept a respectful distance from one another, and their faces were inexpressive. They gave away nothing about themselves but their caution about appearances. Nothing in the picture spoke of Jitendra's unease with Muslims, nor of his wife's struggles with Jitendra's financial choices. In the cabinet were trophies, a poster, a picture of dancers, a picture of someone eating and small conches carved from stone. There was a calendar for the year 2017 from Karuknit Arts and Crafts Emporium, and two plastic babies with tan skin in a miniature plastic chair. The apartment had an air of ornate neglect and forgotten accumulation.

The pane rattled and finally screeched open. He reached in. 'These are my father's books,' he said. 'I'll show you what they are.'

A painting of Hedgewar fell out of the pile: questioning eyes, round face, a luxuriant white moustache, a satiny reflection on the tall black cap that marked him as RSS. Hedgewar had died young, at fifty-one, and had since achieved the highest official status an RSS man could be assigned: an avatar. This entitled him to be remembered 'with a sense of divinity and admiration that reaches the level of God-worshipping', Banerjee wrote in his book. The flatteringly lit portrait had official approval, and went for up to Rs 1,500 online. The books were stories of valour from the RSS's publishing arms. They were gifts to Jitendra on his wedding day from a legendary RSS leader, Eknath Ranade, who had organised protests against its ban after Gandhi's murder, but had himself escaped jail. The moniker 'Underground Sarsanghchalak' was applied to him in admiration for his leadership in hiding. 'Many of the books are in Marathi. Old-timer pracharaks [propagandists] knew Marathi because it was primarily a Marathi organisation. Now it has taken a different shape.' Jitendra, a thoughtful soldier, had translated them into Bangla.

Partha separated postcards that his father had collected and bound with tape for some reason. He spread them, revealing the stars of the RSS pantheon. On one card was Golwalkar, his uncut hair and wild beard conferring instant holiness with an aftertaste of asceticism. Another was of Sarada Devi, the wife of Ramakrishna, the Hindu leader whose teachings had inspired Vivekananda. In the painting she wore a white sari, and her covered head was framed by a soft halo. A third was filled with the Maratha warrior king Shivaji, his orange flag fluttering behind him. These images of the ascetic, the divine and the warrior were printed by the West Bengal branch of the RSS. Looking them over in his palms, Partha said, 'The entire discussion is about Hinduism, nothing else. Nothing exists for them but conservative Hinduism. If I came first in an RSS essay competition, the prize would be a biography of Hedgewar. I mean, how boring is that?'

After Gandhi's murder, a while after the mass arrests, Partha's father was among the 'big people' from the RSS who were released from jail, he said. Jitendra was a studious Bengali in Benares, and had abandoned his future to join the campaign to fill jails in response to the RSS's banning. His sacrifice was acknowledged by Golwalkar, the bearded, bespectacled man at the very top of the organisation, the man who saw himself as Nehru's equal. Golwalkar knew Jitendra's name, a fact that was its own reward.

Since the start of the RSS's protest against its ban, more than forty thousand volunteers and members of the public from Delhi first and then villages outside it had been persuaded to fill the jails by turning up at Connaught Place, Chandni Chowk and other locations. Police officers and intelligence agents called it 'an index of their self-conceited prestige'. In Golwalkar's opinion, the arrests reflected the supreme selflessness of his cadre. When the ban on the RSS was lifted in July 1949 by the deputy prime minister, and the men were gradually released, the RSS's leaders quickly gave them work to do. At public and private meetings, Golwalkar urged his troops to go forth and sign up new members, develop new outposts and join political parties to 'infuse the Sangh ideology in those parties'. Senior leaders encouraged followers to raise funds for the defence of Hinduism, a thousand here, two thousand there, membership fees set and then reduced when there were few takers, and then reduced a little more before finally settling at two annas.

Others were instructed to play regimented games with their peers regularly, a way to keep the troops together. Golwalkar rallied his listeners, saying it would not be long before Hindu members of Nehru's Congress party joined his movement. It was a busy time, and seen one way, the burst of activity reflected the organisation's popularity and spread. That was how most followers perceived matters. But a frantic desperation undergirded these actions; the RSS's leaders were scrambling to keep their soldiers occupied. Reeling under the reaction to their association with Gandhi's murderer, and barred from government jobs for life, thousands of men trained in weaponry and close combat had emerged from jail 'restive' and eager to know the organisation's plans, an RSS official told his government interrogators. 'A great responsibility devolved upon us, the leaders of the organisation. It is incumbent on us to keep a dynamic and vigorous mass of young men under effective check lest they resort to irresponsible adverse acts for which the organisation may get defamed and may have to answer.' After he was released, Jitendra oversaw the organisation's branches, called shakhas, for a while before becoming the RSS's first propagandist in Bengal, Partha said. In return, the organisation found him employment with one of their own. It was a mercy, for the world was not kind to an RSS man after Gandhi.

Information on Jitendra's propaganda for the RSS outside his translations and an essay he left behind was scarce, but the early months of 1950 in West Bengal would have kept him happily occupied in motherland and Hindu unity work. Twenty thousand Hindu and Muslim Bengalis were trading one country for another daily. They left hurriedly with papers, clothes, jewellery and cash, and with luck they gave up only a few things on the way. Partition was not in the past here, despite the prime ministers of India and Pakistan diplomatically urging each other to control their people. Liaquat Ali Khan, then prime minister of Pakistan, advised Nehru that peace would follow if he curbed the activities of organisations that had advocated 'the reunion of India or Pakistan or have been demanding a separate homeland for Hindus in Pakistan'. He wanted assurances that the RSS's roving squads were not terrorising hapless Muslims in West Bengal. Nehru in turn reminded him that Pakistani Hindus too were subjected to 'frequent killing, arson and looting and abduction of women and all the rest of it, and demoralisation of vast numbers of human beings who have been and are intimately connected with us'. The restraint in the prime ministers' critiques masked, at least for a while, their bewilderment at the scale of the crisis. From January to March 1950, explosions of communal violence on the eastern borders had propelled nearly half a million refugees into India, and a slightly smaller number had burst into Pakistan. Each day elapsed at the pace of a burning fuse attached to catastrophe.

Nothing about this moment was rational, Nehru thought. Refugees arrived with shock in their eyes and disaster on their lips, and on the basis of their personal stories people obliterated their neighbours and demanded that their prime minister take on Pakistan. Meanwhile, the populace in West Bengal was primed for roiling by the usual suspects. In such an environment, Nehru wrote to the chief ministers, 'When people are excited and their minds are full of hatred and anger, then any lead from the Hindu Mahasabha may lead to mischief . . . even a slight incident may grow to big dimensions.' He begged them to stop the Mahasabha—which had at least a hundred and fifty-five branches in Bengal—and probably other reactionary Hindu parties who demanded that Hindu populations be exchanged for Muslim ones, and who held public meetings where threatening speeches were made. Tired of their ceaseless rumour-mongering and incitements, he repeatedly warned state leaders that, left unchecked, communal conflagrations would catch them all by surprise. Nehru grasped for control, praising ministers who quelled unrest, scolding ministers who were ineffective. What he was really battling, he sometimes articulated, was a 'medieval state of mind'. By this he did not mean just the Hindu parties, but members of the government and the public at large. On 3 March, he addressed the country on All India Radio and tried to make his listeners understand. To uproot tens of millions and deposit them in a strange land was a colossal endeavour fraught with misery, he said. 'How can we deal with these matters and decide the fate of millions of people in the excitement of the moment and without the fullest thought to all possible consequences?' he asked. He wished that Indians would stop seeing Muslims as potential Pakistanis. But how could they, when the Hindu parties, which had a 'remarkable way of saying or doing the wrong thing', persisted with their propaganda?

Nehru wrote to ministers and friends that in one way or another, the Mahasabha—and by association the RSS—were closer in nature to Pakistan than India, for the Hindu policies they adopted were 'exactly similar, in reverse, to Pakistan's'. He found the Mahasabha's policies, especially towards Muslims, abhorrent, saying that it came out 'from time to time with the stupidest of proposals'. But he also noticed that 'stupidity has a market, if it puts on some kind of a nationalist garb'. The slow creep of the Mahasabha's ideas worried him. 'I find that progressively we are being driven to adopt what is essentially the Pakistan or the Hindu Mahasabha policy in this respect,' Nehru wrote.

The 'medieval state of mind' Nehru fought was on full display in the early months of 1950, a reactionary mind that was quick to act, but slow to consider consequence. Muslims in Bengal and the state of Assam, many of whom cultivated jute, were hunted and chased into East Pakistan. Across the rural countryside, their fields were left abandoned. The crop had led to prosperity and resentment: poems and other writings from the time described Muslim homes whose spotless tin roofs glistened in the sunlight, signs of wealth that raised the cost of living all around. As the cultivators were driven out, Nehru fretted about an acute crisis in jute production during the economically significant harvest season. In their place came Hindus from Pakistan, expert cultivators who were regardless treated with hostility.

The medieval mind could see only one part of a larger picture. In parliament, a member rebelled against Western customs and suggested blowing conches and ancient Indian instruments upon the president's entrance. Nehru asked the member of parliament if he would prefer to 'use weapons which were used five hundred years ago, or weapons that are used now?' But as the killings continued across Bengal, and refugees continued to arrive by train or steamboat, his writing lost its stillness. The correspondence spun from his office took on a manic anger particularly on 26 March, when he learned that the president of the Bengal Chamber of Commerce and his driver had been killed by Hindus. He railed at everyone he wrote to that day, whether Pakistan's prime minister or a friend. His instinct to punish arose acutely once more. He wanted the imposition of jail time and collective fines, and an end to empty rhetoric. By 1 April, Nehru's cabinet was hours from suspending the fundamental rights assured by the Constitution and adopted not five months before. The president of India begged him to reconsider, lest the Muslims panic and Hindus feel emboldened. People who despised him wrote anonymous letters calling him an Islamic tyrant. A member of the Indian parliament composed a letter that began 'Dear Maulana Nehru' and ended by accusing him of betraying India by accepting its partition. The term Maulana referred to a learned scholar of Persian and Arabic, but its application to Nehru implied his sympathies lay with Muslims. The disparaging term would stick. Seventy years later, the descendants of his Hindu critics would frequently call him Maulana Nehru on Twitter. Even as he held on tightly to his idea of the country—the 'noble mansion of free India where all her children may dwell'—he sensed it slipping away in early 1950. 'I see every ideal that I have held fading away and conditions emerging in India which not only distress me but indicate to me that my life's work has been a failure,' he wrote to his deputy. 'It is this inner rot that is the most distressing symptom of today.'

Partha's father, Jitendra, worked as a secretary in an outpost of the RSS's brand new political wing, the Jana Sangh, a body created to make overt what was previously furtive. Partha recalled walking up the office's creaky wooden stairs with his father, and the racket Jitendra's typewriter made as he churned out party correspondence that would be delivered by hand. It was a small workplace, and energised with audacious dreams. But for their dreams of a Hindu nation to reach fruition they needed more capital. The Mahasabha, which was also preparing itself for the general elections, paid a formal visit to American diplomats in March 1951 to ask for 'direct assistance' in its election campaign to keep the communists and the Congress from power. Ashutosh Lahiri, one of the Mahasabha's leaders, requested them to pressure American companies to purchase advertising space in Mahasabha publications in West Bengal. The outrageous request was turned down, and American and British bureaucrats exchanged cables about the approach.

There was work, but little if any money for the rank and file, Partha said. The cost of Jitendra's commitment to the RSS was borne by his wife and children. The only real excess they experienced was ideological; the patriarch had an abiding and ruinous belief in the organisation's destiny. 'My father gave up everything, a good academic career, a decent well-to-do family, their homes, mortal pleasures, everything,' Partha told me. 'My mother suffered greatly because of that. I suffered greatly because of that. We ended up living in poverty all our lives. But that was the RSS.'

That was the RSS. The organisation's members placed great store by suffering, maintaining not only a ledger of their own sacrifice but a complete accounting of everyone they knew. The nearness and innate understanding that helped them watch out for each other in times of crisis also ensured they kept close watch on each other, noticing what they wore and ate, whether their manners had suddenly changed, whether they were less committed, whether they had come into money. No hardship or possession went unrecorded. Years after Partha followed his father into the RSS, and then wrote his way out of it, he too was touched by this habit. And so while he remembered his father ignoring his financial responsibilities, and remembered that other members also 'starved sometimes', subsisting 'day after day on a bowl of rice or chapatis and some potatoes', he saw nobility in the voluntary renouncing of comfort, in going without. It was evidence of detachment, a value ranked above almost every other in his hierarchy of admirable traits.

'They were not greedy, they were not liars, they were not corrupt,' he said. 'They were like saints.'

That was why he became a member and stayed with them for decades, despite 'their hatred for Muslims, communists, and Christians, and their racism, and their extremely conservative thinking, and their anti-intellectual ideologies'. He wanted me to understand that while he did not support Islamophobia, disparaging Dalits and gender discrimination—especially after he understood the RSS's true nature—the people he knew who formed the RSS's most loyal cadre 'were very honest personally'. The purity of their hatred was the result of 'following their own doctrines honestly', he said.

But no belief is without its questions, and the traces of scepticism that lingered within him were his mother's doing. She came from a family of Congress supporters, the party of Nehru, and her distaste for the RSS was so strong that Jitendra rarely discussed politics at home. She was not formally educated, Partha said, but her own family influences had led her towards the Congress's largely secular outlook. She watched with despair her son's decision to follow his father, afraid he would walk away from his education and then his humanity, and leave behind a legacy of rationalism and spirituality for the intoxication of religion. 'My mother never liked the social patriarchs and the chauvinist big talkers of the RSS,' Partha wrote. She questioned the organisation's influence on the family. They inflated lost men, women and children with stories, and used a man for his energy and his time, and when he was done, they were done with him, she said.

Jitendra knew this to be true, but he did not feel exploited. He told his son that his work as RSS was for the motherland, and this god-given duty was all the sustenance he needed. This baffled his son, because Jitendra was not a religious man and performed none of the rituals associated with faith. He wouldn't even walk downstairs to a pandal across the street during Pujo. 'His faith was abstract,' Partha said. 'It was detached from everyday spirituality. He would never participate in religious functions, but it was like, "Hindus must be strong, and we must come together, and we will become militant Hindus, and only with these weapons can we bring our country together, this country that is only for Hindus and no one else."'

His belief in a unified Hindu body was more enduring than in Hinduism itself. The idea had not come to him naturally, through a process of enquiry and deduction, but through repetition and rote learning. He was a vessel for concepts that the RSS leadership had espoused for decades. I opened one of his books, a celebration of the centenary of Vivekananda's birth, and read an introduction written by Jitendra's acquaintance, the RSS leader Eknath Ranade. The book was a compilation of the spiritual leader's teachings, and Ranade listed some of them. 'The national union in India must be a gathering up of its scattered spiritual forces . . . a nation in India must be a union of those whose hearts beat to the same spiritual issue.' He explained that Vivekananda asked people to give up 'imbecility, superstition, pettiness of mind, mutual quarrels and bickerings about trivial things', and instead acquire great power through organisation. 'And thus by coordinating our separate wills we should build up a future far more glorious than our past.' Reading Ranade's words, it occurred to me that the chimera of a national unity of the highest order, pure and responsive to one Hindu logic, was unattainable, and as long as it was beyond their grasp the organisation's workers had something to reach for, and somebody to blame for their failures. In the quest for perfection in purity, conflicting desires and choices were viewed as foreign and impure, obstacles in the path of a striving nation.

Partha said that his mother had been right. After Jitendra died in 2017, Partha visited an RSS office in Kolkata to meet with old-timers who had known him as a child. He spoke up for his father, reminding them of Jitendra's sacrifice: he had left college for them, rebuilt the organisation in Bengal after Gandhi's murder, he had burned incriminating documents when Indira Gandhi suspended civil liberties and sent her officers after the RSS, and had gone to jail for them. He argued that Jitendra deserved a worthy memorial for his evangelism and his translations. But he found them reluctant. What they offered was not good enough for Partha. He now understood that the building with the unattended steps and noisy typewriter, and the men who wrote letters and carried them by hand had all faded away. His father's last decades were spent in reflection on his life and choices, and in the isolation he finally gave himself permission to openly admire the work of Rabindranath Tagore, whom the RSS had once forbidden him from seeing. Occasionally he put on his dhoti and kurta to attend a special RSS meeting, but he had otherwise grown distant from those ideas. He admitted to Partha that he could no longer bear the group's extreme views. He had questions about their involvement in the razing of the mosque in 1992 and in the pogroms of 2002 in Gujarat. Each act of destruction contained the origins of further tumult. 'He wasn't the same old adamant arrogant RSS man,' Partha said. He had mellowed, and was at peace with the realisation that the organisation needed nothing more from him. In the end, fifteen or sixteen veterans showed up for the funeral, and there was a brief mention of his death in *Swastika*, the RSS's Bengali journal, Partha said.

Partha was six years old when Jitendra first led him to a shakha. It was 1962. He was kept busy, pulled into the orbit of the shakha's routines and the lives of its members. He played games, sang songs and heard stories. But what games they were, and what stories were told: every activity had mythological references, or was somehow related to Hindu culture. There was no room for Western games such as cricket or football. The local designated education officer, the Mukhya Shikshak, would arrange the children in a circle and tell them stories about Hinduism and its icons, fencing in their view of the world. That every lesson carried the faint sound of blown conches and temple bells was by design. The RSS's teachers assumed the role of intellectual mentors, but the education they imparted was primarily based on the teachings of a single religion. 'You're not talking about Einstein, of Charles Darwin, or climate change,' Partha said. They spoke of Muslims in the usual way, he said, and discussed the role that men and women were traditionally assigned. The consensus was that men were natural leaders while women were supporters. By the time he was nine or ten, he located the desire to beat a couple of Muslim children at school. The people around him seemed to think it was fine, but he did not disclose the matter to his mother, afraid of what she would do to him.

One time, Golwalkar, the supreme leader, heard him leading prayers in mangled Sanskrit and summoned him to his room. After some questions about his father and his studies, he ordered Partha to take a crash course with a senior RSS leader to fix his pronunciation. 'I was being groomed that way.' Small moments of improvement and leadership, of brotherhood and belonging at the shakha, the gradual inculcation of a warrior spirit serving Hinduism, gave Partha a sense of purpose as a young boy, drawing him tighter into the organisation's orbit. The lessons, exchanges and conversations all seemed calculated to create an organisation man working for an irresistible client: the motherland. The inevitability of his rise was conveyed in so many ways that even now he thought about his fantasy life as a lifelong RSS man serving as a member of parliament in his sixties.

Between the late 1960s and early 1970s, growing responsibility led Partha to believe that he was destined for a higher office within the organisation. His bosses sent word up the chain that he was a rare worker: he carried out orders without question, and was a capable recruiter to the cause. The positive impressions of him accumulated, and he was designated the education officer of his shakha. In his late teens, he encouraged hundreds of children from his north Kolkata neighbourhood to join the RSS. When new recruits visited, Partha would accept them and absorb the circumstances of their life. He would ask what school they went to, the class they were in, where they lived, what their father did, how many siblings they had. Their preferences, quirks and secrets were all subjects of interest to him. In those first days he was careful not to talk of religion or politics. The skin he presented himself in was devoid of ideology. In that cloak of harmlessness and respectability he would ask the recruit's permission to meet his family. An invitation for tea or a meal would be extended to Partha. It was his experience that families were delighted to have an RSS functionary visit them at home. After shakha he would go along with an assistant teacher to meet the parents over the excuse of a cup of tea. Sipping on their chai, the parents and the teachers would assess each other, one party looking for safe harbour for their child, the other searching for potential officer material.

Over the meetings with parents and siblings, Partha gradually subjected them to his calculated curiosity. They were often flattered by his interest, while he tried to see the recruit through the family's all-seeing eyes and all-feeling hearts, and mentally map their circumstances and fears. By making their concerns his own, he could demonstrate the limitless resources of the vast body he represented in this corner of the city. He would find a way to show them he was indispensable. 'You find out how he's doing in school, what exams he's doing for his school final. Are you doing all right with maths? Do you have a teacher? I can send someone to help you with maths. I'll find someone who is good at maths in the RSS and send him to help him out at home for free.'

With every new recruit the work was constant at first. Partha made sure to visit each family at least every week. Soon the familiarity paid off, and 'very quickly this kid, this newcomer, is not a newcomer any more. He's a part of the RSS family. You have to show people sincerely, not in a fake way, that I like you as a brother, and I really care for your life and your family. You start believing me, and you know that I am someone that you can count on. That I am going to be there for you in times of need. I won't give you money, but I will look out for you. And your mother knows that you're not going to be doing internet porn after school. You're going to be in good company with a bunch of kids who play together, sing together and talk about the country and the nation. And if you did not go to RSS, then you would basically be like a stray kid, like on the roadside, talking to a bunch of kids and smoking and doing drugs and womanising.' Earnestness was the method he employed, the 'trick' that prospects found irresistible. 'You've got to be genuine, you know? People understand in two seconds whether you're a fake, or if you have eyes for his sister.' (This approach was vital to the RSS's success, the author Akshaya Mukul told me. 'They create a last-mile network so that they're in your life. They need to reach ordinary Hindu homes,' he said. 'I call them the paterfamilias.')

For all his success, the attempts at conversion were largely unsuccessful. Of every ten recruits, he estimated that nine were 'yanked out before you know it' by families invariably sympathetic to Congress or the Communist Party. 'They already knew what RSS was about.' The ones who remained were largely illiterate and unaware. 'If you are not an enlightened family, I am your enlightenment,' he said, referring to the RSS. 'I'm teaching you about Hinduism, I'm teaching you about Vivekananda, I'm teaching you about India and its many different states and its many different languages and songs.'

Between the exercises and the quiet chats, a view of the world, of Islam and of women seeped into them. Partha thought it was mass conditioning. 'People there groom a vast number of individuals they think will not be able to ask questions because they have absolutely no knowledge. For lack of a better term, it's really a lack of thinking, you know, a lack of intelligence.'

I asked him what would happen if someone asked a question. He replied that there would be a reply of some kind, but the questioner would often lack the critical skills necessary to assess the response—not merely because of their young age, but because of the quality of their education, Partha thought. His dismissiveness about the intellectual capacity of the RSS's rank and file was startling. Partha said assuredly, as if it was one of the foundational truths of maths or science, that 'there is absolute detachment from curriculum-based education and powers of reasoning'. Partha did not blame the RSS's members, but he did not spare them either. He saw the RSS's foot soldiers as limited by their intellectual experiences, 'like, really sub-par intelligence. Ninety to ninety-five per cent of its members are practically brainless idiots,' he said to me.

He believed that the arrangement worked well for the organisation. It needed followers to carry out commands across its vast network, it needed the execution of its instructions without interruption. 'They dumb you down so that you are not allowed to think, question, or challenge. You just blindly follow directives from leaders. The local leaders get instructions from district leaders, and the district leaders get it from the national leaders. The national leaders get it from the Sarsanghchalak or the Supreme Leader, and nobody questions it. There is no process of questioning anything; you just follow with folded hands.' Besides inventing answers to earnest questions, it was common practice to club a troublesome question with two or three queries so that it was forgotten in the reply, a former RSS volunteer who served as city secretary in Shillong said. 'They would say things like, "We'll talk to you later", or "We'll speak with you in private".'

At fifteen or sixteen, Partha was invited to the annual Officers' Training Camp, and then assigned leadership of the local shakha. He continued the regimented traditions that thousands before him had been given charge of across India. In their little fiefdoms, where few people witnessed their practices, Partha and the leaders diligently unfolded and hoisted the orange flag, said their morning prayers and oversaw exercises. They were alone, but across the country at approximately the same time Partha's peers in the RSS were engaged in the same activity. They drew a kind of strength from this synchronicity, a motivation from the feeling of partaking in a larger common activity. On days when the Maoists and other enemies threw homemade bombs at RSS shakhas, Partha conducted his duties alone, confident that his local friends in the Communist Party and the Congress would not kill him, even if they despised the RSS. Their two weapons were death and ridicule, and since murder was out of the question, they laughed at his silly khaki shorts and the foolish workouts he conducted in a corner of a park. 'But you do not care what they are thinking about because you are so blindly driven. You think that it's like a god-given mission that you are carrying out,' he said.

Neither weather nor violence interrupted the shakha's routines. It was the most basic unit of the RSS and its affiliate groups, and its presence was vital. In times of peace, this representation of the RSS—a place where children gathered and learned exercises and discipline daily, where they were taught values of brotherhood and honesty, and told stories of their heritage—was what people saw. It was the front desk of an enormous conglomerate. Even if people disparaged it, the shakha was necessary. From there its centrality to human life would flow. And the shakha itself had a centre, too, in the form of the orange flag, placed and given the respect of the idol in the temple, the book in the gurudwara. To its saluters, the flag in the shakha was sacred. Its flag had to flutter, it had to be saluted, it had to be the centre of worlds.

Partha's work matched his potential, and he rose to joint secretary of the RSS's student wing. He could walk into an RSS office and people would chat with him for hours, complaining about Muslims doing this or that. They always had time for him. He made speeches across the state, fixed meetings, assessed the group's popularity on other campuses and went on marches across Kolkata. The rally he had organised in the courtyard of Calcutta University, perhaps the largest in the history of the student body, just had to be seen, he said; the city's number one newspaper placed it on the front page the next day. During the Emergency, a time of martial law imposed by India's prime minister in the mid-1970s, he convinced RSS members to fill the jails as they had done a quarter of a century ago. While they submitted themselves to the harshness of prison, Partha decided not to follow the same path. 'I was about to go to prison, but changed my mind at the last minute,' he said. The RSS was outlawed again, but, just as before, its members continued to meet under the guise of other activities, and new organisations with enlightened names continued its work. Partha helped establish one such organisation. It was 'the RSS in camouflage', he said. 'We all worked under a non-political platform with an innocuous name: the Bandemataram Chaterbesh Committee.' The name was associated with the national song and deep-rooted feelings of revolution and nationalism. 'We even brought in a judge from the Calcutta High Court to be the president. When it was the RSS, he could not join because he was the Chief Justice. But who can say no to the Bandemataram Chaterbesh Committee?'

His work brought him renown. He had done enough for people to know him not just as Jiten's son, but as a man marked for stardom. And then, when it was all going so well, he surprised them by leaving in 1981.

Partha had been growing detached from the RSS. As to why, his answers were a jumble. He explained that his mother's painful cancer had made him reconsider his life. Additionally, his questions to the RSS's leadership went unanswered. 'From time to time I would be completely depressed and detach myself from the organisation, and not keep in touch with them for months. They would religiously talk to me and try to bring me back. This happened from time to time over the last few years,' he said. He had been reading Tagore, watching Ray and Ghatak, and chatting with leftist friends. In the talking, reading and watching, he grew, and grew apart. Then he moved to America. 'I left behind hundreds of very good friends whom I may never see again in my life,' he said. In his book, he described the departure as a cleansing, a dip in the Ganges that absolved him of his sins.

While he worked on his PhD in a rural part of America, he did not feel the urge to check up on home, as new students normally did. Even if he wanted to, there was no internet. Then in 1995 he moved to Albany, and caught up on the news from India.

'I was shocked,' he said.

The Hindu future he grew up hearing about from his father, in shakhas and in training camps was suddenly here. He was convinced of it when he read about possessed men, joyous men, standing atop the dome of the Babri mosque before bringing it all down. 'I felt they were materialising their long-term doctrine that India was for Hindus.' Partha corresponded about Hindu fundamentalism with writers and researchers such as Asghar Ali Engineer, and read independent riot investigations. Many of them pointed to truths he knew and understood intimately—riots were incited by newly formed communal organisations which consisted of people associated with the RSS and its political arm, the BJP. The organisations were not usually RSS, but the people were, and they operated as representatives of newly formed bodies. As he read what had been written about the organisation, he realised they were outsider perspectives. Scholars understood the RSS theoretically, but they did not really understand it. 'I thought, "Oh, my god, I have to do something about it because I know them so well, and nobody knows what I know."' He wrote his book, a slim volume based on his experiences. He did not explain his work in any detail, instead focusing on the small things about life within the RSS. But it contained enough for his father to feel betrayed by the book.

The possibility that Modi's party would win a third term in 2024 had convinced Partha to visit India for longer than usual. He wanted to travel the country and tell people all about the RSS. 'They are turning India upside down into a fascist state, just the way Hitler did it in Germany,' he said. 'Their entire functioning has been so boring and dull and drab that it has helped them to build a very powerful national network of people who cannot think. And people who cannot think are prone to following the dictates of leaders without question. That is the RSS's main strength. Nobody really knows much about it. How many people read history? A vast majority of Indians simply do not have any idea what the RSS is all about. Most people are illiterate in the first place, and what do they know about Hitler, Mussolini, Franco, Tojo, World War Two, the SS and Brownshirts? There is absolutely no discussion in mainstream media. How many times have you actually heard mainstream media discuss RSS history, for example? Never, never. Because it is so uncomfortable that it is definitely going to create a conflict between media corporations and RSS-BJP leadership, and they have figured this out really quickly.' The party in power and its ideological parent insisted that they were independent of each other, an explanation that Partha thought so little of that he hyphenated them.

As a result, from his home in America he had watched the familiar blights spread: misleading information, made-up histories and armed groups setting the rules of civic life. He said that racists who had been, 'you know, in hibernation', were now fully awake under the new regime, whose encouragement of unrest had made them virtually arms of the government.

All of this had worked to Modi's advantage, he said. 'The BJP has created an illusion about Hindutva and Modi's India. With all kinds of propaganda bullshit they've created an illusion that India is moving in the right direction. The entire system is run by a beautiful doctrine that wants the mass to live in a bubble.' He thought of the writer Aldous Huxley's description of an ideal totalitarian state, a condition he thought applied to Indians: they were inside a prison whose walls they could not see.

Jitendra's love had led Partha towards a life of uniforms and yes-sirs. It was a small world, but it was one he knew. By asking questions and demanding answers, Partha could see the limits of the worldview his father had bestowed. He grieved for the rigid boundaries of his father's curiosity. 'For his entire life, my father did not care to know about the rest of India. He never cared for an India that was not within the realm of the RSS. How sad is that? And he's an intelligent, educated man.' Jitendra, five years gone, was here in the room, present for as long as Partha invoked the RSS. Left unsaid was the question, *What would have happened if Jitendra had not listened to them? Where then would we be?*

Before I left, he hesitantly requested that I show him his words before I published them. He had lost enough friends already, he explained, and did not want to risk upsetting anyone further.

# 2

# Parents and Children

The canal burbled and flowed slowly between embankments of refuse. Residents of East Delhi's various Vihars were convinced the sludge carried effluents, cancer and other miseries from the denim factories upstream. The substance emitted a constant sourness, like the smell of cables burned for copper.

Down the road from the metro station at Gokulpuri, near the home Nisar had run away from, a young man was shuttering his medicine shop for the afternoon. It was the second time that week he had seen me, and noticed the notebook in my hand. He said he was a biotechnologist by training, but did not enjoy it. His love was cricket, and he played professionally for clubs in Delhi. His face betrayed a shadow of the inevitable acceptance that I knew well. He was on the cusp of a choice between passion and expedience. 'The game is unaffordable for middle-income families,' he said. 'The bats professionals play with are made of English willow, and they cost between twenty-five and thirty thousand rupees. If you add the costs of coaching and other equipment, the average expense is between twenty and thirty thousand each month. How will someone middle class play? Only the rich can afford this game.' He had considered alternatives, such as detective work, but had no guidance. His options were limited to biotechnology, a field alive with promise, or the shop, where the KitKats were refrigerated, but the medicines were not.

After some time, when this line of conversation had been exhausted, he again asked what I was doing there.

'I'm interested in religious symbols in public spaces,' I said, pointing at the orange flags. 'I could make out two things distinctly on the way here on the metro. Cell phone towers and orange flags. They outnumbered the Indian flags.'

'Yes, there's a lot of that here,' he said, looking down the street.

He said with some force that he was a religious man, but not a violent one. It was something he stayed away from, meaning the demonstration of religiosity and anger. As evidence of this, he showed me with pride the absence of flags or markings outside his shop. He smiled when I asked if stickers and flags were forced on people.

'This is something people choose to do. No one forces them.'

There is a tension in the give and take of observation and experience in the aftermath of a riot. Both the journalist and the observed are strangers, and they withhold from each other what would otherwise be shared more freely. I had walked around Bhagirathi Vihar and Mustafabad several times to better understand their nature and culture, but exchanges were guarded. I was careful not to ask questions that would make people withdraw, but regularly, as a conversation unfolded, someone would realise what was happening, and that they had probably said too much. First one person would ask questions about me, and inevitably a cascade of queries followed. The crowd would become cautious. The encounter with the man closing his store was different. He was openly curious and eager to explain, and I was relieved to meet someone peaceful for a change, who did not view the asking of questions as a hostile act. Although I did wonder how the riots had left their impression on him. Slowly, returning to questions of not just belonging but of active participation, I asked if he visited Muslim neighbourhoods. He had Muslim friends, he said, but he thought for a while and said that 'those Mohammedan people' kept their surroundings unclean. Although many others had constructed their sentences this very way, it felt out of place from the mouth of this calm man. I left him soon after and walked towards Bhagirathi Vihar.

The neighbourhood was a slice of land hemmed in by two canals, in which residents delivered their garbage. The stench was overwhelming, and transported by the hot wind many streets away. People lived there, fixing things, welding, sitting by the window, sleeping on the steps outside their homes. A block away, the forlorn operator of a large metal frame trampoline waited for customers to bring their children to him. He would charge them a rupee for every minute inside, and take their money joylessly. All he could think about was the instalments on the loan he had taken for the trampoline. Cars and small trucks wide enough to enter the alleys rattled on the mottled tar over shirts and underwear placed for wheels to squeeze moisture from. How they looked did not matter to the wearer, for the clothes were grey and tattered. Along every road, there were small temples and shrines built between houses. Cows munched on trash outside them, and hoardings advertised gangs with names that invoked gods. Above doors and on rooftops of small houses that were shops and offices, the black-orange negative image of a furious Hanuman flew on triangular flags, outnumbering the houses flying the Indian flag. The flag was a show of allegiance to the Bajrang Dal, a militant affiliate of the RSS. Its proliferation in the area was a sign that Gandhian values would not be welcome there. The divine representation had begun appearing nearly two decades before, on the backs of car windows and rear bumpers.

I had intended to meet the mother of a suspect in the Delhi riots, a man caught in legal purgatory. Three years after investigators picked him up from home for 'a few questions', he was nowhere near release. In the meantime, every misery that could have befallen him had done so. Since his father had died, he was the only earner in his family. There was no earning in custody. Then, three years into his incarceration, his wife, who was in her early twenties, died suddenly. His mother was undergoing chemotherapy for breast cancer, and she spent her days catching her breath, unable to move from the living room to the bedroom. His three children were separated and distributed among family members who resented the stretch on their finances. One of those children mopped the floor while her grandmother rested. In the afternoons, tired from studying and cleaning, she would fall asleep immediately after lying down. The suspect claimed he had done nothing; he had been falsely accused. His lawyer thought it was likely he would be released. Neighbours said the mother's medicines were paid for by the RSS. For these reasons I wanted to meet her. But on the way to her, as I was about to cross the small four-turn bridge that zigzagged from Ganga Vihar to Bhagirathi Vihar, I noticed a young man on his motorbike outside a temple, and thought to ask him where the local shakha was. Nisar had mentioned the shakha now and then, claiming it was where several of the rioters he had seen attended RSS morning exercises. He had pointed to a bare patch of land on a satellite picture of the canal in the vicinity.

'It's by the peepal tree. I'll take you there,' the man on the motorcycle said, shifting forward to give me room.

I noticed the orange angry Hanuman decal on his headlamp. 'Don't worry about it,' I said. 'I'll go there myself.' He calmly told me to get on. The man had time, and he was determined to be generous. 'There's no one there right now, and the person in charge lives in one of the lanes behind. We'll find out where he lives.' Down the road, from where I had just walked, he stopped near the house of the local Bajrang Dal leader. 'Call out to him,' he told me, giving me his name. He switched off the engine and waited beside me.

I knocked on the open metal door until an old man looked down from the second floor of a house with a tiled exterior to ask what I wanted. He heard me out and said to wait. Then a man leaned out of a third-floor window with a phone to his ear, and shouted, 'straight, left, and right', pointing down the alley. I was sure I had seen him on a poster for one of the local groups loosely affiliated with the RSS. There were no questions for me, and I thanked the men above and beside me, hoping that their need to be helpful had been met, and that they were no longer concerned for me. The Bajrang Dal leader went inside, but the motorcyclist watched me go down the alley to the house of the man who led exercises at the shakha.

The streets were torn up all the way, and piles of shattered tiles lay spread across them. There was no treading lightly, no stopping and thinking outside a person's door. The noise ensured that every act, even one of simply standing still outside a door, was watched. The man's door was shut. There was no sign of his affiliation but for a sticker of a goddess representing India, and some words qualifying patriots. I rapped on the door and inside a dog howled.

'Oye, chup kar,' a man shouted at the dog, silencing the animal. 'Who is it?' the man said from behind a thick mosquito net. I could not see him, but he could see visitors clearly.

I introduced myself.

'Come back tomorrow.' Then he thought to ask what I was doing there. I told him the usual story: that I was researching the aftermath of the riots there. A pause, a consideration, and he then asked me to wait while he opened the door. He was a short man, in middle age, and clad in a tight orange dhoti. His face was round and tired, and his feet were bloated like a salt pan worker's. He held out a small hand to help me cross the open sewage channel between the street and his home. He limped into a side room and said I could have a chair. I apologised for disturbing him at his time of rest.

'Oh, it doesn't matter. I keep answering phone calls anyway,' he said. He shouted for a glass of water, and a plate of biscuits appeared. I protested meekly, but his son smiled and said, 'No water without something to eat.'

The man's birth name was Dhanilal, but his acquired family called him Dhaniram affectionately, and that was what he preferred. He straightaway invited me to the morning shakha the next day. 'There are lots of people there. Lots of people. They will all talk to you.' His son, Sachin, who was named after India's greatest batsman, Sachin Tendulkar, said, 'They're from the public sector, professors from the teaching line, from corporates, some police.'

Seeing my surprise, Sachin said, 'There are three types of shakhas here. One for schoolchildren below the twelfth standard, one for professionals and one for people who are retired or old.'

'People aged forty and over,' Dhaniram said. 'We look at them through the filter of their experience.' He had lived there since 1990, he said, squeezing his knees. He supplied gas cylinders to hotels for a living, loading them on a scooter or a truck and taking them around North East Delhi. There were eleven cylinders in the room, stacked up behind the bed and in the corner behind him, below a picture of Hedgewar. 'I'm not able to do this the way I used to,' he said. 'My knees have a problem,' he said, revealing swollen knees.

'Tell me what happened here three years ago,' I said.

'It happened before corona,' Dhaniram said, and we nodded together, that, yes, this was something we could all agree upon. 'It was terrible here. That is what people say. What date was it when the fighting began?' Sachin said the trouble started after Kapil Mishra spoke. But he did not blame Mishra.

'You remember how those people jammed the roads and protested there? It all happened due to the CAA protests only. When Mishra said that if you people don't get up from here we will make you move, that day only I was delivering a cylinder in the Mohammedan area, and when I was returning from there, people had started throwing stones. They were throwing stones at buses and started beating the police. As I returned home I saw that the violence was spreading. I got on my moped and hurried home. Meanwhile they had started coming here into the Hindu locality. People from here began going out as saviours. If they hadn't done so, they would have invaded us.'

Dhaniram did not stay at home. Although he could not remember exactly what happened, there were specific details he recalled: which side the Muslims came from, which petrol pump they burned, the one man being treated at Mohan Nursing Home for a bullet wound. 'Nobody knows how and when it began, only the Mohammedans know. That day Mohammedan wives and women withdrew their children from Rajdhani Public School early. It's in Mustafabad side. Even the headmaster of one school didn't understand why they were doing so. One by one, they came to him saying "give the children a holiday". They had prepared slingshots, and kept them on their roofs. And you know how every rickshaw has a chassis? They used them as slingshots.'

I did not understand how this was possible, and he explained. 'Say you make a petrol bomb. If you use a slingshot it goes farther. That's what they did.'

'They were prepared,' Sachin said.

'Prepared. And we had no idea,' Dhaniram said. 'All these things are not a part of our society and culture, but if some unknown people arrive you have to be prepared. Isn't that so? What happens if they turn up suddenly?' For reasons he would not say, people called him for help and protection during those days. He accompanied a priest to a late-night wedding during the stoning and shooting, and he sat by the man's side. But the story now flowed, and Dhaniram remembered more clearly. 'See, the Hindus also became more active then. It wasn't like they killed or cut anyone, but they blocked the roads and stopped cars. And the Muslims ran out of their cars in fright, and jumped into the canals and drowned.'

'Did many people go this way?' I asked, playing along.

'Their corpses were extracted,' he said. 'The fights actually happened over in the Mohammedan areas, but over here there was a larger mess. Some were also killed by us, but that I saw later. They came over here, and got scared when they saw the sticks and weapons we had. We do keep these things with us. It's not like we're sitting quietly. We do reply.'

It was difficult to follow the thread of his claims, but this is what he wanted to convey: that Muslims had arrived here as aggressors, but when they saw armed Hindus they killed themselves out of fright.

'The police moved away the cars that were abandoned, the burned cars,' he said. 'And all the cars were of only one community. Ours.'

I could not place the reason for Dhaniram's grief, although it had the ring of truth. The memories he recalled were from a larger institutional bank, a collection of experiences and recollections that encompassed every riot that had occurred for over a century, offering him a familiar vocabulary. It was either entirely free of his own thought, or laced with ready language adapted to his experience. The words could have come from Hedgewar, Moonje, or the hundreds of leaders who had advanced the idea that Hindus were under collective siege. In public they had spoken on a stage, from behind a podium, or in newspapers and journals. This was how they had done it in private, I thought. The way blame was first hinted at, and then carefully placed with a series of details, observations and hearsay. Listening to him for long enough, saviours and villains would emerge clearly through the haze of his doubt. He edited himself as he spoke, once saying, 'We let a Muslim family go,' before remembering it as 'We saved a Muslim family.'

'Look, some people would have killed them,' he said of the family. 'But the Hindu is merciful. He will try, with his heart, to save people. That much is guaranteed.' In his memory there had been peace before riots, but fear of the worst among them. He told me about Muslims stoning buses after the mosque was razed in 1992. 'It's the same thing today.' Faced with a Muslim of any degree of Muslimness, Dhaniram reached for some unrest to tether the person to. 'Tomorrow is Eid. I usually go to Mohammedan areas, but not today. There will be bloodshed there today,' he said, referring to the slaughter of goats. 'They will have a line of buffaloes.'

'And what parts they can't eat they will throw out on the street,' Sachin said.

'This is demonic behaviour, no? Yes, we used to eat animals, but since we became enlightened, haven't we stopped eating animals?' Dhaniram said.

'Our religion, our sanatani religion,' Sachin said, referring to its timelessness, 'is a way of life. And it recognises all other religions.' He intoned in Sanskrit, remembering the instructions, 'Sarve bhanvantu sukhinah, sarve santu niramayah, sarve bhadrani pashyantu. We recognise all other religions, but they recognise no other religion.'

As Sachin spoke, Dhaniram patted Shampoo on the head with such force that I wondered what the dog had done. 'Ghazwa-e-hind,' he said, turning to me. The notion that Muslims would strike first in the war to control India.

'Ghazwa-e-hind,' his son said. 'If you don't follow their religion, they call you kafir. And you know about love jihad, of course. There are several instances of it. There was a recent movie, *The Kerala Story*, that talked about it. I haven't seen the movie, but I know what it says.'

'Not good,' Dhaniram said, picking up from his son. 'It's not good for our religion. The thirty-two thousand women who were converted from our religion. I mean, the story was made up. It changes your mind. I take it as the truth, and it is the truth. It tells you the story of three girls, but it could just as well have been the story of three thousand.'

There are battles history cannot win in the arc of a single human life, a frame of time so small that a reckoning with our beginning comes only towards the end. Charu Gupta, a history professor at Delhi University who has written extensively about Hindu-Muslim marriages in India, once told me that love jihad as an idea had grown out of a portrayal of Muslim rulers as decadent manipulators in popular nineteenth-century literature. In the 1920s, between the movement to coalesce sects, tribes and castes under a single Hindu banner and the movement to persuade Indians of every denomination of their Hindu ancestry, the suspicions and assumptions once targeting Muslim rulers broadened to include all Muslims. 'They were called abductions then. Even elopements were seen as abductions,' she said. These abductions effectively provided 'one of the glues for Hindu unity' in a country divided by caste.

Now, in the year 2023, near the site of a Partition refugee camp in North East Delhi, the idea was as real as the gravel on the roads, the smell outside, the rising and setting of the sun. The lineage of its spirit seemed to stretch into the distant past, even preceding the personal-preference-becomes-cultural policy of Dayanand Saraswati. The mind that embraced it had so much in common with those of witch-burners and creationists and people who feared eclipses—a mind primed to take conspiracy seriously. I told Dhaniram I would meet him at the shakha in a day or two and said goodbye. I wandered down the street, not looking back. At the end of the lane a blind man sat with his cow, a yellow identification tag lanced through its ear. He gave me permission to touch it. The animal smelled my palm while I stroked its head and took comfort in its eyes. Who could turn believers away from a belief held this deeply when all the evidence they needed—the word of people they loved and trusted, and from media with suspect editorial prerogatives—told them otherwise?

# 3

# A Murder in East Delhi

It was a day like any other in Bhagirathi Vihar: it may have been warm or cold or rainy, but I was paying close attention instead to the gutter-spill and tripwires, the low-wires and smashed glass, the concrete protrusions in its alleys that could send a person hurtling into other concrete protrusions and smashed glass and low-wires and tripwires and gutter-spill. Still unfamiliar with its topography, I watched the ground carefully.

The street names suggested order, but lane 3 in block B led to lane 6 in block C, and the numbers on walls skipped unexpectedly, vanishing entire homes and lives. In one of those houses lived Harender Thakur, the father of Himanshu Thakur, another young man who had been accused of crimes during the Delhi riots. When I found the house and explained myself, Harender gave his permission to come inside. The house, narrow and boxed in, was resistant to daylight. Harender's parents were in the nearest room, and they offered me a place on a bed. We talked in the dim glow of a single white light. Harender was certain that his son was innocent, that it was all a mistake. 'They have no proof,' he said. His son Himanshu worked as a driver. He was travelling to work on the February day when the riots began, and decided to turn back. On the way home, a friend of his, Vivek, gave him a smartphone he had found on the ground; the streets were full of things people had dropped in panic. Himanshu accepted it because his phone was outmoded. While his friends tapped on smooth glass, he still used a keypad. He used it happily for about a month, when several men in plainclothes from the crime branch came to lane no. 3.

'They asked me, "Where is your son?" and I said, "He is here, playing in the lane outside." I called out to him and he came towards me. My son had not gone anywhere. Why would he? He had done nothing. If a man murders someone in the 2020 riots, he isn't going to be sitting at home, is he? I had no idea that police were here because of the phone.' The men grabbed the phone from Himanshu and hustled him into a police van. They promised Harender that they would ask him questions for a couple of hours at the crime branch in Nandnagri and let him go. He followed them on a bike to the crime branch office, where he was told that the phone in his son's possession had belonged to a murdered man. That was the last time his son, who was then eighteen, was free. 'They filed eight-eight, nine-nine cases against him. Three and a half years have passed,' Harender said. 'There's no evidence. If you see him, you won't believe that he could do such a thing. The people in jail sing his praises so much that you can't get them to be quiet,' Harender said of his boy. 'My son doesn't get involved with anyone inside. He keeps to himself.'

Himanshu studied, he wanted to do more, he was not friends with the awaaras who did nothing all day, his father said. Now he was in Mandoli Jail Number 11, so emaciated that he was half his normal size, and the underside of his eyes had become dark and baggy. 'He says to me, "When I haven't done anything, why am I here?".' Harender was certain that Himanshu was tortured in custody. 'He was taken inside a room with a large plastic rod and a leather belt the size of my arm with a wooden handle at one end.' The whole thing was a travesty, he said. Children were being made to sign blank documents under the threat of further cases filed against them. 'They even tried to make him pick up a dagger. My boy told them, "Sir, file however many cases you want against me, I'm not going to do what you want".' He claimed that Vivek, the friend who had found the phone, had taken money from the police to become a government witness. But he had no evidence of this.

'Can you tell me what happened during the riots?' I asked him.

'I wasn't here for a week, but the children kept calling. They were frightened, and were saved by the skin of their teeth. A party of a hundred Mohammedans had come from Mustafabad and were cutting right through people. I wanted to come back, but I was told to stay away. A friend told me that Muslims would throw me into a car and set it on fire. And all the roads I take to come here are ruled by Muslims. They've infiltrated blocks A and B in Bhagirathi Vihar. Only blocks C and E are still ours. Otherwise they cover every other place. If the Hindus had not come from Ganga Vihar to protect us, not a single child would have survived. You wouldn't have recognised their faces. These places were completely vulnerable to attack.' Sometimes there were a hundred Muslims in his recollection, sometimes two hundred, a number he said he would bet everything on. Family members surrounding Harender bolstered his recollections with little comments about numbers and dangers he had forgotten to mention. 'People were calling the police, but they never came.' He was, like everyone else who had suffered, a critic of the police's investigative work. 'All the children they picked up are middle class or poor. Their parents are daily earners and don't know the law,' he said. 'They are illiterate, so they had cases piled on them. The police needed to show they were doing something, so this is what they did.'

I asked him for the names of the other children who had been detained without evidence, and one by one he named the men Nisar had pointed to in court under oath. 'Their parents are also labourers,' he said. Nisar had often said that he was surprised to see the boys in a crowd. They were not killers, he said, not ordinarily, so what made them join a crowd that wanted to kill? Nisar would ask, over and over and over, who was behind them, and why were they not the ones arrested?

Harender was grateful for the RSS's work. 'The government provided RSS lawyers to the defendants, and the RSS is also giving money and medicines to a few families whose children are in judicial custody,' he said. 'I didn't use one, but the others are represented by RSS lawyers.' He said he didn't use one of the RSS lawyers because he feared that lawyers paid by other people could have other priorities. He imagined them leaving unexpectedly at some point. He wanted someone accountable, someone he could pay. 'I think the BJP provided RSS lawyers because they know that the people arrested are children of daily wage earners who don't earn more than ten or twelve thousand, so how will they pay?'

Harender's mother began to speak, and both men looked down from the bed and told her to be quiet. She frowned and said nothing more. I asked if the Bajrang Dal or the RSS were on the streets at the time. 'No,' he said, immediately. 'Neither the Bajrang Dal nor the RSS were here at that time. You know how it is. When a crowd forms for protection, it has no face.'

As he spoke, my phone rang repeatedly. It was Nisar. I was surprised by his persistence, for we had an unspoken arrangement that we needed to call each other only once. I panicked, thinking that he was in trouble—perhaps his assailants from Bhagirathi Vihar had finally found him. When we spoke, his voice was strained and at a lower register. With no hi or hello, he dived right in, 'Bhaisaab. I'm at the Dayalpur police station.

There's going to be a riot. Come quickly.' He mentioned that it was over a stabbing by the Brijpuri mosque. I told him I was in the area, luckily, and would be there soon.

The story was everywhere: the previous night, a young drunk, Zaid, had stabbed a bystander named Rahul at an ice cream stand, and then attacked a friend of his. Zaid was detained but managed to escape, and Rahul was taken to a hospital, where he recovered. But the story that spread through the neighbourhoods of Mustafabad, Dayalpur, Ganga Vihar and Bhagirathi Vihar took on other forms. Aashiq, a dairy farmer who lived on the outer road of Bhagirathi Vihar, had excitedly spoken about a deadly Hindu-Muslim lafda, a big kerfuffle, that had taken place near the mosque the previous evening. His friends told him to be there, but he refused to get involved. In another part of Bhagirathi Vihar a retiree from a state phone company said all he knew was that Muslims had stabbed Hindus. There were other versions of the story. The only constant was the conviction that a man had been killed.

The religion of the attacker and the victim came into it within minutes of the stabbing, when men keen on revenge appeared on the lane to Brijpuri mosque, whose imam had been blinded during the riots. Shopkeepers were surprised by how suddenly the stabbing receded in danger, and how quickly a new threat emerged. The men wore clothes identifying their senas, private armies that advertised themselves every few metres in East Delhi. Some were from the Bajrang Dal, some were from other militant groups. The men in the crowd constantly weaved between each other, winding themselves up, before pouring into a lane a few feet wide, where they overturned motorcycles and sprinkled threats on any Muslim they saw. They stopped rickshaw drivers carrying passengers from the mosque to the main road, and beat their drivers. In videos filmed from a safe distance, there were hundreds of young men in the crowd. They dispersed when the police arrived, but the threats and body language suggested they would return. 'We made a mistake by not finishing you off last time. We'll complete the work soon,' a young man shouted at a store owner recording with his phone from a rooftop.

Nisar had heard of the trouble, too, but he realised the full extent of its seriousness the next morning when he drove to the police station at Dayalpur to resolve a financial matter. A large mob had gathered to demand that the police find Zaid, or else they would take control of matters there. 'I recognised a Bajrang Dal leader there. "What's this bastard doing here?" I thought.' The man's presence usually meant trouble. That was when he called, hoping I would see how groups aligned to the RSS exerted pressure on the police.

We met halfway, beside the Brijpuri mosque. It was June 2023, almost a year after our last meeting. The summonses had nearly stopped since his testimony had been recorded. But a judgement was nowhere in sight. He was slouching, and less defined than before. He wore the same white linen shirt and grey trousers that he had in court. His car was parked in a narrow lane between the mosque and a canal. Nisar reversed it into a wall, ignored the crunch and swung it around in a single move.

He slowed down along the way, taking in the unusual sight of soldiers called out to the street as a precaution. An entire company of the Tripura State Rifles stood in single file, from the maroon-tiled corner mosque to the main road where helmeted men had thrown stones and shot at the residents of Mustafabad. The Rifles were a paramilitary force created to counter insurgencies and keep order. Their work that day was relaxed. A curfew was in place around the area, and the groups had gone underground. So they watched their phones and laughed outside the school where the stabbing had occurred.

Nisar stopped at a kitchenware shop up the road. The middle-aged owner of the enterprise, a small and dignified trader, clasped his fingers behind his back and spoke gravely with ten worried men about what could still happen after sunset. The consensus was that the trouble would begin once the soldiers had left. The store owner said he had been greeted by a thin young boy passing by in the morning. 'He said to me, "Kyun, tu khush hai?" *Tu* khush hai? Just see how they talk.' Had the boy been respectful and used the word *aap* instead of *tu*, the question would have been about his contentedness that day. *Tu* laced the query with menace, implying that the man's peace would soon be over. He remembered in particular the boy's smile, and the words spelled on his shirt: Karni Sena. A couple of men grimaced at the Karni Sena's mention, aware of its reputation for extreme violence. In 2017, members of the Sena attacked a Mumbai filmmaker directing a story about a fictional Rajput queen, seeing it as an insult to their Rajput community. Later that year the Sena's chief threatened to cut off the lead actor's nose. Over the following months they vandalised cars, cinema halls, malls and allegedly attacked a bus ferrying schoolchildren. Its members worked with other extremist groups, served as press liaisons for the BJP, demanded a Hindu state and called for the murder of their ideological opponents.

Nisar listened quietly as the men in the kitchenware shop convinced themselves that the worst was yet to come. The sight of hundreds of troublemakers appearing all at once had disconcerted them. 'It's coordinated,' someone said. What was left unsaid was the role of the very paths that surrounded them. As wave after wave of migrants settled there, flattening trees and grasslands to erect their homes, lanes formed and connected erratically. These familiar paths acquired menace during disturbances, for they became conducive to quick arrivals and hasty dispersions. Shouts and gunshots reverberated in the narrow alleys. Groups of men could jam them and make trouble in them. For anyone chased by the groups, every turn held peril, because every turn was blind, and other groups and their sympathisers could lie around the corner. Merely living there added to the sensation that the riots had not achieved what was desired, and that something more was still left to happen.

Nisar often thought about how fortunate he was. He liked to say, 'God has saved my life for a reason.' He had come to believe that the purpose of his newly extended life was to stop communal violence where it threatened to erupt. One day in October 2022 he called me to say that a BJP minister, Parvesh Sahib Singh Verma, had demanded a 'total boycott' of Muslims to 'fix their head and set them straight'. Listening to the speech had filled him with a tension that made him want to stay at home. He said he would meet the new police commissioner the next day. 'I'm going to tell him that it can't continue like this. These people will spark a fire.' Every week brought some new assault on his notions of fairness and freedom, and he considered the range of his options, from political to legal.

Now, with Dayalpur on the verge of another riot, he hurried to the police station. Landmarks of violence lay around him. Ahead of him was the gate where the helmeted men had come in, and to his right was Mohan Nursing Home, from whose roof the BJP's supporters had fired guns during the riots. He accelerated and squeezed between other cars, almost all of which were larger and sturdier. Seeing as I was doing nothing in the passenger seat, he pulled out his phone and searched for a video that had riled him up.

'Sister-fucking anchor. What is he doing?' he said.

An Aaj Tak news anchor wearing too much make-up announced in Hindi: 'Big news from Delhi. In Brijpuri a twenty-year-old has died. A man by the name of Mohammad Zaid has murdered Rahul. Zaid also seriously attacked Rahul's brother. Mohammad Zaid killed Rahul with a knife.' The feed cut to a journalist who asked Rahul's sister what had happened. She said he was alive, and that he had no enemies. As the line of questioning began to clear the air, the channel cut away from the story. But the headline and the anchor's words were what viewers responded to, and soon more channels echoed the same line: Muslim man (Zaid) fatally stabs innocent Hindu (Rahul).

Years of watching speeches that imputed motives and incited riots had given Nisar an instinct for editorial trickery. The unsettling feeling that came from watching something insidious, something not quite what it was presented as, showed on his face. The anchor's repetition of Hindu and Muslim names meant that the story was no longer a simple news report. It joined the stream of stories about Muslim deviations from the norm that ended in Hindus suffering, adding another layer to the feeling that Hindus were under siege. I looked online for commentary about the incident, and found a series of tweets that were depressingly, and unsurprisingly, about the subject of what ought to be done with Muslims. As I looked, more tweets arrived. It was more of the same. Other channels were also reporting that a death had occurred.

The local police station stood on the right bank of the burbling canal from which cranes had lifted bodies three years before. It was late in the afternoon, and the mobs had left. Nisar was disappointed, but then noticed a tall man in a white kurta walk out of the building with a man on either side. There was an air of politics about him, his deep, tired eyes ringed by a chronic deficiency of vitamins or sleep. 'This is the guy,' Nisar said. This was the man he claimed to have seen at the bridge, the man whose presence brought bad tidings. He had once represented Mustafabad in Delhi's legislative assembly, and was a leader of disrepute—and not just in Nisar's opinion. After the pogroms, survivors filed official complaints that the riot's leaders on the ground were heard receiving instructions from him as they burned their homes and the nearby car spares market. He denied the allegation, and was not questioned by the police. Now he walked out of the Dayalpur station and said, 'I'm here to check up on the stabbing investigation,' before getting into a car that was driven away.

The man had just met Dayalpur's new station house officer, the SHO, then six weeks into his assignment. Nuisance groups came to him regularly to show their strength and estimate his tolerance for their activities. Public lawlessness in a jurisdiction occurred because the SHO allowed it to occur, and if trouble evaporated it was because the SHO had made it evaporate. The previous night was an example of what the SHO could do. People came out to make trouble, and within half an hour the SHO made them disappear by declaring that they were in the way of his investigation. The groups slunk away. All night long and for most of the next day, the locals I spoke with praised him for his work.

When Nisar and I entered his office he was chastising a large man whose complaint was wasting his time. 'So tell me, really, why do you want to see me? I'd understand if you were a pretty girl, but you're not.' The SHO smiled as he did this, but it was a frightening smile probably brought on by a lack of sleep. It had been a long and fretful night, with his seniors demanding regular reports on the stabbing situation. When his phone rang, he extended a thick arm and jerked the device to his face. 'Jai hind, sir,' he would say, and then follow it up with a recounting of the characters involved. 'First the Bajrang Dal guys came. Then some other Hanuman group came. They're saying they will do something at 8.30 if we don't catch the man,' he said, 'but even if we do I think they'll be here.' The assistant commissioner of police was pleased by how well the SHO had handled the matter so far.

The SHO had accounted for Mustafabad's politics of communalism by reducing large and unruly groups to their most basic imperatives. Making a fuss was in their nature. When they came to him to show their strength and assess his tolerance for their activities, he heard them and addressed them respectfully. But afterwards, when the door closed behind them, he would call them 'bhopus', loud and full of air like a bulb horn. The groups were replete with opportunists and the unemployed, poseurs who did nothing helpful for society. He did not worry about them. They mattered very little in the hierarchy of forces that dictated how he spent his days.

'Sir has encountered people,' Nisar said in awe, by way of introduction. The SHO's eyes met mine, and he discussed the merits of extrajudicial killings. 'What can we do about hardcore criminals, about criminals who cannot be reformed?' he said. These were incorrigible men who frequently made life a misery for women. 'They go into jail, and then they run their sultanate from inside.' The best way to resolve that menace was to encounter them, he said.

'What about laws?' I said.

'You don't have to agree with my point of view,' he said with self-aware charm.

Nisar was critical of the Delhi police's investigations, and often said they were compromised, but he had a fatal weakness for police who conducted extrajudicial killings. No one I knew had more to say about the Constitution than Nisar; no one I knew ejected it faster when presented with an efficient cop, if efficiency was measured in dead criminals. All talk of the rule of law was set aside, as if extrajudicial killings were an extension of due process. He was captivated by them, and his dreamy expression reflected a mind gone elsewhere. Nisar referred to an encounter specialist's kill count as if they were pushing the boundaries of human achievement. As the SHO talked about the circumstances under which encounters were justified, Nisar sat transfixed, as if his amazement came from knowing that he would never possess the kind of power being discussed here. I wondered if his arguments for the Constitution's primacy were because he was a victim. A hard country made it tempting to dream of easier paths: of instant justice, of what citizens would do if they were prime minister for one day, of the corruption that technology would solve, of all the change only a strong leader could bring. In the unlikely event that dreams came true, how would Nisar's rule be remembered?

The SHO's soliloquy about orchestrated killings was interrupted when the door swung open and nine men and women entered in a blur of white and saffron. They represented the United Hindu Front, an organisation whose founder once belonged to the RSS family. The founder, Jai Bhagwan Goyal, took pride in being among the first to raze the mosque in Ayodhya in December 1992. 'He is one of the forty-nine accused in this case,' the UHF's website explained. It had the same aims as other extremist organisations, namely the organisation of Hindu society, but with one added feature: it openly called for a Hindu nation, following which India's 'internal problems will be removed'.

The workers spread out across the room and asked the SHO how his hunt for Rahul's attacker was progressing. He told them he was confident that the culprit would be found. The men in the front were in charge. One of them wore sunglasses indoors. He wore a saffron-colour shawl around his neck and a red tilak on his forehead. I had moved to the back of the room and could not hear the discussion clearly, but from the odd word it was apparent they were talking about the logistics of finding the man. Less than a day had passed, but they wanted to know why it was taking so long. Then one of the women spoke up in an attempt to hurry things along.

'The boy's sister was threatened!'

'Wait a minute,' the SHO said, stiffening as he looked at her. 'How do you know? Where was the threat made?' He said it like an accusation. His size was suddenly apparent to the people trapped in their seats: large and broad-shouldered.

'He told her,' the woman said.

'On email? Phone? Personally?'

He looked at her and only her, and did not blink.

'Personally,' she said, a little softly.

'Wait,' he said, glaring at her. A woman beside her placed a hand on her forearm in warning. This was not an advisable line to pursue. 'When exactly did he threaten her?'

The woman mumbled something. Her colleagues picked up the slack and declared that if the culprit was not found that day, they would return to the streets.

The SHO tore his eyes off her and interrupted them. 'Look, the problem is that we're being very broad-minded. That's what is leading to problems,' he told his visitors. There were some nodding heads. They might have understood the warning. Then he smiled at their leader. 'Look, let's all work in a way that I can entertain you while my team does its work. If my people start entertaining your people, the work will stop. Just think: they're doing their work, but it will stop because of you.'

The leader was not adequately submissive, and so the SHO made a throat-clearing threat. 'Look, if you keep my people busy, I'll do a pen-down strike. Then it's all up to you.' He would halt the investigation altogether.

For once, the possibility that the police would not do their work frightened the mob. At this they all shouted versions of, 'Arey, no, no, please, don't do that.' He looked around the room from one person to another with a triumphant smile. They said they would behave, shook his hand and left.

When the door closed behind the last of them, he said to us, 'We have to keep an entire company on the streets because these people don't like peace. They won't pay for your child's education from nursery to the fifth, but they will come to the street for you,' he said, disgusted. 'To show "we are with you". It's an operation for them.'

I asked if he foresaw any problems with the UHF.

'I don't expect trouble from them. They have just one purpose: "Jai Shri Ram! Jai Shri Ram!"' he said, pumping his fist in the air. 'They just want to be seen. Look, this was a fight between two individuals. But these people are turning it into a fight between two communities.'

Perhaps because of exhaustion, or because of the adrenaline from making the group look silly, the SHO felt chatty. He looked at me and said, frowning, 'You're too formal.'

I mentioned the news report by Aaj Tak, and asked what he thought of the media's role. He was aware of the report. 'Your TV newswaalas have killed him,' he said.

'Will you ask them to correct it?'

'The elephant walks, the dogs bark. I don't want to open another front,' he said.

He ordered chai and gave us a tour of the station. Not two months had passed since his arrival, and already he took pride in his legacy. He stood outside the child-friendly room; its friendliness had been upped with blue Spider-Man wallpaper and posters of babies. The houseplants that now dotted the station's glum interiors were his enterprise. 'I did this,' he said, admiring the ferns and money plants that lined the staircase on which two men were helping a horribly beaten friend limp upstairs.

He stepped outside and ordered a constable to move a car blocking the station driveway. Within minutes, a row of vehicles with blaring sirens delivered a high-ranking police officer to the station.

As the cars went past him, Nisar grinned. 'For such a small matter,' he said, and watched the SHO stand straight and salute someone in a car.

Nisar wanted to show me something on the road back to the Brijpuri mosque. He stopped his Maruti at the mouth of an alley. 'Look at that,' he said, pointing down the lane. All along the narrow path, from buildings on both sides, jutted dozens of luminous orange flags. They contained an illustration of the god Hanuman beside the words 'Jai Shri Ram', and glistened against the setting sun—Bajrang Dal flags. 'This is all new,' he said. I looked around and noticed other markers. There were posters of gods, orange flags and hoardings for small armies that represented a god—all markers of religion, but not religiosity. It occurred to me then that we had spoken to shopkeepers and the police, and understood what the Hindu groups wanted, but I knew nothing about Rahul's family.

'I want to visit Rahul's home,' I said to Nisar. He said he would wait in the car.

The friends, family and assorted sympathetic stragglers who had gathered on the rooftop of Rahul's home sat around his parents mournfully. The parents sat on plastic chairs beside their landlord, a thickset man with fingers covered in rings and stones, and wrists coated in rudrakshes. Rahul's father, Ram Swarup, clutched his head in pain from a headache. She said that her son had been eating chow mein and minding his own business when Zaid swore at him for no reason. Rahul and his friend asked why he was swearing. 'He was drunk. He said nothing. Just took out his knife and put it in his stomach,' his mother said. 'We don't know the boy. All we know is he rents a house close by. Then he pulled out a knife and struck him. He was a Muslim. He was trapped, but then hundreds of people came and rescued him.'

The landlord was eager to talk. The extra security on the roads outside was because trouble could happen. 'It is a Muslim area. The adjoining areas are a mini-Pakistan,' he said, twirling his finger.

'It's a mishin. It's a mishin. A mishin,' Rahul's drunk uncle said. His name was Sanjay Kashyap, and his speech slurred. If you leaned in to hear him better, he sprayed you with spittle. 'It's a mishin to rescue them all.' He made no sense, but I nodded seriously because a few dozen people were watching. A group of tough young men sat on a cord bed and sniggered at him.

Reporters from NewsX and India News turned up and asked to interview Rahul's father, who yelled that he had a headache, but Rahul's mother screamed at him, 'This is their duty! Talk to them!' The cameraman said he was ready.

'Tell me,' a reporter said, pointing his mic towards Rahul's father, 'did Rahul ever say that he and Zaid were friends?'

'He never said anything of the sort. They didn't know each other. This boy came out drunk, took out his knife and stabbed him.'

The reporter turned to Rahul's mother, while the father said loudly, 'He's a Mohammedan. He stabbed my son. And then a hundred and fifty to two hundred Muslims came here and freed him.'

'What would you like from the government?' the reporter asked him.

'The bastard should be hanged,' he said.

'Their boys are teasing our girls,' his aunt said. 'Hindu girls are dying.'

'This is their daily work. Our girls who go to school every day are teased,' the drunk uncle said. 'Tell me, what are you going to do with all this? What is going on here? What is going on here? What are you here for? Haven't you come here to take down our testimony?'

'The government is unable to control things,' Rahul's aunt said. 'I'm afraid. All we want is for him to come home.'

Behind them all, Rahul's father clutched his head and mumbled to himself while he walked listlessly across the rooftop.

His wife sat alone, lost. The landlord had disappeared. In the corner, the group of boys laughing were now speaking to each other softly, with fury on their faces, as if they were about to do something terrible.

# 4

## The Hindu Awakens at 6 a.m.

The shakha Dhaniram had invited me to was easy to locate. Everybody knew it was on a muddy clearing along the canal, close to the bridge where the violence had begun in February 2020. Nisar knew the place too. He had lived a few minutes' walk upstream before his eviction. He had mentioned to me in passing that some of the boys in the crowd downstairs on the day of his escape used to attend the shakha, but the significance of this did not seem to register in him.

It was still dark when I arrived. The gate to the shakha was barred by bamboo lathis, leaving just enough room for people to walk in. Of course there would be room. It made no sense to keep participants from a shakha, I thought. The whole enterprise would fall to pieces. Inside, beside an immense peepal tree, the kind whose age would almost certainly be exaggerated, Dhaniram was hunched tragically over his phone, his countenance pure lament. Sachin, his son, was nowhere to be seen, and neither was his dog. He was stoically negotiating with recalcitrant RSS volunteers still under their blankets, calling each of them and asking, 'Ram Ram. Coming, no?' Not yet dawn and he was already tired. Such is the life of the RSS foot soldier: how can he awaken Hindu society when his friends refuse to wake up?

He noticed me and said to come and sit.

'The rain messed up everything,' he explained. 'It's been raining since 1.30. They'll come. They're late, but they'll come.' The shakha had almost two hundred and fifty members, of whom ten or twelve showed up every day, except when it rained. 'There were nineteen yesterday.' He was somehow more energised and mobile since our last meeting. The swelling in his knees had subsided.

I talked about what wet and cold nights did to a person's resolve to rise early, but my empathy sounded defeatist to him. He laughed politely and continued calling. Rainwater had collected in pools across the ground. He considered them with concern, and wondered aloud whether there was room for the day's exercises. Then a man arrived with two sleepy children in pyjamas, a heavy lathi, a long steel pipe and an iron stake with an alarmingly sharp end. It was a sariya, a rebar used in building construction. Survivors of the riots in the area had recalled men clutching sariyas among the mobs. A sariya could make short work of padlocks, shutters and people, they said.

'Ram Ram,' the man said.

'Ram Ram. What's the matter today? Nobody's coming. It must be because of the rain.'

'Where's Mahesh ji? And Shekhar ji? And Sachin ji?'

'Mahesh ji is at a meeting. Shekhar ji is sleeping. He's using the rain as an excuse. Sachin ji is also at a meeting.'

The children were a picture of dazed commitment. They tottered in sleep, waiting to receive further instructions after the adults finished their business.

'Should I make the mandal?' the man asked. Dhaniram told him where to put it.

The man found a place under the peepal tree's foliage and marked a spot in the mud with his finger. Turning the metal pipe and the sariya into an enlarged protractor, he drew a circle four or five feet in diameter, walking along with the sariya as he did so. Then he laid the stick in the centre and halved the circle with his finger. He gave himself fully to the task. His eyes did not move, his arms and fingers held their angle and shape as he turned his body into an implement. He cleared the circle of leaves. He pressed a thumb into the centre and created half a circle above the line in the mud by using it as a pivot for his outstretched little finger. Finally he drew straight rays around the half-circle, transforming it into a rising sun. Dhaniram complimented him on his illustration while he drove the iron stake into the centre and placed one end of the steel pipe on it. With the sun made, he stood up straight, dusted his hands and smoothed his track suit bottoms, and took five steps south to draw a line in the sand. A pole was then planted on the sariya, and the bhagwa, the swallow-tailed orange flag that meant everything to the RSS's members, was revealed, unfurled and hoisted on the construction at the centre of the dawning sun. The wind would not cooperate that morning, so what held them like a deity, a reminder of higher aims, was a drooping flag. Fists clenched, backs straightened and mouths closed in a valiant attempt at military tightness. The attention to detail and the sudden rousing were traits common to rituals before religious ceremonies. When a god is the object of devotion, love is seen in deliberation and in the slow bathing of an idol, the straightening of a cloth, the exact placement of a coconut on a copper vessel, the clean steel plate under unlit incense sticks. The flag received such adoration. They formed a small line facing the pole, with Dhaniram inspecting stance and foot spacing. I fell in line between them, which pleased him. Dhaniram held his right arm horizontally across his chest, the flat of his open palm facing the ground. We walked up to the line one by one, and saluted the flag this way with bowed head while I worried whether an act of civic duty on a tourist visa made me a citizen. I remembered a book explaining that anyone who saluted the RSS's flag was counted as a member.

It all became Potemkin military very quickly. Men limp-marched up to each other in large and uncertain strides at odd angles, corrected their trajectory with a sidestep and saluted each other before running back to be saluted by someone else. Dhaniram led morning exercises with the canal at his back. First we ran in a large circle. Then, standing beside one another, we stretched our arms sideways, then above, or ahead, in repetitions of four. The model of instruction was based on second-standard PE. Under Dhaniram's gentle encouragements, we loosened our necks and stretched away our stiffness. The movements gradually became more complicated. Arms moved one way, the body another. Ten people attempted to follow Dhaniram. One exercise was synchronised mayhem: a leg forward, followed by hands that swung to the left, and the lower body followed. Dhaniram's smile suggested he had no expectations. Failure only hardened the resolve to be at one with the group's choreography. There were four chances to get it right. Each time, I thought with some satisfaction, I had improved a little.

After three quarters of an hour, someone suggested they play a game called mantri ji, bringing a cheer. A slim older man with a kind gaze and gentle voice took charge of the game. He was dressed in a neat white safari suit and slippers, a contrast to the sloppy loungewear around him. His instructions were transmitted by an extended finger, which the others watched and moved left or right until they had formed a perfect circle. He then pointed directly at the man who had assembled the flag, who walked away from the group. When his back was turned, the finger pointed at Dhaniram, who started clapping. Almost instantly the rest of them followed Dhaniram, clapping loudly with serious faces, while the man turned back and prowled the centre to identify the group's leader. The replication of Dhaniram's movements happened in less than half a second, as if they were joined to the same mind. Certain that he was safe, Dhaniram raised his hands above his head for others to follow, but the man swivelled his head and caught him doing so. Dhaniram limped out of the group while the finger assigned another leader. The new leader clapped his hands and rubbed his nose for the others to follow, and they all forced a laugh at each of Dhaniram's mistaken guesses. When the young boy's turn arrived, he found the minister on his third try; his face was radiant. From behind the wall that ran along the ground came the sound of car engines and scooters, and the rattle of small trucks on the neglected road outside. For the people inside, there was still time to enjoy the sensation of surrounding someone who did not know what they knew, the sensation of holding a secret in an organised activity. The crowd knew something he didn't, and took care not to reveal who the leader was.

When the game was done they took off their slippers and sat in the mud. Partha had left the organisation decades ago, but it was as he had said. One of them sang a song off key, and the others repeated each verse with no attempt at melody:

*When the Hindu awakens the world will awaken,*
*humankind's faith will awaken.*
*When the Hindu awakens the world will awaken,*
*The Hindu has forever been a friend of humankind.*
*We have accepted it all through our roots.*
*We recognise one god,*
*whichever path we have tread on.*
*When the Hindu awakens the world will awaken,*
*humankind's faith will awaken.*
*Discrimination and darkness will disappear,*
*immortality will reign.*
*Hindu awakens, humankind awakens.*

The song went on to describe their relationship with god, country and politics. It spoke of what the Vedas said, what the

Upanishads had taught, of the knowledge they would all receive in religious monasteries. The children had memorised the prayers, and they led the singing. At the end, after Dhaniram had removed the flag and folded it lovingly into a tiny flap of cloth, he gathered the group around the peepal tree.

'Brother here wants to know the truth about what happened three years ago, and that is why he has come to us,' he began. 'That's why he has come to the Sangh.'

Shekhar Bharadwaj, a tall, bulky, serious man, assumed responsibility for my education. To understand the riots, he told me, 'you must begin with local demographics'.

He wistfully recalled the days Mustafabad was culturally familiar. As soon as he said this, some of the men who had gathered there murmured about Mustafabad's downfall. 'I don't know where these people come from,' he said, perplexed. He said that so many Muslims had moved in that the Hindus stood no chance. He presented me with a fable he hoped I would believe: the riots of February 2020 were a conspiracy to cleanse the neighbourhood of Hindus. 'The violence was well planned.' In his story, Muslim shopkeepers who knew that riots were coming wrote slogans denouncing the Citizenship Amendment Act and the National Register of Citizens on their shop shutters. The slogans were on the lips of citizens protesting injustice, and therefore on placards, boundary walls, sidewalks and tweets: NO CAA, NO NRC. But the words harboured a darker meaning for Bharadwaj. 'It was a sign to Muslim rioters that *this person is ours, and we should not burn his shop*. The shops that didn't have a slogan, they targeted. In my case I know I was a special target,' he said. Bharadwaj was a member of the BJP and the RSS. 'Word must have got around that this man organises Hindus, and if we get rid of him it will be good.'

Bharadwaj said he watched his burning shop from a distance. There were men in light blue motorcycle helmets taking down

CCTV cameras and doing damage, he said. 'It's a matter of shame that there is no one to protect us in this Hindu land. The government doesn't let us keep arms at home. It doesn't give us permission to be violent. Our hands are tied because of the law.' But his complaint was not simply that policy failures had led to this state of affairs. A civilisational flaw was the ultimate problem. 'Hindus are taught from the beginning that you have to live in peace with the world, and our wrists are bound with this knowledge. We do the same thing to our children. Meanwhile, those people are taught from the beginning to live in an atmosphere of death and destruction. I feel sometimes, how can we live side by side? How can people of such different cultures and thoughts live together? There is no sense. We have nothing in common, not the way we live, not the food we eat, not our thoughts. You tell me. When they start a business, or sell vegetables, they give their shop a Hindu name. What does this mean? That you cannot run a business with your own name! They want money from Hindus, and then they want to kill those very Hindus.' He paused for precisely one second before something occurred to him. 'One Muslim can live among one hundred Hindus. Nobody will call him Mullah. They will call him Mullah ji out of respect. He can wear his cap and go out. It doesn't bother anyone. But if two or three Muslims live in a Hindu locality, they start planning. They throw animal bones on the roads, and tease young girls. They say they want brotherhood with us. But I feel they are the brothers, and we are the hoods.'

The crowd erupted in agreement.

'Remember the Muslim councillor who kept stones on his roof?'

'Remember the boy at Anil Stores whose hands and feet were cut off?'

'Remember the Muslim in E block who was taken to safety by Hindus?'

Some men frowned when they spoke about Muslims, and one or two of them were so distressed that they sat down and murmured things loudly.

'They threw petrol bombs!'

'They burned a thousand cars!'

'Two thousand!'

Mulayam Singh, a small man with a tobacco-inflected voice and stained teeth, had lingered on the edge of the gathering until that moment. The others fell silent when he spoke about a girl who had been assaulted and then mutilated. 'The police has not investigated it yet,' he said, clicking his teeth with a dark red tongue. 'What can they do? It was a riot crime. Then there was the policeman who tried to stop the abduction of a Hindu woman. They stabbed him.'

'Four hundred times,' someone added.

'Four hundred times.' Singh shook his head and clicked his teeth. He had a dead look that felt dangerous. 'And the member of the RSS. What was his name? Never mind. Just because he was a member of the RSS they broke the gate to his home and entered it. Now tell us, based on just these three incidents, how can we ever live together? Lane number four is Mohammedan, and there's also the main junction. They would collect there and tease Hindu girls. Dhaniram rescued some of them,' he said, glancing at Dhaniram. The Muslim boys wore their hair long, as was the fashion, Singh said. And the girls would go off with them. 'But we are with the Sangh,' he declared, 'and we could not abide by this. We thought, how can one stop them?' He gathered a group of seventy RSS men to stand near the Muslims and read the Hanuman Chalisa every day 'until the Hindu girls were left alone'. For someone like him, North East Delhi brought untold opportunities to be a holy warrior. 'Remember Mishra ji's daughter? He lost one to a Mussalman on the same street. No one was able to do anything. Rakhi was the girl's name. We came to know that she had left. We—me, Dhaniram, all of us—managed to stop her. I went to the boy and told him that if you ever come this way again, it will not be good for you.' The men's outrage superseded questions of consent and choice; there was of course no recognition that a woman's desires mattered at all. They conferred with and encouraged each other into ever wilder declarations in support of a more constricted existence.

'Their main target is to remove Hindus from here and kill them when the time comes,' Singh said.

'This is more dangerous than cancer,' a man said. 'Does anyone ever want to get cancer? That is the main problem.'

'It happens a lot over here,' someone in the crowd said. 'Seven or eight cases of love jihad here.'

'Love jihad, love jihad,' an old man with a sweet smile said at the back, amazed at its frequency.

Bharadwaj spoke up from the back. 'Love jihad? Man, it's lund jihad going on,' he said, pointing at his crotch.

'This is a regular occurrence,' Singh said. He had kept track of elopements in the neighbourhood. 'In the last four to five years, two girls have left Johripur, Sanjay Colony has lost three or four girls, three from Ganga Vihar. And there's a boy, Asif, who is married to a woman from Bihar. He extracted one in the last couple of years. He was a friend. Used to wear a big tilak on his head. He wooed her and brought her over. As soon as she died, he eloped with a married woman from here. The streak on his head was the god Bholenath's. Now you tell me.' The concerns in Singh's complaint included impersonation, elopement, inter-religious marriage, a lost Hindu, callousness, deceit and all Muslims.

'I have a friend, a Muslim man,' he said. 'I met him recently. I asked him where that girl who went with him was. Look, if it's a beautiful woman that they elope with, you won't know what they've done to her. He said she died. Where did she die, I asked. He said he didn't know.'

'These people keep names like Sonu and Monu, and wear a tilak,' Bharadwaj said. 'They wear the bracelets Hindus wear. They hide their own names. This is all to deceive Hindus, marry their women, and produce children to enlist in jihad. This is what they are taught. This is what they are taught in their madrassas.'

The constitution of the men changed. The quiet ones moved to the back, the younger, more restless ones swayed at the front, pacing back and forth as they tried to find the words. But all they could summon when they spoke was a faded list of complaints: *beautiful girls, elope, Muslim man, baby machines, conversion, love jihad, death*. All the tropes in these matters were brought out as evidence for their visitor. I wondered if the whole thing was an act that we all knew about and yet continued to participate in, propelled by some irrepressible impulse to speak and record. I allowed them to ramble on, checking on them occasionally, but reluctant to break the unhinged flow. I had heard and read the words before, and what they were saying would come as no surprise to anyone who read the news, but the newness was in hearing *these* men say the words *now*, in *this* corner of New Delhi. It was like testing a different stretch of the same river, and being unsurprised when the dipstick demonstrated toxicity.

Now Bharadwaj paid homage to his moustachioed patron saint, the reason the men and children were gathered there. He said he was grateful to Dr Hedgewar for creating a platform of last resort for Hindus. Because of him, every ordinary person knew that the RSS stood behind them. 'The Sangh has always been there to help people,' he said with feeling. 'It helps Hindus, of course, but even Muslims when we feel sorry for them.' Then he was off once more, referring to a rail tragedy where his brothers from the RSS were killed by Muslims they had tried to help. I had no idea what he was referring to. 'Now how do you save them when they're trying to kill you?' he said.

'And the government is worried about the Muslim vote bank. So if somebody says that we should live together, I don't think a formula for that has been imagined. Because these people plan. And they have funders outside the country.' He told me a long story about medieval Muslims chopping Hindus in half, and unsuccessfully trying to terrorise them into submission. When that failed, they distorted history, he said. 'And now what we study is completely wrong.'

It was understood that my chief function was to grasp the broader sentiment, not hold each claim to the light. When the men invoked victims of various jihads and primeval Islamic impulses, their recollections had an impressionistic tenor, like friends at a pub remembering Wasim Akram's skill with a cricket ball. Accuracy was set aside for emotional consensus. The larger outcome was to prove a siege by the Muslim team on the Hindu side. And now these humiliations and schemes existed so vividly in Bharadwaj's mind that his face took a hard, determined form when he spoke about them. His sat straight and glared after talking himself into a fury.

I asked him to elaborate on the Muslim funders he had mentioned. But he was in a mood where the opportunity to say something became an opportunity to say anything. He declared loudly, 'I'm not saying this. It was in the papers. But just before the riots began they received one thousand two hundred crore rupees. And after the damage was done, if a Hindu lost ten million, he would get compensation of one or two hundred thousand. But if a Muslim had damages of fifty to sixty thousand, he would get paid one or one and a half million. Isn't this corruption?' I looked for reports on the money later, but could not find any. Then he moved on to another subject. He singled out the Congress party and the Aam Aadmi Party—among the BJP's fiercest rivals—as desperate for Muslim votes, but it was a momentary diversion from the corrupting influence of Islam, to which he returned. I was reminded again that a conspiracy theorist's mind is capable of unfathomable leaps between truth and allegation, the mere existence of which is reason enough for connection.

'Look at land jihad,' he said, to encouragement from behind. The word 'jihad' denoted a righteous struggle, but Bharadwaj had adopted the meaning preferred in this neighbourhood: a war, specifically a war on Hindus. The idea that Muslims were waging a secret war by occupying public land illegally was once the domain of extremist Hindu blogs. It was the typical way movements began—with a mention of a strange discovery or phrase in an obscure place, and then made alive through repetition. After Modi's election in 2014, news channels such as News18, Republic and Times Now gave the 'land jihad' phrase credence by reporting its utterance without scrutiny. On one occasion, Republic, the newest of the major news outlets, dedicated nine minutes to a story about the subject. Its headline was, 'Has land jihad begun in Rajasthan?' For the first two minutes and nineteen seconds, suspenseful music played over footage of women in saris protesting outside closed shops, and a man in a salwar—a Muslim—speaking on a phone. When the correspondent asked a woman the reason for her protest, she replied, 'They've made living here complete hell. Day and night they swear. Men go out to work, and women can't step outside. Our freedom has been restricted. The environment has changed.' Another woman cried, 'They've put up cameras. And . . . umm . . . I'm troubled. How can we stay here?' Her voice broke, and the correspondent said, 'You can see here the tears in the eyes of these women.' The story eventually revealed that a single Hindu selling a single house to a single Muslim had started the trouble. In this way the phrase ricocheted across platforms with large audiences and no ethical restraint. They had names like News Nation, IBC24, Citti Media, India TV and Zee News. Newspapers quoted BJP ministers on the dangers of land jihad, but did not provide the political context of the words, leaving it to readers instead. Context was dangerous, for it inserted the newspaper between a man's words and a reader's ears, making it liable for how the words were received. But without context, most readers saw the allegation as worthy, for it had been printed in national newspapers. Without the calming influence of context, the phrase's repetition seeped into Bharadwaj's mind.

I started to say that land jihad was a made-up phrase that meant nothing, but stopped myself. 'If this place was empty,' Bharadwaj, the man driven mad by the spectre of various jihads, said, 'you would have had a mosque here by now. It would have been in no condition to take a walk in. Bangladeshis would have settled down here by now. Pakistani infiltrators would have settled down here. Afghanistanis would have settled down here. The Rohingyas would have come here too.' Infiltration was one of the reasons Muslims had protested the CAA and the NRC, Bharadwaj said. It would have led to their discovery. His objections were like countless connected roots. He did not want to share his country's finite resources or stop thinking about it for a moment. Something had convinced him that he could go nowhere else, and be nothing more. 'This is the only Hindu nation. It's not on paper, but it is understood that this is the only place where Hindus can live,' he said.

In the same breath he wondered why Muslims were so desperate for freedom. 'Where is the government saying that they cannot stay in this country?' Bharadwaj asked. 'Why do they feel unsafe here? That is for them to introspect and answer. All right, let's say that Hindus are persecuting them here. Tell me, who is persecuting them in America, in China? The Christians are sick of Muslims. In Arab countries even Muslims are sick of Muslims. I really fail to understand this sickness that exists in Muslim society.'

The sounds of morning life had begun outside the shakha. Trucks juddered, drills went off, temple bells rang, people said their prayers, locals came to be near the peepal tree. The crowd expanded and contracted, sometimes to eight or nine people, sometimes to thirteen or fourteen. They were eager to talk, and waited for the slightest break in the conversation to speak. Only one of them said nothing. He sat on a bench away from the group, but within hearing. I noticed him glaring at me with sealed lips. After an hour of listening, he said, 'I have a question, but turn off the recorder first.'

He had questions about my past and my family. I told him I grew up in Dubai.

'You've been interviewing people for a while, and they've told you what they think,' he said. 'But what do you think? How can we live together? Give me ten points.'

'I don't have ten points. I have two,' I said, confidently winging it. 'Education . . .'

'Yes, education,' he interrupted. 'Physics, chemistry.'

'Not physics or chemistry. But critical thinking. The other is media . . .'

'Yes, media and books,' he hurried me, shaking his head to say, *what else, what else?*

'No, media and news coverage,' I said. 'Communal news coverage can affect people. People become . . . emotional.'

He was sceptical. 'What you said about critical thinking. Surely you've collected data on Muslim education. How educated they are, how many women are educated. How many people are educated among Hindus, how many are educated in the North East? What loopholes exist in education today?' I thought he had misunderstood me, but he understood perfectly that I was referring to the ability to dissemble news. It was not to his liking. He wanted me to focus on Muslims. 'What loopholes are there in madrassa education and government education? According to the census. Surely you've done this work.'

I said that my work did not depend on the census, but if he needed a figure I recalled one about Muslim literacy from the 1911 census, a document I had recently looked up. I floated a number that felt familiar. 'About eighteen per cent, I think.' (It was only later that the weirdness of recollecting figures from a century-old survey struck me.)

'One minute. Stop for a moment,' he said. The tone he used felt like an escalation. He took control over the gathering to make a point I could not discern. 'You have good data. Give me numbers for the Hindu population and the Muslim population and the literacy variation.'

'This is all connected to education,' an old man said. 'Because when one of their children turns three, they send them to a madrassa where they are taught that the kafirs have to be killed.'

Someone shouted, 'The answer is that a Hindu Rashtra should be announced, and leadership should only belong to Hindus.'

The young man's line of enquiry was thoroughly derailed, and he sat back scowling. But Bharadwaj had gathered his thoughts, and he was ready to present them.

'Rahul ji,' he said, 'Brother, all I'm saying is that they have representation. They have reservations even in government jobs. But if you don't study, how are you going to get jobs? Then you beat your chest and say you get no work. Arey! Where can I employ you if you don't study? You don't study. You have no wisdom. You collapse systems in protest. You have two sons, two parents and a husband and a wife in your house, and then you bring in six more people for some reason. Won't the system collapse?' Bharadwaj was deeply affected by his country's inability to support its citizens. 'And you're fighting with others while you live here? Why can't you respect other ways of life? Why is there this incessant campaigning from you lot? Love jihad, land jihad, all of that? This country is our father. If a son goes off on the wrong path, how long is the father going to tolerate this?'

'They have fifteen children and say it is Allah's gift,' Singh said.

'All they think about is how to divide this country. And Hindus? Cowards. If one of those people is hurt, ten more arrive. If they have a mosque nearby, twenty people will turn up. Our Hindus, meanwhile, are nowhere to be found,' Bharadwaj said.

'You know, one of them just killed two Hindu boys and ran away,' someone said, referring to the incident that had nearly caused a riot.

'They're alive,' I said. 'Religion had nothing to do with it. It was a small matter.'

Bharadwaj did not allow this unexpected piece of information to dent his worldview.

'Rahul ji, let's say you and I have a fight and it goes out of hand. I'm not talking about them. I mean you and me. Could we go to such an extent that we end up killing each other? You understand what I'm saying. Okay, it was chance that the doctors saved him. He did not die. But what if they couldn't save him?'

His raised eyebrows, head nod and hand gestures suggested I had not considered an alternative. 'If they couldn't save him, he would be dead. Brother, that he survived was luck. If not for luck, those people had killed him.' His hand fell like a hammer, and then thrust out in a stab. 'One knifing in the wrong place and he would have died! It's not an attempt to murder. It's murder! *That's* the only difference between section 307 and 308 of the criminal code. In 307 we say "this man died". In 308 the dying man says, "this is the man who killed me". He gives his own testimony. He is a witness to his own murder. And he survived today, but someone will kill him on another day. *That's* what I'm saying. The thing that's in their veins, in their blood . . . Look, nobody's removing them from this country. But yes, every house needs to clean its trash.'

Singh started to leave, but turned to me after something had occurred to him. He came close and asked, 'Is your name really Rahul? You must have an I-card?' I showed him a library card, and he seemed satisfied. 'There are campaigns against us,' he said. 'Rahul bhai, I have a code in life. I make friends with lots of Muslims. So much so that they sit like Hindus at weddings. But what is in their heart? When my friends heard I was with the Sangh, they withdrew from me, but that's another matter. Anyway, two or three of us were sitting together. They were drinking. I said I don't eat non-veg and I don't imbibe. They offered it to me and I said okay, fine, I'll have non-veg, but I'll get chicken. They said sure, get it. They started drinking. There was an Abdul among them. I said, Abdul bhai, tell me something. Why do you have six kids? And he said, we produce ten-ten kids because whether we starve or not, we spend the same on ten children as you do on two. I asked how that was possible. He said you Hindus have to buy milk and fruit and things for their health all day. Meanwhile we just have to cook meat once a day and that's all they need. He said to me, our main plan is to become fifty per cent and we'll laugh as we take over Hindustan. I said how will you laugh and take over Hindustan? He said, there's no unity among you people, nor will there ever be unity. But we are one. He said, the day the parliament, the prime minister and the president are ours, you will become our slaves automatically. That's what he said.'

While I listened to the men and tried not to show my weariness, I thought of a phrase the writer Alok Rai had coined for the RSS. 'It was an aggregator of resentment,' he told me. The men's stories could have been real or false, but that did not matter. All the complaints and injustices were 'part of a carefully articulated and false knowledge that added up to create a framework that blocked out the world', he explained to me at his home in Allahabad.

I noticed the children through the thicket of legs. They were ignored, and idled nearby, listening closely to animated adults talk about holy rescues and dark plots. Their father, the flag man, had let them be. He was at that moment more invested in the fate of his faith than the earthly matter of school. They were no longer sleepy in these early morning lectures about Muslim cruelty and subterfuge by grown-ups they trusted. They were not yet ten. The curriculum of their everyday life was chaotic and undesigned, but as the men piled allegation and mistruth upon each other like unaligned blocks, I saw how this moment could harden their minds and close their hearts, turning them cynical. I wondered if the children would see the cracks in the constructs they were expected to operate within. Would they question the stories that surrounded them and emerge with a different explanation for their life? It would take unusual luck for the children to find their way out, and even more so for them to understand that they had to escape in the first place.

# 5

# Reading and Misreading

'They peddled hate, but did it very, very sincerely. It was almost like god's work,' a former RSS volunteer told me. I had known R— for years as a perpetually bootstrapped businessman in Bangalore, and we had chatted on occasion, but I only learned of his past during a conversation with a critic of the Sangh's ideology who simply said, 'Just talk to him. He has stories.'

R— agreed to speak over the phone, and when I asked if the anonymous nomenclature of tech entrepreneur suited him, he sighed and embarked on an extensive justification. 'Four or five years ago, I'd have said put my name in. But things are really different now.' As late as 2019, R— frequently posted criticisms of the Modi regime on Twitter, but his childhood friends who worked for the BJP urged him to be careful online. They indicated that he was on a watchlist of dissidents. He quickly concluded that social media was overrated for advocacy anyway. Every week, though, he continued meeting with those old friends, some of whom lawmakers relied on for their policy inputs, and some who were built for rough persuasion. 'They were literally going around breaking bones,' he said.

But only four years after the warnings, in 2023, his conversations with those very friends had taken an even darker turn. 'They're being told that any hint of dissent should be crushed mercilessly.' Over beer one evening, his friends had told him the unfortunate tale of a proprietor of a small internet café in Mangalore who printed pamphlets reminding voters that an incumbent had not kept his election promises; the printing equipment met an untimely end. 'There is no tolerance for any sort of dissent,' R— said. 'It's not even dissent, for god's sake, it's social work. If the threshold for what is considered dissent has come down to that, then I really don't know.' He was haunted by the silhouette of federal enforcement agencies, present in every potential action. Critics he knew personally were sent notices scrutinising their accounts for years-old transactions. Mere suspicion was enough to warrant a raid or a search of home, workplace and electronic devices. Arrests needed no public explanation. (An income tax officer told me, 'A friend of mine was told to profile a comedian. It was like, "Find out where we can punish him." It's crazy.') As a businessman navigating complex foreign currency and tax regulations, the entrepreneur felt that even the slightest mistake was material enough 'to badly screw me if they want to. Five years ago I'd have said we'll contest their notices. But now I know they can keep me on the hook indefinitely. The cost of opposing people in power was not this steep.'

R— was not yet a teen when he joined the RSS, a decision that his father, a leftist who saw nothing redeemable about the organisation, helped him come to. It was the early nineties. While pundits wondered about the political effects of the Babri mosque's destruction, the entrepreneur was worried about games. His Muslim friends had disappeared from playgrounds, and from the squads and reserves of football and cricket teams that once buckled with their numbers. His father blamed the RSS, saying, 'You demolish their mosque, and you think they'll play with you as if everything is fine?'

Day after day, R—'s father placed India's travails on the organisation's doings. 'For him it represented everything that was wrong with the country. I would ask him questions about why he blamed them for everything, and we would reach a place where he would be unable to answer,' R— said. Still years from attending the Indian Institute of Technology and from becoming an entrepreneur, the son signed up at the nearest shakha at the age of ten in Bangalore. The outpost was then in the midst of a slum, and eventually overrun by luxury housing. It consisted of Dalits and members of lower castes who noticed the entrepreneur's bicycle and his English. The shakha was led by a kind Brahmin who addressed Dalit students directly, but did not eat with them or drink water from their home. His attention was enough. Although there were deeply ingrained caste lines he would not cross, he was protective of the boys he oversaw, and kept members of the Sangh's vigilante groups away from them. 'He was clearly focused on building the next generation of RSS cadre,' R— said.

For close to an hour after the daily shakha meeting, children would be encouraged to stay awhile and have open discussions. The shakha served as a community centre and daycare where parents left their children in good hands while they worked. Children were safe there, exposed only to traditional values by men considered upstanding citizens. Sometimes the pramukh, the man in charge of R—'s shakha, would invite a priest to tell the children all about the stars and sidelights of the Hindu mythological canon. 'Meanwhile other shakhas would have these conversations about Bollywood showing Hindu priests raping or molesting someone in a temple, but they would never dare to do that in a mosque,' R— said. 'The leaders of other shakhas would tell children that a temple is a holy place, and usually such people would not be rapists. And then, if there was a moral science lesson, it would devolve into "the Muslims ruined everything".'

By 1994, when he was thirteen, he ran the shakha. He was smart, and his English did not hurt, but the practice of giving children responsibilities was institutional. At fourteen he was invited to attend the annual RSS jamboree in Mysore for a day. Although R—'s father was hesitant about sending his child away with men he fundamentally disliked, he assented to the trip. 'He hated them with every fibre of his being, but he wouldn't come in the way of my education,' R— said. He was soon in a convoy of Matador vans travelling to Mysore. The men and children in the vans were excited. They had talked about the event for days. It was the largest gathering of RSS members in the state each year, and important men spoke in breakout sessions. He thought it was like a large fair, and he stayed by the side of his shakha leader, absorbing the discourse on offer for the day he was present. But as the sessions went on and he heard one speaker after another touch upon the same set of concerns, often to do with religion and persecution, he realised, perhaps for the first time, that the men he was listening to were stuck in time. 'Their entire existence was limited to pockets of time when Hindus were oppressed.'

On his return to Bangalore, he asked questions. He didn't know where they came from, or why he was sceptical about the stories the RSS leaders told, but suspected the trait was related to his reading habits. His father was a collector of newspapers and magazines, and if he saw an editorial he liked, he tore it out to keep. Over time, his collection of clippings grew to 'a few hundred kilos'. Many of the articles he shared with R— were courageous editorials from the mid-seventies, when civil liberties were suspended during India's first Emergency. He remembered seeing among them a blank page published in protest by a newspaper that now, in the latest siege on Indian democracy, lent its pages to RSS ideologues, making their ideas appear reasonable.

He remembered an imaginary line drawn between himself and the other children—they were pliable, and followed orders unconditionally, while he had endless questions about history. When he 'pounded' his seniors with his doubts about brutal campaigns run by Hindu and Buddhist emperors—'How do you reconcile what the Marathas did in the north of Tamil Nadu, that the Cholas destroyed Vishnu temples? Why are south Indians depicted as monkeys and bears in the Ramayana?'—their replies were not conclusive. He demanded to know why Ayodhya was important to the RSS, and what made them certain that the Babri mosque was constructed on the birthplace of Lord Ram when there was no evidence of it. 'I asked them how they knew. They mentioned something about excavations and British-era historians who confirmed what they knew. I would ask them why Muslims were seen as enemies, and they would talk about Abrahamic faiths and how idol worship was looked down upon. Then I would ask why Islam and Christianity weren't at odds. I mean, Muslims consider Jesus to be a prophet. That's when the mask would come off a little. They would talk to me about a civilisational society, about how Hinduism was above it, how it had the space to accommodate different manifestations of god.'

His elders at the shakha answered his questions patiently, and he now marvelled at how much they had accommodated his questions, but also remembered that their replies did not satisfy his curiosity. The answers withered under sustained questioning. 'For them, Hindus fighting each other is dharma, or holy duty, or part of a nationalist movement to create a Hindu nation,' he said. 'When it comes to Muslim kings, it is a vicious invasion. A religious war. I was like, boss, you either really believe this, or you know it's a complete lie, that it's propaganda.'

The shakha was a recruitment office, as well as an outlet for the RSS's views of the world. As an organisation, it committed very little to paper—a long-time journalist recalled receiving an 'official statement' from a senior RSS leader on a sheet without a name or a letterhead—but the elements that formed its philosophy of life were recorded most clearly in its own magazines. A reader browsing the RSS's current affairs magazines would have encountered a world impersonating reality. Its most renowned English language publication, *Organiser*, was a journal of ideas—fringe ideas, bizarre ideas, distorted takes on lived experience. Its pages declared, without saying as much, that the truth had been hidden from readers, a truth that its readers had always suspected was kept from them. Early issues of *Organiser* carried stories about forced conversions and marriage, about the racial unrest in America leading to the creation of a 'Blackistan' and the threat of an Urdu revival. The *Organiser* picked up local news of elopements and neighbourly disagreements and depicted them in civilisational terms. It ran stories with headlines such as 'Indian Muslim x-rayed' and claimed to report on conversion activities by the Peace Corps. On page ten of its 3 August 1968 issue, readers learned that 'Muslims prefer Nazis'. The magazine published a fortune teller who concluded, upon coming across a picture of a dead man's palm, that murder was the cause of death. With no bylines to hold them accountable, writers published anonymous theories that ran the length of the *Organiser*'s tabloid-size pages. A surgeon was granted space to write that contraceptive pills would give women beards (his doctor prefix made him a general expert). Another writer said that Mandarin, with its seven thousand characters, had contributed to illiteracy, and therefore 'no other language—or script—in the world is as scientific as our Sanskrit'.

But hatred was only one of the rails on which the RSS's opinions were disseminated. The other was efficiency. Threatened by an Urdu revival in the 1960s, the *Organiser* asked how a poor nation could afford to offer instruction in three languages. It published tracts urging people to follow 'the Vedic injunction to live together and move together, think alike and act alike' to recover greatness. Efficiency could be discerned when it called for population control, or its foot soldiers complained about unpaid taxes and welfare benefits allocated to undeserving beneficiaries. An efficient society was a pure society, and purity was a sign of efficient processes. There was little self-reflection or correction visible; its stances and truths existed in a state of suspended animation—an opinion held in 1949 was likely to be held in the year 2023.

'The basis of the Sangh's knowledge contains enough reason for 99.99 per cent of the population,' R— said, 'even though the moment someone challenges the limits of their knowledge, the whole thing falls apart.' As we spoke, he grew sombre on considering the insignificance of his opposition. 'We're in such a small minority that it doesn't matter in the larger scheme of things. Electorally we don't matter, in terms of collective intellect we don't matter. Because at the end of the day, a thousand dumb people indoctrinated by someone smarter with certain talking points will always overwhelm a hundred smart people.' The propagation of alternative histories was not left to chance. The RSS and its affiliates were buttressed by an operational structure whose frictionless nodes and pathways had impressed R—. He described it as 'a nice neural network' that conveyed messages and coordinated financing activities at surprising speed. 'When there were donations to be collected, the pramukh would get a call on a mobile phone paid for by the Sangh and he would tell us to go around the neighbourhood and ask for a certain amount of money within a day. If we had fallen short the next day, he would already have a list of locals who would make up the gap.'

Messages went up and orders, money and products came tumbling down chains he could not see. He remembered a Sangh member visiting the shakha to discuss the logistics of an upcoming pilgrimage he had organised. The visitor told the leader that he wanted locals to join the pilgrimage. The leader asked for a thousand pamphlets, which arrived neatly stacked the next day, a Friday, and were distributed by the children over the weekend. 'Forty or forty-five people went, based on the thousand pamphlets,' he said, still amazed. 'It's a fantastic hit ratio, if you think about it. It's better than the best you can hope for in any mass-marketing scheme. I grudgingly admire that these people do it of their free will.' This was familiar: the former RSS member who notes its regressiveness but fondly recalls the dedication and superior organisation of its members.

I asked if he thought the network could be used to spread rumours.

As an answer, he told me a story.

When R— was thirteen or fourteen, the leader of his shakha had said they would raise donations for the Ram temple, to which R— suggested a library as a more fitting tribute. The leader discussed the idea with the organisation's Bangalore chief, and within a fortnight of R—'s suggestion it had become a state or a nation-level priority, he said. 'We suddenly had pamphlets and ID cards and forms to collect money for it. They printed out file numbers, form numbers, shakha IDs, contributor IDs, collector IDs. All in two weeks. It was like, you just need to think about it, and it will manifest.'

Almost thirty years had passed, and R— was still struck by the organisation's ability to share information and produce what was required; it was a young boy's astonishment at being taken seriously that quickly. 'I can only imagine how scarily the infrastructure has evolved with the infusion of technology into the system. If one was to use the same infrastructure for violence, I'd imagine it could happen really quickly.'

FOUR

# TECHNICAL DIFFICULTIES

# 1

# The Visionary's Toys

The procession began in Gujarat, on India's west coast, at a temple that had been sacked for its treasures by Mahmud, the sultan of Ghazni. A thousand years had passed, and it was being ransacked once more for an even more valuable belonging: its reputation as the site of Muslim barbarism.

At the caravan's head was a Toyota truck decorated to resemble Ram's war chariot. Rose petals were strewn across its roof, as if it was a vehicle for prayers. There were speakers on its flatbed, and an elderly man's voice rang through them, 'Every child is a child of Ram! We swear on Ram the temple will be built only there!' Followers coated in blue paint, the colour associated with Ram and other deities as vast as the sky, danced around the vehicle as it trudged along. They were held back from unfettered exuberance by the presence of police. Lawyers and electricians in their sunglasses carried swords and shouted, 'Jai Shri Ram!' Boys dangled their legs over balconies to watch the procession. A photographer on an upper floor captured wave upon wave of believers. Halfway up the picture, by the tenth row, their faces lapped one another, and their features were indiscernible.

Armed with the thousand-year-old grievance of the temple raid by a foreigner, the convoy set off in September 1990. Its organisers aimed to reach the northern town of Ayodhya in the state of Uttar Pradesh by the end of October 1990, where the crowds hoped to build their monument to the god. The procession was called the Rath Yatra, the chariot's journey. For weeks it moved in a raggedy line across central India, covering three hundred kilometres a day, and slowed down in cities and towns to drive its message deep into the local culture. Along the way, the procession's leaders repeated the claim that the Babri Masjid mosque in Ayodhya stood at the birthplace of Ram, that it had been built on the rubble of a temple. For there to be a temple once more, the mosque would have to come down. Much later, the procession's most immediate effects would be quantified in lives taken by rising tempers and boiling blood. On 27 October, fifty-two were killed in Jaipur. On 29 October, eighty-eight killed in Bijnore, Rampur, Lucknow, Howrah, Ranchi. By 30 October, sixty-seven dead in Colonelganj and Hyderabad.

At the centre of the commotion, on top of the Toyota truck that resembled a chariot, was Lal Krishna Advani, the sixty-three-year-old president of the BJP, a party whose representation in parliament seemed to grow faster when voters were polarised after communal riots. Each new agitation widened social rifts, bringing it closer to absolute power in India. But the riots of previous decades had been intensely local. Independent India had not seen an agitation larger and more potentially dangerous than the one Advani was now leading. 'For the first time, a countrywide movement based on the deep religious devotion of millions of Hindus has been organised with an out-and-out political purpose in view, with amazing skill and astounding subtlety so as to touch the Hindu psyche deeply,' Narasimha Rao, who would soon be prime minister, wrote under a pseudonym in early 1990.

From a distance, Advani seemed avuncular, even harmless. He was a tall man, bald on top, smiling and respectful in person.

His aura was of culture and education—not a man of the people, but one people liked having around anyway. Advani's erudition and love of Wordsworth were a part of RSS lore. Old hands spoke of his intuitive grasp of image and song: he knew what power movies held, and he knew how effective rhymes could be. He was a master of the cutting phrase aimed at the heart of democratic aspirations: his 'pseudo-secular' was a reductive but catchy attack on modern India's foundational ideas. His father owned two movie theatres in Karachi; when he was a child, he would slip in to watch them, and that led him to write film reviews. He learned his English at a Catholic school, and later in life he wrote catchy songs and poems that poked fun at Congress policies. He set up libraries that stocked RSS books. Because the written word was his jurisdiction, he was put in charge of the organisation's intellectual cell in Karachi.

Advani was never far from matters of communication and communalisation. For over a decade he honed his craft as an editor and frequent contributor to the RSS's *Organiser*.

The publication, like other journals associated with the RSS, created links and justifications where none existed, and invited readers to do the same. The practice leapt off the pages, into everyday action. The temple in Somnath and the mosque in Ayodhya had no historical connection, but as president of the BJP, Advani imprinted on them a historical image of successive Muslim invasions and the destruction of Hindu property. He would quote Swami Vivekananda: 'Mark how these temples bear the marks of a hundred attacks and a hundred regenerations, continually destroyed and continually springing up out of the ruins, rejuvenated and strong as ever!'

*The Advent of Advani*, a 1995 biography based on the accounts of Advani's family, friends and peers within the RSS, revealed that one of Advani's greatest influences was a tract written by Savitri Devi, who wrote poems in Hitler's honour and roamed about Germany in the 1950s, prophesying his return. Her book, *A Warning to the Hindu*, 'made a lasting impression on him', Advani's biographer wrote. The treatise was packed with advice urging Hindus to stand together, and 'sacrifice caste prejudices at once and live and . . . rule India once more; or else, stick to caste prejudices, and, under the pressure of a formidable tide, growing every day, become Mohammadans in a generation or two'. Hindu nationalism's survival depended on 'an all India Hindu consciousness', Devi wrote. In his own book, Advani would say that the BJP was 'committed to India's all-round national resurgence, based essentially on a non-sectarian Hindu ethos'.

Chief ministers of various states privately urged each other to stop Advani. The prime minister, V.P. Singh, asked the leader of the Communist Party to meet Advani and reason with him. 'But I could not convince him,' the communist leader, Jyoti Basu, told an oral historian. 'He was talking about the Moghal days as to how [Muslims] destroyed our temples. I said, but was it right what they did . . .?' Advani gathered from Basu's question a concern that his yatra was a similarly violent act. 'He said, "No, there is no question about destroying anything. Mine is a peaceful rath yatra,"' Basu said.

Even though Advani maintained that his campaign was a movement without harm, the images of Ram as a baby, the slogans shouted, the religious songs shared on audio cassettes, all charged the crowd. He was followed by other BJP leaders and a convoy of open-top jeeps carrying RSS supporters, and these supporting actors were less constrained by appearances. During the procession, they shouted a violent rhyme in Hindi, 'Just one more push, break the Babri mosque.' For that reason, no matter what he said, the crowd's drum beat to faith, not reason. The men's minds were engulfed by songs, and women danced in a frenzy. One volunteer stabbed himself with a trident and smeared Advani's forehead with his blood. A hundred of them reportedly presented him with a vessel filled with their blood. An army captain told a reporter that the men he commanded were Hindus, and said, 'I may have to order them to fire on fellow Hindus in a religious procession. I do not like it.' Everywhere, blood was either drawn, or promised to be.

Seeing the unmistakable drift towards calamity, twenty-five prominent historians argued in an article that the 'claim to an ancient sacred lineage is an effort to impart to a city a specific religious sanctity which it lacked'. The only document narrating the destruction of a temple, they wrote, was within a nineteenth-century historical sketch that offered no evidence. Based on the available material, there had not been a temple where the mosque stood. The whole endeavour was based on a fiction. But the cavalcade marched on.

The BJP had descended from the Jana Sangh, the political party created by the RSS after Gandhi's murder. Over time, the relationship between the two organisations had slackened. The political leadership feared that Indians would find the RSS's ideas too extreme, and chose a more centrist approach for the BJP. The RSS and its affiliate groups, such as the militant Vishwa Hindu Parishad, meanwhile made demands for a temple. 'For years, the RSS and VHP had demanded that the Ram temple be built in Ayodhya. And all the while, Atal Bihari Vajpayee [the BJP leader who would eventually become prime minister] had been vacillating. Then in 1989, when Advani became the BJP leader, he took a calculated risk [with the yatra]. That was the only way to impress the Sangh parivar,' Abhishek Choudhary, Vajpayee's biographer, told me. 'But it's like a family. Even if you're distant, you talk. It conveyed to the Sangh that the BJP wanted to come back to them.'

Two years after the procession, on 6 December 1992, hundreds of volunteers stormed the mosque compound and took apart the holy site. Advani said he was dismayed by the violence. He had not called for it, he clarified.

A day after the attack on the Babri Masjid, my mother picked up the phone and arranged a trunk call from Dubai to Bombay, to her sister, a professor. 'Nothing will happen here,' my aunt reassured her. 'Whatever happens will happen in Ayodhya.' But when she stepped out of her home, the streets were empty. She remembered saying these things three decades later.

The phone at her office in south Mumbai, several kilometres away, was ringing when she arrived. It was a call from parents asking permission for their children to skip college. Then another parent called, and then another. 'Then a Muslim friend of mine called up. She said, "Go home! Why are you out of the house? There's going to be a terrible problem. There are going to be riots!" I thought, if a Muslim is calling me up to say there are going to be riots in Bombay [it] means something's wrong.' She went downstairs to find a taxi, and a dozen men noticed her. She remembered how they ran to her and demanded: '"Who are you! Where are you going!" I said I was a teacher, but I heard everything was closed, so I'm going home. "Where do you stay? Who lives with you?" I told them I had an old mother who needed help, and asked them to find me a taxi. One of the boys stopped an old Fiat and ordered the driver to take me home.'

The driver tried to dissuade her from travelling, but she insisted. 'If there's trouble on the way it's not my responsibility,' he told her.

As she left, a young boy broke away from the group and walked to the open window beside her. He said with a smile, 'Just look at your luck today.' The way he said it frightened her, and she placed her hand on her chest when she remembered him. The temples on the way rang no bells, store shutters were down, building gates were locked, windows were shut. 'There wasn't a single soul outside. Not even police. The whole city went blank,' she said.

As they crossed a narrow lane in a Muslim neighbourhood by the sea, the few men outside turned to stare at her car until it disappeared.

At the end of the road was a church with a large cross that lit up blood-red at night. Just there, before the cross, the driver shouted, 'Madam! Get down! I'm going to race the car! I don't care if four or five people come under the car! Just don't look up!' She ducked first, but then looked up. A crowd had seen them come up the straight road and was now coming their way. She noticed the sticks and swords in their hands, and estimated there were fifty people. The driver accelerated, and cut through them all 'like a banshee'. She noticed a burned bus and a charred taxi, and the smoke that rose from a shape in the front seat.

They witnessed nothing more until the northern suburb of Juhu, where she lived. The enclave's inner lanes, with its film star homes, were usually quiet and sunny, with sand carried by the wind from the nearby beach. Hundreds of men had taken over the main throughway. The driver turned to her to apologise: he couldn't take her any further. 'I'm leaving the car here. I'll find safety somewhere,' he said, and left her.

'My house was four buildings away,' she said to me.

She described moving slowly, sheltering in a hollow beneath a staircase in the nearest building, and plotting her way back through a neighbourhood park. She crouched behind shrubs and took refuge in bushes. 'I remember hiding hiding hiding hiding, panicking. It took me three hours to cover that five-minute walk.' Someone opened the back gate of her building to let her in. Inside, the residents of her building were taking down Muslim nameplates and replacing them with idols of the god Ganesh. Men had formed groups to keep watch on the terrace. They filled empty bottles with water to drop on anyone intent on causing them harm.

The killing started the next morning. The building's residents called out to each other to look out their living-room windows at the low slum across the road. Young men were running into the mixed settlement, finding a Muslim and dragging him outside. 'They were bringing them out and thad, thad, thad, cutting them like that,' she said, her arm working in slashes. 'They were knocking on every door and asking if Muslims lived there. It was the worst thing.' The killing was efficient. It was all she could remember. No one could safely say which neighbourhoods were on fire, but rumour and the burst of sirens provided direction. In the throes of it, traumatic violence seemed eternal. There were stories of how people braced themselves: oil was boiled and kept prepared for tipping out of windows if armed men turned up below. Kashmiri chilli was stirred into pots of hot water in kitchens. She must have said more on the phone with my mother, but this is what I remember.

Their conversations were usually warm, and crackled with teasing and laughter, but now, from start to finish, my mother seemed to hold onto her sister as long as the conversation would allow. What's happening now, she kept asking in one way or another. What happened today? And what happened after that? I would listen from behind a wall to the short, sharp burst of questions that a child recognises as signs of trouble at the other end of the line. At the end of those conversations my mother would put down the receiver and be silent while my father reached for her. Sometimes she would notice me and ask me to go inside, but as time went by she let me stand in the hallway and just listen.

'The flames catch on in several parts of the city and the whole of Bombay is aflame from the next day,' the official report on the riots said of the events of 6 December 1992. By the end of the next month, nine hundred people were dead, and over two thousand had been injured. One in five people in Bombay were Muslims, but where riots occurred, when stabbings happened, when fires broke out, and when mobs gathered, they bore the brunt of it.

When it was done, people who studied the violence remembered how easily Muslims were found. Jyoti Punwani, a journalist who helped write the official report on the Bombay riots, told me about the way Muslims were identified, and recalled a harrowing account in the report. I found it; it was as she had said. One night after the mosque's demolition, men claiming to work for the city housing authority went door to door in Pratiksha Nagar, a mixed-religion neighbourhood near Bombay's eastern shore, to conduct a survey of residents. They left chalk marks on Muslim homes. A week later, seven trucks filled with armed men entered the slums, took away what they could from the marked homes and set them on fire. Men entered the home of a mixed couple and demanded that the Hindu woman hand over her husband, who was hidden inside a box mattress. If she spoke with anyone about what had happened there, they said, she would be 'stripped, raped, and killed'. The police inspector she complained to said to her, 'If a Muslim dies, there would be one Muslim less.'

The fact-finders did not include several such incidents in the report 'for reasons of space', Punwani said. As we talked, she remembered that men from the Shiv Sena, a nativist political party then closely aligned with the BJP, had visited her home before the riots to ask who lived there. Punwani was taken aback. 'Because it was them asking, I knew it couldn't have been for good reasons.'

I asked Anand Patwardhan, who had made a documentary about the temple campaign, about the way Muslims were discovered during the violence. 'The Shiv Sena were in power, and they had access to lists,' he said. 'They would give out lists of Muslims. Everybody in the neighbourhood knew. You would know who lived where. In that period of the riots they even attacked upper-class neighbourhoods. Because I remember people changing their nameplate from Muslim names. Even Parsis with Muslim names changed their nameplates because they didn't want to be accidentally attacked. But you can say they made lists like the Nazis, who made lists of where the Jews lived.' In a scene in his documentary *Ram Ke Naam*, Patwardhan gently interrogated a lawyer and an electrician wielding swords. They proclaimed with gusto their inclination to defend the faith. Patwardhan probed them gently at first, and then with greater insistence. Finally, he asked them when Ram was born. Several of them could not say, and one winged it, saying that only people immersed in history would know. 'So you don't know?' Patwardhan asked from behind the camera.

'I blame Advani squarely for what happened,' Patwardhan told me. 'But I don't know if he had hatred for Muslims.' Muslims were collateral damage in Advani's political journey, he said.

Advani said afterwards that he never called for violence. What India had witnessed, he said, was an outpouring of suppressed national sentiment. Years later he would write in his memoirs, *My Country, My Life*, that precipitating 'a vigorous national debate on the content of Indian Nationalism, and the true meaning of secularism' was his greatest achievement. Behind the lofty rhetoric, a successor Advani had picked, Arun Jaitley, later explained the party's focus on hardline Hinduism as opportunistic. But the gambit worked, and from 1991 to 1999 India witnessed five general elections, each one rewarding Advani's political ambitions a little more. The Bharatiya Janata Party he led grew from two seats (out of five hundred and fourteen) in 1984 to a hundred and sixty-one seats by 1996, becoming the largest in India. It found even greater success in the next two elections.

'In private, Advani used to say that Vajpayee's centrist ideas were not going anywhere,' the political journalist Neena Vyas told me at her home in Delhi. Vyas had been a correspondent for the *Statesman*, and for a time she spoke with Advani every day. Advani thought he could control the mosque's demolition, but she wasn't sure. She worried about the tone the procession's followers were taking, even as Advani distanced himself from impending violence. She saw posters with the pejorative 'katwa'—circumcised—and remembered telling him, 'You've unleashed all this. You're not going to be able to control it.' He said nothing, she recalled.

It was early in June 2022, almost thirty years since the mosque's destruction. A few days before our meeting, a spokesperson for the BJP had set off an international crisis by implying on a news channel that the Prophet Muhammad was a rapist. A bench of the Supreme Court called her a threat to national security, and held her responsible for 'setting fire across the country'. Not long after, two Muslim men filmed themselves beheading a Hindu tailor who supported the spokesperson online. 'I'm not at all surprised at the ideology of the politics,' Vyas told me. 'I'm surprised by the speed and openness of the politics—openly saying that we should kill Muslims. I didn't see that coming. You can never be prepared for something like this. As we speak, detention centres have become acceptable. As we speak, a Muslim must be getting lynched. The government bulldozes houses built on government money, and someone can open my fridge and claim that I'm eating cow meat,' she said, referring to the circumstances that led to the lynching of a fifty-two-year-old Muslim man in September 2015—the year after Modi became prime minister.

In memory, certain deaths freeze the world around them in time. Mohammed Akhlaq's was one such end; he had the misfortune of coming to represent the moment and its murderous mood. The story had begun with a village temple announcing that a cow had been killed—news to wind up the prickly. Men had entered Akhlaq's home, assessed that the meat he possessed was once a cow's, and beat him to death. An initial police case was made out against the dead man for cow slaughter, and many months after the meat was sent off for forensic analysis, it was found to be mutton, a substance with no holy links. A year after the murder, the police announced that no cow had been slaughtered in the first place. Vyas's dismay was as much at the killing as at the aftermath, a surreal landscape of broken laws and abandoned duties, a place with no moral anchor. There was no trace of propriety after the crime, no assertion of law's rule, only a vacuum. It was now a time of confusion, a time when the expression of anger justified anything, even death, and standing in the way of that expression was to impinge on the rights of the righteous. Vyas noticed evidence of it in the groupthink among relatives and friends on WhatsApp groups, the arrests of victims, the surrender of the dailies, the faint scent of feudalism everywhere.

'Their thoughts haven't evolved. It's like they're in a time warp. They're still where their leaders were in the 1930s,' Vyas said, echoing other close observers of the BJP and the RSS. Instances changed, but the ideas and methods that undergirded the cause remained the same. 'I still don't know how an ideology this stupid came to dominate us. It's amazing,' Dhirendra Jha, the historian of the RSS, had once said to me.

I wrote to Advani's daughter a few times, to no response, and also to his former speechwriter, Sudheendra Kulkarni, who would agree to meet or talk, but then ignore my messages. Now that Advani was in his mid-nineties, his protective circle was smaller, but tightly packed. Finally I wrote to his personal aide, Deepak Chopra, who people simply knew as Deepak ji. He asked me to meet him at his office at Thalassemics India in Delhi.

The office was in a bungalow on a dusty lane in Nizamuddin West. When I arrived there, a guard handed me to a woman who took me to a room with a large table and a chair. Chopra arrived after a brief wait. He was tall, with a face that was gentle and free of the varnish of age. He was seventy-five, and his hair was white and thinning. His moustache resembled Advani's. Chopra had started the organisation after his son's thalassemia diagnosis. Now lists of patients and letters seeking aid were on his desk, and medicines were stacked beside the conference table.

He made clear at the outset that it was Advani that he owed everything to. 'It's not that I'm disloyal to the party,' he said, 'but my first association began with Mr Advani, and my loyalties are hundred per cent to Mr Advani. He created the party.' For over three decades, Chopra, who was nineteen years his junior, had been by Advani's side. He was central to Advani's affairs, which meant that he lingered at the periphery of significant political events. His ghostlike presence haunted official photographs, watching from behind on birthdays, often the only other participant given room in Modi's photo-ops with Advani. Sometimes his was the head behind the bouquet on the table.

Advani's prime ministerial ambitions ended when Modi became the party's candidate for the 2014 elections. There was much conciliatory talk about blessings sought and advice still required, but it was clearly Modi's moment. Advani's final years in politics, when he was in his eighties, were marked by unceasing news that the party wanted energetic leaders in their fifties and sixties, even though Advani's electoral victories only grew larger (in his last general election, in 2014, he won sixty-eight per cent of the vote in Gandhinagar, where he campaigned).

But age was only one reason for his absence. While Advani's popularity with the electorate was never higher, his standing within the BJP had diminished as the memory of 1992 waned, and the party lost two successive elections in 2004 and 2009. The RSS's hardliners were critical of his attempts to moderate the party; without an adherence to Hindutva, there was no difference between the BJP and any other party, they said. An RSS spokesperson, Ram Madhav, told a diplomat that the organisation had called for Advani's removal as part of a series of 'systematic changes to ensure that the RSS core ideology is not diluted'. They were concerned, above all, with 'ideological erosion'. Advani railed against this outcome. His dreams of leading India ran so deep that he could barely contain himself. On his eighty-fourth birthday, when asked what he had received from the BJP, he replied, 'Party has given me so much all my life that when somebody says you have to become the prime minister, I say becoming prime minister is not more than what I have got from the party.' During an online Q&A in 2009, an interlocutor wondered whether India needed a younger leader who understood modern India and the global situation, to which Advani replied that he could 'humbly claim' to do both. But Chopra wanted me to know that despite the public record, Advani had not longed for leadership. 'He was not a chess player,' he told me. It was clear that although Advani could no longer make history, his friend would rewrite his place in it.

But there were no more moves to make. When I asked him why Advani might have lingered, Chopra said, 'It's not like Western politics. Politicians in our part of the world usually stay until the last drop of power has been extracted, like juice from a sugarcane.' The last drop of power had been extracted. With Modi's rise, Advani slipped into the final role of Indian politicians; his feet were for touching, his hands for ribbon-cutting, his presence not really necessary. 'He may not be in any position today, but the party still considers him to be the seniormost leader of the BJP. A stalwart,' Chopra said.

The words had the ring of a lifetime achievement award. He

told me he saw Advani at home every other day for a couple of hours to keep him company. They no longer spoke about work. 'There are some memory issues now. And as he has nothing to do on a daily basis, I pep him up, have a cup of tea with him, read him a paragraph, do some chit-chat. It's to keep him on, you know? When I greet him he has this smile on his face, and when I leave he says to me, "Oh, you're going?"' He put on a face of childlike innocence—raised eyebrows, a surprised smile, a soft voice. 'I enjoy it, and I think he does too. But I don't prick him with the issues of the day. He's done his best.' And then, once more, a firm reminder that his legacy was settled: 'He created the party. He brought it up to this point.'

Their association began over thirty years ago, in 1989. Five years had passed since Indira Gandhi's assassination, when a wave of sympathy for the Congress left Advani's party with only two seats. Advani was assembling a team to manage his first electoral campaign. He was sixty-two then, and wanted everything to be just so. He phoned Chopra, whom he knew socially as an engineer and salesman for a remnant of the East India Company, and invited him home for tea and a chat. Advani's home was bustling with energised campaign staff when Chopra arrived. Advani had just four months before he committed the party's support for the temple in Ayodhya as a way of consolidating the Hindu vote. He surprised Chopra by asking him to join the campaign. When their families met every now and then, Chopra told me, Advani would corner him and ask about his work selling water pumps for agriculture. 'He'd want to know where I'd been, how the crop was there, what I'd done there. He would want to know what was happening in Uttar Pradesh. He would ask, "Tell me how farming is different there from Kashmir."' Advani was eager for all kinds of information, and full of questions, but barely spoke about himself. That was why the offer was unexpected. 'I would produce pamphlets for him.' Immediately he saw that Advani was a details man. 'I would submit something to him after two or three proofreads, but he picked up errors straightaway,' Chopra said. Advani was deeply involved in the specifics of political communication. He had a reputation as a backroom man, someone more attuned to details than soaring rhetoric, and he would fiddle with poster layouts, typefaces and font sizes. They grew closer in victory. 'He took a fancy to me. We were destined to meet,' Chopra said.

The following year, Chopra accompanied his friend on the yatra. 'Frankly speaking, I didn't know how large it would become. It was like a thriller—and great fun. We were on a chariot, and people were coming to see us. It was basically a fun element. But as we went from one city to the next, I'd think, "People have gone mad. We're reaching a city at two in the morning and people are still sitting, waiting for Advani." That gave a pretty clear message that India was passing through a change.'

The squatters on the roadside past midnight had chosen to be there on their own. 'These were not people bought out with a hundred rupees,' Chopra said. 'They had passion and commitment.' He was proud of his friend for engineering the movement. 'He was talking about a temple at the birthplace of Ram, which no other political leader had ever mentioned. The VHP had been campaigning for it, but its reach was only to the monks. The BJP was the political branch, and its reach was across India.' Chopra said that the Rath Yatra had focused the Sangh's arms—political, spiritual, logistical, militant—on the same objective for the first time. As a result, he said, the cleavages that had thwarted the mobilisation of Hindus as a single body in the past were finally overcome. 'The yatra brought together all the castes, which had never happened for Hindu society.'

Chopra had taken a sabbatical from work for two years to work on the yatra. He intended to return once the journey was complete. But he was swept away in its power when he saw the ecstatic faces around the convoy and heard their cheers. He enjoyed the political confusion it caused. All around him was an awakening, and it exhilarated him. He decided to stay beside Advani, even though the political effects of the yatra on the BJP's fortunes were unclear to him then. 'At no time did I imagine that they would become a party of power.'

I asked him how he justified the riots around the yatra. He winced and said, 'I would not put it that way. There are bad elements and good elements. Those bad elements wait for opportunities.' In Chopra's mind, the yatra may have 'created some small opportunity' for violence. Whatever had happened then, he couldn't recall. 'To only read those books and journals that say so many people died in communal violence after the Rath Yatra . . .' He could not recall when exactly violence occurred, and whether those instances could really be connected to the yatra's progress; the connection between provocative speeches about religion and communal violence was tenuous to him. He made sure to tell me that communal riots had even happened in states far from the yatra's route, but that was how India had always been. 'It has always been happening. It is still happening. Maybe the yatra worked up people. But these elements are prevalent in society in good times, bad times and vulnerable times. Maybe it got sparked off and someone said, "Oh, the 1990 Rath Yatra was responsible for it". I wouldn't say that the yatra led to communal violence. If you heard his speeches, there was no hatred.'

I recoiled. Chopra then seemed like yet another product off the conveyor belt that had produced Hindutva leaders and their justifications for nearly a century. Men who sought no atonement for the chaos left behind them, who put it all down to some awakening, as if victims were an afterthought on a larger journey. They absolved themselves of everything. They had all just minded their own business, doing something perfectly lawful, and could not be blamed if the visceral reaction to their lawful acts was illegal; they maintained that illegality lay in the reaction, not the provocation. Like Advani, he hid behind India's strictly legal definitions of hate speech. The law was simple: a person who, 'by words, either spoken or written, or by signs or by visible representations or otherwise, promotes or attempts to promote, on grounds of religion, race, place of birth, residence, language, caste or community or any other ground whatsoever, disharmony or feelings of enmity, hatred or ill-will between different religious, racial, language or regional groups or castes or communities', or who 'commits any act which is prejudicial to the maintenance of harmony between different religious, racial, language or regional groups or castes or communities, and which disturbs or is likely to disturb the public tranquillity' would be charged with hate speech. Of course Chopra was confident that Advani's speech contained nothing that could be defined as hate speech. Advani knew what words and images could imprint on a person's mind and soul, and he managed to inhabit the slack just outside the boundaries of hate speech. And yet, after Advani's procession had run its full course, more than a thousand people were dead.

Because Advani chose his words carefully, he could deny it all. He could sound reasonable when he wrote in his memoirs that the volunteers who had brought down the mosque had damaged the Hindu cause. In this matter he was defended by Chopra, who spoke with disregard about the yatra's penchant for cutting lives short. The most that Chopra would allow was that the yatra might have caused some 'excitement' among attendees. 'There may have been people' who said vile things on the stage Advani spoke from—but not Advani himself, he said.

I listened to him, afraid of showing him how disoriented I was by the casualness of the description, and by the dismissive look on his face, as if he was saying, *it's a minor matter*. Upon taking my leave, I immediately tried to capture his expression on my phone camera outside his bungalow gate while it was still fresh in my mind and emailed it to myself as a reminder: his raised eyebrow and narrowed eyes and mouth open in a slight smile. But it was unnecessary, because in the year that followed I never once forgot his face.

Chopra was right if one went by a strict interpretation of what was said. It was the familiar refuge for too-clever men, that space between words and implications where he found safe harbour for Advani. But Advani sought to disassociate his actions from his words, and he wanted only his words to be judged. He had shared the stage with those very men, who crossed lines with their oratory, their invitation to take the Rath Yatra's promise forward. He spoke of building a temple on that spot, but left others to speak of demolitions; he spoke of Hindus contributing bricks, but left the talk of killing to others; he spoke of the pain inflicted on them, while they spoke of inflicting pain.

The crime was all over him, speaking plainly. The crime was in the absence of responsibility. It was in the promise of a spectacle, the tingling sensation of certain victory in a fight. He promised them the spectacle of a temple, but the path to it lay through hatred. He insisted that matters of the heart, such as the temple, could not be litigated by the courts, it had to be done by people. He gave them a sense of their own superiority by reminding them that no court could decide what lay in their hearts, only they would decide. The hatred lay in inviting them to a lawlessness justified as doing god's work. The god they were protecting, Ram, was depicted as a baby in propaganda around the yatra—that was who they were all defending. He had found an emotional frequency that pulled them away from law. The hate lay in his guiding them to the belief that their sentiments mattered. He said and did all this in the absence of moderation. In the pictures of him, police surrounded him in protection. In journalistic accounts, there were enough police who approved of it all. The awakening was an engineering of hatred, the creation of a reality in which the laws of god took primacy over those of men.

As Advani developed plans for the mosque and a Hindu 'rejuvenation', observers noticed a characteristic in him that was uncommon to parliamentarians at the time. Reporters' eyes would light up three decades later when they remembered how 'techno-savvy' he was. 'In 1991, huge computerisation was taking place when the prime minister'—Narasimha Rao—'wanted to digitalise parliament. They brought computers to the parliament annexe,' the journalist Jayanta Ghosal told me. 'But only two parliamentarians would go to learn how to use computers: the prime minister, and Advani.' The computerisation was one thing, but with the average parliamentarian aged nearly fifty-two in 1991, learning to use computers was quite another. Advani asked the prime minister to arrange for classes, and the prime minister wondered if anyone was likely to attend. 'If nothing else, I'll attend,' Chopra remembered Advani saying. He was wary of revealing too much about the yatra, but spoke without hesitation about his friend's interest in consumer technology. He recalled that every evening at five, Advani would be the first to class, where a young woman trained two of India's main leaders in a largely empty classroom; soon younger members of parliament signed up as well. In his office, Advani showed off his laptop, boasting to visitors that he kept his 'diary on the computer'. When a friend from Hong Kong brought out a PalmPilot-like device, Advani was enamoured of its capabilities. A new device just for him arrived a week later, and he read each line of the manual, insisting that he would personally transfer phone numbers and appointments from his pocket diary to his new toy.

It was only a matter of time before his enthusiasms crossed paths with his concerns. On his trips to the border state of Assam, Advani preyed on the insecurities of his audience by raising the subject of illegal infiltration. Migrations and border crossings were personal concerns in Assam, inseparable from questions of pride and prosperity. In the borderlands, the lines between nations and states shifted and disappeared, and the significance of the land itself changed according to when a particular ethnic group or tribe had migrated there. Identities constantly shifted; people who counted themselves as Assamese speakers in one census answered differently in the next.

'Migration in Assam is a continuous process that has been going on for centuries,' a retired senior bureaucrat, S.D. Majumdar, told me at his home in Delhi. 'Tribes came from as far as the Tibetan plateau and China.' I asked him about the roots of the paranoia over migration in Assam, and he proceeded to give me a history lesson from memory, naming dozens of groups and their bloody conflicts, slights over language and employment. It was the old story about status and opportunity, about who gained and who lost. Watching me become overwhelmed by the details, Majumdar simplified it for me: 'Migration takes place for economic reasons and political reasons. It is not a bad word, it's only a question of the time it took place.'

And so, when Advani referred to the stresses caused by migration, he knew that some of his listeners harboured grievances against Bengali Hindus, that hill tribes did not consider themselves citizens of India, that children absorbed from their parents stories of the best jobs going to educated outsiders. 'On the western front enough had been done,' Chopra told me, referring to the boundary with Pakistan. 'But the eastern borders were so porous. One could never tell if a guy had always been there, or was illegal.'

In 1983, elections in Assam were announced on the basis of newly prepared voter rolls that included recent migrants. This angered local groups who had demanded citizenship only for residents of the state before 1971, the year of Bangladesh's creation. The new country's birth had been violent, with thousands coming across the border into Assam. But the new voter rolls were seen as an affront, and prominent Assamese leaders called for a boycott of the elections. There was violence between 'pro-election and anti-election ethnic subgroups', Sanjib Baruah, a professor of political studies, wrote in 1986. In one place, Lalung tribals killed Bengali Muslims. In another, Boro Kacharis fought Bengali Hindus and Muslims. In another place, Hindus killed Muslims. Elsewhere, Muslims killed Hindus. In yet another, Hindus and Muslims together killed Bengali Muslims. '. . . each community that was a victim in one place was a predator in another', a journalist wrote.

Over the decades, Hindu leaders had found it useful to remind their Assamese audiences of their perilous state. In the 1940s, Moonje had said, 'If the people of Assam remain indifferent and sleep over the matter they will be doomed forever.' In the 1960s, Arya Samaj leaders such as Prakash Vir Shastri alleged that 800,000 'infiltrators had made their way into Assam alone during the recent months'.

Advani was no different. 'Assam as a whole today is fighting for survival. And the threat to its survival has come from a flood of illegal migrants from neighbouring Bangladesh. If this flood is not controlled, Assam will face extinction under the inundation caused by foreigners,' Advani once said, adding that they—his Hindu listeners—ought to vote for the BJP. In this way history was propped up and kept alive, not to light a path to peace, but as a constant reminder of fissures, deprivations and impending danger. Disaster was always over the horizon.

If anything, the arguments made by the leaders of the Hindu right were measured, hinting at but not stating their main problem: Muslims. The part left unsaid was only spoken in private by the RSS's members, and that too 'in one-to-one conversations', Soumen Chakraborty, a one-time RSS worker from Shillong, the former capital of Assam, told me. 'After the partition of Bengal, home for many people disappeared into East Pakistan. So there was a hatred of Muslims. The RSS exploited it. They said, "we are with you". They would bring clothes, food. They ran refugee camps.' After Gandhi's murder, the RSS took up seva, service, for Hindus for a time. They gave food, shelter and water to refugees, and helped them find work.

The refugees 'became an important base for the organisation', the political scientist Malini Bhattacharjee found. The social service was a gateway into RSS ideology, Chakraborty told me. He stayed with the organisation for about twenty-five years, and watched them lend quiet support to Assamese against Bengali Hindus, even as they told Bengali Hindus that Muslims were the problem. 'They are developing hatred across communities,' he said. 'They are turning cultural nationalism into political nationalism.' He was no longer with them. His association began to fray when, like others, he asked questions of them.

In 1998, an alliance headed by the BJP came to power, and the protection of India's borders fell to Advani as home minister, the person charged with the country's security. But in May the following year, Pakistani soldiers disguised as shepherds crossed the border and occupied a strategic Indian peak, initiating the Kargil War. For over two months it endured, five thousand metres above sea level. By the end, India had lost more than five hundred soldiers, with a thousand injured, while Pakistan said that nearly four hundred of its own were killed. During every session of parliament that followed, ministers wondered what would become of residents on the front lines and how much to pay them; they asked questions about what would become of the families of the dead, and what would be done for the soldiers who suffered at enemy hands before they were killed. Advani was ordered by the prime minister to join a group of ministers and review India's national security system. And then, while they worked, before the end of 1999, five members of the Harkat-ul-Mujahideen, a terrorist group in Pakistan, hijacked an Indian Airlines flight from Kathmandu to Delhi with a hundred and ninety-one on board. After stops in Amritsar, Lahore and Dubai, the hijackers forced the pilots to land in Kandahar, territory controlled by the Taliban. For seven days they negotiated the release of fellow militants imprisoned in India, and proved they were serious by killing a passenger.

'When the plane left for Kandahar, we had no option but to negotiate,' the former chief of the Research and Analysis Wing, A.S. Dulat, said to me at his home in Delhi. Dulat flew to Kashmir and pressured the chief minister, Farooq Abdullah, to release two prisoners held in Jammu and Kashmir. Advani was against any dialogue with the hijackers, 'mindful that a hostages-for-terrorists swap would be politically damaging', a national security reporter wrote, but his colleagues in the foreign ministry prevailed. On 31 December 1999, the hijackers' demands were agreed to, and the crisis was over. In Dulat's recollection, Advani was deeply unhappy. 'He kept saying, "We are a weak country, we are a weak country."'

Dulat sipped a cup of kahwa as he told his story. 'I am trying to give you the sequence of events that I remember that add up to Advani's thinking,' he said. It was about this time, after the Kargil War and the hijacking, Dulat said, that he heard talk about an identification card within government.

On the eighty-seventh page of the report the ministers produced after the Kargil War, they wrote that illegal migration had 'assumed serious proportions', and that it was time to compulsorily register every person in India. They recommended a national identity card that would serve several purposes, without specifying what those purposes were. The country's borders would be covered first, then the middle, and finally its interiors; national safety lay in identification. All the while,

Advani was personally preoccupied with thoughts of identifying 'infiltrators', Chopra, his friend, said. (Several people who worked with Advani at the time said it probably meant Muslims. 'Advani was Hindu-minded, not very different from Modi ji and Amit Shah,' Dulat said.)

During one of his visits to India from the United States, Advani's brother-in-law waved his social security card around when they were in the back of a car. *What is it?* Chopra recalled Advani asking. *What does it do? Does every American citizen have it?* He was fascinated by the idea of it. Chopra said that after this conversation, Advani began to ask out loud in meetings, 'Why can't we have something like that?' The men around him had ideas about several cards that could fulfil the purpose, but Advani disagreed with them all. He didn't want a simple identification card, but something more complex, capable of doing several things. 'He was like, "No no, it should be one card",' Chopra said.

By August 2000, Advani's ministry announced it was considering registering citizens in a new database. The ministry would then issue them 'Multi-Purpose National Identity Cards'. It had invited companies to investigate if the creation of a national database of citizens was feasible, and had already chosen one company from the eight who had made presentations. The recipient of the project had submitted a comprehensive feasibility study about the subject, and the government was scrutinising its recommendations. No decision had yet been made.

The study was the work of a small group of consultants at Tata Consultancy Services, India's largest software services firm and one of the vanguards of India's outsourcing revolution. At its head was a thirty-four-year-old man who led around six junior consultants barely out of college. Chopra watched the presentations from the sidelines, 'but I thought Tata's pitch was the best, if I recall', he said. 'They covered more areas.'

# 2

# The Architect

In 1998, a young consultant from Tata Consultancy Services was dispatched to the authorities overseeing India's census, an immense effort carried out once a decade. The company was propelled by the concern that once computer dates ticked from 1999 to 2000, all the IBM mid-range computers it had used to stop the banking system from collapsing and planes falling out of the sky would have no work worth their capabilities. The consultant was twenty-three at the time, and told to suggest that his company could help process the census's data. But the man in charge of the census was conservative in his thinking, and enamoured of things as they had been done for the past century. He indicated that the 2001 census would be done by pencil on paper too.

The consultant asked for a meeting with a senior official in the home ministry, a joint secretary who advised him to forget about the census, for there was a bigger concern: the government was considering a national identification system to help them manage unauthorised migration. The consultant recalled that representatives from Unisys and IBM were at one of his meetings. He relayed the message to his boss, who assembled a small team of consultants to work on a concept report for the ministry. She was leaving the company, and installed as the group's head an unpredictable thirty-four-year-old with a dim view of the company, who preferred fishing and going off to the mountains instead of doing whatever consultants did. When she thought of him decades later, she remembered his excitement at the work.

I flew to Delhi twenty years later to meet that thirty-four-year-old. The ornate wrought-iron fireplaces scattered around Viraj Chopra's office provided no evidence of his life's great contribution to India's trajectory, and neither did the detachable spectacles imported from Italy that he had once imagined a market for in India; they lay limp around his neck like a regrettable decision. Viraj was past fifty now, and had the bearing of someone whose failures were inconvenient, not ruinous. His face was soft and gently lined with a glossy tan, and fixed in a smile, like everything had been taken care of. His office had more space than a Mumbai flat, and it sat unobtrusively at the edge of a roomy estate in central Delhi. He told me about his detachable spectacle business that hadn't worked out, about the barely profitable fireplace business, about the corner he wanted to lease out to a bank, about his investments, about the sure-shot stock I would be a fool not to invest in (a tip to ignore, in hindsight), about the new Jeep he had bought, about the fly-fishing trip he had recently taken in the mountains. At one point, he interrupted himself to dart outside and watch a woodpecker that had appeared on an enormous tree in the garden. His was a life in repose.

Viraj had attended Doon, an all-boys boarding school set amid the Himalayas. Its students became writers, prime ministers, Olympians, authors, business tycoons and, when the opportunity arose, authoritarians. One declared prohibition. Another, Sanjay Gandhi, Nehru's grandson, forcibly sterilised approximately six million of India's poorest men in 1976.

Viraj ate with the sort of people who effortlessly converted large industrial lots beside highways to residential land, a challenge beyond the abilities of most Indians. He told me he was supposed to be at lunch with friends from the Indian Administrative Service—bureaucrats—who said to him, 'You're ditching us for a journo?' A few hours later, someone visited his office to declare that 'the problem' had been handled. After she left, Viraj explained. Someone had asked a chief minister's son for help. The chief minister's son rang a judge. The judge called the police. Only then did the police finally arrest the employees of a large bank over a million-dollar fraud. 'There was no money in the favour,' Chopra said.

Years of working alone will give anybody unusual habits, and his was removing a matchstick from a box and rolling it in his ear as he remembered the events of twenty years ago, when he was a management consultant at Tata Consultancy Services, and was asked to design the identification system that Advani so badly desired. The basic plan was to give every person in India a number that would be used for taxes, driving licences, bank accounts and almost every other service, he said.

Before we began, he wanted me to know just how difficult it was to get a phone connection in India twenty years ago. 'I had just wanted to buy my wife a phone,' he said. He rattled off the documents the phone company had asked him for. 'Passport, electricity bill, rent agreement, house purchase agreement.' He was struck by the work getting a single phone line entailed, and calculated that India lost up to 'two hundred billion hours every year in furnishing documents'. Going by this assessment, every man, woman and child spent over eight days every year proving their existence. This was consultant-speak, an exaggeration whose logic could be disassembled in one or two calculations. Viraj took such pleasure in telling his story that I grew sceptical.

He said that when he met the government administrators back in the nineties, he sold them on an identity card that served several functions. Its chief utility was in reducing paperwork and proving once and for all that a person could be verified electronically in seconds. It was a stunt, unthinkable to bureaucrats obsessed with paper, he said. (Nothing roused him like bureaucrats, and he wanted nothing more than to 'disintermediate the bureaucracy'.) A thing on paper could always be explained. Paper was protection. The bureaucrats asked him to put his thoughts down on paper. But another consultant in the room remembered it slightly differently. 'The home ministry,' which was led by Advani, 'said we needed to have a national ID system, something technologically heavy,' he said.

Yet Viraj shuffled from meeting to meeting, watching them for a tell. He could see, in the way some of them looked at each other, the way they shifted in their chairs, which ministry was interested. As they talked, tossing about variations of the US social security number, they reached a consensus on the nature of identity itself. 'It came down to this: our identity is the sum of our transactions with the country,' Viraj said. 'Transaction number one is your birth.' He received the budget he demanded for the feasibility study—thirty lakh rupees.

At some point, the home minister himself started attending the meetings. Advani, who was often clad in a dhoti, watched the proceedings with interest. Viraj had sent six team members to regional transport offices across the country to record the bribes people paid to get a licence made. He put the numbers on a graph for Advani, and explained that a new kind of identification was required. 'We conceptualised the national ID as a slab. And we designed identity pillars that supported this slab. One pillar was electoral records, birth and death records, all kinds of different IDs. Transaction one is your birth, transaction two being school. Other transactions include your ability to drive, ability to vote, ability to go abroad. And all these transactions build up your identity. These are the transactions that support your identification.'

The bureaucrats watched Advani closely for direction. Advani hoped to be prime minister one day, but he lived in the moment, taking pleasure in his reputation as India's strongman, the power behind the power. Questions of citizenship were on his mind, and so they were on the mind of the consultants as well. A senior team member interpreted the ministry's concerns: '. . . there was this feeling that internal security, to a large extent, was being threatened by illegal migrants in the country', and that they were drying up 'scarce resources'. After a meeting with a high-ranking ministerial secretary, another consultant remembered thinking, 'Clearly one of the things on their mind was migration from Bangladesh.' Viraj recalled a paper about unauthorised migrants written by the governor of Assam; officials in Advani's ministry shared the paper as recommended reading, he said. The paper argued for identification cards, higher border fences and deportation. I read it and found its author concerned by the possibility of annexation by Islamic forces. 'The influx of these illegal migrants is turning these districts into a Muslim majority region. It will then only be a matter of time when a demand for their merger with Bangladesh may be made,' he wrote.

'This report was important because in these meetings with the ministry, illegal immigration came up several times,' Viraj said. 'The question was, are you going to issue the illegal immigrants a card? It's a debilitating thing. Because there are 500,000 Bangladeshi Muslims in Assam, 1.3 billion of us are going to suffer.'

The consultants wondered if national security was reason enough for citizens and residents to adopt another form of identification. Indians had ration cards, passports, permanent account numbers and voter IDs. When the consultants thought about it some more, they decided that the identity project would succeed if it offered the people something in return for their compliance. 'We were saying that there has to be a carrot. We did not want to push it down people's throat. We wanted them to want it,' one of the consultants said to me. That carrot, they agreed, could be welfare. They calculated that by transferring money directly into accounts linked to an identification number, the government's public sector wage bill could be reduced to a tenth, and that the measure would find support among recipients of welfare.

The consultants designed it as the only identity anyone would ever require. Passports were trustworthy, but few Indians used them. Driving licences could be forged, and a person could have several tax identification numbers. Their creation served one use only, Viraj said: to identify a person. No other government agency or private enterprise would ever have to create a database all their own ever again. They would only have to check a single database. Chopra saw efficiency in this if the government allowed private interests to manage it.

Advani, meanwhile, saw in it a means of furthering India's interests. He believed it would thwart the 'demographic invasion' by Bangladeshis who strayed across the border, he later wrote. The lines between Bangladeshis and Muslims were blurry; one word could stand in for the other. Viraj recalled pushing back, and telling Advani that a card would give immigrants legality. 'There's no difference between people from Uttar Pradesh coming to Delhi to work, and Bangladeshis coming to India to work. They're all human beings,' he remembered saying. The world Viraj imagined was oddly frictionless. He threw out possibilities and scenarios with the enthusiasm of a married man explaining efficient parenting to his homebound wife. This was evident when he said, 'It doesn't matter if every ten years you take five hundred million illegal Mexicans, make them Americans, and pay them a legal wage'. The suggestion was devoid of context and possible effects.

I asked Viraj what Advani was like in the meetings. 'He's a nice guy, actually,' he said. 'Soft-spoken and gentle. It's the bureaucrats who are the bane.' He remembered that 'When they saw that Advani was vibing with me and not listening to them, they tried adeptly to put me down. One of them asked, "How will your card help us with illegal migrants?" So I looked at Advani, who was sitting calmly in his dhoti, and I replied, "Why don't you ask him?" and Advani, fuck, he just woke up, jumped up, and blew the shit out of the guy.' Viraj claimed that at another meeting, Advani 'got up, hitched up his dhoti, and said that he wanted this boy to meet the prime minister'.

'I don't think he's a bad guy. Compared to Modi and Amit Shah he's a polished man. Compared to them? I would call him a statesman.'

When it was done, the consultants called the programme NISHAN, a word that meant identity in Urdu. 'In front of thirty bureaucrats I told Advani, "You've got this overly Hindu image, and nishan is a beautiful Urdu word."' Then, finally, Viraj unveiled his winning idea: the identity made tangible. He showed them a card designed like the national flag, and embossed with a portrait of the prime minister. The cardholder's name and face were relegated to one side of the card. 'Imagine this in every pocket,' he said to them. It could be swiped on a bus, or at a railway station, or at a polling booth. The card would bind a person tight to their identity, with no question about who they were, or where they lived. Everything about them would be known.

A few hours into our interview, Viraj reached for a magazine above his desk. It was a February 2001 issue of *Dataquest*, a tedious industry magazine. He pointed at the headline—'Taming the billion'—and said, 'I came up with the words.' I bristled at their meaning. The one true pastime of the country's managerial class was complaining: about queue-breaking, lane-cutting and signal-jumping, spitting, polluting, the trash on the streets, the hooliganism, the overcrowding and the general absence of Western refinement. They saw the public's behaviour as the source of the problem, rather than a response to structural barriers. Such simplistic diagnoses resulted in unimaginative solutions. The easiest course of action was to order the population, a task far easier than reforming governance. Inevitably, it came out in such conversations that a strong leader was necessary—a choice preferred by a large number of Indians, polls showed.

Within the story, Viraj was the technologist who sees himself as a saviour. The magazine article was an advertorial, a faithful reproduction of a corporate plan. An accompanying illustration depicted 'the legacy systems', crumbling pillars of information that held up a slab breaking under its own weight. 'Little wonder then that the country's national fabric is weakening,' the article's author wrote. It was a stark way to look at driving licences and passports, documents for getting around and getting away.

The report was more than two inches thick, with over a hundred pages of 'district habitat dispersion' matrixes that classified districts by their patterns of consumption. But aside from the benefits to the underserved population, the consultants saw a commercial justification for it. One of them said that the identification project was 'based on the market-driven franchisee model', and that 'if the project could generate sufficient revenue by commercially exploiting the database, the burden on government would get substantially reduced'.

Viraj had a pleasing manner, a brotherly lightness that laughed off troubles and burdens. Twenty years and there was still the residue of a technocrat in him, not an inventor's technocrat as much as a consultant's, who did not excavate the struggles behind intractable problems, who saw them instead as a failure of resolve and imagination. He liked blaming bureaucrats. If they were done away with and their power was curtailed, everything would right itself, he seemed to say. If people had a card, they would save time. If the government allowed private players to manage it, the enterprise would be profitable. If this, then that. The laws of his optimism were as neat as a light switch. Perhaps it was the oppressive air, or the citizenship protests outside, because I was hungry for hope, and susceptible to reveries as he described how easy it could all be. This velvety cheer wrapped around me from time to time as I listened, and I would forget that technological optimism often conceals a blunt instrument. He had so many stories of the ministry's intentions and the company's solutions that I realised, to my surprise, that he hadn't said a word about privacy, and to my dismay, that I had neglected to ask him about it. Even between us it was an afterthought.

'Was it a consideration?' I asked, eventually.

'Not that the Indian right is too interested in my privacy, but it came up a bit,' he said. 'But my view at the point was that privacy was a secondary factor to those thirty to forty per cent of people who didn't have transactions. And now, come to think of it, our life has changed in twenty years. Who wants privacy, man? There's no privacy. Google knows everything. Everything is known.' It was an old justification, one I would hear more frequently in the two decades after he wrote his report: everything was already known, so what was a little more?

After the consultants submitted their final report, they heard nothing further from the ministry. The BJP had miscalculated its popularity, produced an ad campaign around the theme of a shining country, and by 2004 the Congress returned to power. 'Nobody ever thought we were not winning the election,' Chopra, Advani's aide, told me. 'We thought we would take up the identification project when we came back. But we did not win.' Viraj left consulting to enjoy his time on earth and in Delhi: fishing, and taking his son shooting.

The conversation with Viraj had gone on for hours before he stretched and said he had to be elsewhere. He walked with me to the gate. It was dark, and raining, and the condensation from our breath was illuminated by the headlights of passing cars. Ten days had passed since the police attack on the students at Jamia University, and the protests against the Citizenship Amendment Act were spreading. There was a pervading sensation of living through history, of every word and course of action being part of some historical record yet to be set. 'It's mad, what's happening these days' was all he said, and then he turned around and shut the gate.

The following month, January 2020, I found a member of Viraj's team who had been present in the meetings with Advani. He had settled in Singapore for some years, and was dismayed by the turn his country had taken. He had absorbed from afar the detention camps and the university beatings and the movement to isolate Muslims. It all seemed like a remaking of society based on a new accounting of citizens. But he spoke about it oddly, setting aside the question of citizenship and discrimination. He wondered why a new database was necessary. India already had enough databases, he said. At that point, I asked him about the identification system he had helped design. 'We did this project to just create a tool,' he replied. 'I really don't want to get into how it is used.'

The government's silence was mistaken for inaction, for the report by Viraj's team and its conclusions surfaced occasionally in different forms during the next few years. For weeks I scoured news databases, government websites and private archives, and hoarded stories and documents that illuminated the nascent technology. I had hoped to create a rough chronology of the idea's metamorphosis. In 2001, Arvind Virmani, a former World Bank economist on India's Planning Commission, suggested using 'smart card technology' to reduce 'leakages' in welfare. Two years later, Advani's ministry began an experimental project to issue identification cards to millions of people in thirteen border areas. But as I read each line of these documents, I noticed a register of suspicion. The economist's concern for leakages implied theft. And in a document meant for official information vetters of the experimental identification project, the first lines set the tone for the terms of engagement: 'As Indians we feel proud in making proclamations that we are Indian Citizens. Surprisingly till now we have been exercising all rights of Citizenship but many of us are not in possession of any valid document to fortify our claim of Indian citizenship.' From the very beginning, in the way documents were phrased, certain citizens were seen as disingenuous. Technology would force truth out of the suspects.

Ideas and attempts at identity burbled for some time until June 2009, when the government of India, under the Congress party's rule, announced that Nandan Nilekani, a wildly successful technology entrepreneur, would be the first chairman of the Unique Identification Authority of India (UIDAI), an independent authority tasked with giving every resident of India an identification number. Nilekani's company had been one of the eight contenders for the identity card feasibility report during Advani's time. He had lost out then, Chopra told me, but in June 2009 he stood on top of it all, on the verge of creating the world's largest identification system. He announced immediately that it would be everything to everybody: it would streamline welfare, and would benefit the security establishment too. The worlds it had to straddle did not faze him. Difficulty seemed to spur him on, he said. India was a challenge anyway, and government departments worked in silos. He reasoned that he could try to bring them together in the way he had brought separate departments in his company together. He would draw up simple rules that could be easily understood, he said, and he would 'persuade everyone to agree'.

The job had little to do with his past; the Congress government had been keen to recruit him to do something, anything. They had offered him the ministry of human resources, which he accepted, and then the offer was revoked when they realised 'it would be too radical to give someone from corporate India the role of education minister', he told a reporter who shared his notes of the interview with me. He had since grown familiar with how government worked. He was given ministerial status and a desk, but facilities for his staff were neglected. He was moved to the premises of an insurance company. Overlooking all this, he said he was excited. 'If it achieves what it sets out to achieve, it will be a very important step into the future,' he told an interviewer. With this single technological feat, he hoped to upend the welfare system and give his compatriots the means to participate in the country's growth, to add to its economic value. He wanted bank accounts and mortgages and loans for them, he said.

He told people who worked for him that the identity programme—not the millionaires he had made, not the company he had helped build, not the industry he had launched—would define his place in history. The impossibility of registering over one billion people all made it seem worth his while. Such was Nilekani's reputation that well-paid executives at software companies and consultancies took sabbaticals to sign up as unpaid volunteers. Not long after, he announced that the identification platform would rely on biometrics—the whorls on fingers and the blood vessel patterns in eyes that set a person apart from every other.

The similarities between the new system, called Aadhaar, and the one he had imagined were too great for Viraj to ignore. 'It's eerily similar to Aadhaar because it is! The idea was that we need a fucking transactional ID for people to just transact in this country. I want to say it's a coincidence. It's the same. It's exactly the same thing,' he said. Chopra, Advani's aide, had no doubt that the biometric project was the old system that Viraj and TCS had designed. He made sure I knew that 'the basic work had been done during the BJP government'. He wanted credit to be given to the party responsible for it.

# 3

# Towering Visions

Barely four months into his appointment, at the end of October 2009, Nilekani arrived at the open skies and sprawling lawns of the Indian Institute of Advanced Study in Shimla. The mountain town was no longer beautiful in the way old honeymooners remembered it, but the clouds still swept across the institute's grounds, and the land fell away at the edges so that only the treetops were visible. He expressed a desire to return to it some day, when there was more time. He had been busy recently with meetings across India to win approval for his identification project, to somehow find common ground and turn sceptics into allies. The people he encountered knew the national significance of his work; in the normal course of business, their lives would have little reason to cross. They had read the stories and the interviews about him and they knew of his renown. Who did not? He was the billionaire co-founder of Infosys, one of India's largest technology companies, a maker of stock-option millionaires, a representative of India at Davos, a man on first names with journalists and editors, and recently the most inside of insiders within the government—a man the prime minister himself wanted to see succeed. When heads of state and other dignitaries visited India, they were shown Bangalore as a sign of the country's progress, and in Bangalore they were shown Infosys's premises, and on the premises their guide was inevitably Nilekani. He was the official tour guide to India's possibilities.

Nilekani could be a charming man, and people who spoke with him came away with the impression that he was open and frank, regardless of their ideological differences. They did not know how much Nilekani put into his preparation for encounters of consequence, which is to say every encounter: if he met you, something had to come of it. For that reason he was prepared, and insisted on preparation from the people around him too. He schooled marketing staff at Infosys on the proper way to make an impression, teaching them that every meeting was an opportunity to be memorable. An aide of his told me that he took 'networking classes' that lasted days, during which he ascribed the company's success to relationships. Nilekani urged his people to know everything they could about the people they met. 'What does he read? Does he go to the theatre?' a person who worked for Nilekani recalled him saying. 'It was a pleasure to take him to meetings. If he spoke to a client CEO as a friend, I could talk to them as a friend.'

When he walked in and smiled at the wizened historians, activists and social scientists in Shimla, the person they noticed was fused with the persona he had built for over two decades. He was a businessman philosopher, a public-spirited entrepreneur, the sum of generous headlines and glowing tributes. On matters of economy, foreign correspondents found Nilekani to be a thoughtful subject. *Forbes* had him opine on the 'unintended consequences of globalisation' and jobs of the future. The *New York Times* presented him as one face of globalisation (Al Qaeda was the other they picked). He was on the Charlie Rose Show, explaining that his role models were American business people 'who also played a larger role in public affairs', such as the philanthropist Edward Filene, or Eugene Meyer. After spending an afternoon with him, Tom Friedman found a thesis for his book about a flat world. Journalists lost their bearings around him when he seemed to share confidences. He told a *Forbes* interviewer that working on the identification project was like being the 'guy in an all-night poker game, who at 3 a.m. in the morning . . . puts all his chips back on the table and plays one more round'. He all but told the journalist that the risk was entirely his, but to this admission the journalist could only say, 'For the sake of a billion Indians, we hope Nandan wins this round.' In these interactions he was less a representative of commercial success than a singular man of technology, a figurehead who stood in for the aspirations and achievements of a country. His lineage was from Vikram Sarabhai, the father of India's space programme, and A.P.J. Abdul Kalam, who led missile development, and others who had ushered in the telecoms revolution—men associated with significant national advances. A business journalist who admitted he had gone easy on Nilekani in the past explained that coverage of the billionaire was often fawning because he was 'one of corporate India's darlings'. He was the chief beneficiary of a press ecosystem that existed to celebrate corporate leaders by granting them easy interviews, empathising with their failures, glorifying their achievements and conferring awards: in short, an environment that took men fortunate in business and made visionaries of them.

I wanted to understand him, not through his words, of which there were plenty, but by examining the places he passed through, and the people who worked with him. One morning in 2018, I visited the Indian Institute of Technology in Mumbai, from which Nilekani graduated in 1978. He was twenty-three then, and leaner, he freely admitted much later.

A graduate from the institute in the seventies recalled that what they learned and how they were taught was an extension of school, an arrangement of horrors and regimentation. The graduate was in his sixties when we spoke, and a few days from retirement. His recollections came in a combination of vignettes and stinging insights. He remembered the unending exams, the rudimentary courses, and how there never seemed to be enough time. He remembered the competition, and the brilliance of the students. They took the same courses, ate the same food and suffered from a lack of research. 'It was a place for people to teach,' he said. What he remembered of Nilekani was his talent as an organiser.

A classmate from the electrical engineering department wrote about Nilekani's penchant for emerging as a natural leader among small groups, and of his talent for delegating work to those best suited to it. During a planning session for the institute's annual festival, his classmate Kamal Sinha wrote, 'It was remarkable to see how Nandan started slowly but gradually took control of situations and before long he was telling them what to do and they all followed him without any protest.'

Several people graduated first class with honours, the class's yearbook shows. Nilekani was not among them. Neither did he stand among the ranks of first-class graduates in 1978. Of the two hundred and eight students who received their degrees and diplomas in the Bachelor of Technology programme the year Nilekani was conferred his certificate, he was one of forty-six students who graduated second class. I did not find his name among the theses collected in the institute's library, where each bound book was a strand of obscure expertise.

But twenty years later, it was Nilekani whom the institute honoured as a 'distinguished alumnus'. (The only graduate that year who has outshone him since was the mathematician M.S. Karmarkar, whose algorithmic work at Bell Labs revolutionised logistics in the airline industry.) Nilekani's contribution was not scientific, but directional and monetary. When a school of information technology was required, Nilekani made one of the largest contributions the institute had seen. He funded a technology business incubator inside it, offering advice on its design and how it could work. An institute guesthouse by a lake would not have been built but for his generosity. A chair in his uncle's name supported the research work of professors. All these things required a speck of his fortune. For this he was so cherished that the institute said it would name the guesthouse after him. But Nilekani insisted otherwise, and the institute said that at the very least an air conditioner should be installed in a dorm room in Hostel No. 8 so he could rest in comfort for all of one afternoon. Twenty years later, it remained the sole air conditioner in Hostel No. 8.

Nilekani had lived for three years in that very hostel, which was situated a ten-minute walk from the main gate, down a wide central avenue pressed between walls of foliage. On every side was a vast green openness, and tennis courts—reminders of the privileged life the institute bestowed on its students. The hostel manager told me that Nilekani had asked to see his old room on his visit to the institute. When I asked the manager to show me the room, he sprang up immediately, pleased by the request. It was not a busy day, and he left his station, from where he watched who went in and out, paying particular attention to their gender. He took me to room 278, on the second floor of the hostel's perimeter.

The facilities were basic and rundown, but students had beaten off competition from thousands of others to be there and nowhere else. One year in the mid-1970s, over ninety-one thousand students had applied for admission to the IITs across India; students worked so hard to gain acceptance, said Vivek Borkar, a professor who had been a student at the time, that 'many people burned out by the time they entered'. And while they were among the best in their schools, they would arrive at the IIT and realise there was always someone better. Admission was not assured. If a student's grades dropped, they were 'thrown out', he said. But while they were there, they learned 'the basics at a higher level of understanding'.

Competition was accompanied by a constant reaffirmation of their skills and abilities. Outside the gates of the IITs lay a risk-averse country, expectations of safety and security. But inside, Borkar said, 'it was a place where everything felt possible. People outside didn't strive. They were not trying to get ahead. But the people who were trying to get ahead were at IIT.' Students were repeatedly reminded that they were unlike anyone else. 'They were constantly told that they were the best.'

On 3 October 1978, the convocation ceremony began at four in the afternoon, the usual time. The convocation hall was a broad concrete edifice made starker by meandering cows beneath the rain trees. Students arrived there on foot and by cycle, and skipped down eleven steps to a grassy plaza, and then inside, their dust-tipped shoes hidden below shiny polyester bellbottoms. One man arrived with his shirt unbuttoned and a broad grin, a cheerful kiss-off to an education system a former student thought hard before describing as 'more of the same'. Behind the wood lectern, row upon row of stern-faced academics wearing glasses slouched on floral print chairs. Their hair shone under the lights. It would be years before the wood benches in the auditorium were replaced by soft red seats, and ducts cooled the room. The students graduating then were so used to the discomfort and the stuffiness that it hardly bore mention.

Dr Atma Ram, an ageing scientist, was the commencement speaker. A white Nehru cap sat like an upturned paper boat on his head, and his jacket was closed at the neck. His speaker's robes reflected patterns of wheat. Ram was the principal adviser to the prime minister on science and technology, and the institute's director introduced him to the students as 'an ardent believer in scientific research for economic development'. He 'always endeavoured to give practical effect to this philosophy', the director said.

Ram was the government's emissary, but he was kept waiting

because the chairman spoke next, describing in detail the school's latest scientific projects. The mathematics department was looking up laser beams and plasma, he said, and the humanities and social sciences department was investigating the law of karma. There were discoveries about zinc and new manufacturing processes. The deeply specialised knowledge emerging from the institute was arcane for a population used to scarcity and regulation. There were questions about whether the institute and its sister concerns were worth the investment. The defensiveness showed in the chairman's annual addresses, in which he reminded students they were emerging from an institute of 'national importance' where teaching and research had 'a bearing on the industrial and technological life' of India. 'We are playing our legitimate part in nation-building activities by imparting education and training in sciences, engineering, and technology,' he told them.

Ram told the students that engineers were responsible, in no small part, for the superior quality of life found in advanced nations. Developing countries similarly needed their engineers to show up, he said, reminding them of their obligation. 'Roads have to be laid. Water and sewage systems have to be organised. Irrigation and drainage facilities have to be provided. Electricity has to be taken to rural areas. Technological changes have to be made. The engineer has a magnificent role to play in this great challenge of ambition to match action. We should respond to this challenge because it is at once socially preferable and personally rewarding.' Ram said that the institute had been designed to meet 'the socio-economic requirements of modern society', but that 'most part of our society is far from modern'. In trying to blindly match prestigious Western institutions, he said pointedly, the institute had seemingly forgotten about what was relevant to India. 'The attraction of the West is felt all the way. Can we ensure relevance and appropriate returns for the country this way?'

India and its state of hopelessness was a subject that students, professors and the institute's governing council thought about all the time. Year after year, like a ritual drumbeat, students were brought to the altar of their country's needs, unspecified and incalculable as they were, and massively guilt-tripped for harbouring anything but complete obeisance. Yet, at the first sign of possibility, the finest minds in the country shot down the tree-lined main avenue, past the sentries, to the airport a few kilometres south, and out of the country. 'I worked for one year after graduation, and then left. There were no jobs then,' Rajiv Dattatraya Kane, a student from the class of '79, told me over the phone one night in October, thirty-nine years later. 'You only had basic programming jobs. Most of us migrated to the US,' he said. Kane had built a life in San Jose, and while he noticed the growing confidence of technologists in India, he hadn't been tempted to return. Some of his classmates had. 'The cutting edge of technology is still Silicon Valley,' he reasoned.

Ram was among those who asked the graduates to stay, assuring them of their pre-eminence and their criticality to national progress. It was 'exceedingly important that we have an adequate number of engineers who not only handle their assignments with skill, but also help the country to make appropriate choices in matters of technological implications'. The words reverberated: go forth and guide society. This was the message the class of '78—Nilekani's class—heard.

Had they stayed one more year, they would have received a less giddy and nationalism-infused estimation of their expertise. When Dr K.R. Narayanan, the vice-chancellor of Jawaharlal Nehru University, read them a sobering observation from Winston Churchill's first scientific adviser, Solly Zuckerman, he was advising the graduating class to doubt any feelings of superiority they harboured: 'The better the scientist, which is to say the more fundamental and far-reaching his discoveries, the less does he feel able to foretell the consequences of the new knowledge to which he has given birth.'

By the time Nilekani arrived at the Institute of Advanced Study in Shimla in 2009, he was among India's richest men, and self-made too, in an industry that punished satisfaction. Infosys had grown almost uninterrupted into an information technology behemoth worth a hundred billion dollars over four decades, growing at forty per cent a year for several years, and employed so many engineers that smitten business papers reported on its quarterly attrition rate in percentages ('25%'), not hard numbers: fifty thousand. But India's 'demographic dividend' was a treasure, Nilekani liked to say, and there was an endless supply of youthful prospects ready to be sized up by the company's HR department.

At Infosys, Nilekani was a giant—its face, its chief enabler of relationships. A manager, one of the company's earliest employees, related an anecdote, with a caveat: 'Please remember, I heard this from someone who was there.' The story was this: in the course of a business meeting, Nilekani unexpectedly assured the boss of a Swiss bank that he would devise ways to save the bank a billion dollars on its information technology budget within three months. He said it so casually that his colleagues protested loudly outside. And, so the rumour has it, he said to them, 'Well, I said it. Now you guys make it happen.'

I was struck by how vividly the manager remembered the events of that day, events he had personally not witnessed. Perhaps it was because he disparaged the direction his former company had taken. He told me how the company changed on Nilekani's watch, leaving inventing things for inventing new realities. 'A powerful marketing message is more important than reality' at the company, he said. 'It becomes a reality in our mind. It doesn't matter what reality is. The culture at Infosys was: make the marketing message, and pretend it's already there. The guy who makes the statement that resonates is the important guy.' He was unhappy about the reduced emphasis on innovation. 'When you start believing in your own marketing mantras, you lose touch with reality.' The ex-employee thought that the company's leadership had grown used to consequence-free decision-making. Nilekani and the company's chairman 'believe that if leaders spend too much time worrying about the consequences of their actions, then nothing will get done,' he said. 'So you have to be decisive, and take a call on how to get what you want. If some indirect consequences happen, so be it.'

The story had stuck in his mind: outside the room, after his colleagues had protested that to find such savings was unreasonable, Nilekani schooled them on the difference between what was done and what was remembered. Even if the savings fell well short of the promise, as long as something was saved, as long as the client saw some benefit, they would feel goodwill towards the maker of the promise.

'A large number and a simple message,' the manager recalled. 'We did that all the time.'

That was the kind of story people remembered about him. It may not have been true, but it certainly *felt* true, because Nilekani's was a world of favours and exhibitions of power. In the telling of his confidants, it was also full of promises that stuck and outcomes that did not. It was a world whose dynamics he had mastered; even his mortal enemies admitted that he was good with people. His memory was said to be 'elephantine', his ability to convince his listeners unparalleled. 'You should have seen him at meetings,' a man from human resources said. 'How he remembered things.' An executive assistant said, 'One time he remembered meeting this man on a bus in China twelve years before. Not just that, he remembered what they did that afternoon. You should have seen the man. He was zapped. Just stopped talking. He became a listener.' Another time, he said, Nilekani recalled the name of the server at the canteen, startling him. 'That's what Nandan does,' he said. The manager likened him to something out of science fiction. 'You know those films where you see something from a robot's point of view and there's a lot of data that comes up on both sides of the screen? That's him. He's probably got some radar for people, more than anyone I've met in the world.'

As I interviewed people around him, they spoke of another aspect of Nilekani's personality: the sensation that he had his eye on some future they could not see. 'Men like him are looking thirty or forty years' into the future, an employee at his philanthropic foundation said. 'They're operating on a timescale we can't begin to think of.' The employee had kept his distance out of cautiousness, and was troubled by what he saw as an avoidance of everyday concerns. Nilekani had a technocrat's aversion to the friction of daily life, he said, and the fortune to fuel his visions. He was filled with his ideas for the future, an ability to articulate them, and look beyond their immediate effects. This confidence sprang from the certainty that his intentions were pure, and his knowledge complete. 'This is not a view that encourages doubt,' the employee said. 'For him, using illiberal means to attain liberal societal outcomes thirty or forty years from now is not an issue. His fear is that if he uses liberal democratic processes alone, illiberal undemocratic factions will take over.'

'The power of intent matters with him,' the employee said. The future had been decided; the present only had to fall into line. With this kind of worldview, public dissent cut him deeply. The people who knew him spoke of him in awe for the most part, but they feared his influence upon their livelihood, and would only share their criticisms anonymously. And even in anonymity they were conservative about what they said. I heard from them that he was a good man, a lucky man, a man with deep connections. But he was also a man with more money than his employees could imagine, and the causes he backed, someone who knew him said with a laugh, were funded by 'the interest on the interest on the interest' of his primary investments. After a reporter wrote a critical story, he claimed, Nilekani sent him a polite SMS to say that their association had ended. The writer of a somewhat critical op-ed about a Nilekani project recalled him pointedly mentioning, after months had passed, that he had read it. A senior official privy to the company's deals remembered a columnist writing that 'although he's very smart, he wears a suit like a small-town bank manager. He wasn't too happy about that. So he made sure that his suits were specially tailored from then on.'

The occasional jibe aside, press about Nilekani was largely glowing. His warm, open manner and prompt replies to requests endeared him to reporters and editors. Nilekani was articulate, and full of the kind of hope that editors found intoxicating; even if he was not in the room, they would empathise with him. Wherever he went, he conveyed optimism about India's prospects in terms that a global audience would understand. During his TED talk, he sauntered around in a loose suit on the stage, a hand in his pocket, a face without expression, like he did in conference rooms and client meetings, where he rattled off large numbers and political ideas in broad strokes. His message was about how the unstoppable force of young energy would alter India; democracy had become 'embedded' because 'everybody has realised the benefits of having a voice; the benefits of being in an open society'; globalisation was good; everyone knew cities were 'engines of innovation' and caste was a 'policy gridlock'. His 2008 book, *Imagining India*, was a treatise on the immense potential of the subcontinent's demographic dividend—the millions upon millions who would soon join the labour force. He was a businessman-philosopher, and his optimism was tied to wealth. That was why his argument was about improving execution. Execution was a neutral idea, with no heroes or villains, only people who had to do better. It hurt no one's feelings to hear that India needed better execution. His manner was forgiving and encouraging, as if he was saying, *Everyone has the right idea, we've just got to implement the stuff we already know*. Padmini Ray Murray, a technology researcher and engaging cynic, described this techno-optimism as a 'libertarian wind blowing through Bangalore'.

First, the country. Nilekani worried about an opportunity that could curdle if it was not seized immediately, a concern on the mind of anyone with a whit of foresight. In the sixties and seventies, at a time of scarcity, Indians saw their endless numbers as a burden to bear. But with opportunity they had become assets, human capital. This change was a fundamental one in India, brought on by the rare gift of the demographic dividend, he explained to an audience in California. India was producing large numbers of young eager for work, even as fertility rates were falling. As it arrived, India would be the largest young country in an ageing world. But this dividend was uneven. The south and the west of the country would be 'fully expensed' by 2015, he believed. The bulk of them would come from the north. The dividend would only be as good as the 'investment in human capital'.

He didn't say outright that the north made for depressing reading on every parameter that counted. But he was referring to it as an Indian businessperson would: in language so eager to avoid offence that it clung to economic metaphor. Fewer children made it to the age of five than in any other part of the country. If they made it to school, classrooms had almost forty students for every teacher. Away from the cities, even teachers skipped school. One out of every five kids dropped out before the sixth grade. And although education spending had increased a great deal, fewer than two in ten children in the third standard could read a first-standard text. Without the investment, Nilekani said in the sprightly tone of a man who doesn't burn bridges, disaster would follow. This was the country that confronted him, the country he wanted the experts in the room in Shimla to see.

Nilekani had come prepared for the civil society groups, social scientists and activists in the meeting room, and knew what they would say to him. From its inception, people had worried about what the identification programme would become, and wondered what its limits would be. They had written editorials about the identity project, calling it a Trojan horse for a capitalist takeover of welfare, and accused him of not understanding his country. 'Some have argued that ID cards can be used to profile citizens in a country and initiate a process of racial/ethnic cleansing, as during the Rwanda genocide of 1995,' Professor R. Ramakumar wrote. An agricultural economist at the Tata Institute of Social Sciences in Mumbai, Ramakumar noticed that officials discussed the project in generalities, as if they were describing a building but not sharing its floor plan. He had read the claims and that it would improve attendance, its health benefits, how welfare corruption would stop, how the identity number could become a mobile number. The project made him uncomfortable, and a while later he articulated four reasons why. It was a threat to privacy, the technology it was based on was fallible, the costs were too high, and, lastly, 'this might be a neoliberal ploy to undermine' India's welfare system. A month after Nilekani's appointment, Ramakumar published an article in *Frontline*, a magazine he wrote for frequently, and found that it 'got a lot of traction among people who were sceptical'. The critique had attracted Nilekani's attention, and he invited Ramakumar to Shimla for the discussion. Nilekani had a memory for critics and their criticisms, people who worked with him told me. But that day and the next were to give reassurance and make friends for the programme.

In a meeting room within the institute, sitting around a long oval table, his doubters awaited him. Then the room's doors closed, and Peter DeSouza, the institute's director, welcomed him and the retinue of bureaucrats and researchers from the Unique Identification Authority of India, the new government body Nilekani was in charge of. The identity project would almost certainly change India in some way, the director said to the social scientists and the Authority's officials, but he couldn't say how that change would manifest. 'I don't know if you've had other conversations with social scientists in a formal setting, but if this is the first such conversation, it's fitting that it happens here. This place is for people who want to ask the larger questions.' The institute, housed in a red-brick colonial structure, was born of a desire for pure learning at a perilous time—the years after Nehru's death, when the country could have lost its way, the director explained. He saw the institute's existence as evidence that India had survived 'the dangerous decade'.

Nilekani listened quietly. He had grown up in thrall of India's first prime minister, and remembered standing in a crowd when he was four, a crowd captivated by Nehru as he went by in a car. 'His greatest strength was that even as the rest of India doubted its own capacity as a nation, Nehru never did,' Nilekani wrote in his first book. 'These romantic notions of his were backed up by an iron will and a remarkable ability to bridge disagreements.' He came to appreciate, in particular, 'the great gift of his charisma: he could talk persuasively and build towering visions'.

The social scientists gathered there that morning hoped that Nilekani would properly explain the towering visions he had built around the identity project. They had read the newspaper stories about it, and were familiar with the interviews he gave on television, but its shape and scope eluded them. How would it change the way money and food were delivered to people whose lives depended on the regular appearance of sustenance? What of the inevitable unintended consequences of the programme? What about the technology to support the identities of a billion people? And would the project allow different classes of people to be sorted more easily, and facilitate discrimination? Dreams and all were fine, but they wanted specifics.

'As a political scientist, it's clear that we're on the threshold of something revolutionary,' the director said. But he wondered if there were unresolved tensions. 'Is this a new state in the making?' It was an academic's way of confounding a simple question: would the project change the balance of power between citizens and the state? 'Civil liberties are not straightforward,' he said.

Nilekani began peaceably, stating the most fundamental truth about his programme. 'It's about giving a number to every individual, a database which has one record for every Indian resident,' he said. 'There's really no desire to keep profiling a person.' He assured them repeatedly that the programme was a government project, which is to say it had the weight of public opinion behind it. He did not address their fears as much as glance by them, saying that the project's architects would 'consult a lot of people to make sure we do it properly'.

He appealed to their humanity, telling them about how millions of Indians could not open a bank account and receive their share of food because their papers were untrustworthy. Meanwhile, cheats and imposters roamed through the country's welfare delivery systems, pretending to be someone they were not, pillaging food and money that wasn't theirs to take. 'Unless we get our hands around this, we won't be able to do social welfare,' Nilekani explained. He did not specify then what kind of social welfare he envisaged. Nilekani explained that the cards and passbooks people carried with them were ineffective and bore an expense for society. He walked them through the large numbers India misplaced on each of its many welfare programmes, and gave them a big number and a simple message: the bill probably came in at over a few billion dollars. He wasn't entirely sure, and couldn't recall any official studies on the subject. 'I mean, who wants to admit there's a problem, right?' he joked. It was a strange way to create public policy—to act on a premise without evidence.

Nilekani explained the coming era of devices that would capture 'fingerprints, retina, and even DNA' and end the scourge of 'ghosts' in the system, those nameless men and women who stole rice and dal and gas cylinders. The scholars patiently listened to him talk about a process called 'de-duplication', a procedure of elimination so complicated that Nilekani simply said, 'It's a massively complex technology. I won't spend time on that.' It was a struggle, he said, but 'once we create the database, we have a powerful tool to make sure welfare reaches the right people. I think we all can agree that if we can be more efficient, it's a public good.'

Even as he showed them how the project would rescue welfare, he revealed to them its other uses as an aside. The number 'would make it easy for people to move around the country'. And as the number's use spread, 'it will be that much more difficult for someone who has bad intentions to be doing these things because they will have a number, and therefore they can be identified'. Realising what he had just said, he added, 'We have to do this carefully because we want to make sure we don't create the surveillance thing . . .'

He assured them, again, that the system would not spin wildly out of control. It would be completely voluntary. If it was useful, people would demand better governance. Meanwhile, democratic processes would keep its uses in check. A soft-spoken sceptic rose, introducing himself as a student of 'social reality'. Sanjay Palshikar, a professor of political science at the University of Hyderabad, had read enough about identity projects to have serious concerns. He said the number was similar to the practice of branding criminals. 'Because of tech, the past is again indelible. Governing authorities can go through your past. With technological breakthroughs, it's possible to have a dynamic view of your life, where governing authorities cannot just look at your past, but also the future—the kind of illnesses you are genetically prone to, et cetera.'

The professor's voice was toneless; his sentences digressed like footnotes, and his apprehensions came bullet-pointed. The identification project officials caught each other's attention and exchanged winks, smiling at the wildness of these speculative fears. Ramakumar remembered the look on their faces. 'They gave you the feeling that he was speaking about something completely irrelevant. The typical scorn that bureaucrats have for academics. Like, the fears being raised were completely baseless. It might have happened in some country, but to think of it happening in India? *Complete nonsense*,' he said. The academics were surprised that the possibility of misuse was not a factor in the Authority's calculations.

More scholars spoke up. One said there had been no proper debate before the project began. Another wondered if the discrimination rampant in India would be given new legs by identification technology. Mukund Padmanabhan, a newspaper editor, declared, 'This is dressed up in terms of volunteerism, but nothing prevents the state from making this mandatory.' Yet another registered that citizens would be punished for providing incorrect information, but the government could use private information however it wanted.

One of the professors said, 'How are you going to ask people for their date of birth when even they have no idea?'

'Who doesn't know when they were born?' an official from the Authority asked, genuinely confounded by this information.

'Much of India,' said Ramakumar, the agricultural economist. He explained that dates were of so little use to most rural Indians that they marked time by larger events—the month a prime minister died, the year after a great flood. The room burst into terrible disagreement.

The resistance took Nilekani by surprise, and he spoke rapidly and forcefully. 'All these civil liberty people have not been asking about why voter data is online, why tax information is online? How come nobody asked these questions before and suddenly they wake up with civil liberties?' His questions did not take into account the main worry: that the number and everything connected to it put citizens at the mercy of the government. It would make the processes of governance more efficient, but what if the processes themselves were oppressive? Would a tool meant for efficiency deliver oppression more efficiently? He reasoned with them loudly, agitatedly, presenting the clearest distinction between his vision and theirs. 'I think the question is: are the unintended consequences of this programme sufficient not to do this? If there's a social benefit we can give three or four hundred million Indians on the margins, if that means we potentially build a system that potentially can be subverted, and therefore it's a reason for not doing it? That's not a clear argument. A mobile phone can be much more oppressive than this. I know exactly where you are sitting right now by using a tower. So then should we not have mobile phones?'

The exchange left the scholars uneasy. They had thought Nilekani had come to Shimla to take their apprehensions into account, but it became clear that the identity programme's course had already been decided. When they left the mountainside town, a hardening of positions had occurred. And mistrust only grew when the Authority published a version of events that mentioned the disagreement in passing, but captured none of its fire.

Nilekani spoke of the solutions identification would provide in private gatherings and in front of entire halls that paid to hear him speak. He told business leaders, and he told people who possessed little power. Nilekani filled them with an idea he wanted to grow inside their minds until it had become an ideology. He was certain that an ideology's journey led to policy and, finally, action. All the more, he felt in his bones, India was ready. In just twenty years, he said to them, India's desires had grown: the old refrain of 'roti, kapda, makaan'—food, clothes, home—had become, in an instant, 'water, roads, electricity'. Change had come so quickly, he thought, that even that refrain's time had passed, and India was now on the threshold of 'identification number, mobile phone, bank account'. He insisted, in the voice of a man with an idea to sell, that the market had moved on from the bare necessities.

These proclamations, defining in one swoop the movement of a billion people, would have seemed pretentious coming from anyone else. But Nilekani understood that India saw in technology a miraculous portal to opportunity, to governance that it could only dream of, and transparency in matters of money (in this, it felt as if the chief familial imperative of budgetary concerns, job prospects and a smoothly run household were projected across the running of the country, elevating some concerns over all others). He nurtured the idea that technology would help them avoid repeating the mistakes of the West, and show the country a better way towards development. What if India, still a low-income country, could avoid the diseases of rich countries? he said. What if all those mistakes could be avoided? What if a new system could be injected into the bloodstream before the environment grew more calcified? When he unveiled these visions, it was because he wanted people to dream with him, and understand why they were paying for his vision. They would only understand what he was doing if they imagined the country the way he had. He would reshape India by giving it 'tools of opportunity'. He would reshape Indians because the future he imagined demanded it. And the foundation of that future was a number that identified them. It would be the base on which a new society would be constructed.

When they spoke of its possibilities, members of the team that built Aadhaar compared the identity to electricity, to roads, to the internet. In its possibilities, the project provided a foundation for purposes known and unimagined. 'Nothing like it existed anywhere,' one of Nilekani's first employees told me. 'We were trying to hit so many things in the dark.'

But when it came to its possible misuses, they spoke of it defensively, comparing it to a knife or a gun; the project's use depended on the intentions of its owner. Still, they only dealt with concerns about it when activists or social scientists or economists raised them. The rest of the time, the men who designed it saw themselves as revolutionaries, upending old systems of power and patronage, making government answerable for its fund allocations and upsetting outmoded economic ideologies. The employee told me that he had asked Ramakumar for a meeting to understand his reservations. Ramakumar said to him that creating infrastructure to identify people for welfare was a mistake, and that the answer lay in strengthening the social sector. The employee—whose background was in operations management—concluded that the economist was ignorant of how administration worked, and questioned his intentions. 'He wanted unaccountable administration,' he said to me.

In the first year, about fifty employees (they were no longer volunteers) worked in nine or ten divisions in eight offices across India. The government employees deputed to the Authority came from the Indian Administrative Service, the defence accounting, the Auditor General, a government telephone company, from the Reserve Bank of India. Some handled enrolment processes, some designed processes to authenticate the fingerprints and iris scans that they believed would make the system efficient, some bureaucrats used their familiarity with bureaucracy to clear hurdles for the Authority. What they were trained in and what they built were not necessarily connected, two personnel told me; the enterprise had the spirit of a startup, and staff were directed at problems and challenges wherever they arose.

One evening, over tea in central Mumbai, I asked a staff member who had worked on the system's enrolment processes how his education and work experience helped him design it. He replied confidently that background did not come into it; he was a problem-solver confronted by a problem, which he resolved 'by reflecting, talking to people, and creating proofs of concept' and then releasing a series of iterations until the problems in the software had been fixed. (The unknowing testers, of course, were the population.) The emphasis was on speed, he said, and on working with commercial initiative and resourcefulness within a framework defined by the government. 'The bureaucrats were responsible. They were assisted by the private sector. We were effectively consultants.'

Nilekani, meanwhile, went from state to state, meeting leaders and senior administrators, employing flattery and giving them the gift of his attention. In the official telling, chief ministers and bureaucrats fell in line after seeing the undeniable logic of the programme. 'We didn't convince them, we created awareness,' the staff member said. 'Nilekani would tell them what the ID system was and how they would benefit from it. Each department had its own whims, fancies and ideologies.' He was a convincing salesman. In one short stretch in 2010, from 17 June to 28 July, his organisation signed agreements with eight states and territories. Nilekani explained to a reporter that his approach was to make 'the first move in reaching out to various organisations and departments inside the government and public sector' to allay any anxieties people had about him. He was on the outside of his own effect; it wasn't a simple anxiety people felt about him. A former government auditor named Sowmya Kidambi described the excitement of her peers during a meeting with him. 'Nilekani's social clout was so great that when he dropped in to have a chai and tell a small-time officer somewhere in some small department that he was the only person who could do a particular job for the identity project, the officer would lose his mind a little. "He's so down to earth!"' she mimicked administrators.

This new identity descended on India like a cosmic drape, immense and everywhere at once, an achievement only possible because of unrivalled coordination. In less time than an election cycle, Nilekani had herded dozens, if not hundreds, of politicians and administrators into promising him their support. It was the government's idea, he told political rivals, but it would benefit them too. He explained that the project would create a list of citizens underpinned by an advanced technology. They heard him talk about the money they would save, and how easily they could reach citizens in the most inaccessible parts of their districts. He raised the spectre of corruption, and explained how the system he had helped design would make corruption harder. Government offices were officious, grey places with flickering tube lights and stacks of files bound with shoelaces, and people addressing each other by the abbreviation of their designation, an impenetrable code. Nilekani applied his disco ball imagination to the future of administration.

Soon the volunteers who had signed up to his project were sitting in government offices with consultants and tech companies, working side by side to connect the new system to their processes. They built databases in each state, giving administrators there the means to know each person who resided in their territory. The database was sorted and could generate lists of people, revealing their Aadhaar number, name, address, gender, date of birth and much else. Everyone had a use for the data his project would collect. It would 'help in creating a Digital Citizen Profile which can be used by various Departments for delivering several citizen services', an official five-year plan from the government of Gujarat noted (reading it in 2023, I thought: police services and enforcement directorate services). All of this was because of him. 'You have to use a lot of tact,' Nilekani explained later. 'Like any other evangelisation process, you have to have a clear vision of what you are going to do, articulate that vision and sell it to them: Why is it mutually beneficial to be partners?'

Besides the personal outreach, UIDAI asked marketing experts to put together a communication strategy. Early in 2010, a confidant of Nilekani's called an experienced advertising man, Santosh Desai, to ask how they could sell the idea of the new identity to people 'who had a difficult relationship with any arm of the government' or who were normally not reached. Desai understood little of the technology, but when he imagined people in villages and forests suddenly becoming visible, as if the technology was a radar that located humans, it occurred to him that the national identity programme was 'a direct form of democracy'. He could not resist the lure, in his words, 'of being on the inside of something that meant something'. In the spirit of volunteerism, he agreed to advise the Authority without pay.

Desai found the appointment flattering. 'Somebody takes you seriously enough to do something important, you know,' he laughed. He met with the communications team a few times to discuss how the nebulous project could be made solid, and then they returned to their daily lives. Desai came away uncertain about how it would work. He had questions about the technology underpinning the system, about the ability of phone networks to work in rural India, about how people would be verified, and other nagging concerns that he couldn't quite articulate. The responses did not satisfy him. 'We kept getting piecemeal answers. They had this technology hand wave,' he said, waving his hand, 'where they'd say, "Oh, this has been taken care of. International companies are coming and the entire network is being set up." I'd say we were sceptical, not suspicious.'

They were advertising men, he explained, not well versed in techno-speak, and saw it as an article of faith. His only glimpse of the project's size, complication and financial investment was at a 'pointless, boring' conference session on identification in Delhi which was 'full of important-looking white people in suits who were representatives of different technology companies. It struck home that there were a lot of people very interested in this programme from a commercial perspective.' He was left wondering about his own role in the process, and about the wisdom of the exercise he was undertaking. 'You don't run communication campaigns to popularise passports, right?' Why, then, was a campaign necessary for an identification number? He had heard nothing more in the decade since, and when I showed him a communication strategy sixty-seven pages long that thanked him and a few others, he flipped the pages in surprise and said, 'I've never seen this.' The message the report recommended for the population was one of opportunity, rather than duty. The Authority's communications would 'provoke a dialogue in the mind' with songs catchy enough for children to recite at home. It concluded that 'with this number, the poor will no longer be invisible to the state . . . [and will] recognise the existence of each poor individual by registering their identities with the government'.

The message largely spread by the press was that people were signing up to have themselves numbered at unbelievable rates. One million people a day on some days. Volunteers organised enrolment camps in apartment complexes, schools and colleges. Cheery drives were hosted for people with disabilities, and fairs were held for labourers. The population's numbering became an event. People voluntarily stood in line outside bank branches and post offices waiting for one of the tokens released that day guaranteeing them a place in the enrolment line that morning. A few minutes late and they were told there were no more tokens. They returned voluntarily. Once they were inside, they volunteered a copy of their existing identification papers or voluntarily declared their relationships, voluntarily submitted themselves to a photograph and voluntarily had their fingerprints and irises recorded for digital posterity. Receiving the number was like coming up behind a breaking wave: you bobbed gently and watched others reckon with the deluge. And like this, within four years of enrolments beginning, five hundred and sixty million people had voluntarily received their numbers. That enrolment was voluntary, completely in the hands of the people, made the explosive rise all the more noteworthy, revealing the deep need for identification. Nilekani and other Authority officials had insisted that people would be denied nothing if they did not have the number. They said that Aadhaar's enrolment numbers, therefore, were proof of its centrality to life, a necessity born of the urge to be seen. People were exercising their right to choose.

But among people who lived in details, who noticed the fine print of governance, a pithy phrase began to circulate. 'Voluntary mandatory' described a choice that wasn't one; the people standing in line were under duress. Bureaucrats who silently followed orders, and networks of researchers and developmental economists who studied welfare, spoke of official 'nudges' that turned the voluntary number into something like a diktat. Inside government offices, on their computers and on encrypted chat apps, district magistrates and administrators overseeing geographies or welfare departments were ordered to link welfare recipients to a number. They were given harsh enrolment targets, and their performance was subject to unceasing scrutiny if they failed to enlist a certain percentage of the district population by a given date.

'It was pushed heavily from the top,' Kidambi said. 'It was about meeting targets. When Aadhaar-based payment systems became a priority, officials were told that there would be state reviews and government reviews if the jobs guarantee programme was not linked to Aadhaar. They would be told, "If you don't link Aadhaar to bank accounts, the state will not pay you." You would have messages from the top that said, "Performance found to be unsatisfactory. Please improve on these parameters." People would come crying to me.' She despaired at the heartlessness of it, and spoke in a most unbureaucratic manner about it.

Reetika Khera, an economist who for years studied the welfare delivery system, told me that 'bureaucracy found a thousand different ways' to coerce welfare recipients to sign up for the number. She recalled visiting a district where a well-meaning administrator whose faith in technology was absolute modified an official welfare form to make the number mandatory, despite explicit orders from the court. 'Unless you create the fear that the poor won't receive pensions, that the jobs programme will stop, that they will not get rations, why will they stand in line?' Khera guided me through the sequence of events and pressures that would lead to the system's acceptance. 'Once you make the poor do it, it takes on a life of its own. You make it out to be that Aadhaar is good for these things, and you sell it to the middle class. You create elite consensus for the programme.'

Ten years after the meeting in Shimla, I called Sanjay Palshikar, the professor of political science who was one of about twenty people in the room, to ask for his impressions of the day. He distinctly remembered the dialogue's unusual tone, and the sensation that the man who wanted to assuage his fears was in no position to dictate how it would be used. Nilekani and his team spoke to sceptics 'in a language that was very new to us. The assurance they gave us was that it [Aadhaar] would not be misused. The information could be misused, but "we are not going to. Governments, however, can misuse it." I was left speechless.' The words had unsettled him so much that they were fresh in his mind. Palshikar wondered how matters would have turned out if Nilekani—who he now remembered as cordial and open, answering almost every question warmly and immediately—had been confronted not by professors and their scholarly references to the past, but by someone who could conduct a technical interrogation about the workings of the system. 'We didn't have computer experts,' he said, ruefully. 'We needed one, just one, solid technologist.'

Ramakumar, the agricultural economist, realised that the meeting in Shimla was a pitstop for the Authority, and that it allowed them to claim that members of civil society had been heard. Before them, Nilekani had met with support groups for the homeless, and after them, he and his team would meet with women's groups in Ahmedabad, civil society organisations and 'thought leaders' in Pune, and students and leaders in India's North East. Official records of these meetings were useless. In one instance, the UIDAI recorded, 'The meeting was very interactive and a number of issues were raised by the participants which were important feedback . . .', and published three generic pictures of women at the meeting. Incidents like these, of which there were several others, contributed to the feeling that the technologists were not being straightforward. When I called Ramakumar, it turned out we lived down the road from each other in northern Mumbai, and he invited me home for a chat one evening in June.

'Nilekani didn't see himself as the government,' he explained. 'But he *was* the government. He was responsible for how others would use the data he collected.'

Soon after the meeting, individuals unsettled by the project began to seek out the like-minded. They read each other's opinions in the papers, or someone shared a video link of a talk that broadened their understanding of the platform. Each of them seemed to understand a different aspect of the project—not necessarily its architecture, but its effects and general drift. A security consultant who once sold biometrics-enabled safes to diamond merchants in Mumbai showed Ramakumar how the project's technology could be thwarted with a little glue;

the consultant was trotted out before members of the Planning Commission, the government body that planned India's priorities in five-year increments. Along the way he met a legal researcher in a sari who was convinced Nilekani knew nothing about the poor; it was to this woman, Usha Ramanathan, that dissenters found themselves drawn. When Ramanathan and her husband, a respected judge, hosted parties at home, Khera would attend; she had worked on food welfare, and calculated that the savings that supporters claimed Aadhaar would lead to were based on 'unrealistic assumptions'. In Bangalore, a retired missile designer found a contract signed between the Authority and a defence contractor with close ties to the Central Intelligence Agency. 'We don't know where all this data is going,' he said. 'It's a black box.' He found Ramanathan too.

There were others: lawyers, activists, security professionals, developers—all of them were on their way to her, even if they did not know it then. The worries they carried were worries about hunger and other exclusions from progress, about gerrymandering and fiddling with political boundaries, about security, about a corporate takeover of the government, about the World Bank's effect on domestic policymaking, about the relationship between citizens and their country becoming even more imbalanced. In these discussions Nilekani was sometimes a mastermind, sometimes a puppet, sometimes just lucky. They spoke of him with contempt; he could not be separated from his invention. It was why their opposition to the project felt personal at times; their criticisms of the project stemmed from the fear that the concentration of power it would enable would threaten the idea of India.

The one book everyone seemed to have read, or said they had, and insisted everyone else should, was *IBM and the Holocaust*, a reported account of the corporation's role in the genocide of Jews. 'When IBM Germany formed its philosophical and technologic alliance with Nazi Germany, census and registration took on a new mission. IBM Germany invented the racial census—listing not just religious affiliation, but bloodline going back generations. This was the Nazi data lust. Not just to count the Jews—but to identify them,' its author wrote.

Why the book resonated was easy to see. There was no confidence that a numbering technology unrestrained by any law would be used wisely. From time to time, during conversations with friends or family, someone would voice approval about Hitler's determination and drive, an admiration devoid of all context. There was no telling what a country obsessed with efficiency, bureaucracy, and the idea of public order—which took from Nazism the lesson of national strength—would do with such a tool, or where its limits would be drawn. Everything could be escalated, as it often was. *Mein Kampf*, a bestseller, received glowing reviews online: 'Great book.' Targeted violence occurred frequently, following familiar patterns that each new generation grew inured to—the rental accommodation denied on religious grounds, the laws that required inter-faith marriages receive parental approval, the decision of a mob about who to lynch, and who to let go. Everybody understood that voters' lists shared with angry groups ended unpleasantly. In time there would be men standing beside canals and metro stations in East Delhi asking for Aadhaar cards to decide who they would attack.

And so, when they felt charitable, the people I spoke with ascribed callousness and ignorance to Nilekani: that he did not understand India, he only knew how to sell the promise of it. That he was ignoring how dangerous it could be.

For three or four years, over hundreds of conversations, these critics in various cities explained what they knew. I would meet them in cafés, in dark living rooms on plastic-covered sofas because that was where they worked, in parks during lunch breaks, in labyrinthine Delhi colonies, in courtroom canteens between hearings, in underground garages for fear of being seen, in stifling basement offices near Mughal tombs. They worried that the contours of the project were ill-defined, both morally and legally. The easy explanation, that technology was a necessity in this case, was difficult for them to accept; it felt incomplete precisely because technological optimism requires disbelief of its audience, it requires forgetting expertise and lived experience; it requires a wilful lack of scepticism.

An editor I had once worked with patiently heard me pitch a story exploring the system.

'Excellent idea. What has it done?' he asked.

'Nothing yet, but it can be a device for surveillance,' I said, feeling the weight of the words lighten immediately, as if there was nothing there to explore. *Can be* was not the same as *is*.

He called the fears of the system theoretical. If something had not been caused by it, there was nothing to report, he said. He was right. I found it difficult to argue with an experienced editor, a class of newsgatherer more at ease with autopsies than anticipation. There was nothing for him to work with. I struggled to tell him then that the event could not be judged on the timeline of breaking news. It was geological, more present in the air. In a country where violence was inescapable, where it was present in the marrow of lived experience, how could it be theoretical?

# 4

# Viscera

As far as India's states went, Jharkhand, a state in central India, lingered on the edge of my consciousness, for the longest time associated with a general word cloud: extraction, tribals, Maoists, army, revolt. But even within it, there were places outside the jurisdiction of a person's attention. It was in such a place, hours away from the state capital, far away from hills of coal and a charcoal-coloured sky, that a woman died of hunger early in December 2017. A group of researchers were informed by local sources about the cause of her death, and they raided her village to recreate her final days. It was their job to keep track of public welfare, a job they had given themselves. They became familiar with the people and circumstances of her last days: in her last days Premani Kunwar was mad with a hunger that took her to her neighbours in search of food they parted with grudgingly. Gulbaso Kunwar gave her a kilo of rice. Lilavati Devi shared a bowl of cooked rice. Her son brought home rice from school. She had last eaten dal a year ago. For two months she had gone without vegetables of any kind. They found cooking oil, but nothing that could be cooked in it. Her bank account contained nothing.

For two months, she received nothing that she was due. When she had strength in her legs, she walked down the mud path between the wheat fields to visit the ration supplier, a man occupied with building an extension to his house, a man with a full stomach, a man who grew deeply worried when someone unfamiliar asked him not for food but answers. The villagers knew him very well, and they called him a bastard. It was a long walk from her hut to his house, but she would go there to demand her entitlement. She was due 35 kilos of dal, rice, sugar and salt every month by law. The sack she took away, when he chose to give it to her, was often lighter. Sometimes he would tell her that the month's allocation had not been delivered to him, but villagers suspected he sold their share in the market.

He turned her away in August, saying the food had not come. That was the start. By November, her strength had left her. A village practitioner put her on a drip, and her sons carried her to the supplier once more. He said that her food would arrive in December, and told her to put her thumb on a device. Someone, somewhere, would surmise that she had come for her food, and that by placing her thumb on the glass she had received her due. This was how the system was designed. It should have been obvious that the intentions of human beings cannot be boxed in by code.

By her final night, Premani lay on the floor of her hut, and her son lay sleeping beside her. Uttam Kunwar dreamed about his mother's passing even as she stopped breathing. After news spread that Premani had died of hunger, her body was taken away to make sure. On a table in the district's mortuary, the official autopsy concluded that hunger was not the cause because a few grams of something were found in her stomach; it was the only thing she had left. The state refused to see it. Hunger was not supposed to happen in 2017, a time of technological efficiency in systems delivering food and money to people who were finally visible.

When the researchers visited her local bank, the branch manager was surprised to discover that the six-hundred-rupee widow's pension Premani received each month had been diverted to another account. He asked the researchers to look at his computer screen. The owner of the account Premani's money had gone to had been dead for twenty-five years. Someone had managed to link the account to Premani's Aadhaar number; the national electronic system that handled pensions sent Premani's payment to the newest account linked to her identification number. Premani knew none of this. She would rail at the bank officials and return home in tears. The manager told one of the researchers that he thought she was crazy at the time.

By the time I visited her son, Uttam, three months had passed. It was February 2018. He lived in a mud house. Cut wood for the funeral pyre lay in a corner. It was a gift from his brothers, who had been estranged from their mother. Without his mother to remind him, Uttam had already begun to doubt the usefulness of going to school. He disappeared for hours in the day, sometimes stopping to do cartwheels by the river, sometimes stopping to fight, sometimes doing nothing but wandering. An activist lent him money for a phone recharge so that he could buy minutes to call his relatives; it was the first house the activist had visited that contained truly nothing.

Uttam had assembled a punching bag of coal wrapped in cloth and hung it on a bicycle chain. A single bulb hung above him. There was no food, of course, and no containers to store food either. Slowly, however, food began to arrive. It was unclear if the sacks arrived as compensation, as show, or as an apology. On most mornings, there was barely a sound from him. Uttam had stopped speaking to everyone but an uncle and aunt, and a tailor at school. He was given a blanket by some official for his misfortune.

Villagers gathered outside Uttam's home and brought out three chairs for the activists I had accompanied. They sat on the floor and described how the police came for one of Uttam's brothers. They jailed him for two months on the charge that he had altered Premani's bank records, diverting her monthly pensions to another account. They could not prove how he did this, and a judge hearing his case said there was no evidence to support the police's claims. 'If this man is arrested,' the judge said, 'the branch manager should be arrested too. If I give my number to the manager, will I get money from the bank too? Did he offer his thumb? No. Did he sign anywhere? No. So how did he get the money? When the judge said this, the advocate for the government was silent.' Uttam's brother was released within two days. His family asked a friend in the police why they had filed a case against him, and he replied that there had been pressure from above. 'They wanted to close it and call it a family matter, and that's what they did in their report,' a woman said. Then they took him to jail, and asked for his Aadhaar number as they locked him up.

Inside the house were barrels, a cycle, pots from the funeral, an old bottle of Sprite, an empty water bottle, cowpats, wood and one bed. Premani withdrew less than four thousand two hundred rupees over six months. I had spent more in getting to her village that day.

For at least two years, food campaigners had watched in alarm as Aadhaar took root in India's bureaucracy. Jharkhand's food distributors installed biometric readers that did not read biometrics, and the number of people claiming their monthly allocation of food plummeted. 'Why have the deaths happened here in Jharkhand? Because people here are anyway starved. They're at the edge of survival,' Swati Narayan, a researcher who had tracked starvation deaths for three years on a spreadsheet, told me. She said that there had been 'a wave of deaths' when welfare recipients were told to link their benefits to Aadhaar. The previous year, in September 2017, a child died after her family's ration card was deleted because they hadn't linked it. A paralysed woman who couldn't visit the ration shop for an Aadhaar fingerprint authentication died of hunger, as did a seventy-five-year-old man after his daughter's biometric authentication failed. In all three cases, as in others, the government denied that starvation was at fault, often blaming sickness instead. ('Yes, she was sick,' one of Premani's neighbours told me. 'But she fell sick because there was no food.') Later, when I looked at the caste column of the victims Narayan had found, it brimmed with India's marginalised: Muslims, Dalits and tribals. I asked her why the state did not admit to starvation deaths.

Her reply was immediate: because starvation was proof of a broken system. Narayan was optimistic that change would come. 'Right now, only a hundred million people have been affected, so it hasn't hit the news. Imagine what will happen if it's rolled out across India.'

That week I stood on a sandy roadside lot while village women in saris gathered on the outskirts of Ranchi, the capital of Jharkhand. Activists wrote slogans on placards and passed them around. It was a blazing morning late in February in 2018. Women from across the district came by train, bus and on foot to the grounds of a temple. They carried babies and umbrellas and walked past volunteers from the Right to Food campaign distributing wooden pickets from a pile. A drummer from the Communist Party of India adjusted his blond wig and tested his drum while the grounds filled up steadily.

Jean Drèze, a developmental economist, watched the march he had organised finally take shape. He told me the campaign had gone door to door in each nearby village, urging everyone to make it for the march. 'I've never seen this kind of anger,' he said, pointing out the significance of the women's presence: they had skipped a day of work to be here. Their unhappiness was directed at the shift in welfare to direct benefit transfers. No one had consulted them before the switch had been made, and now the underlying system, which was based on Aadhaar, was malfunctioning.

The previous year, the local government had announced that it would conduct a limited experiment: instead of giving people food, it would deposit money directly into accounts linked to Aadhaar. Campaigners told me they heard of the scheme, called Direct Benefit Transfer, when villagers began to protest. The idea of linking beneficiaries of welfare to Aadhaar had come from a government report overseen by Nilekani shortly after he took responsibility for the identification programme. The government-appointed task force he led recommended that the public distribution system for food required 'IT-enabled reform'. The report was sixty pages long, and awash with abbreviations and dubious action-speak. When I asked Narayan about Nilekani's frequent references to ghosts, beneficiaries, welfare claimants who only existed on paper, she guffawed—a laugh so deeply felt that it surprised even her. 'For me, the worst was that students would be declared ghosts if their biometrics don't work, or if they don't have an Aadhaar which is linked to their school card. What they don't seem to understand is, because they do everything online, they're basically looking at the best-case scenario, and assuming everything will work.'

The protestors' plan was to walk eight kilometres to Ranchi's centre, and provide a list of demands to the governor. As the march shuffled forward, I caught up with Drèze, who had run up and down its considerable length to check in on the marchers. He stopped to smile and speak to the women, many of whom recognised this tall, rangy white man with unkempt whiskers. Drèze was keeping watch on the mood to prevent it from becoming too political. The Congress and the communists were political rivals, but had come together to call attention to the flaws in the way benefits were transferred. Both had brought muscle. The comrade in a blond wig summoned a heart-pounding drumbeat. An imitation Dhoni ran his fingers through his hair and strutted around like India's famous cricket captain. The drummers handed out pink pamphlets with the hammer and sickle. I asked a motorcycle rider at the rear if he was a party member, and he asked a friend who they were with that day. 'Today we're with the Congress,' he replied.

The march began soon after eleven, and as it entered Ranchi three hours later, the air grew warm and dusty. The crowd compressed, weaving around honking cars and uneven pavements. The slogans shouted out of giant loudspeakers on trucks grew less inspired, but they still kept going. A sloganeer caught me taking notes and, deciding I was a writer, ordered up a few catchy rhymes. He made a sour face when I shook my head. Then the slogans swerved towards calling for the government's removal, causing Drèze to wince and gesture to someone to shut it down. Without warning, the motorbikes broke away from the march all at once towards a petrol station, and Drèze watched them, unimpressed. He suspected that a political party had offered riders free petrol. 'They wait for opportunities like these,' he said.

As they drew closer to the governor's bungalow, the marchers began to find their voice again. The protestors sat down facing tall barricades. Behind the fencing, security forces held guns and tear-gas canisters, and plainclothes police from the Special Branch took down names of any journalists in attendance. One by one, people rose to speak about the new digital system. They didn't want cash in their accounts. 'Remove DBT, save the ration, come to your senses, come to your senses,' a chant went up. Someone sang a song about food being a right. 'This country runs on money while we get slapped with cases.' Finally, a woman rose, adjusted her sari and asked for the mic. She screamed, 'These are only sparks, not the fire.' The crowd's approval was loud. Drèze stood by the barricades, near the guards, grinning and clapping. He said he was busy that day, and suggested we meet at the university after a few days.

Two days later I found him waiting for me outside his office building. He unlocked the main gate, and then locked it behind us, and then unlocked a gate to a corridor, and locked that behind us. It reminded me a little of motorcycles parked in the living rooms of houses I had seen on the city's perimeter. He made a weird little joke. I recognised it later as nervousness; personal questions unnerved him. The other day he had been unburdened during organisation, but now with questions to answer, he was tense. He was a tall man who made himself smaller to reassure people around him. He listened carefully. He preferred dark denims or corduroys to go with a kneelength kurta. The hemline of his trousers was slightly frayed, and his cracked heels were the colour of the soil he happened to be on that day.

Drèze grew up in Belgium and arrived in India in 1979, when he was twenty. He joined the Indian Institute of Statistics, where learning leaned towards measuring inputs and outputs. But Drèze was moved by the effect of intangible things, such as caste and education. After reading a book on hunger and famine by Amartya Sen, he began a correspondence that turned into a productive research partnership; they authored several articles and papers on hunger, development and opportunity. Between all this, in 1989, he helped plan and carry out a squat at an empty London children's hospital destined to become luxury apartments, the details of which he wrote in a published diary titled *No. 1 Clapham Road—Diary of a Squat* (which he made free to prisoners and the homeless). 'The Belgrave Homeless Project' was a place where any homeless person could find shelter and kinship. While he took heart in spreading the word that the 'unimaginably large number of empty buildings' in London could be reclaimed, he was uncertain of the effects of this societal repossession. In a letter to a friend, he wrote of his realisation that 'homelessness is not just about not having a roof, it's also about not having a job, not having a place in society, not having a lover, fighting alcohol, drugs, the police, social workers, the hooligans . . .' He wondered whether the promise of a roof would even find takers among homeless people. Drèze was not given to clean answers; there were no great leaps into the future, only a series of hesitant steps.

The taste for unmediated experience stayed with him. Drèze taught in Ranchi University's department of economics and required his students to live in villages as much for frugality as for experience, a former student told me. He believed that the problems he witnessed were a natural outcome of the vast distance that existed between policymakers in Delhi and villages scattered across the country. 'I wish these technologists would go and see villages to understand what's happening,' he said to me. When he stepped out of his room to take a call, I flipped through a crumbling copy of Bertrand Russell's *Power*, which lay on his desk. Within it some passages were underlined so hard that the nib had pierced the page:

> opinion is the ultimate power in social affairs. But this would be only a half-truth, since it ignores the forces which cause opinion.

> nationalism is a stupid ideal . . . The best solution is to disguise it under some international slogan, such as democracy or communism or collective security.

Drèze said he disliked labels, but if one had to be applied to him, he preferred 'left-libertarian'. This came from his belief in 'individual freedom and social responsibility', he said. 'I have a principled opposition to any concentration of power.' I wanted to know more about him, about organising, about what he had seen. I realised I wanted him to keep talking, because he seemed to be the most reasonable person I had met in months. It was tempting to view him as some kind of oracle, as if he possessed some sacred knowledge. In this I was not alone; his co-authors and students spoke of him with such affection that at times it felt as if they were in love with him.

His opposition to the accumulation of power included the biometric identification system, whose threats he had been late to see. He explained that he first heard of it at a meeting about food security and welfare reform almost a decade before, when a bureaucrat close to Nilekani attempted to persuade him about its benefits (money directly into bank accounts, the end of corruption). 'It's one thing to see this idea in a room, another to see it on the ground,' he said to me. But then he saw it at work in Jharkhand, where it did not work, where the new technology replaced governance with absent customer service, where the women marched out of frustration. He wrote to the banking regulator to ask for adult supervision of a technological landscape in which electronic wallets and bank accounts were opened without a person's consent, and bank accounts were frozen suddenly and pensions were wired to mysterious new accounts. He found them unhelpful.

Drèze was aware that the delivery of welfare was a delicate act, and he knew as well as anyone that its old form, the form that Nilekani depicted as an irredeemable monolith, did in fact leak. But he tried to understand its nuances and see where the gaps were. In 'Understanding Leakages in the Public Distribution System', a 2015 paper Drèze published with Reetika Khera, whom he had mentored, they showed that in 2005, over half the benefits the welfare system delivered to twenty major states had been siphoned off. But Drèze and Khera also showed that leakages had fallen by a quarter within five years, and that most of the pilferage did not occur in welfare schemes for the poorest, but for those above the poverty line. It was not difficult to see why: the closer a person was to total deprivation and desperation, the more likely it was that they knew their rights. People who were not as poor simply did not know what they were due—that was where welfare was intercepted and sold on the black market. These systems of misappropriation were organised and entrenched, but Khera and Drèze found that states that initiated major welfare reforms broke through and experienced the biggest drops in disappearing welfare: the drops were anywhere from sixty-seven to eighty-two per cent.

Drèze also knew that administrative errors cascaded into catastrophe, a discovery anyone could have made if they had asked. One evening after the march, I travelled to Upar Kudlong, a village near a coal plant a dozen kilometres west of Ranchi. It was in proximity to urban life, but the wide fields and scattered trees gave it a more idyllic appearance. A person who experienced it only visually would have given in to wistfulness, because its beauty flooded the senses so completely that its deprivations were not immediately apparent. Our car stopped on a rough road where chickens scattered, and a woman named Salgi Devi hushed her teenagers as she spoke to me. She said that she had learned about the new ration system when her food didn't arrive through the normal channels. No one had told her that money would be deposited in her account. As we spoke, others gathered around to say that they had received neither money nor food, and had visited banks several times over half a year to no avail. At the banks, officials couldn't say why the money hadn't come. And if money had arrived, account holders were told they couldn't withdraw less than ten thousand rupees, an unthinkable sum for villagers in the area. It would take them several months to earn that amount. One man said he stood in a winding line for three days to withdraw a thousand rupees—to him, the line represented three days of missed work. In three months he had taken ten days off to stand in a queue. The woman beside him was startled. 'Ten days in three months!' Two young men on motorbikes stopped by. They hadn't seen their money either. 'We'll be seen as a state with no poverty if they take this experiment across Jharkhand because no one is going to get their rations,' one of them joked.

When Drèze spoke to bureaucrats, they admitted in private that the technology applied this way had failed the poor, and had broken welfare too, and they tried to extricate themselves from the boggy system. This was also true in other parts of the country, where auditors found that, despite the biometric system, money due to labourers was still intercepted by the middlemen it was expected to make redundant. Kidambi, the lead auditor of a report examining technology failures in the state of Andhra Pradesh, told me that an identification system this hopeless for welfare was probably a tool for surveillance. 'One per cent of fingerprints don't match,' she said, and asked me to calculate how many people experienced biometric failures in real terms. The answer was around eight million people. 'Is that not an issue worthy of discussion? But if you bring it up, they say things like "oh, activists are so negative". Oh, fuck you! I'd like to leave them in penury and then see what they do when they have no money.' Kidambi's fury was startling, but she was not alone in feeling that a system vital to survival had been treated with something approaching callousness. The team of auditors she oversaw wrote in a report that if payments did not reach people in time, they would lose faith in the welfare programme itself.

Drèze recalled meeting Nilekani and voicing his fears about surveillance, but was met with arguments that he felt Nilekani had made before. 'He was already saying things like, "If we want to track you we can do it with a mobile phone, why would we need Aadhaar? In any case Aadhaar doesn't make any difference because technology is already there."' Drèze submitted an editorial to the *Hindu*, writing that the system enabled the possibility of widespread surveillance. 'Most of the "Aadhaar-enabled" databases will be accessible to the government . . . It will be child's play for intelligence agencies to track anyone and everyone—where we live, when we move, which events we attend, whom we marry or meet or talk to on the phone. No other country, and certainly no democratic country, has ever held its own citizens hostage to such a powerful infrastructure of surveillance.'

Few people knew of the identification programme's origins before it was tasked with solving welfare—when its purpose was to know them as the sum of their transactions. Even fewer knew that the project's promise was first articulated as a tool to aid internal security in the ministry led by Advani, whose campaign had mobilised Hindus at the cost of social peace. And even though they did not know of the origins and ideas that had led to the programme's creation, people whose business it was to think of rights and transgressions worried about its potential to cause damage they could only imagine in theory. The threat of a surveilled society had been a pressing concern for as long as there had been an identity project. To understand it in practice required an open discussion of its vulnerabilities and dangers.

But whether its critics were journalists or economists or computer scientists or cryptographers or activists, no matter who they were, and what they had seen with their own eyes, they found themselves constrained from critiquing the system or shedding light on its mechanics in some manner. Each of them felt isolated and mystified in their own way, and some of them even acquired a conspiratorial edge, convinced that there was an organised effort to not hear them. They could speak, but the response they expected—the public questions, follow-ups and journalistic investigations—did not come. A junior organiser of the first major meeting critiquing the programme told me that several journalists covering the event had left their names and numbers on a sheet that disappeared; the next day they were surprised to see how little coverage there was in the papers. Khera, the economist, said she knew that journalists in national newspapers were being dissuaded from reporting on

Aadhaar, and said that most critiques were only printed in the opinion pages, giving readers the impression that crucial facts were a point of view. Journalists at the *Hindu* and the *Economic Times* told me about unusual editorial friction in publishing stories about Aadhaar—writing about the subject was made harder by a tightening of editorial standards that did not exist for other stories. When researchers at the Centre for Internet and Society discovered millions of identification records exposed by databases linked to the identification programme, the UIDAI accused them of accessing data illegally and sent them legal notices. It became common knowledge that the Centre's funders were under pressure to withdraw their support, which its leaders said was true when I spoke with them. Two critics, Chinmayi Arun of the National Law School in Delhi, and Osama Manzar of the Digital Empowerment Foundation, told me they were blacklisted from a government-run cyber conference they had helped organise in Delhi. The bureaucrats who gave them the news were apologetic, but said they were following orders.

For nearly three years, I regularly wrote to a reporter who worked with the *Economic Times* in the early 2010s to see if we could talk. Then, towards the end of 2023, Vikas Dhoot, the reporter, finally decided to describe his experience writing about the identification project.

His first story was about impropriety. The organisation's financial adviser had executive powers. That was published, and so were the next few stories. Seeing his work, government officials who knew more about the project and were disturbed by its direction shared what they knew. He learned from them about a turf war between the finance minister and Nilekani on one side, and Advani's successor in office, the powerful home minister P. Chidambaram, on the other. The trouble was over establishing which of two fledgling databases—Aadhaar and the National Population Register—had primacy over the other.

While writing his article about the turf battle, Dhoot asked Aadhaar's managers for their side of the story. His editor insisted on Nilekani's response for the sake of completeness. Days passed in waiting. After he received Nilekani's response, there was further editorial feedback: the ministry's response to Nilekani's response was necessary too. More days passed. Dhoot relayed the full sequence of events as dryly as a newswire report. 'Eventually *Economic Times* did not carry it, and television news did some superfluous reports. I told my sources to share their knowledge with other reporters because I was getting stonewalled.'

Some weeks after the 'story's slow murder', Nilekani arrived at the *Economic Times* office in New Delhi. In a corner room where the staff converged for news meetings, Nilekani explained the project's progress, reiterating how it would change welfare forever. 'He said he wanted to dispel some myths about Aadhaar,' Dhoot said. 'It was evangelist spiel.' The reporters and editors heard him mostly uncritically. When the meeting was over, an editor escorting Nilekani downstairs asked him how he was spending his time. Perhaps Nilekani was unguarded then, or felt he was among friends, because he gestured at the street outside—a reference Dhoot took to mean the many newspapers with offices in the vicinity—and said, 'A lot of time goes in environment management.'

Dhoot found the phrase demeaning. It was loaded with hierarchy and intimations of power, this idea that journalists and what they hoped to make public required manipulation. He had found the experience of writing about Aadhaar 'deeply frustrating', and he watched other newspapers take editorial stances on Aadhaar in line with the talking points of the system's architects. He wondered if this was due to Nilekani's relationships. The result of these interactions was that 'an element of self-censorship' crept into his work.

Activists shared their discoveries about the system's fault

lines and failures—where the system's programming fell short of its creators' intentions—but Dhoot did not think his work would be approved. 'If the big fish stories are not going through, I knew I would hit the same wall with nuanced stories. I told them, "I love you and love your work, but I'm struggling to get your voice out. You're wasting your time in my case."' They stopped sending him their research papers and sharing their findings. 'You give up,' he told me. 'It takes a toll.'

The abdication consumed him for a while, but he no longer showed his anger except when under the influence. Then his thoughts were properly lubricated, and they flowed in an unprintable torrent, in words that would have injured his employment prospects. Like any reporter in this country, he had made the adjustment to his station in the hierarchy of news. He was not near the top, not even remotely in its vicinity, and replaceable. The conclusion he drew from this experience and others like it was simply, 'They pay me to write the news, not print it.'

It exhausted Dhoot to think that readers knew little about the technology they had lined up for. There were facets of its architecture and creation that required public scrutiny, but reporting stories had been such a struggle that there was nothing more he could say. It felt naïve to point out that traditional channels of information no longer served the public interest. 'The whole situation outside and inside the newsroom enabled Aadhaar to ride roughshod over systems of checks and balances, and that was unnerving. Because you don't know what else the government can unleash.'

# 5

# So Much Power

Aadhaar's proliferation was by no means guaranteed. In fact, its existence was threatened when Narendra Modi became prime minister in 2014.

Modi had spent the previous year presenting himself as a dynamic prime ministerial alternative to the old ways of the dynastic Indian National Congress party, while Nilekani, a hero to Bangalore's technologists, had stood in that very election as a Congress party candidate in opposition to a local candidate from Modi's party. He had positioned himself as a selfless visionary, and called his BJP opponent a part of the 'pro-corruption, anti-development forces'. When he declared his candidacy for the constituency of Bangalore South, the specifics of his fortune were revealed. He had over twelve million dollars in his bank accounts, ninety-one million in funds, and his share of the software services company he owned in part was now worth over five hundred million dollars. His wife, once a journalist, now a philanthropist, had assets equal to his own. He was three times wealthier than the next richest candidate in India's 2014 general elections. The idea that Nilekani stood for the people had some faint echoes of truth because a life in politics was seen by many as a path to unimaginable wealth and power. But Nilekani already had both.

The campaigns Modi and Nilekani ran were unlike any Indians had seen before, despite vying for different positions of power. From the start, Modi had a glorious tale for every waking moment. His scars had origin stories involving crocodiles. In biographies and puff pieces written by friendly writers, Modi was the son of a tea seller, who grew up in a house the size of a train compartment; the floor of his home was matted with dung, and despite having no money, the family took care of a Muslim child for a year; he swam across a lake three times a day to touch the flag on top of a temple, evading twenty-nine crocodiles whose tails cut like swords; an astrologer saw greatness ahead, but for years he was a recluse; he wandered the Himalayas for a time, sleeping with his clothes under a pillow so that the creases would be ironed out by the next morning; he kept a beard at the suggestion of a swami. In these stories, he was touched by holiness. Heroism, athleticism, kind-heartedness and reflection came to him easily. Like Dayanand Saraswati and other sages before him, he was free of attachments, and distanced himself from the past by burning what he owned.

In 2009, Haima Deshpande, a journalist with *Open* magazine, found an overlooked attachment. Deshpande visited a village in the state of Gujarat, where Modi was then chief minister, to meet a woman known to be his wife. Jashodaben Chimanlal Modi was fifty-seven, a much loved primary school teacher who lived in a tenement with no bathroom. She was eager to tell her story, but soon the school she taught at was visited by men who dissuaded her from speaking with journalists. She ran away. Deshpande wrote, 'People close to her say that she longs for that phone call from her husband, the call asking her to come and live with him forever.' (Modi acknowledged their marriage in his nomination papers during the 2014 elections.) The appearance of distance from the weight of dependants gave Modi the aura of a man dedicated to service. 'I have no family ties, I am single. Who will I be corrupt for?' he said during his election campaign. About him, a reputation grew: of spartan tastes and nights spent tackling intractable problems. After years of corrupt excess, the messaging implied, India could choose a man who wanted nothing. He spoke words that Indians responded to: he would provide ten million jobs, reform the notoriously complex taxation system, build bullet trains and hydroelectric power plants, retrieve 'black' money from Swiss bank accounts and implement market reforms. 'When people are hungry, you talk development, not [Ram temple],' a BJP official told a reporter in 2009.

The viability of Modi's message of progress hinged on his ability to keep the electorate's attention on the future, a safe distance from his past. On 27 February 2002, barely five months after Modi first became chief minister of the state of Gujarat, religious pilgrims and extremist Hindu organisation members arrived on the Sabarmati Express. They had attended a religious programme held in Ayodhya. In their own eyes, they were faithful sevaks—servants—of Ram. The train halted at a station in Godhra, a municipality east of Ahmedabad, on tracks marking a sharp division: the northern part was dotted with Hindu temples, while mosques speckled the south. The train began to leave, and then stopped once more. Someone had pulled the emergency chain. Words were exchanged between the Hindus on the train and the Muslims outside, followed by stones. A fire started. The blaze burned a compartment, and dozens inside were killed. In those early hours, every claim was disputed. Was it fifty-seven dead, or sixty? Had the pilgrims beaten a Muslim vendor at the station and forced a Muslim woman into the train? Why had the train stopped there? Had over a thousand Muslims ambushed the train? The headlines in the morning papers were written to incite: '1500-strong mob butchers 57 Ramsevaks on Sabarmati Express', the *Asian Age* splashed. Other front pages were just as provocative.

Over the next few days, Hindu mobs seemed to have the freedom to do as they wished, while the state's security apparatus was nowhere to be found. Modi, the chief minister, stayed silent. Ehsan Jafri, a Muslim member of Gujarat's parliament, reportedly called him several times after armed men surrounded his home. A witness said, 'Finally, Modi picked up the phone and used an abusive word for Jafri, and said he was surprised Jafri hadn't been killed already . . . I saw him being dragged away by the mob. They hacked him, poured petrol over him and set him on fire.'

After the VHP called for a shutdown in a Muslim suburb in Ahmedabad, the Bajrang Dal ran wild while the police watched. 'The crimes in Naroda Patia were among the most brutal in the state,' Human Rights Watch found. 'An eyewitness to the murder of a six-year-old boy named Imran . . . described, for example, how "petrol instead of water was poured into [the boy's] mouth. A lit matchstick was then thrown inside his mouth and the child just blasted apart."' As in previous riots, BJP functionaries crossed over to become activists for the militant groups, confirming the belief that there was little to separate the RSS's political arm from its enforcers. The names of the organisations were different, but they shared the same personnel, giving members who went door to door seeking votes during elections the freedom to take as many lives in any manner they chose.

A Bajrang Dal member named Babu Bajrangi told an undercover journalist how the massacre at Naroda Patiya happened. 'Narendrabhai had come,' Bajrangi told the journalist, referring to Modi respectfully. 'He didn't come inside Patiya. But he had a firm grip on what was happening [on the day of the massacre]. The police didn't make a sound, and that was because of Narendrabhai. Otherwise you won't believe how many policemen were present on the scene. If they wanted, they could have killed us.' Over several hours, approximately five thousand men, armed with 'swords, hockey sticks, pipes . . . diesel, petrol, acid', killed at least seventy people, raped women and children, and set houses on fire. Bajrangi told the journalist, 'There was this pregnant woman, I slit her open . . . Showed them what kind of revenge we can take if our people are killed. They shouldn't even be allowed to breed . . . Whoever they are, women, children, whoever. Nothing to be done with them but cut them down. Thrash them, slash them, burn the bastards.'

Witnesses found their testimonies had been changed, and discovered that the police had instead charged them with crimes. 'The police did not record any names in the [report],' one witness told Human Rights Watch. Other witnesses were reportedly bribed, or recanted. Justice was so elusive that the father-in-law of the pregnant woman Bajrangi killed said, 'Even if they don't get punished a lot, they should at least get punished a little.'

After Modi called for early elections, he was re-elected with an even larger margin.

By 2013, Modi was everywhere: on WhatsApp in distant countries, in holograms in distant villages, on news channels for everyone in between, and most of all, inside people's heads. He told the story of who he was, and reminded people of the life they could lead if only the Congress party, whose six decades in power had been worthless and corrupt, was removed. He appealed to them to choose a 'Congress-mukt Bharat', an India free of the Congress party. Every morning people woke up to catchy messages about him, and short clips of his speeches. In Mumbai, one advertising agency claimed to have produced over two hundred films and a thousand other advertisements, all about Modi. 'Research indicated that Narendra Modi's recall was higher' than his party's, the agency's creative director said, and so they focused on him, rather than the developmental messages they would have in a normal election. At the same time, technologists rejuvenated by the possibility of change offered their skills and built Modi's party databases, and young men flooded social media platforms with messages promoting Modi as the only rational choice for voters. In return for promises from Modi's colleagues that they would protect Hindu traditions, Baba Ramdev, a robed businessman whose televised yoga sessions had a large viewership, commanded his army of followers to spread the word about Modi's prowess all over the country, and collect phone numbers to harvest for political messaging. A software entrepreneur with a reputation as India's most prolific spammer assisted the campaign by hosting websites dedicated to propagating alternative histories of Modi. Online, Modi's campaign managers worked with Facebook to flood a constituency of undecided voters with clips of his rivals stumbling over their words. Meanwhile, Modi attended 'over 5,000 events and 470 political rallies'. His party members organised street plays and political stand-up acts.

The outreach and literature had been years in the making. An entrepreneur who created software for political parties said he was surprised by the sophistication of the BJP's organisation when he visited its data centre back in New Delhi in 2009. 'They had all their processes catalogued like HSBC's IT department,' he said. The party was in the process of transforming how it communicated with its members, in ways that would define future elections. Its million volunteers prided themselves on the party's discipline, but didn't check emails, and couldn't be reached for sudden vote calls. The party aimed to form the government, and it needed technology to strengthen its ground game. It wanted a secure instant messenger, 'like WhatsApp', for its workers and bureaucrats, one they could use to spread party messages immediately, and ensure they spoke with one voice.

The entrepreneur built the party a platform to share data and fetch internal knowledge for candidates, and he attended weekly party meetings. 'They had this clarity, and were dependent on tech.' But the party's discussions on how they would use technology made him uncomfortable. 'Identifying an enemy was very important' was all he would say, alluding to conversations about religion.

While Modi campaigned for national office, in the early months of 2014, Nilekani left his small glass-fronted office on a quiet street in Koramangala, a Bangalore neighbourhood, to walk the streets of Bangalore South, stopping by local resident welfare associations, making promises that were more modest than Modi's. He assured his listeners that he would build them local parks and put an end to the persistent mosquito problem. The promises were hardly novel, but Nilekani and his young campaign managers believed that a promise by him was worth more. 'It was like, "we get it done",' Anshuman Bapna, a volunteer, said.

When he went to voters, it was not as a technology billionaire or a visionary, but as the man responsible for creating the largest identity project in history. It was because of him that when a person opened a bank account an officer asked for their Aadhaar number. It was because of him that a person on welfare no longer had to prove their identity every month, only press their thumb onto a fingerprint reader and receive their due. It was because of him that phone companies verified new customers in seconds, not days.

Within five years of Nilekani's appointment, government departments had enrolled over six hundred million Indian residents. 'What he did, and the speed he did it with, was astonishing,' a professor of computer science at the Indian Institute of Technology in Delhi told me. (He was a critic of the programme.) This work enshrined Nilekani's reputation as someone who could execute plans within government, the hardest place to get anything done. That made him, in the eyes of his campaign team, uniquely suited to a political moment with corruption on the agenda. One of his campaign managers told me: 'It was like the stars had aligned.'

Inside their office in Koramangala, a team of bright young campaigners, trusted advisers, data scientists and consultants strategised Nilekani's path to power, replacing the grassroots activists and politicians found in other campaigns. They would turn him from a man admired for his business acumen and achievements to a leader worth voting for. To begin with, Nilekani's face was on ads and websites, and his campaign flooded the radio. They used electoral rolls and added new information beside each name. Volunteers with phones went door to door and asked, 'What are your local issues? Have you lost your job at any point in the last few years? Have you struggled with any illness over the past year?' His campaign staff struggled to describe just how omnipresent he was in Bangalore South. 'Everywhere. He was everywhere,' a sceptic who worked on the campaign said. Charged with spreading the word about their candidate, they were then overwhelmed by him. They could not scroll down a webpage without seeing him on some advertising placeholder. If they had once been dubious about his intentions—one volunteer suspected it was a vanity campaign—they had since come to believe that Nilekani's campaign represented a new conjoining of politics with corporate effectiveness. Some worked on ways to clean up voter rolls. Some worked on making door-to-door campaigning more effective. They were optimistic. The postal code Nilekani had decided to campaign in had 'the most educated, most forward-thinking people in the country', Bapna, the volunteer, told me. More than eighty-four per cent of the men living within its borders were literate. While literacy in individuals was no marker of their participation, research showed that more educated neighbourhoods tended to have a higher turnout.

Bapna, a graduate from Nilekani's alma mater, the Indian Institute of Technology, had admired him for years. He recalled the day Nilekani noticed him hauling a heavy computer up the stairs at a hotel and helped him. And he never forgot how, when he needed advice on a problem, but was uncertain about whether he had succumbed to the habit of seeing every problem through the lens of technology, Nilekani told him not to shy away from what he knew. He remembered Nilekani saying, 'When you're trying to make large change happen, you have to play to your strengths.' The time was ripe for what he could offer, he told Bapna. 'The current establishment does not understand the disruptive power of technology. And because they don't get it, you have a window of opportunity to execute. But the time they wake up to the fact that it's going to change things dramatically, you'll have embedded tech deeply into the ecosystem.' Bapna respected Nilekani, and took this to heart.

Nilekani's campaign was designed to minimise failure. His staff were advised by Barack Obama's former campaign manager, who educated them on which datasets to keep and discard, and how different databases could be integrated with one another. He had a legislative plan for his first hundred days in office, created especially by a consultancy company. Internal polling showed the approach working, a staff member said: the difference between Nilekani and his opponent was less than five per cent.

And yet, when his campaigners stepped outside to ask the voters about their candidate, they were surprised by how anonymous a famous person could be. 'About seventy-five per cent did not even know of his existence. They simply didn't know him,' a data scientist told me. He said that the office they worked out of was a bubble that separated them 'from the concerns of people on the ground. It really made Nilekani feel even more of an elitist.' Nilekani sat among his constituents while they talked, unsure of his Kannada, the language of the state. His authenticity was in question. 'This is a man who walks among billionaires and heads of industry. He doesn't have a sewage pipe overflowing outside his house and smelling up the place.

He doesn't have mosquitoes to deal with. So when he talks to people about the mosquito menace, it sounds wrong,' the data scientist said.

Nilekani's approach had other problems. A Congress party volunteer claimed that his team spent about two hundred million rupees on the election, but the money did not reach the volunteers or tools that helped bring out the vote. The volunteer was taken aback by the naiveté on view. 'Someone would tell them that he needed books, and they would say, "What do you need books for?" The person would have to clarify that, by "books" he wanted money. They just didn't understand,' he said. He drew a parallel with another famous Indian who discovered the country's habits and preferences. 'It's said that Gandhi learned about India by travelling on its trains. Nilekani should have spent years on trains before doing this. He needed social scientists. He needed people from the humanities. But he got volunteers from McKinsey, from INSEAD.'

Nilekani did not foresee how much the 'Modi wave', as editors and Modi's party called it, would overwhelm reasonable campaign promises. Nilekani lost badly in Bangalore South, by over 200,000 votes. Although he wished his opponent well and declared that he would not quit politics, he was privately disappointed with the lack of support he received from the Congress party, the volunteer said. According to one strategist, at a meeting with two Congress politicians who made him promises, Nilekani clammed up and only smiled, 'as if he was saying, "you people say one thing but do another".' I asked the strategist how he would define Nilekani's campaign, and he replied immediately, 'Nilekani found new ways to look at data, but he had too much faith in what that data could do. He didn't touch the people who needed to be touched.' Another told me, 'He was the right man, but in the wrong party.'

The disappointment of the election made way for another concern: Aadhaar was under threat. This scepticism had, until then, spread no further than a loose collective of critics. But as the 2014 election campaign rolled on, and the likely outcome became clearer, members of the BJP turned against the identity project. 'Lock, stock and barrel, it will be thrown into the dustbin,' declared Nilekani's opponent, who also happened to be the general secretary of the BJP. He said that the project had not been debated adequately in parliament nor discussed enough with citizens, the money spent on it had been wasted, and that the US and the UK had rejected similar identity programmes. Modi joined in, tweeting, 'On Aadhaar, neither the team that I met nor PM could answer my Qs on security threat it can pose.' Up and down the chain of leadership within Modi's party, the identification programme was subject to scrutiny.

Modi's opposition took the programme's critics—many of whom were ideologically opposed to the RSS—by surprise. They were concerned with rights and freedom, which Modi, they were certain, was not. As chief minister of Gujarat, Modi centralised power. He picked key personnel, compromised independent institutions, and there was also the matter of 2002. The programme's opponents briefly considered working with the RSS to roll back the programme, but decided against it, the missile designer Colonel Mathew Thomas told me. 'The left liberals do not like the RSS,' he said.

At the end of June, a month after Modi became India's undisputed leader, Nilekani asked for a meeting with him. He had heard there were plans to finally fold the programme into the National Population Register, a list of every resident of India. After the elections, Nilekani told a journalist 'there was a vacuum' in which the home ministry, which handled internal security, had attempted to take over his creation. After all the work he had put into it, he said to the journalist, 'the thought that Aadhaar could be irretrievably shut down was heartbreaking'. At noon on 1 July 2014, he entered the prime minister's office.

There, he later told the reporter, he explained the project's achievements to Modi, and showed him the potential it still had. He talked about how inexpensive it was, and the money it could still save by reducing corruption. According to accounts of the meeting, Modi had questions about the legal challenges to the programme that threatened to curtail its progress.

In his notes of the meeting with Nilekani, the reporter described Nilekani responding that the problem could be easily resolved. Nilekani recalled saying that a bill giving Aadhaar legal sanction was kept ready and only needed Modi's approval.

Nilekani told the reporter what he had said to the prime minister. 'If you wanted, you could get it passed in this session itself. Once you pass the bill, the Supreme Court will lay off the matter.' Nilekani left the new prime minister with a big number. If the programme was left alone, he said, it would save Modi seven billion dollars by identifying 'ghost' beneficiaries and plugging leaks. Translated into crores, the largest common unit of measurement conceivable to most Indians, it formed a pleasing number that Modi could take to the public: fifty thousand crores. According to the reporter's notes of his meeting with Nilekani, Aadhaar's creator emerged from the room confident that he had done enough to ensure the programme's survival. It had taken half an hour.

After the meeting, Modi expanded and asserted his control over the project. He told ministers that he was in charge, and that 'surely [they] had no problems working under the prime minister', Nilekani told the journalist. They heard the implicit threat and fell in line. A newspaper reported that not only was Modi no longer an Aadhaar sceptic, he wanted to enrol a billion people quickly. He told his finance minister, Arun Jaitley, to sort out the project's entanglements so that it would be constitutional. Two days later, Jaitley's first budget included a three-hundred-million-dollar allocation for the project, a significant rise over the previous year. Modi later declared he hadn't been against the project, only its inadequacies. Besides, he said, his predecessors lacked imagination. 'We expanded the scope, amplified the scale, and augmented the speed,' Modi said. He claimed that due to the expansion, the project had saved India over seven billion dollars.

The only accounts of what took place in the meeting between Modi and Nilekani have come from Modi, Nilekani and 'sources close to' the men present in the room. In the minds of people who watch the identity project, the meeting has achieved a singular significance. Little is known about what was said, and yet, after it took place, everything changed. The project was renewed, and was more hungry than ever for data. A programme that had been introduced as voluntary now expanded into every facet of life in ways that made opposition to it almost impossible. They had met in June 2014. By October that year, Modi had ordered that phone numbers should be linked to Aadhaar. The following August, newspapers reported that the government was 'considering' joining educational records to the number to help students and employers, and 'tackle the fake educational degree menace'. Within weeks, the number was mandatory for starting a new business.

All the while, the population received clarification upon clarification from media, officials, the courts and Aadhaar's overseers that identification numbers were not compulsory, and that denying anyone services in its absence was wrong, possibly even illegal. Still, the Aadhaar number proliferated, propelled in mysterious ways, reaching into lives in unexpected and unpleasant ways, turning unlucky individuals into examples of the fate that would befall resistors. Bank customers who held out complained that their accounts had been frozen without warning, sometimes all at once, and sometimes a woman without a number gave birth outside a hospital's gates, and in the hours after a person's passing, their family would learn that a number was required for a death certificate. The interruption of grief, the interference with comfort and the halting of routines all focused the mind on the number's significance. In this way the number's necessity was communicated, while the population was assured that their suffering was not sanctioned by law.

I phoned Jawhar Sircar, a writer, politician and former government bureaucrat from West Bengal whose enthusiasm for plain speaking had made him a valuable source for insightful and entertaining commentary on bureaucracy and the government. Sircar immediately lived up to his reputation as a buttoned-down administrator with no time for niceties or tradition. He had it in for Modi, blaming him for compromising the reporting structure of India's public broadcaster, an organisation he had led for four years. I listened to him rail against the prime minister's lack of 'propriety and shame', and explain 'how much Modi hates compromise', I asked him what it would take to change Modi's mind.

'It's not possible to change his mind,' Sircar said. 'He is looking for ideas to publicise. Style and presentation matter to him. Substance is boring to him. You have to understand, he's not a normal human being.' He went on, describing the prime minister as ravenous for credit, hungry to inaugurate infrastructure projects that had nothing to do with him.

What could Nilekani have said that changed Modi's mind about Aadhaar during the meeting, I wondered. Sircar took the opportunity to vent his feelings about the prime minister.

'You now have, for the first time in the history of the world, such great details, oho!' he said. His mind leaped at the possibilities, knowing what he knew about how information was used within government. 'That data gets you a master database. Then you have smaller databases for everything. One links to the other, the other links to the other. The data comes out popping. You have a super database. Nilekani probably had to hold on to [Modi]. "So much power!"' he imagined the prime minister's breathless reaction in Hindi. '"So much power without doing anything?" Nilekani would have held him, and said, "Yes!"'

There are people who know their place in the world and accept its humbling ways; signing up for the number and marking themselves forever is a rational decision, given the alternative. Who wanted the jhanjhat, the khitpit, the thousand minor irritations that resistance to unexplained government imperatives caused? It was the easier thing to do, because then the banks and phone companies would stop calling many times a day for weeks on end, and days would go by pleasantly and without confrontation, and a person wouldn't feel like a deviant and at a remove from the majority for not having an identification number. What could one say if someone asked why they didn't have their number? Even the absence of the identification number revealed something about a person. Explaining meant showing you disagreed with consensus, with the idea behind the number's necessity and, by extension, with the state. All this when the political party ruling India saw unity in conformity.

Putting down the phone after yet another demand for identification and an annoyed exchange, I would spend hours wound tight, as if I had been in a fight.

*Have you linked Aadhaar to your account?*

*No.*

*When will you do it?*

*I don't know.*

*Your account will be frozen.*

*The court has judged that you cannot do this. It is illegal,* I would say hesitantly, unsure of what exactly the courts had said.

*We have orders.*

*From where?*

*Above.*

*But your bank already has my ID. I have been your customer for fourteen years.*

*Even so, sir.*

Two or three times a day, weeks and months on end. There was no resolution, only an impasse, because my refusal was in defiance of an entity that did not see defiance as an expression of independence. That was why the act of refusal felt heroic one minute, and utterly pointless the next. My defeat, looking back, was assured by the manner in which the number's necessity was communicated. However personal the quarrel was for me, my persuaders were faceless, limitless and motivated by daily targets. To them I was an unnumbered inconvenience. They would call and repeat the words of their predecessors on the line emotionlessly, as they had been trained to do. Holdouts I knew shared notes about how they were coping with the number's insistence in everyday life. One year, when the number was still voluntary, the annual tax form was designed to make it mandatory. Without it, the form could not be submitted online. Who had done so? Who knew? The actions of individuals were absorbed into the larger spectre of a government department. The community of holdouts shared a secret sequence of numbers that thwarted the requirement. These moments of satisfaction were rare, and passed quickly. They offered each other advice about using the right tone and sequence of words to deal with inflexible officials and get some minor task done. But that these conversations were happening at all was a sign of a tightening life, like a condition that could not be cured, only managed.

For some time, I was puzzled by the intensity of my angst, and why the loss felt irreversible. I think it was this: over time, the country's impositions on choice and expression had grown heavier, as when beef was removed from restaurant menus, and audiences were provoked by people who did not stand for the national anthem in cinemas when they were under orders to do so. (There would be more impositions still: Modi would announce one evening that to counter the proliferation of unaccounted wealth he was withdrawing large currency notes at once, sending people to queue outside banks to exchange their notes for weeks across the country. *It was for the good of the country*, people told each other. He would appear once more to announce a sudden lockdown at the start of the pandemic, catching the country unaware and leaving them with four hours in which to travel home before the trains were halted, the roads cleared and state border crossings closed. Migrations greater than even those during Partition would occur. *If Modi has done it, he must have thought hard about it*, people said to themselves.) Those impositions could still be managed, by travelling to a different state, or standing outside the cinema while the anthem played. The restriction on choice could be thwarted by exploiting the gaps and duplicity of leaders who made different promises and imposed different restrictions in different constituencies. The number, however, was universal and more personal, aimed not merely at individual choice, but at the body itself. There had been no meaningful dialogue about this, no real attempt at persuasion, just the blunt force of government instruction. My resistance and ideas about the programme were an inconvenience because the compact these callers wished to enter into was with my identifying markers, as if they were someone else. And so, when the day came in 2017 or 2018, I dragged my body to a bank and it flung the papers the registrar needed to verify my identity one last time, and when he told it to look at the camera it opened its eyes reluctantly, and placed its digits on the reader when he told it to do so, although it thrashed around a little and smudged the glass in anger. I accompanied it outside the bank later, and we stood on the pavement and stared at the traffic and tried not to think about what had just happened. Something had been taken away by force, and there was no one to complain to.

Some weeks later the number arrived on a card, and we buried it under a pile of papers in a drawer we rarely opened.

Even then, I wondered if I was making too much of it, especially when few people around me were as troubled. They seemed to manage the arbitrary foisting of rules so much better than me. For most of them it was just another thing to accept, and they moved on. When orders came from 'above', that catchword for a mysterious authority, the only realistic course—a course free of trouble and potential repercussion—was to fall in line. Perhaps one day trouble would come, but that was a fifty-fifty matter, while causing trouble would invite trouble one hundred per cent guaranteed. They did not necessarily think about how the number would be used, or the utility that government departments would see in it, or about oppression in the distance. It seemed that way because the voices that spoke up about such things were decried as elitist or Luddite, and out of touch with the needs of a developing nation; when food and housing were still a problem, a matter like privacy receded in importance.

The CEO of a small Indian bank who had been in the business for over three decades told me that banks thought the number was as legitimate as a social security number. That, and 'government also pushing the number', was why they called endlessly. 'It was the best way to prove your identity. From an account monitoring perspective, it told us that you were a genuine person.' He began by listing its many benefits to me, including its utility in reducing fraud. Since each account was attached to the number, he said, 'with the number linked to your tax number, your accounts are automatically known'.

I tried to draw him out of his caution, asking if the links made by the number revealed a person financially. He laughed, agreeing immediately with a corporate euphemism. 'It was left unsaid that it provided a financial overview.'

The authorities in charge of the tool's oversight concerned him. The ability to identify account holders accompanied an arsenal of punitive tools ranging from arrest to financial ruin. 'If the powers that be want to lock me out of my accounts, I'll be helpless. I've seen cases of corporates having accounts frozen, and their entire cycle of payments is thrown out of gear. It has had serious cascading impacts that even triggered bankruptcy.'

Even as he thought about the number, he wondered about the prerogatives of the ruling party. 'Protecting you from the protector is the challenge. It's very difficult to take them on. We all know this, and we don't want to talk about it. It's like, "You enjoy your own place, and don't take on the powers that be". That is the reality. The point is that people think that all that's happening is for the larger good. You hear that your concerns are elitist. But for a nation to be really developed, there have to be different viewpoints. It can't be my way or the highway. At the end of the day I feel I have a right to meet who I want to. This is, after all, supposed to be a democracy. That level of tolerance comes with maturity. But the people we have given power to . . .' It was understood that a person's friendships and acquaintances were grist for questioning loyalties and alleging seditious behaviour. Meeting people freely and attending protests was hazardous.

He paused, and then said haltingly, 'Playing the religion card and linking it to the overall development of the country is dangerous. That narrative gets dangerous.' The discussion's political turn was unsurprising. For those who cared to think about it, for those who picked at the thread of identification technology, they soon found themselves thinking about politics, nationalism and communalism. But only if they cared to think about where it led.

# 6

# The Case for Identity

A woman blazed through the checkpoint, her robe flying behind her. A constable started after her but stopped and shouted, 'Ma'am, you forgot the biometrics!' The biometrics was a little box hung on a wall by the gate. Visitors to the Supreme Court complex paid it homage with their thumbs. It was about nine in the morning, and clerks, copyboys, lawyers, surly tellers, petitioners and respondents all stood in a line to enter the Supreme Court complex, when a woman blazed through the checkpoint, her robe flying behind her. A constable started after her but stopped and shouted, 'Ma'am, you forgot the biometrics!' The biometrics was a little box hung on a wall by the gate. Visitors to the Supreme Court paid it homage with their thumbs. The constable's conscientiousness marked her as new. A male guard, seated, reclining, old and experienced, spoke slowly: 'It's her problem.' At the court's highly guarded entry points, the biometric age had dawned with a stutter.

The lawns were renewed by the overnight drizzle, and a festive scaffold had sprouted. Court reporters waiting for calls from their editors sat on the lawns with their cameras positioned on tripods and pointed to the Supreme Court's distant dome and the fluttering flag above it. It was September 2018, in the middle of Dipak Misra's final week as the most troubling head of the court in recent memory. Earlier that year, four Justices had called an extraordinary press conference to say that Misra's decisions had failed to protect the institution of the Supreme Court. They were 'convinced that democracy is at stake'. The immediate reason for the press conference was Misra's allocation of a sensitive case connected to Amit Shah, Modi's chief strategist and the president of the BJP. Misra, the master of the roster by dint of his position, had allocated the case to a man considered sympathetic to the BJP.

Misra had left the most pressing issues for his final week: temples, taxes, the identification project. Long cloth partitions were being erected for his farewell lunch on the lawn. A row of cooks on a row of tables smiled and laughed as they cut rows of vegetables in preparation for the meal. It was festive, adding a touch of good riddance to the goodbye.

The court was built of red and tan sandstone held up by 5,000 tonnes of steel. It was constructed in the fifties, when Delhi's public works department had its first Indian chief architect. He made it in the overbearing style of the departed colonialists. Now law students wearing shiny shoes but no socks took photos of themselves under the giant flag. The room directly below the dome was Court No. 1, the courtroom of the Chief Justice. Only registered journalists and people with matter before the court could enter. A guard outside the room looked at my documents and, pointing to the doors, said, 'Your pass allows you entry only until here.' When the doors opened, a thick brown curtain fluttered out, revealing the judges.

The best place to stop and watch was not the exposed yard in front of the main court, but down a corridor on the left. At the entrance of Court No. 5, a weary old guard was seated outside the room all day on a metal bench, and he rose only occasionally to hold the door open for famous lawyers. His lanyard marked him as Delhi police. It was only eleven, and already the guard was conserving his energy. His body searches started at the waist and ended at the thigh, with his palms moving in the air like a security wand. Watching him was harrowing, and his role made no sense. The room beat like a heart, inhaling and exhaling lawyers every second. They nudged each other, slid past each other, shook hands over other heads, stretched their necks to catch the judges' words, and ran out while the guard performed the task he had been given.

The cause list outside detailed three hundred and fifty-nine cases for the day for this one courtroom alone. At 11.40, an hour after the court had opened, a digital sign above the doors announced that the judges were hearing their eighth case of the morning. In the next five minutes, they would adjudicate three more cases. Case numbers appeared and disappeared in minutes. Within four minutes, the morning's twelfth case was before them. Outside the court, even more lawyers stood around for hours, waiting for the seconds that the court would grant them. These were mostly junior advocates assigned the task of waiting, watching and warning their seniors as the numbers on the digital sign ticked towards their case. As their number drew closer, the main lawyers would materialise, often with a phone held to their ear. As I watched the lawyers and their clients rush around in the corridor, I remembered a chat with a relative my age on a balcony that overlooked a cricket field in South Bombay. He had been entangled in a decade-old court case over a property deal, and his hair had turned white prematurely. Looking at the unlit field, he said, 'You wait all your life for fucking justice and it's suddenly fucking done.'

As I watched, files started to appear. Income-tax matters hauled in on large trolleys were wrapped in brown card paper and bound in white cord. They had once been dog-eared from use, but now they had no ears at all. They were dumped beside the guard in fifteen piles that were each four feet high. The guard said expressionlessly that every day was the same. All these people, all these files, all these old disagreements had to be heard by one courtroom that day, between 10.30 a.m. and 5 p.m., not counting the hour the judges left for lunch. The next day would bring new piles. I walked around the court's corridors, registering its rhythms, the way lawyers moved from one room to the next, where they ate, the dark sports shoes they wore beneath their robes. At about 4.30 p.m., a legal news website announced that the Aadhaar case judgement would be delivered the next day, 26 September 2018. My phone began to ping with messages from lawyers and others I had spoken with. For the rest of the day it flashed notifications from friends, family, technologists, designers and activists. They were relieved that the day had arrived, and anxious about what it would bring.

In comprehending the speed with which cases were dealt with, the abnormality of what took place in 2018 became more apparent. In the matter of *K.S. Puttaswamy v. Union of India*, as the cases against Aadhaar were collectively known, throats were cleared, schedules were emptied and time slowed down in the court of the Chief Justice of India. At the outset it was decided that the matter of the identity project would be settled once and for all. And so, between 17 January and 10 May, for thirty-eight days out of the seventy-three that the court was in session, a constitutional bench that consisted of the Chief Justice and four brother Justices heard arguments for and against the identification system from morning to early evening in Court No. 1. Only one hearing had lasted longer in the history of independent India.

One young lawyer, Rahul Narayan, described a path to the Supreme Court that was so bumpy and frustrating that it had turned him cynical; for six years the petitioners had approached the courts, and were confronted by the judicial system's inadequacies. 'The number of judges who have heard [our arguments] and have moved on, either because of retirement, or because different benches have heard it . . . and to explain the entire thing over and over . . .' he said. 'I don't know if at the end we'll jump off [a building].' Another lawyer, Apar Gupta, told me about a senior advocate who for weeks had unsuccessfully asked the courts to begin hearings on the right to privacy, a vital part of the Aadhaar case, and was caught in traffic when the hearings finally began.

The delays gave the Authority time to spread the number, and the additional enrolments then made it more difficult to argue against. Narayan said that the delays were likely a ploy. 'It was clear by 2013 or 2014 that the government's strategy was to stretch it out for as long as possible, enrol as many people as they could in the meantime, and then tell the court, "Look at how many people have enrolled."' The weight of the numbers would exert pressure on the court's decision. 'If they strike it down, they will have to face criticism that the government has already spent a thousand crores on it.' The court had only the Constitution behind it, and was wary of the limits of that support before public opinion; it could not be seen as profligate.

A constitutional lawyer, Menaka Guruswamy, saw in the case a threat to the questions about the nature of citizenship. She broke it down into a series of questions when I called her: who are we to government? Who are they to us? How are we seen? As ourselves, or as our habits? How much are we seen? What is in our power? 'Time and constitutions rule how these questions are answered, but here the court has to consider an additional question: how did a national identification system to which registrants offered their retina scans and thumbprints affect the answers?' Guruswamy told me. 'Few cases in India have been as crucial.'

When the Aadhaar hearings took place in January 2018, Shyam Divan, a senior advocate, arrived early at the court. He had been uncertain about the case at first, Khera, the economist, told me. He said that a judge would see straightaway his discomfort with matters of welfare. His expertise was in commercial law and, because he came from a life of comfort, he would not be convincing. He was born into a family of distinguished lawyers, and lived in a large New Delhi house made of smooth grey stone and glass, outside which stood a row of expensive cars, and just beyond them were trees, grass, birds and a small park where elders assisted by helpers walked slowly in the mornings. In the way he spoke, in the way he carried himself, you could see white tablecloths and glinting cutlery and heavy gold-nib fountain pens and quiet libraries. When Khera visited him at his office, she noticed his immaculate large desk, the impressive monitor that lay on it and the window that looked out onto his garden. She remembered him behind it, in a short-sleeved shirt, his brusque manner; not the buttery reserve of the New Delhi elite. She saw him and thought: such a South Bombay boy. She wanted Divan to see that when the identification project was applied to welfare, trouble followed. She invited him out to Jharkhand to see the problems with the identity system, a trip they made with Drèze.

And then, at ten in the morning on the seventeenth day of January in the year two thousand and eighteen, Divan, who represented thirty petitioners, finally laid out the combined understanding and fears of the economists, legal researchers, privacy activists and others as he stood before the judges to explain the foundational problems of the identification project.

No democracy had adopted a tool this capable of upturning civil liberties, Divan said. No tool in any democratic society had even come close, and those tools had been rejected for their potential to cause harm. Permitting Aadhaar to continue would twist the Constitution's aims and protect the state rather than the people of India, he explained. The matter he was slowly coming around to, the matter that lay at the heart of most objections, was that the system enabled unparalleled surveillance. It sought 'to tether every resident of India to an electronic leash', he said. 'This leash is connected to a central database that is designed to track transactions across the life of the citizen.' His words echoed the language of Viraj Chopra, who had envisaged an identity as the sum of a life's transactions. But Chopra's vision was at the very beginning, before the system's use and performance could be assessed. The advocate explained what was possible when the idea that life was a series of recorded and measured transactions reached fruition. He argued that the project gave the government a 'switch' to turn off an individual's identity, causing their 'civil death'. He spent the next six days building the case against Aadhaar, and said that the case was to challenge the constitutional validity of the programme. Along the way, he wanted the court to declare the rights a person had over their own body, and declare, once and for all, that citizens had the right to ask for no record of their transactions to be maintained. He then made way for other arguments.

The hearings concluded on 10 May. With nothing to do but wait for the judges to decide, the petitioners, lawyers and others I spoke with announced with great seriousness that the judgement was imminent. This would be shared in confidence, in a low, wavering, giddy tone, as if they had a direct line to the source. Their information turned out to be wrong, of course, but I saw the need to imagine a date of resolution as desperation for firm footing, for a semblance of security amid all the uncertainty about government, technology and institutional processes. After all, if it was a time when wisdom truly prevailed, if there was no crisis within the Supreme Court, if judicial orders were followed in letter and spirit, if the law conducted its work with propriety—if all these things had worked, the judgement date would have been less significant.

In this wait, imaginations turned to the judges, whose leanings were speculated over. I heard that the youngest judge on the bench had drafted his opinion first, and the rest were continuing to do so. I heard that the youngest judge had written the majority judgement. I heard that judges were sharing each other's opinions and rewriting their own. Every rumour and hint was scrutinised for revelations about the future of the republic.

One evening, during the long silence before the court delivered its judgement, Narayan agreed to stay back at his South Delhi office for a chat. I found him quiet and full of doubt, not just unsure of the probable outcome, because he no longer took for granted that courts would do the right thing, but about whether the case had changed him in some way. When he first took on the case, he followed his own best practices: to be at an arm's length from his clients, and to listen but not buy into their arguments. That distance helped him distinguish effective arguments from outlandish ones.

But over time, as the cases against Aadhaar were heard and delayed, and any public criticisms of Aadhaar were quickly followed by rejoinders in newspapers, he found himself accepting the idea that the identity project was dangerous because it was fuelled by delusion. He was particularly bothered by a surreal moment in court where one of the government's advocates declared that Indians had no fundamental right to privacy. It was one thing to oppose the identity project's critics in court, he said, 'but this is a kind of scorched-earth tactic, you know? I mean what does this mean that there is no right to privacy and how can the government say something like this?' The declaration ground the proceedings to a halt so that the court could decide on whether the Constitution offered a right to privacy. The arguments and stances bothered him deeply as a lawyer but also as a citizen. 'You don't believe—at least initially I didn't believe—that the government is evil and out to get you, that they are going to destroy you in whatever way they can, [by raising] every single constitutional, legal and moral hurdle, like they seemed to have done at the end,' he said. 'It radicalised me.'

When he spoke about being radicalised, he suggested that his experiences in court had made him consider more outlandish theories, an admission that embarrassed him. What he really wanted to tell the judges, although he couldn't bring himself to say it to them—he stuttered along, aware of how it might sound to a listener—was this: he had wanted to fill his argument against the project with references to Nazism. 'But no, nobody wants to do that because it sounds . . .' he said. 'I mean, the Holocaust was such a unique event in human history that to compare anything to it casually is ridiculous, no?'

It was not widespread corruption that had brought the republic to that point, Narayan thought, but the overblown perception of corruption. The bogey had grown so large in the minds of his fellow citizens that it overtook other concerns, such as privacy, he said. 'If corruption is the biggest thing, then all moves to end corruption, whether farcical or effective, tend to be justified by the public regardless of how brutal they are. So even if civil liberties are destroyed on the side, well, you know, *corruption is bad*.' He mimicked the tone of the system's proponents: *Who cares about privacy? If you have nothing to hide, then what is your problem?*

'I think to a large extent all of us should question ourselves about the quality of public disclosure in this country. When we talk in generalisations like, you know, oh, technology is the answer to everything, or that, oh, corruption is evil, are we oversimplifying problems and leaving ourselves open to grand solutions that don't really make much sense?'

He thought the support for Aadhaar was connected to a dissatisfaction with the country's progress. This amused him, because its most ardent supporters were 'people in the middle class who lead reasonable lives, lives which are not full of anger, misery and unhappiness, but [who want] a great amount of destruction for a new India to be born. If I were a poor tribal who has lost all my land in Orissa and who is being victimised by the Maoists on one side and the government on the other, I would be angry and upset at the way the government is structured, and maybe I would do something about it.' He wondered if people took the progress India had achieved for granted. 'Much of the way things have evolved is crap, I agree, but it can be remedied. It needn't be destroyed and built from the ground up, like Pol Pot did in Cambodia. I don't know. I mean, is it a liberal viewpoint or a conservative one that you shouldn't destroy the past completely?'

I mentioned to him the case of Teesta Setalvad, the human rights defender. After the 2002 riots in Gujarat, Setalvad placed the blame for the violence on Modi. Over a decade later, when the national government changed and Modi was elected prime minister, authorities opened cases against her and picked apart the details of her life. That they would build a legal or criminal case against her was widely expected, for that was what happened to human rights defenders, but I was alarmed by how her private financial decisions and purchases were given wide publicity as moral failings. The police account gave the impression that she had squandered donations meant for the poor on alcohol, an allegation her lawyer disproved immediately. The judgement these stories were meant to influence were not the court's, but the public's.

His mind went to the databases, and he brought up National Socialism again. 'The Nazis, you know? The first thing they do is make a list of everybody. Just imagine how much more precise our riots would be if you know how X is owned by a person who is from a certain religion, and how a particular person is personally related. When all of this information is readily available in one particular place, it is not safe from that point alone.' In August 2018, when we spoke, the words had the air of possibility. When I went over my notes of the interview again, in 2023, the possibility had come to pass. Within two years of our speaking, just a few miles from where we spoke, men in East Delhi would precisely target Muslim tenants in Hindu homes, and burn Muslim shops but leave Hindu shops untouched.

On the night of 25 September 2018, hours before the judgement, there was calm, but no peace. A technologist in Bangalore who had provided quiet support to the petitioners decided he would turn off his phone. He suspected the judgement would not be a happy one, for some of the judges were near retirement, and they would not risk the prestigious sinecure that awaited them with a decision hostile to the government. The technologist announced that he would surface a few days later.

In Delhi, an anti-Aadhaar campaigner since 2014 was filled with foreboding. He could understand why someone would submit to the identification system willingly. Probably because they imagined the government was benevolent, he thought. 'We're simply handing power over our lives to them,' he said to me. Once upon a time, he believed the courts would agree with them if they understood how invasive the system was. Now he was not sure. These judges had allowed a PowerPoint presentation created in support of Aadhaar as evidence, so what hope could there be? At his wedding reception, he and his partner, a digital rights campaigner, decked their hall with posters saying, 'Resist the Aadhaar' and 'Aadhaar FAIL!'. On this night, he huddled with other members of Rethink Aadhaar to envisage the future.

In Ahmedabad, Khera planned for the day of the judgement. Over a decade of activism, she had designed a single-page guide to attracting media attention. It was all of fifteen points, a tiny but focused weapon in a meagre arsenal. Her memories of the court were not good. She attended the court at first, writing notes diligently, but stopped after nearly yelling 'liar!' while listening to a government official provide testimony to the judges. 'I couldn't take it,' she said. She had felt the poison, mistrust and steady erosion of decency over years of battle. And so she was grateful for the decision's arrival.

That evening I met with Apar Gupta, one of more than a hundred and seventy advocates on the case, to see how he was feeling at the precipice. Gupta was, by every account, among a small cast of young lawyers who had researched, guided and shaped arguments on the case in recent years. A website called them 'India's Justice League'. Gupta smiled broadly when he emerged from his room. 'This isn't over. I mean, it's just the start,' was the first thing he said. He was referring to the identification project as the first wave of a series of technological challenges that would soon become clear. He was dressed in his black and white court attire. He had sixteen sets of this uniform stitched every year. 'It's a better fit, and I get a good rate,' he said.

He took his place behind a large desk and made me understand that the court case was a result of failure. The problem, he explained, was that planners had created systems without regard for how they would be used. He connected it to an unquestioning belief in technology that saw rights as friction, and an inconvenience. As he spoke I noticed the painting on the wall behind him: a cross-hatched face of a man with a burst of oil paint over his right eye; he looked to the side with his remaining eye, worried and watchful. 'It helps spur more inspiration, less innovation,' Gupta said, smiling. I did not understand. An hour had passed, and he counted over three hundred messages, several of them from journalists reserving his time for comment after the judgement tomorrow.

After I left, Gupta changed out of his white shirt and black trousers and left for a late evening run at Lodhi Garden. He used to be able to run four rounds of the park when his knees were stronger. Gupta turned on his music and ran between the trees until he was soaked. The act of it helped him think better, but also helped him stop thinking. The appearance of calm he usually presented was misleading: he was on edge. By the time Gupta returned home, his parents had finished dinner. They did not mention the next day, and neither did he. They had once asked him to get his Aadhaar number at a nearby registration camp, but became more sceptical after reading his op-eds. He spent the evening speculating about the judgement with other lawyers on a chat group. They had worked together for years, and were anxious about the results. It always happened before a large case until someone or the other remembered that the judgement was only hours away, and there was no point in torturing themselves. He was certain there would be no decisive victory for either the government or his side. There had been such a wide range of objections to the project—from surveillance to its commercial uses, and from its requirement for welfare to the contentious Act of parliament that gave it life—that there would be no total victory or defeat. Parts of it could favour them, and parts could go against them. The 'cause list' for the court announced three separate opinions in the case. He and the other lawyers wondered how each judge had ruled. What would true victory look like? Was it to be found in the moment? Or would it be found over time? He was of the opinion that all the great constitutional victories had been great because they created new legal doctrine, instead of deciding victory and defeat. He ate and bathed, and prepared for an early bedtime: it was 11.30 p.m. His clothes for the court were already ironed and folded on the weekend, a habit formed over ten years of attempting to be more efficient with his time.

The next morning, Gupta woke up before eight, had his breakfast and left for court. It was usually a half-hour drive, but he seemed to encounter more red lights than on other days. He kept checking and responding to his messages until he arrived at the court, where there was no space to park. It was early, about 9.15, and a crowd had already begun to form between the middle sandstone columns outside Court No. 1. Guards turned away dozens who hoped to cajole, bribe and wangle their way in. If only they could pop in for a second behind the large doors and the thick curtains? What if they squeezed against the walls? 'Not allowed,' the sour guards said, proud of the power they possessed at doorways. By now there was not only no room to sit—the seventy-seven chairs in the well meant for lawyers and petitioners were taken, as were the twenty-two in the visitors' gallery; there was no place to stand either. A sea of black robes and serious faces filled the immense space, as dense and stoic as a Mumbai train compartment. They lined up in the aisles, and on every permitted edge of the room, leaning against the waist-high bookshelves. Gupta struggled to get to the front, where the petitioners were, and smiled from across the room when he saw me. He wanted to be right in front, but held back out of respect for the other advocates present. He couldn't presume his work was more important.

About this time, when all the chairs were taken, and there was no more room in Court No. 1, a woman with slightly wild grey hair announced herself to the sentry. The guard saw her light green sari, and then he saw her. Something about her made his authority evaporate. His posture changed, and he stepped aside. 'The media is allowed in, and Usha Ramanathan is allowed in,' a man waiting outside said to a friend. Young advocates enveloped her in a cordon of respect and affection and helped her inside the courtroom with no room. Inside, when they saw her, counsel gladly made way for her. She touched shoulders, made jokes and, near the long black table where lawyers had made arguments she had teased out of theory and intuition, someone sacrificed their chair for her. She asked for the floor instead. Ramanathan, who had recognised a decade before that a troubling new age was emerging in India, one in which citizens would become 'transparent to the state', sat on the floor of the room, and waited to hear if the judges had recognised it too. When advocates and economists could not answer a question, they recommended speaking with her.

Shortly before eleven, the murmur subsided noticeably. A door behind the judges' bench had opened and the curtains at the entry were held aside by turbaned court marshals. Within minutes, five judges emerged, greeted the room simultaneously with palms pressed and sat on maroon velvet chairs that the marshals slid forward. Chief Justice Misra, whose court this was for two more days, sat between the judges. There was the judge D.Y. Chandrachud whose detailed questions during the months-long hearing had convinced Ramanathan's side that he, of all the judges, understood them. It took two court masters to lift a bound copy of their ruling. Their struggle to place it gracefully before the judge who would read it, Arjan Kumar Sikri, was in vain, and he offered to help them.

'Boss, that's a fat judgement,' a lawyer muttered to a man beside him.

From where the case lawyers sat, it appeared four inches thick. All five men considered it at first, as if they had only just realised how mighty their individual work was when put together, and allowed themselves to break character and look happy. Sikri glanced about the room with a smile and reassured the lawyers that the document included written summaries. But on seeing the bound volume, the young lawyers around Ramanathan became subdued. When judgements were written in an expansive mood, all kinds of baffling things happened. One of the young lawyers had explained, only weeks before, the problem with sprawling decisions. 'Thick judgements bring confusion, and often require clarification.' The ruling he had in mind had been made a year earlier, in August 2018, when nine judges agreed that, by birthright, Indians could choose not to be observed and disturbed. That judgement on the right to privacy, which the lawyer believed would sow confusion, was five hundred and forty-seven pages long. The one before the judges now was one thousand four hundred and forty-eight pages long.

Then the judge began to read the first lines of the majority judgement. 'It is better to be unique than the best. Because, being the best makes you the number one, but being unique makes you the only one.' Narayan, who stood in the left half of the court with the other lawyers, had been smiling only moments earlier. As the words were uttered, his face tightened and he stroked his beard and looked at the seal of the Supreme Court above the bench. His gaze swept a wide arc around the judge's chair, landing everywhere except on the speaker. I recognised it as him bracing for disappointment. Justice Sikri was a 'fair and even-tempered judge', a centrist in demeanour and expression, but as soon as Gupta heard the words he knew the opinion, which spoke for the majority of the bench, would 'lean towards the constitutional legitimacy' of the identification programme. 'To my mind, it was a way to indicate that his opinion would not only uphold the legal validity of Aadhaar, but also approve the necessity for it,' he later told me. The lawyers made an effort to remain expressionless and maintain their composure; they practised in this room, and expressing their thoughts like sports fans would have had adverse effects, they feared.

Justice Sikri read from the majority judgement, a block of white with pink Post-its poking out. He said the identity project was unparalleled. 'There has been no other subject matter in the recent past which has evoked the kind of intensive and heated debate wherein both sides, for and against, argue so passionately in support of their respective conviction,' he said, reading from the judgement. 'The petitioners in these petitions belong to the latter category who apprehend the totalitarian state if Aadhaar project is allowed to continue. They are demanding scrapping and demolition of the entire Aadhaar structure which, according to them, is anathema to the democratic principles and rule of law, which is the bedrock of the Indian Constitution.'

'Even outside the Court,' the judges wrote, 'there are groups advocating in favour of the Aadhaar scheme and those who are stoutly opposing the same. Interestingly, it is not only the commoners who belong to either of the two groups but intelligentsia is also equally divided. There have been number of articles, interviews for discourses in favour of or against Aadhaar. Those in favour see Aadhaar project as ushering the nation into a regime of good governance, advancing socioeconomic rights, economic prosperity etc. and in the process they claim that it may make the nation a world leader.'

After Sikri had spoken for almost an hour, he struck down provisions allowing private companies to use the programme to identify their customers. The judges also ruled that children could not be coerced into registering themselves for the project, and that metadata—data that described other data—could not be stored without judicial intervention. 'Human dignity has always been considered from the individual's point of view. We have enlarged the concept of human dignity,' he said. Soon after, he declared that Aadhaar would continue to exist.

From the perspective of civil rights and others who wanted Aadhaar destroyed, Narayan's face was a barometer. He frowned, mostly, watching years of work slip away. He stood hushed and still, raising his eyebrows, muttering 'what?' as the judge spoke. Gupta, meanwhile, thought the point about metadata would make surveillance harder.

Once the judgement was read, three of the five judges signed it. They concurred. The stack was then put before Justice Dhananjaya Yeshwant Chandrachud, the youngest judge, who was on track to become Chief Justice. He was thought of as a liberal judge ('within a framework', a lawyer clarified) and he immediately made it clear that he spoke a different language. 'We need to scrutinise the programme for it affects the future of freedom,' he said. 'The notion that power is absolute is unconstitutional.' Chandrachud called the manner in which Aadhaar had been made mandatory 'subterfuge' and said it was unconstitutional.

Across the room, the lawyers for the petitioners stood rapt, nodding, tweeting. On occasion they recognised a line of argument they had made, and whispered to each other excitedly. 'We were counting our victories,' Gupta told me. 'We knew that the court has a history of dissents becoming majority judgements. It corrects itself over a period of time. It wasn't a hollow expression. It was grounded. When he was reading out parts, they were important methods of reading the Constitution.'

'Dignity ... of individuals cannot be made to depend on algorithms or probabilities,' Chandrachud concluded. 'Constitutional guarantees cannot be subject to the vicissitudes of technology.'

At 12.22, the judges rose, acknowledged the room and left. At the very back of the room, near one of the doorways, I found myself behind two men in safari suits. The lanyards around their necks announced them as officials from the ministry of home affairs.

One said, 'Not bad.'

The other replied, 'Much more to be done.'

Outside, Gupta and the other lawyers were jubilant. 'Do you know what this means for phone tapping?' he screamed. 'They need a judicial order from here on!' Narayan was somewhat subdued.

'They're going to pass a law,' someone said of the Central government.

'What? There's not going to be any parliamentary session before 2019,' someone responded.

'Now it's a fucking political hot potato,' Gupta said.

'I expected no compassion for children, so that was really

progressive,' a journalist who worked with the petitioners said. She was exuberant.

'If Chandrachud had got the majority, they would have struck down the project. That would have been unbelievable,' Narayan said softly, in wonder. 'They don't do it to projects this size.'

'Why couldn't they concur with him? What was stopping stupid Misra? He's retiring this week, right?' the journalist asked.

'He's retiring this week. That's why,' one of the lawyers said, implying that the Chief Justice would be given a comfortable post in retirement by supporting the right side.

The journalist asked the lawyers if they should have emphasised welfare instead of privacy during the hearings. 'We didn't speak on privacy. We spoke about personal liberty,' Narayan said. 'That there is a chilling effect on your activities, the fact that you will be tracked everywhere. And that your identity is separate from identification. Identification is what a state does to you. Identity is what you do to the state.' Narayan's thoughts came fully articulated, with immaculate punctuation.

They left in high dizziness, in a blaze of plans for that evening and the night. Nobody could say what would happen next. No one could truly explain the true effects of the order. They could only see what they wanted to see.

Later, the judgement came from everywhere at once, all one thousand four hundred and forty-eight pages of it. At the offices of the Indian Women's Press Corps in Delhi, the lawyers and activists swarmed to its different parts, attacking it to understand what laws had changed, what laws remained, and what was gone. Someone made the discovery that the main judgement was only forty-seven pages long. As they read it, their cheer began to ebb, and a fury rose in its place. The judges' justifications, one of them pointed out, seemed to have a lot in common with a government minister's talking points during the hearing. That's not the judges' voice, the journalist researcher said, staring at her screen, it belonged to a slippery minister. She shook her head in disgust.

One day, a year after the judgement, I wrote to Ramanathan by email, her preferred mode of electronic communication. Her friends and colleagues were affectionate and protective of her; they would talk and talk about her wild driving and shake their heads at how they communicated with her, but if I asked about how the case against the identity project came together, economists and lawyers who thought nothing of writing searing opinions in print told me 'it would be better' if I spoke to Ramanathan. The project was large, and the tentacles of its complications spread into law, governance, speech, privacy, welfare, banking, disability and many other places. The popular perception was that 'Usha' possessed the imagination and breadth of understanding to grasp them all because she was at the centre of the opposition to the project.

Ramanathan's husband was a Delhi High Court judge, and they lived in a nice bungalow in Lodhi Estate, a nice part of Delhi. The lane outside was quiet but for the sounds of snipping and clipping from behind the compound walls. These sounds of shaping and trimming hinted at luxuries and choices common to places where power resided in Delhi, where someone opened the gate, someone else swept the leaves, a person trimmed the trees, a worker mopped the floor, a helper brought a finger bowl, a cook made the best breakfast that you just had to try. It was accommodation fit for a senior judge, not ostentatious, but sprawling, with enough people around to ensure no discomfort. It was not fancy by Delhi's standards, but there were birds and foliage and a large lawn filled with lemon trees. They hosted parties here. I noticed Ramanathan sitting in an outer room with one leg heavily plastered and resting on a stool. She waved me in with a warm smile, and told an eager cook to get tea and biscuits. Her arms and head moved with her sentences, expressing question, exclamation and full stop. She grimaced in her chair and stretched out to touch her leg. 'I was doing the exciting business of walking,' she said, embarrassed. There was something in her manner that felt familiar, and I imagined she made friends and allies quickly.

In 2011, the *New Yorker* profiled Nilekani, who made clear his irritation with Ramanathan, already his chief critic then, by accusing her of not owning a cell phone. 'That's what I heard,' he said, likening it to choosing to 'go back and living in a cave'. When I asked about her aversion to phones, Ramanathan said that she couldn't afford a landline at home during her first decade in Delhi. 'So what? Who cares? It didn't stop anything. I did my work, I went to the library, I did research, I went to the field. They call a phone convenience. That's what makes it so weird. It's not convenience. It's not convenient to be overheard, to be tracked. It's not convenient to be on call all the time.' Her opposition to the identification project was not the result of an aversion to technology, but from an understanding of its implications. 'We may not know the technology, but we know the meaning of power, the meaning of the market, the meaning of global ambition, the meaning of so many things,' she said, passionately.

Ramanathan signed off her essays and papers as an independent legal researcher whose gaze was set on the jurisprudence of law, poverty and rights. In an *Economic and Political Weekly* essay on eminent domain and displacement published in 1996, Ramanathan scrutinised a colonial-era land acquisition law's shortcomings: 'a law that does not acknowledge displacement and its traumatic overtones, does not mention resettlement, and is unwilling to take the responsibility of rehabilitation, what can be seen in its rooted presence in this field of human suffering is expediency, callousness or arrogance,' she wrote. In the same journal the following year, she explored the effects of manufactured morality on Pakistani women. The expression of that morality was inevitably left to law enforcement, 'specifically the police, and the legitimation of the abuse of this power'.

These papers, along with others that Ramanathan wrote, were at first glance about the interpretation and application of law, but within them lay detailed studies of power, poverty and injustice. If knowledge is constant searching, the papers were her tugging at the roots of systemic failure to understand what had gone wrong.

Although Ramanathan knew about Nilekani, and had read the stories about his appointment, she did not notice the project at first. She had come by the agricultural economist Ramakumar's articles about it, but details about the programme were scant; there was not enough to judge, she said. Then, just as the Authority's representatives had met with representatives of civil society organisations and social scientists at Shimla, they invited Ramanathan for a gathering at the National Law School in Bangalore. Before the meeting, the Authority sent her a draft of the agenda, which she read in alarm. 'It was a horror. It was basically saying, everybody get on to my database. And there was an implicit threat that if you were not in there, you didn't exist.' She imagined that the meeting would clear her doubts about the project. When she arrived there, she noticed that lawyers and biometrics specialists were present. In her recollection, Nilekani wanted a problem solved: the Authority needed resident data from various states, but it had no legal standing of its own. 'So he was like, make a law that will allow them to give it to us,' Ramanathan said. 'It was like a task given to different people to complete this work.'

She remembered snatches of information from the encounter: that the project was a 'tank' of names and identities, for instance. There was an unsettling combination of words. 'What Nilekani said in his presentation made it very plain that there is no innocence to this project. Because he was talking about three words: unique, ubiquitous and universal. That's the first time that I heard those three words being used the way they are being used.' But these generalities were all she was left with—the sensation that 'what is being marketed is not what the project is about. And we don't fully know what the project is about,' she said.

Nilekani and others spoke about the benefits of a Unique Identification, but the details of this UID mattered to Ramanathan. 'You have to think of the whole, and not just bits and pieces of it,' she told me. 'There were no explanations, and there was no document. So it was somebody's utopia, which may be our nightmare. Even at that time my thing was, listen, we need to know what this is. You can't just carry on with a project like this. And you put the poor onto something like this? They don't even know what's happening to them.' Years of working on poverty had informed her views of identification. She remembered being alarmed once before, when voter IDs were issued for the first time in the nineties, and she had imagined the ID would be used to 'map every person', but those fears did not come to pass, because people used it as a form of identity. But the project promised to track the poor, bringing them into the light. This was not necessarily a good thing, Ramanathan said. 'When you work in the area of poverty, you know that the poor are in the twilight zone of legality, and so they need shadows. And we were worried that this kind of finding, identifying, putting them on databases, will remove the shadows.'

She bristled at the audacity of the UID project's creators, frowning with her eyes wide open one moment, smiling incredulously the next. 'They started it without telling us anything about it. And when they started telling us about it, they told us what we needed to do. They didn't tell us what it was, and what it would do to us.' She determined that the project was a danger, and read every document about its internal systems and architecture, its contracts and memorandums of understanding.

Ramanathan, Ramakumar and a number of concerned citizens became part of a group called No2UID. It began as a repository of stories they found in various newspapers and magazines, but soon became a hub for worried journalists, lawyers and other questioning sorts. Understanding the system's details became simpler when expertise and information were collected. 'Once we all got together, we were sharing things, it became much easier [to track the project],' Ramanathan said.

In early 2010, she decided to speak with lawyers about the project. She told me that she did not anticipate a legal challenge just then, but wanted them to grasp its meaning. If she did not prepare them by turning their attention to it immediately, she feared, it would become too large to comprehend. She identified constitutional lawyers, not just public interest lawyers, and asked for meetings with them. It was an opportunity to explain what she had seen to people with set ideas; a chance to understand where they struggled, and understand what they could not see. 'It was a test for me, that I had to convince a lawyer that there can be a problem. If I can't, then maybe I'm not getting it right,' she said. One of the first lawyers she met with, Divan, eventually became the lead lawyer on the case against the system, but she had trouble explaining the system's problems to him at first. He heard her out, and then asked why the poor getting an ID was a problem. 'I said, "Okay, we've got to start from scratch."' In meetings like these, during conversations like these, Ramanathan clarified her objections until Divan and other advocates began to notice the system's transgressions.

All the while, Ramanathan travelled, spoke at seminars and lectures, wrote op-eds titled along the lines of '[Aadhaar] is about data for surveillance, profit, not serving citizens', and managed the coalition's growing areas of expertise. She sought out potential allies and flattered them, as she did a sceptical technologist in Bangalore who later conceded to me that she 'was on the right track'. She visited Aadhaar enrolment centres and discovered a flawed registration process: NGOs would 'introduce' migrants who were complete strangers to the Authority for registration, and lend their address to the migrants, but have no way of contacting them; the identification cards would arrive, but there would be no trace of the migrants. She continued to insist that a profound change was occurring due to the system: 'The use of science and technology to practise the politics of suspicion is a possibility that is finding its way into becoming a fact,' she wrote. These jabs at the system and the Authority were accompanied by a thorough examination of every instruction book, code specification and marketing guide that the Authority published; using the language they contained, she ascertained that the Authority could collect extensive data, that its officials had immunity from prosecution and that biometrics were still an untested technology.

The criticisms were heard and registered by the Authority, according to Ramanathan and others. The sceptical technologist recalled a meeting with one of Nilekani's hires in which just the mention of Ramanathan's name soured the mood. 'He was generally a very cool character, and he just lost it at that point. As far as he was concerned, Usha Ramanathan was some kind of fraud.'

Nilekani's annoyance had amused people I spoke with, and even Ramanathan had stories about the times he had avoided her. When she learned that he would be addressing the National Advisory Council—a group of academics, lawyers, former bureaucrats and representatives of civil society chosen by the prime minister to offer advice on the creation of laws—she told its members that she would sit outside the gates in protest if they didn't hear an alternative point of view. The council invited her to speak. Nilekani did not turn up, however, and a senior emissary from the Authority was sent instead. When members of the council told her that Nilekani would speak with each member individually before a significant presentation to the full council, including Sonia Gandhi, the leader of the ruling Congress party, she decided to do the same. 'I said, okay, two can play this game,' Ramanathan said.

She put across her point of view to nine of the fourteen council members. She was certain that her outreach contributed to Nilekani's absence from the presentation. 'Because if they raised questions with Sonia Gandhi there, it would have been embarrassing. So he just cancelled out,' she said. In Ramanathan's stories, people asked hard questions of the identification programme when Nilekani wasn't their only source of information. But disseminating that information had been challenging. She remembered the months the *Times of India* sat on an opinion piece, the time the editor of a weekly magazine 'sweetly' told her that nobody would publish a negative story about Nilekani, the newspaper editor who said his publication 'was no longer accepting' articles about Aadhaar. 'What is this?' Ramanathan said, her fingers spread out in a question. 'Are you a newspaper or what?'

As she spoke, I sensed a deeper objection to Nilekani. In Ramanathan's opinion, he deserved the Nobel Prize for marketing, his ideas found purchase in surprising ways even among smart policymakers, and he brooked no questioning. But those were minor irritations when compared to the damage he had done to the body politic, Ramanathan said. 'In the last ten years, no one has done more to spread the idea that citizens are criminals than Nandan Nilekani, and for this I cannot forgive him.'

Guests living in her home interrupted apologetically to ask for a driver or to introduce themselves, or just listen to her speak. The cook came in with tea and biscuits, and some hours later with lunch. All the while, Ramanathan talked, sometimes breaking into Tamil. Her answers were practised, but as time passed, and she established my concerns about the project, she relaxed and dug deeper into her own experiences. She told me of her exasperation with economist friends and well-meaning ministers who bought into the idea of an identification project without considering its other effects. She told me about encounters and confidences I could not write about, and people I could not name. My usual reaction to something like this is to bristle, but here it didn't feel like a restriction because the people were not the point. Her stories were about failures of imagination and curiosity, and the absence of independent thought. The backdrop to her stories of the identification project's birth was one of extreme vulnerability—an opening for other dangers to come through.

'There's a certain clubbing we tend to do that distorts our understanding,' she said. 'Science and technology, for instance, shouldn't be clubbed. Science is where you are trying to produce knowledge. Technology produces tools. Knowledge and tools are not at all the same thing. Production of knowledge and tools are not at all the same thing. So in my mind, at least, it's very clear that when you produce a tool, you produce it for something. So what is it that you're trying to do with it? The second thing is that, over time, we've been seeing corporate interest becoming state interest. The US is a classic case. The whole Gulf War was about that. So that much understanding I have—that when you allow corporate interests to start dictating state policy and practice, you're not in a good place.'

She pointed to a fireside chat in which Satya Nadella, the CEO of Microsoft, and Nilekani talked about 'the poor being able to empower themselves with data' by selling their own data. This sort of discourse was connected to corporate interests—as opposed to the interests of individuals. 'That's how they talked about the poor [to justify the project]. Because you need something to give it moral legitimacy. And the best place to put it is on the poor. If the issue was really about poor people getting their entitlements, you'd know that they can't handle the technology.'

It was late afternoon, and Ramanathan said she had to show a climate scientist around Delhi. Before I left, I asked her if she wondered whether her discoveries were simply conspiracies. To excavate meaning from policy documents and utterances was treacherous, and the Authority's officials did say that the fears of surveillance were unjustified.

'I'm a researcher primarily. When I say researcher, I do my own thinking. I don't let somebody else do my thinking for me,' she replied. She had seen the justifications for the system, and they didn't make sense to her. That was where her criticisms came from. But she felt that the system's existence itself represented an undiagnosed weakness. 'In the 1980s we had the human rights debate, where human rights became very important for people working among communities. And somewhere in the nineties the corruption thing started. Once corruption took over everybody's imagination, it let all other human rights slide. It has bothered me for the longest time.'

On a rainy day in July 2022, I arrived at a dilapidated building stained by moisture. It was in an older part of Mumbai, called Parel, where ageing and forgotten publishing houses once produced popular calendars, magazines and newspapers. On the second floor was the office of the Public Advocacy Research Centre, and within it I was met by a soft-spoken elderly gentleman named Dilip Karambelkar, a high-ranking RSS functionary. Abhishek Choudhary, the biographer, had introduced him as a man in the know. And so I went to see him to understand how a knowledgeable member of the RSS viewed the identification project's origins.

He was a modest man: grey-haired, with a trim moustache and dressed in mismatched colours—purple check trousers and a pink check shirt. He wore slippers to work. Had I not seen pictures of him beside the head of the RSS, and read news stories about favours and positions allegedly bestowed on him by the BJP, I would not have thought of him as the editor-in-chief of RSS publications in Marathi and Hindi, which he was. Editorial meetings surely valued the tried and tested, because the content of these outlets was the same rehashed fare served in Sangh-affiliated magazines for over seventy years. The main story on the webpage of a monthly publication was a jauntily written cautionary tale about a Hindu woman marrying a Muslim man. It covered the spectrum of clichés and canards deployed by the RSS: Muslim man lures Hindu woman into love and marriage, forces her to cook meat, orders her to wear a burkha, and nearly murders her so that he may marry again without grief.

'It was imagined as a citizenship card and a citizenship number for the North-East states, where a lot of infiltration was taking place, so how could we find out who was a citizen, and who was an infiltrator? It was meant for infiltration-affected parts of India,' he said. At least once every sentence he searched for a word in English, found it in Marathi and continued in English.

He accused Nilekani of a lack of imagination. 'When Nandan Nilekani came in, he had limited thinking. They thought it should only be for beneficiaries of various welfare schemes. They thought of a unique identification so that people [did not get undue benefits]. But under the Modi government it saw wider applications. It was converted to a sort of citizenship card. It is a citizenship card, though it is not said to be a citizenship card.'

The manner in which residents had been registered left him deeply unimpressed. The point of such an identification project was to mark citizens, but it did not do that, for there was no way of telling who a citizen was. And what was the purpose of a citizenship number if it was not connected to useful information? He had thought out a citizenship registry with tiers of privacy. If he offered someone a job, he wanted to know if they had been in jail. That was one tier. The second tier would offer a wealth of information only to constitutional bodies. The third, and most secret tier, could only be disclosed 'to high courts and the Supreme Court'. I listened to this wide-eyed, and let him continue. He imagined an identification number that told planners who passed and who failed their final school exams, what college they applied to, where they worked and how much they earned. 'This sort of data should be open to everybody. It will help us plan.'

He qualified all this by saying that he was no expert, 'but as journalists we are a jack of all trades'. But the project, he insisted, was meant to root out illegal migration from Bangladesh to Assam and West Bengal in India.

At this I asked whether all migration was a concern, or only migration in certain states. I mentioned India's border with Nepal, which ran one thousand eight hundred and fifty kilometres long, and allowed for the free movement of people between the two countries. 'With Nepal, it was only about criminals coming across the border. But Nepal is part of our cultural ecosystem, so there is an exchange of cultures there. With Pakistan and Bangladesh, there is a different culture. There is cultural infiltration. Once Partition happened on the basis of religion, religion became a sensitive issue between nations. Here the fear was that through infiltration, it would change the socio-political map of India. That was the concern,' he said.

Karambelkar abruptly ended our interview, saying he had a Zoom call to take. But before I left, he asked me questions about myself so forcefully that it startled me. He wanted to know about my family, the language I spoke, where my parents were from, what they did, where I grew up, where I was schooled, what I did, how I supported myself, who supported me and where I lived. I wondered if he would take these answers elsewhere, because he said once or twice in a serious tone, 'The RSS has an ecosystem that is vast.' Then he said goodbye and turned away.

When I left him I sat in my car downstairs a while and watched the rear-view mirrors. Then I drove slowly, and then fast, and took turns in odd places, and finally went home, feeling a little silly, but also somewhat relieved.

FIVE

# AN EDUCATION

# 1

# Real History

It was late in June 2023, Delhi was hot as usual, the judges of Karkardooma court were on their annual summer vacation. Rakshpal Singh, the advocate who had failed to disprove Nisar's testimony in Justice Pramachala's court, had arrived at his office from home on a simple motorcycle, removed his black Steelbird helmet and facecloth, and slipped the key, which was attached to a small temple bell, into his pocket.

In an immense building within the court complex, Rakshpal's office was at one end of the fourth-floor corridor, a long passage that reeked like a public toilet. A sticker of Saraswati, the goddess of learning, was on the door to his office, and a stainless-steel nameplate was screwed onto her face. Another sticker offered Diwali greetings from Rakshpal, as well as two advocates whose faces had been scratched out. Only Singh remained: deep and narrowed eyes, a waterfall of a moustache that diminished his lips, a streak of vermilion on his forehead, the clothes he wore during hearings, a stare that suggested it was all taking too long. The room contained two desks but there was space for six clients if they adjusted things a little. Files gathered on the unwashed floor, the desks and the tops of cabinets. The work was not lucrative, but there was a lot of it. Some of it bored Rakshpal, and people seemed to have a habit of presenting him with unnecessary information. On the wall behind him he had put up a sign in Hindi: 'Please don't waste your valuable time by sitting idle.' A young man was presently miserable about possible jail time due to a marital dispute. Singh cupped his chin and listened dispassionately. The man complained that his wife had agreed to a payment, but then changed her mind after speaking with a lawyer for only five minutes. 'What is there to changing minds?' Rakshpal said, closing his eyes, his fingers rising economically and falling. The gesture was subtle, indicating he was unconcerned about this, and that it was no big deal. 'Minds change like weather. Don't the seasons change? Give it time. She will change her mind again.' For this advice the man handed him a few notes, and he pocketed them without bothering to count. Rakshpal's phone rang, and he told the caller, 'The court is closed, but you know how unhappy people keep coming here.'

I asked how he came to represent the men accused in Nisar's testimony.

He gave a little laugh and said he was in charge of the Delhi legal cell of the Vishwa Hindu Parishad. After the pogrom in 2020, the leader of the VHP claimed, as was expected, that Muslims had started it, and he insisted that any Hindu violence was resistance, not aggression. Anyone with a memory knew better its reputation as a moral policing squad, forever checking dark corners of parks for lovers on Valentine's Day. 'I'll tell you. The VHP has a legal cell in Delhi. The legal cell is in my hold,' Rakshpal said. 'I'm the chief. The cases we have, whether about religion, riots, whatever, it's the legal cell that handles these cases.' He said that they had no option but to help assist the men. They were Hindu men, and if that was not reason enough to defend them, they had stood up for the faith. 'It is my moral duty to help the men and, if they have evidence, to even save them. If your parents were sick with something uncurable, you would still treat them, yes? You should never feel like you didn't do enough.'

Rakshpal had no doubt that his clients would soon be freed by the courts. His optimism sprang from predictable developments: a witness claimed that the police had threatened him with jail unless he testified against Rakshpal's clients, and other witnesses had refused to recognise the accused. Rakshpal presented this information to make the case for his clients' innocence. What about Nisar and his testimony, I asked. He was momentarily annoyed, and dismissed Nisar as an unreliable witness. He had complaints about Nisar's recollections, and said that Nisar's testimony did not even match his own son's account of their escape in court. His trust was reserved wholly for his clients—the alleged rioters and killers he represented at no cost as a matter of faith. It was not the simple trust an advocate is obligated to have in a client. It was a complicated and blind faith, because his belief in their innocence also stemmed from their shared religion. 'It is my belief that when Hindu society was under attack—and this will become communal—these boys stood like soldiers and stopped them. If they hadn't stopped the violence, there would have been greater damage. It is my moral duty to defend them,' he said.

When Rakshpal said he was representing them for no fee, I must have revealed my misgivings because he said, 'I don't feel like I should charge them. You might think this is suspicious, because people see these things through the lens of suspicion. I'll tell you. The Hindu community was thrashed for a day. After that, you know what happened.' The fight, the riots, the finding and killing, had been the work of the other side. 'It was entirely pre-planned,' he said, offering the VHP line. Rakshpal told me in remorseless detail how the Muslims of Seelampur and Jafrabad had left their homes to protest below a metro station that was used by everybody. Once they were outside and away from home, they 'launched' their attack. 'They emerged from their territory and brought the war to Hindu territory.' There was a story about a man first bound and then hacked bit by bit until his blood flowed. 'I'm giving you the postmortem,' Rakshpal said, with relish, using his hands and feet to illustrate the progression of violence: 'First here, then here, then a little more.' He told me about CCTV footage that showed Muslims 'coming out of their locality with sticks. Now you tell me.' In this story of Muslims causing havoc, and Hindus standing in defence, the police were absent. Their only role was to gather evidence and produce an account of what had occurred.

About forty-five years ago, in 1978, Rakshpal came here to Delhi from Etah in Uttar Pradesh, filled with ideas his mother had poured into his mind. She may not have been educated, but what she needed to know about the world, she knew well enough. What was wrong with society, what it required—these were also things she had thoughts about, he said. To that end she raised Rakshpal to be a proper Hindu boy. She made him keep a ritual braid all through childhood, and watched his barber's hands as they advanced towards it, and issued firm instructions that under no condition was it to be touched. But in Delhi, Rakshpal lived among kin who had shorn their braids to be inconspicuous, and he lopped off his own just months after his arrival. 'For the first time in my life I felt like "Hindu" was a bad word,' he said, and he remembered her horror when she noticed the braid's absence. There were other markers of her ideas: she had raised him to beware any feelings of friendship he might entertain for a Muslim. She poured into him the certainty that it was in a Muslim's nature to betray. 'They will bury you if you are a friend, and will anyway bury you if you are enemies,' he said, echoing his mother's advice. He disobeyed her and accepted Muslims as acquaintances, but he made sure not to invite them home. A Muslim in a Hindu home was a dangerous situation to manufacture; completely avoidable. Whether a woman was eighteen or sixty, a Muslim would find a way to lure her to his faith, Rakshpal said in the year 2023, when he knew better. He had personally witnessed it six or seven hundred times, he said, not specifying a single instance. 'Every two to three days there's a case. He'll be in a relationship with the mother, and get engaged to the daughter.' Listening to him, I thought that these individual dislikes, each a calumny that could be unpacked and discussed at length, had stacked up into hostility. Under the heat of immediately unverifiable lived experiences and assertions, the Muslim had changed state in his mind, no longer a person as much as a cluster of notions and general principles. The story's moral was that a Muslim man had no shame, and therefore it was a Hindu man's duty to do everything he could to protect and preserve the Hindu advantage in numbers. Rakshpal said that 'women's empowerment' was one of the solutions to the problems Muslims posed.

He reached for an edition of the Quran from a bookshelf. 'I study it closely,' he said. 'There are things in there that will make your head spin. Look, when we read our books, when we advise each other, we say . . .': he spoke in Sanskrit for a while. 'But when they talk, they say to god, "ya Allah, give me strength to fight kafirs".' He blamed the book: 'It's in the book that the day of judgement will not arrive until the world is converted to Islam.' He mentioned a few incriminating phrases in the book from memory; the idea was to show that scholarship had led him to his conclusions. 'Now, if their god says things like this . . . Their book says that the wives and property of non-believers can be taken, and non-believers can be finished off. And it even says that you can make non-Muslim women your slave, and you can sell them in a bazaar or rape them. You tell me, if this is what people hear from their childhood in a madrassa, what happens?'

In 1980, Rakshpal began to visit a local RSS shakha a few times a week. He bought into the ideas they discussed, and found his faith returning. He grew out his braid once more, and wore a sacred thread. He became what he called a 'sanatani', with an originalist interpretation of the Vedas. 'My family was sanatani.

In my youth, there was no focus. What child has focus? I focused after the twelfth, when I joined the RSS. He would do what thousands before and after him had, listening to stories about kings and queens who served as vessels for a timeless Hindu valour, and now he was keen to test my grasp of history. 'Do you know Bappa Rawal? Then what history have you studied? Bappa Rawal was a Maratha soldier. He killed Mussalmans all the way to Tehran. He emptied the place. But where do they teach him? Have you read about Hari Singh Nalwa? You haven't? You haven't studied history. He was seven feet tall, and the governor of a fort in Kabul. He brought back the gold that Ghazni took. Seven times he thrashed the Pathans. They did not have the guts to cross the fort and come in this direction. You know that movie *Sholay* with the dacoit Gabbar? The mother tells her children, "Go to sleep or else Gabbar will come." In reality, that line was stolen. The real line is still spoken today by Pashtun women in Afghanistan: "Go to sleep or else Nalwa will come." Pathans thought they were brave, but they were nothing before him. Read history and you will be proud. Read about the great Ashoka. You'll learn that to run a government you will have to pick up a sword.'

He was curious about history, and did not want to be constrained by what he was taught in class. 'They used to teach us history in school, but it was about Mughals, all of that.' He joined a public library in Delhi to learn what was kept from him. He went to books wildly, without structure, and his learnings were unruly, as if he was his own first teacher. The combination of his interests and the oral histories he heard at the shakha instilled in him the kind of belief that would allow him to discuss with utter confidence his deep knowledge of 'Christian civilisation, Islamic civilisation, Chinese civilisation and Harappan civilisation'. He would strongly recommend reading about the Romans solely because 'the people of Rome worshipped the sun'. He would come to believe that the world began with sanatani thought, and that every breath, every enlightenment and crucifixion, every angel and prophet, was the 'this and that' that had occurred between the beginning and this moment in Karkardooma. It was a study of history in which Hindu primacy was inevitable, and its superiority was by dint of its having reached discoveries and realisations before anyone else. 'When was electricity invented?' he asked me, and then said, 'Sometime in the nineteenth century. But we had a word for electricity in Sanskrit. This means we had knowledge about electricity earlier. Look at the aeroplane. Made in the 1800s by the Wright brothers. But we had the word "vimaan" earlier. And there was a vimaan in the Ramayana too. If we didn't have this technology earlier, why would we have these words? If a word exists in Sanskrit, it means that object was available earlier.'

'What evidence do you have?' I asked.

'The evidence of every society is found in its books,' he said. 'You cannot deny that the four Vedas are the oldest books'—he was stretching it by a millennium—'and the Ramayana, which is between ten and twelve thousand years old, also mentioned aeroplanes'—this was an overstatement too, for the epic was probably written some two thousand five hundred years ago. I listened as Rakshpal talked about the presence of modern weaponry in the epics. In his imagination, the bows and fire arrows that mythologies referred to could have been ancient launchers and explosive projectiles. I wondered how his mind worked, for some readings he interpreted as evidence of ideas he held dearly, and others he took literally as evidence. Primacy and dominance were important to him, which meant that his understanding of the texts did not tolerate the possibility of imagination; the written word had to be true.

Rakshpal staked Hinduism's claims over the past with such certainty and speed that I could only listen. I was unsure of how to respond or what to challenge him on, but certain that all of it was swaddled in wild exaggeration. These stories and their repetition were the RSS's lifeblood. The organisation's centrality to life in India required the propagation of recently created myths and glories extracted from regional stories—but the stories had to be framed as part of a grander Hindu identity, and imparted to unquestioning minds. This allowed for a liquid certainty that consumed most ideas in its path: aeroplanes, missiles, plastic surgery, the origins of Muslims, the origins of species. It was an ideology hungry for expansion. Rakshpal went on and I listened, fascinated by his deep feeling. These things were real to him, they needed to be real.

And then he said: 'I've picked up a little here and there through my readings. I can't tell you where exactly my knowledge is from. But there is nothing that has benefited mankind that we don't know. When we go to a shakha, each of these things is taught to us. We are taught that if we find something new, we should search for a reference to it in our books of knowledge.'

I asked him why it was important to locate modern knowledge in books sacred to him.

'It's important because science is rediscovering what has been proven in our books. Science is re-researching. And they say they don't believe in our sacred books, but it is only re-research. Okay, take a word we have in Hindi: "telepathy". What is telepathy? You are sitting here, and you focus on a mantra. Thousands of kilometres away someone else focuses, and it forms a connection, and you can speak to each other. It is on this basis that telephones work. All science does is repackage what has been proven.'

He talked about his life, and then he spoke about his children. Like him, they worked in law and attended the RSS's shakhas, he said. Rakshpal was proud of this continued chain of tradition; they were on the right path. Now he dreamed, like some parents do, of his children going further than he ever had. 'I want my son to join the judiciary,' he told me. 'Several of my friends have joined the Delhi High Court as judges. Politically, if he does well, and if this government is there in ten or fifteen years, we can get him a high court appointment. It's not a big deal. We have to see if luck is with him. But from our side, it's not a problem.'

After some time, when it was early in the afternoon, Rakshpal said he had to leave for a baithak, a discussion. All day long, in shakhas across the country, an exercise in the coordinated dissemination of a clear message was taking place; the Sangh's officers and volunteers would be given talking points about the BJP's latest legislative endeavour, the Uniform Civil Code. The spectre of the code was raised frequently, but all it did was rouse the party's base at the prospect of Muslim discomfort. Muslims, like Parsis and Christians, were governed by a unique set of personal laws that dictated marriage, divorce, inheritance' and succession. The UCC would result in common personal laws for all Indians, superseding customs and practices they were guaranteed by the Constitution. But details of the code were scarce, and so discussions about it lacked specificity. This did not stop an RSS spokesperson from declaring, in the usual way, that the law was nationalist, and that its opponents did 'not want solidarity and harmony among religions'.

I asked Rakshpal if I could come along. He smiled sweetly and said it was a private gathering.

We took the elevator down and left the building. Two high court advocates noticed him, and they stopped and bowed slightly with palms joined, and said to him, 'Jai See Krishna.' Rakshpal, who sometimes called himself Sanatani Rakshpal Singh for reasons of Hindu identity, was on his phone, and he walked past them with his hand raised in slight acknowledgement and blessing, unaware that the men stared at him in admiration until he had vanished.

For all that evening, the next day, and then all week long, the newspapers and nightly programmes discussed the legislation.

Their coverage was the typical production of noise that occurred at moments of high intensity—of voices so loud and debates so fierce that the observer was transfixed by the husk of news. I thought it was only time before this confusion and chaos grew into an emotional idea in the public mind, transforming the code into something larger and sacrosanct, like the idea of a temple that did not yet exist.

# 2

# This Is Life

A few days after I met Rakshpal, Nisar invited me to his home in Mustafabad. After we had talked for a while, Nisar said he wanted to go to his village, for it had been years. Asma, who was sitting beside him on their bed, said that she wanted to go too, but he told her straightaway that it was unnecessary. It was six hours away and deep in Uttar Pradesh, he said to dissuade her. There was no further discussion. She was disappointed momentarily but buried her unhappiness, remembering that a witness was present.

There had been no resolution to the case. The accused were where they had been a year before. Nisar was prohibited from leaving Delhi for his safety, because the policemen designated to protect him could operate only in the city. The restriction was in its third year, and it made him miserable. He complained endlessly that he could no longer meet potential clients at the speed his business required without a fuss being made about his coming and going from Delhi. He briefly considered applying for formal permission, looked at me for some guidance (a futile exercise), and decided to have a little chat with the minder assigned to him that day. He left early the next morning with a nephew, having arranged for his police protection to come along.

For half an hour he waited outside the Gokulpuri police station with his nephew, sighing deeply and muttering, 'Where is this guy?' He hung out at the building the way teens went to malls, for it was everything to him: the place that filled him with despair and hope. Lately a temple's construction on the station premises had reminded him again that the secular compact was no longer assured. It could be revoked at any time by any authority. 'I have been coming here for thirty-five years,' he said. 'It's the first time I'm seeing this. If they are making a temple inside a station, it should be bust of Ambedkar'—the Constitution's drafter. 'Should there be a temple inside a station or a court? On whose authority are they doing it? They're doing it with their own authority. Why? This is where people get justice. There are already temples outside. People of every faith go there for justice. It's wrong.' He spoke with acquaintances in media and politics who agreed that this was wrong. But there was nothing he could do. 'I can't make an allegation because I'm a Muslim. The community here can't talk about it because the people here are already pressured after the riots. But this means that whatever is happening will continue to happen. The public has come to this level. They are making a big shrine inside the police station. This is what they're working on, just spreading hate.' His minder arrived eventually, and Nisar melted meekly, as he usually did before authority. They shook hands, got into Nisar's car and set off for Uttar Pradesh.

The vehicle was an inflammable offering from a popular manufacturer who did not allow safety features to get in the way of a suitable price point for the average Indian consumer, a target audience that would consider life itself optional at the right price. In slow-motion videos of a crash test, its metal structure turned to dust like cheap glass, adult dummies snapped their necks and infants floated in zero gravity while a child's severed arm flew out of a window. The car promised adventure, and Nisar was there to deliver it. He took off in high spirits down the highway, which was less a road than a series of public-private partnership contracts; every few kilometres the road ended abruptly at one height, while the next segment began a few inches higher or lower, and so the car was either falling or lurching up at every road contract's end while Nisar kept on at eighty kilometres an hour. For a long stretch beside the road was a wall with a sign repeated: 'Infiltrators will be shot.'

As a toll plaza approached, he called out the policeman's name.

'Hmm?' the man said, sleepily.

'Make a small gesture.'

At the toll booth the policeman raised his hand to the operator from the back. She noted the car's registration number, wrote 'uniform' in a field on her screen, and let the car go without payment.

He drove for long stretches in silence while the others slept at the back. He drove in the right lane, keeping his distance from the scooterists who stopped abruptly in the left lane to answer their phones. The cottony monsoon sky had bestowed on the countryside its annual abundance, and the soil had returned with its gifts. The air smelled of fresh grass and manure, and if not for the thermal power plants, the persistent electric pylons and the unfinished walls and pillars of vague ambitions, the green expanse would have stretched uninterrupted beyond the horizon.

'What a beautiful country this is,' he said between rice fields. 'It's such a big country and they've made it so small. They've filled people's heads with rumour and innuendo so they hate each other. In the Quran it is written that wherever you live, you should make it strong. But people don't read. They don't read their own books and try to understand.'

From behind the policeman spoke up: 'The problem is that nobody bothers verifying anything any more. If they verify something right there, the rumour will die on the spot.'

This was his first visit home in eight years, and leaving Mustafabad had lightened his mood. I remembered that he hadn't travelled outside Delhi since the riots. 'I feel free here,' he said. 'My mother was a vegetarian. If someone prepared meat in their house, she would not drink water from their home. All her life she would drink from the house well, not the kitchen, if we made meat at home. You can't force someone to do things. The old books are permissive. You can't force people to eat meat. Some religions say you should not drink. That doesn't mean you should kill me if I drink.' Freed of urbanity's distractions, his gaze located metaphor in the open country. Passing by two women carrying enormous bundles of grass on their head, he commiserated with their burden. 'I'm carrying grass too,' he said.

Hours later he slowed to find the turn that would take him home, but he did not recognise it because a new bridge had interfered with his recollection, but as he rode on something about the land occurred to him. He stopped and looked back and felt that, yes, that was the path. The road disappeared between the fields. Six lanes became two, and then one. Men rode their motorbikes with their stands extended. Men with dusty feet and a tear in their shirts sat on sacks of cow feed waiting for customers. Well-fed children wandered about unsupervised. Marijuana sprouted wildly. Birds taller than Nisar stood unmoving in the fields. 'Look at how peaceful it is here. There's no pollution. There are no chemicals in the mangoes here.' And then, when there were only fields on every side, his nephew and the policeman said and repeated to each other, 'This is real life.'

As Nisar drew closer to the village, he stopped his car and pointed to a large tree in the distance. 'That mango tree. My father planted it. The mango tree,' he said. As he looked about at the fields, his smile disappeared. 'Everything has changed.'

'Everything has changed,' his nephew said.

'Where are we?' Nisar said.

'How do I know?' his nephew said, laughing.

Then an old toothless man doing nothing at the roadside noticed him. 'Nisar!' he said, and shuffled across the front of the car. 'It has been an age since you left.'

'You recognised me?' Nisar said. The man, bony and turbaned, replied, 'Hmmnn.'

When he found his village, he looked about for familiar faces, and found them on a raised platform in the shade of a tree. He parked the car beside them and leaped out into the mud in his polished shoes and ran to hug them. At first there were only three people, but word spread that Nisar had arrived and more old friends emerged to see him. They gave him room on a string daybed while they sat on plastic chairs or squatted, and they asked him if the news about his sister was true. Nisar said it was, and told them about the cancer's lethality. She had lived beside the canal in Bhagirathi Vihar for years, and died within three or four days of the diagnosis. They spoke about the old days, about where they played, what their parents did, his father's field, and the beauty of the home his father had sold. The man who purchased the house agreed. 'It's true, it was very beautiful.' The way they looked at him with adoration and called for biscuits and sweets, the way he patted the sweat on his skin with a kerchief, the way he held a glass of tea with his thumb and first and second fingers, the dhotis and pyjamas they were dressed in beside Nisar's crisp white shirt tucked into grey trousers, and his black loafers—all gave him the air of civilisation, as if he had acquired something long ago and left them behind. His closest childhood friend, Shailendra, ran out to meet him, and pulled him away to meet the village elders whose age no one knew, but everyone agreed was between hundred and ten and hundred and thirty. Every village in the country had one person over a hundred and ten years old whose only job was to smile beatifically and appear wise.

Shailendra dragged him home and ordered the family to bring out food. Each time a plate turned up, he said, 'Completely organic. No chemicals. It's from here.'

'This is not a family,' Nisar said, beaming, 'This is a clan.' When the mangoes came out, Nisar almost shouted, 'Absolutely pure! Everything on the table is from the fields here, even the mustard oil.' He went over each item on each plate, calling out, 'Spinach pakodas, makhana, ghee, pudina chutney, imli chutney, aloo bhajiyas, dal moth, milk, everything is from here.'

The policeman said, 'You won't get this taste in the city.' He ate a little of everything, patted his stomach to turn down more food, but always ate a little more.

Each member of the family urged Nisar to eat. When he was full, someone from the kitchen said, 'Now for the food', and rotis and vegetables appeared before him. The policeman and Nisar panicked silently, but submitted and ate in silence. 'Too much love can be ruinous,' Nisar said.

After lunch he wanted to see the land his father had owned, and Shailendra led him outside the village. Nisar walked like a man from the city, skipping over puddles, while his friend walked through them in his slippers. Nisar's protection followed them. He looked at the vastness of his friend's fields, and identified where the peanuts took root, and asked him to show him where the land was. They walked along a raised bank between the corn and the arhar dal, and reached a spot beside a pond. Something about the landscape seemed familiar to him, and he had just begun to consider it when his phone rang and the moment was lost. While he talked, Shailendra, who adored Nisar, mentioned a recent local election. His candidate had triumphed, a success that pleased him greatly. Which candidate was this, Nisar's nephew asked, and Shailendra replied that he worked for the BJP. From then on the nephew was quiet until he was inside the car that evening, and the car had left the village behind.

And then he said, 'Chacha, Shailendra told us he's with the BJP.'

And Nisar, who remembered the mango tree and the friendships, but nothing else, said, 'Oh.' He looked straight ahead at the road, but he was now thinking, because there was a very particular look on his face.

It was a look that said: perhaps it was not as I remembered.

# References

## 1. AFTERMATH

*Interviews*

Ali and father, Waqaar, Sonia, Minhajuddin, Md Meharban, Anees bhai, Dr Anwar, Shamsuddin, Imran, Nisar, Asma, Ilyas, Ganesh, Prashastika, Tanima Kishore, Anas Tanwir, Bhainswali, Aashiq, graveyard minder, Apoorvanand, Chitranshul Sinha, Tamanna Pankaj

*References*

### 1. They Get no Respect

page 7 *Knowing this is unconstitutional, you're ramming through this Bill*: https:// www.youtube.com/watch?v=TcA-EF8HWN4

page 8 *What are you doing to the constitution?*: https://www.youtube.com/ watch?v=xnS_w7Arw_4

page 8 *Amit Shah's ability to listen*: 'Can Amit Shah, Narendra Modi's Chanakya, fight three tactical battles for BJP?' https:// economictimes.indiatimes. com/news/politics-and-nation/can-amit-shah-narendra-modischanakya-fight-three-tactical-battles-for-bjp/articleshow/39839175.cms

page 8 *They get no respect*: https://www.youtube.com/watch?v= XDDD8v82Sr8

### 2. Tin Roof Refuge

page 11 *Understand the chronology*: https://www.youtube.com/ watch?v=Z__6E5hPbHg page 11*inclusion challenged by a neighbour*: https://www.bbc.com/news/world-asia-india-48754802

page 12 *four million left stateless*: https://www.bbc.com/news/ world-asia-india-49520593 page 12 *CM called for NRC to be cancelled:* https://www.indiatoday.in/india/story/assam-nrc-national-cut-off-himanta-biswa-sarma-bjp-amit-shah-1620965-2019-11-20

page 13 *seizing property and revoking the right to vote*: https://cjp.org.in/why-the-caanprnrc-is-a-toxic-cocktail-for-everyone/

page 14 *'How do we organise?'*: https://www.youtube.com/watch?v=ashAr2ATM1w

page 14 *Is the worth of any human being less than any other?*: https://www.youtube. com/watch?v=r1hgKR-kLRQ (2019)

page 16 *Everybody saw it*: https://www.youtube.com/watch?v=P-VUPenZpPE (2020)

3. The Graveyard

page 22 *Blowing themselves up:* https://maktoobmedia.com/india/over-770-kg-of-explosives-seized-from-local-rss-leaders-home-in-kerala-weeks-before-polls/

*Knowing the Quran*: https://www.newindianexpress.com/nation/2023/Jan/04/gold-ink-quran-ancient-manuscripts-preserved-by-rss-inspired-body-on-display-in-maharashtra-2534606.html

4. Everyone Is a Suspect

page 23 *law, not religion, says Ambedkar: Annihilation of Caste* (2nd edition), reproduced in Dr. Babasaheb Ambedkar: Writings and Speeches, Vol. 1 (Compiled by Vasant Moon), Dr. Ambedkar Foundation, Ministry of Social Justice & Empowerment, Govt. of India, 1979; 2014 reprint, p. 76.

page 23 *Cut off the electricity*: https://www.thequint.com/news/india/abvpdisrupts-screening-of-ram-ke-naam-in-ambedkar-uni (2019)

page 25 *media aligned with the government at Shaheen Bagh*: see, for instance, https://www.newslaundry.com/2020/01/26/shaheen-bagh-and-the-spiralling-hostility-against-godi-media; https://thewire.in/media/rightwing-media-channels-shaheen-bagh

page 32 *MLA warned Muslims*: https://www.business-standard.com/article/news-ani/we-re-80-per-cent-you-re-18-don-t-oppose-caa-k-taka-bjp-mla-spews-venom-120010400341_1.html

page 32 *Anurag Thakur's violent anthem*: https://www.youtube.com/watch?v=FeR23GE6BSU

page 32 *campaign promise to demolish every mosque*: https://www.ndtv.com/india-news/delhi-election-2020-parvesh-sahib-singh-verma-says-no-shaheen-bagh-protesters-mosques-on-state-land-2170674

5. A Call for Freedom

page 36 *COVID being blamed on Muslims and invitation to shoot citizenship act protestors*: https://scroll.in/article/959806/covid-19-how-fake-news-and-modi-government-messaging-fuelled-indias-latest-spiral-of-islamophobia

6. On Their Own

page 39 *The fire at the Gokulpuri car spares market*: https://thewire.in/communalism/gokalpuri-tyre-market-fire-jai-shree-ram

page 43 *Mishra accused the women*: https://www.youtube.com/watch?v=GNCvL9T_TkU

page 44 *Mishra accused Modi*: https://www.thehindu.com/news/cities/Delhi/mishra-calls-modi-isi-agent-draws-bjps-ire/article8440350.ece

page 44 *Mishra accused Kejriwal*: https://www.rediff.com/news/interview/kapil-mishra-no-way-kejriwal-can-be-saved/20240322.htm

page 44 *Mishra's Hindu ecosystem project*: https://theprint.in/india/bjps-kapil-mishra-building-hindu-ecosystem-team-calls-for-recruits-on-social-media/546192/

page 44 *Hindutva proponents claiming old structures*: https://www.indiatoday.in/magazine/indiascope/story/19760930-qutab-minar-was-not-originally-a-hindu-monument-say-experts-819348-2015-04-11

8. Testimony

page 68 *Delhi government's compensation package*: https://archive.org/details/aap-2020-delhi-riots-compensation-package

2. A NEW COUNTRY

*Libraries*

Nehru Memorial Museum and Library, The Asiatic Society of Mumbai, National Archives of India, The U.S. National Archives and Records Administration, Harry Elkins Widener Memorial Library, Harvard Divinity School Library, Countway Library of Medicine, Harvard Archives, Columbia Butler Library, India Office Records at the British Library

*References*

1. In Defence of Faith

page 107 *unsurpassed scientific prowess that made India a teacher to the world*: Prasad, Durga, *An English Translation of the Satyarth Prakash of Maharishi Swami Dayanand Saraswati* (Lahore: Virjanand Press, 1908)

page 107 *deity representing revenge*: *A Year's Work in India: Report of the American Marathi Mission of Western India for the Year 1900* (Bombay: Caxton Printing Works, 1901)

page 107 *elevated local policemen to idols*: *A Year's Work in India: Report of the American Marathi Mission of Western India for the Year 1900* (Bombay: Caxton Printing Works, 1901)

page 107 *begged the goddess of cholera for mercy*: *A Year's Work in India: Report of the American Marathi Mission of Western India for the Year 1900* (Bombay: Caxton Printing Works, 1901)

page 107 *the learnings of that advanced civilization were lost in the Great War depicted in the Mahabharata*: Prasad, Durga, *An English Translation of the Satyarth Prakash of Maharishi Swami Dayanand Saraswati* (Lahore: Virjanand Press, 1908), p 391

page 108 *faraway discussions about the effectiveness of flogging*: The Earl of Ellenborough, *The Indian Mutiny—Punishment of Mutineers* (Hansard, UK Parliament—Volume 148: debated on Monday 15 February 1858)

page 108 *decades would pass before the event was recalled*: Rai, Alok, *Hindi Nationalism* (Hyderabad: Orient Blackswan, January 2001)

page 110 *God is personal, the human soul is distinct from god, and the world is real; drowning books in the Yamuna*: Farquhar, J. N., *Modern Religious Movements in India* (London: MacMillan, 1929), p 106

page 111 *a scold in Sanskrit*: Farquhar, J.N. *Modern Religious Movements in India* (London: MacMillan, 1929), pp 107–109

page 111 *as the champions of Rama dreaded the monster*: The Friend of India (4 December 1873), p 1360

page 112 *Saraswati's arguments were passionate*: *The Pioneer* (13 November 1874), p 3 page 112 *Called them popes in Hindi*: Saraswati, Dayanand, *Satyarth Prakash*, p 37 page 112 *a benediction to themselves*: *The Times of India* (29 March 1876)

page 113 *wandering sanyasi*: *The Madras Mail* (8 January 1875)

page 113 *a paid missionary of the British government*: 'Aryan Reformer', *The Times of India* (9 December 1874), p 2

page 113 *decorated elephant and donkey*: *The Times of India* (9 September

1875), p 2 page 113 *the district magistrate of Benares didn't know what to do with him*: *The Times of India* (3 January 1880), p 3

page 113 *from time to time his men received beatings*: *The Times of India* (20 October 1877), p 3

page 113 *wherever they went, one heard of slander, passion, and unfair methods*: Farquhar, J.N., *Modern Religious Movements in India* (London: MacMillan, 1929), p 122

page 113 *eighteen kinds of disputes in the jurisdiction of courts*: Saraswati, Dayanand, *Satyarth Prakash*, p 207

page 113 *when he listened, it was with a kind of contemptuous courtesy*: Prasad, Durga, *An English Translation of the Satyarth Prakash of Maharishi Swami Dayanand Saraswati* (Lahore: Virjanand Press, 1908), p 18

page 114 *the teachings preached by the Arya Samaj were stolen from Christianity*: *Missionary Magazine and Chronicle—Relating Chiefly to the Missions of the London Missionary Society* (1 March 1881)

page 115 *a British member of the Samaj*, and *the samaj was propagating the most active and public propaganda in India or perhaps the world*: Shaker Manifesto (February 1879), p 39

page 115 *converting two Christians in 1877*: Hardiman, David, 'Purifying the Nation: The Arya Samaj in Gujarat 1895–1930', *The Indian Economic and Social History Review*, Vol.44 (No1), pp 41–65

page 115 *an immense quantity of literature pours from the press*: Farquhar, J. N., *Modern Religious Movements in India* (London: MacMillan, 1929), p 174

page 116 *hundreds of men of the student class believe that the ancient Hindus were far advanced*: Farquhar, J. N., *Modern Religious Movements in India* (London: MacMillan, 1929), p 431

page 116 *a hundredth of their income*, and *the society's remit was not simply cow protection, but society itself*: Saraswati, Dayananda, *Gokarunanidhi—Ocean of Mercy for the Cow* (February 1881)

page 116 *whose stomach turned at the sight of meat*: Prasad, Durga, *An English Translation of the Satyarth Prakash of Maharishi Swami Dayanand Saraswati* (Lahore: Virjanand Press, 1908), p 9

page 117 *the professed object of his cow protection society was humane and politically unimportant*: *The Calcutta Review*, January 1898, p 141

page 118 *preachers calculated the output of such a creature*: *The Madras Mail* (7 August 1889), p 5

page 118 *the bottomless appetite of the English and the foreign were to blame*: Tejani, Shabnum, *Cow Protection, Hindu Identity and the Politics of Hurt in India*, c.1890–2019, p 14

page 119 *administrators noticed that communal riots frequently occurred where the protection societies went* McLane, John R., *Indian Nationalism and the Early Congress*

page 120 *swamis exerted a secret influence*, and *a rabid fanaticism*: *The Pioneer* (31 May 1894), p 1

page 120 *scientist working in a lab*: Nehru Memorial Museum and Library, B. S. Moonje Papers, File 25, p 2

page 121 *music and the communal riot in Salem*: *The Pioneer*, 25–6 August/2, 7, 25 September 1882

page 123 *the police—whose senior posts in South India were filled with Europeans and lower posts with locals*: David, Arnold, 'The Police and Colonial Control in South India', *Social Scientist*, Vol. 4, No 12 ( July 1976), pp 3–16

page 124 *blame pinned on the cow protection movement*: *The Pioneer*, 11 March 1894 page 124 *rumours that English had conducted massacres*: *The Calcutta Review*, January 1898, p 141

page 124 *children in seminaries, meeting houses, loyalty of regiments, growing antagonism through propaganda*: Chirol, Valentine, *Indian Unrest* (London: MacMillan, 1910)

page 124 *actively poisonous seed*: *The Calcutta Review*, January 1898, pp 135–143

## 2. The Book and the Rifle

page 127 *fundamental differences between Hindu culture and Muslim culture and politics* and *when Muslims conquered any country*: Nehru Memorial Museum and Library, N.B. Khare Oral Transcript, p 117

page 127 *graduated with second-class honours*: Bombay University Calendar (1901), 215

page 127 *in 1938, a letter from an Arya Samaj outpost*: Nehru Memorial Museum and Library, B. S. Moonje Papers, File 54, p 180

page 127 *The Book and the Rifle*: Nehru Memorial Museum and Library, B. S. Moonje Papers, File 25, p 10

page 127 *Vedic image echoing cryptic words by Mussolini*: Nehru Memorial Museum and Library, B. S. Moonje Papers, File 25, p 10

page 128 *Queen's South Africa clasp*; *on ship to south Africa with four civil surgeons of Bombay command regiment*: ancestry.com

page 128 *charitable eye dispensary in Nagpur*: *Amrita Bazar Patrika*, 7 May 1905

page 128 *one imperishable point on which the system is based*: Nehru Memorial Museum and Library, B. S. Moonje Papers, File 25, p 16 page 128 *in Moonje's stories, Hindus were vulnerable and blameless*: Nehru Memorial Museum and Library, B. S. Moonje Papers, File 6, p 10

page 129 *overseen thousands of reconversions*: among Moonje's papers related to Moplah page 129 *do Christian missionary professors receive a commission for converting Hindu students?*: Nehru Memorial Museum and Library, B. S. Moonje Papers, File 102, pp 1–2

page 130 *no central distinguishing concept*; *to exaggerate their numbers, Hindu enumerators did a little religious fudging*: Census of India, Vol. 1, Part 1—Report, p 130

page 130 *unity of Muslims due to no caste system*; *fanaticism of acquiring heavenly glory*: Nehru Memorial Museum and Library, B. S. Moonje Papers, File 12, p 31

page 131 *Buddhism's corrupting influence*: Nehru Memorial Museum and Library, B. S. Moonje Papers, File 25

page 131 *I am not a historian*: Nehru Memorial Museum and Library, B. S. Moonje Papers, File 25, p 4

page 131 *Moonje trusted it enough*: Nehru Memorial Museum and Library, B. S. Moonje Papers, File 25, p 3

page 131 *Hindu society had gone through terrible ordeals*: Nehru Memorial Museum and Library, B. S. Moonje Papers, File 25, p 3

page 132 *Mahatma Gandhi perverting Hindu minds with calls for non-violence*: Nehru Memorial Museum and Library, B. S. Moonje Diaries, 20–21 September 1926

page 132 *Moonje applied what he believed was scientific rigour*: Nehru Memorial Museum and Library, B. S. Moonje Papers, File 12, pp 33–4

page 132 *the higher caste deprived of the very material help*: Nehru Memorial Museum and Library, B. S. Moonje Papers, File 12, p 32

page 133 *Moonje at cow protection conference*: Nehru Memorial Museum and Library, B. S. Moonje Papers, File 18, p 1

page 133 *Moonje addressed a letter to the chief commissioner*: Letter from B. S. Moonje to the Editor, 'C.P. Government's Press Note', *The Leader* (3 July 1918)

page 133 *they could easily raise a standing reserve of 50,000 or 100,000*: Letter from B. S. Moonje to the Editor, 'C.P. Government's Press Note', *The Leader* (3 July 1918)

page 133 *warrior queens who leapt on to horses from height*: Nehru Memorial Museum and Library, B. S. Moonje Papers, File 6, p 3

page 134 *the district magistrate of Belgaum wrote about Moonje's plans for Muslims*: Extract from the Weekly Confidential Report of the District Magistrate, Belgaum, no. E.C., 19 September 1935,

Home Department Special Branch, file no. 812–A, p. 89. MSA (B) [Source: *Shaping the 'Community': Hindu Nationalist Imagination in Gujarat, 1880–1950*, Saavedra, Beatriz Martinez]

page 134 *Moonje suggested a few ways to build such a force*: Letter from B. S. Moonje to the Editor, 'C.P. Government's Press Note', *The Leader* (3 July 1918)

page 135 *raise funds for the school*: Nehru Memorial Museum and Library, B. S. Moonje Papers, File 30, p 304

page 135 *Mussolini's office*; and *to experience a landscape*: Ludwig, Emil, *Talks With Mussolini* (Little, Brown and Company, 1933), pp 11–13; Getty Images

page 136 *Moonje description of Mussolini*: Nehru Memorial Museum and Library, Moonje's diary, March 1931

page 137 *in case of dissolution, all assets go to the RSS*: Nehru Memorial Museum and Library, B. S. Moonje Papers, File 26, p 65

page 137 *the Moslems are making themselves a nuisance*: Nehru Memorial Museum and Library, B. S. Moonje, File 57, p 28

## 3. Unreliable Patriots

page 139 *on the advice of Hindu nationalist leaders*: Calcutta National Medical College Examination Results (27 June 1914), p 6

page 139 *Hedgewar graduates from National Medical College*: Calcutta National Medical College Examination Results (27 June 1914), p 6

page 139 *secret societies, Bengal clubs that put emphasis on physical training or mental development, Jugantar, extremists and moderates*: Heehs, Peter, *The Bomb in Bengal: The Rise of Revolutionary Terrorism in India 1900–1910* (Oxford: Oxford University Press, 2004)

page 140 *four emerging methods of writing in Calcutta*: Laushey, David M., *Bengal Terrorism & The Marxist Left: Aspects of regional nationalism in India, 1905- 1942* (Calcutta: Firma K. L. Mukhopadhyay, 1975)

page 141 *'Formation of Bands'*: Heehs, Peter, *The Bomb in Bengal: The Rise of Revolutionary Terrorism in India 1900–1910* (Oxford: Oxford University Press, 2004), p 96

page 141 *inwardly devoted to dissemination of sedition and disaffection among masses; revolutionaries were everywhere*: Samanta, Amiya K., *Terrorism in Bengal, Vol. 1* (Government of West Bengal, 1995)

page 142 *the authorities' surveillance of Hedgewar became RSS lore*: Joshi, Yadavrao, *Glimpses of Doctor Hedgewar, Hindu Swayamsevak Sangh* (http://www. hssworld.org/doctorji/index.htm) page 142 *in one story, Hedgewar finds a man in Calcutta suspiciously friendly*: Joshi, Yadavrao, *Glimpses of Doctor Hedgewar, Hindu Swayamsevak Sangh* (http:// www.hssworld.org/doctorji/index.htm)

page 142 *they were unreliable patriots*: Curran, J.A., *Militant Hinduism in Indian Politics: A Study of the R.S.S.* (Institute of Pacific Relations, 1951)

page 142 *a children's comic book on his life by Gyan Ganga Prakashan*: Raje, Sudhakar, *Dr. Hedgewar* (Gyan Ganga Prakashan) (http://www.hssworld.org/ doctorji/doctorji_ack.wmv)

page 144 *there were fifty-two riots in colonial India between February 1926 and August 1927*: Question in the Council of State Requiring Statement and Comparison of Communal Riots During 1926 and 1927, file no. Home_ Political_NA_1927_NA_F–44_Xiii, National Archives of India

page 144 *113 dead, 1,070 injured*: Question in the Council of State Requiring Statement and Comparison of Communal Riots During 1926 and 1927, file no. Home_Political_NA_1927_NA_F–44_xiii, National Archives of India

page 144 *arrest of B. S. Moonje and Pandit Mohan Malviya, the law of love and punishment, civil war, provocative speeches, labyrinthine commercial buildings, jamadars*: Communal Tension in Bengal Internment of Pandit Madan Mohan Malaviya and Dr BKS Moonje from that Presidency by An Order Under Section 144 of the Criminal Procedure Code and Question As to the Means of Preventing a Breach of Such An Order, file no. Home_ Political_NA_1926_NA_F–187, pp 20–4, National Archives of India

page 145 *a weak and disorganised showing*: Curran, J. A., *Militant Hinduism in Indian Politics: A study of the R.S.S.* (Institute of Pacific Relations, 1951)

page 146 *broad chests, muscular shoulders, big limbs, and tall stature*: Nehru Memorial Museum and Library, B. S. Moonje Papers, File 143, p 2

page 146 *massive intellect capable of grasping any system of science*: Nehru Memorial Museum and Library, B. S. Moonje Papers, File 143, p 2

page 146 *enthusiasm for nationalism in the country was cooling down; its object was that Hindus should have the strength to resist attacks made on their community; poisonous hissing*: C. P. Bhishikar, *Keshav Sangh Nirmata* (New Delhi: Suruchi, 1980), p 7, cited in

Tapan Basu and others, *Khaki Shorts Saffron Flags: A critique of the Hindu Right* (New Delhi: Orient Longman, 1993)

page 147 *chanted an oath in unison*: Nehru Memorial Museum and Library, Delhi Police Records, File 7-419

page 147 *trained in daggers, swords, and wooden staffs*: Nehru Memorial Museum and Library, Delhi Police Records, File 8-417

page 147 *RSS promised locals a glass of milk with thick cream in exchange for support*: Kulkarni, Atmaram, *The Advent of Advani* (South Asia Books, 1995)

page 147 *some gave them time and money, one gave them an airplane; purchased printing presses and fired Muslim workers*: Nehru Memorial Museum and Library, Delhi Police Records, around 1947

page 148 *secret note describing RSS as pan-Hindu Boy Scout movement with physical training; Golwalkar beseeched them to create feelings of hatred toward men of other religions*: Nehru Memorial Museum and Library, Delhi Police Records, File 7-419, Appendix B

## 4. The Mound of Dead Men

(Note: In some cases the exact file numbers have not been mentioned. For reference, this chapter relies primarily on the following Delhi Police records at NMML: 2nd instalment file 9, 225, 3-46, 3-67, 5-43, 5-54, 5-58, 5-136, 5-138, 6-30, 6-32, 6- 148, 7-68, 7-72, 7-76, 7-78, 7-419, 8-416, 8-417, 9-671, 9-674, 6-677, 6-679, 9-680, 9-683, 9-684, 9-685)

page 154 *Nehru's anguished letter to India's president; every foreign ambassador had been visited by mobs looking to kill their Muslim staff; the marks left on the dead felt like personal vengeance; the future appears dark not because . . .*: Nehru to Dr Rajendra Prasad, 17 September 1947, *Dr. Rajendra Prasad: Correspondence and Select Documents,* Vol 7, pp 123–5

page 155 *Inspector-General of Police wonders if violence is organised, Nehru says he is convinced*: Conversation during meeting at Government House, 26 September 1947, Emergency Committee Papers and Minutes, DO 133/62, UK National Archives

page 155 *the RSS had a great deal to do with the disturbances*: Letters from Nehru to various people between 5 December and 29 December 1947

page 156 *RSS offices searched by police in January 1947; walking through Muslim quarters, they shouted slogans against Pakistan; told newspaper editors to cover activities sympathetically*: Nehru Memorial Museum and Library, Delhi Police Special Branch

page 157 *the RSS created a stabbing squad*: *Note on the Sikh Plan*, p 11 (Lahore: Superintendent, Government Printing, West Punjab, 1948)

page 157 *the plans ranged from detailed and specific to outlandish*: *Note on the Sikh Plan* (Lahore: Superintendent, Government Printing, West Punjab, 1948) page 157 *RSS volunteers gathered to learn how to handle bombs and pistols*: Vajpayee, Manik Chandra, and Paradkar, Sridhar, *Partition-Days: The Fiery Saga of RSS* (New Delhi: Suruchi Prakashan, 2002)

page 158 *mischief makers have better intelligence than government*: Nehru during meeting at Government House, 25 September 1947, Emergency Committee Papers and Minutes, DO 133/62, UK National Archives

page 158 *conspiracies detailing plans to kill senior RSS members before slaughtering Hindus; three groups of RSS men hurled grenades and bombs in Muslim tenements; chartering a plane to drop bombs, maps of neighbourhoods*: Printed by the Superintendent, Government Printing, West Punjab, 1948

page 158 *RSS stories recall*: Manik Chandra Vajpayee & Shridhar Paradkar, 'Himachal', *Partition Days: The Fiery Saga of the RSS*, Suruchi Prakashan.

## 5. A Most Unnatural Way

page 160 *a history written in blood*: Vajpayee, Manik Chandra, and Paradkar, Sridhar, *Partition Days: The Fiery Saga of RSS* (New Delhi: Suruchi Prakashan, 2002) page 161 *they would attribute the worst kinds of criminal motives*: Goyal, D.R., *Rashtriya Swayamsewak Sangh* (Radha Krishna, 1979)

page 163 *take notice of none*: Reply from Sardar Patel to Gopichand Bhargava 14 November 1946, *Sardar Patel's Correspondence–Vol. 3* (Ahmedabad: Navajivan Publishing House, 1972)

page 163 *published a Gallup poll*: Nehru Memorial Museum and Library, Delhi Police Special Branch, Non–Current Records, File 5–138, p 45

page 164 *a sort of guerrilla warfare*: Nehru Memorial Museum and Library, Delhi Police Special Branch, Non–Current Records, File 5–138, p 72

page 164 *warned Hindu households not to give shelter*: Nehru Memorial Museum and Library, Delhi Police Special Branch, Non–Current Records, File 8–416

page 164 *Muslims would only quit India when a movement for their total extermination takes place*: Nehru Memorial Museum and Library,

Delhi Police Special Branch, Non-Current Records, File 5–138, p 28

page 165 *communal body with totalitarian outlook*: Pyarelal, *Mahatma Gandhi: The Last Phase,* quoted in D. R. Goyal: *Rashtriya Swayamsewak Sangh*, 1979

page 165 *RSS members would wear a white kerchief*: Nehru Memorial Museum and Library, Delhi Police Special Branch, Non-Current Records, File 5–138, p 36

page 165 *it is a part of the programme of the RSS to contact men in the services*: Nehru Memorial Museum and Library, Delhi Police Special Branch, Non-Current Records, 5th instalment, file 138, p 45

page 165 *planning to contest next election*: Nehru Memorial Museum and Library, Delhi Police Special Branch, Non-Current Records

page 165 *flow of Ganges cannot be stopped by any obstruction*: Nehru Memorial Museum and Library, Delhi Police Records, File 5-138, p 61

page 167 *blaming Gandhi for amalgamating the two races unnaturally*: Nehru Memorial Museum and Library, Delhi Police Records, File 9-680, p 15

page 167 *Pakistan insists that Nehru restrict the RSS and Hindu Mahasabha*: Liaquat Ali Khan to Nehru, J.N. (S.G.), Vol 37 part 1, pp 302–3

page 167 *while Pakistan has followed an intensely communal policy*: Nehru to Vallabhbhai Patel, J.N. (S.G.), Vol 40, pp 85–8

page 168 *I have to face today exceedingly reactionary and bigoted Hindus*: Nehru to B. C. Roy, J.N. (S.G.), Vol 42 part 2, pp 202–3

page 169 *by the end of 1948, 31,268 arrests had been made across India*: BBC estimate, Nehru Memorial Museum and Library, Delhi Police Records, File 9-684 page 169 *RSS sympathisers interrogating RSS volunteers*: Nehru Memorial Museum and Library, Delhi Police Records, File 9-684, p 9

page 169 *operators at telephone exchanges were suspected*: Nehru Memorial Museum and Library, Delhi Police Records, File 9-684, pp 64–8

page 170 *a large number of RSS men have been arrested, probably many of them more or less innocent*: 26 February 1948: Nehru to Sardar Vallabhbhai Patel, J.N. (S.G.), Vol 6, p 137

page 171 *the bills had been scrubbed and painted over . . .'*: Nehru Memorial Museum and Library, Delhi Police Special Branch, Non-Current Records, 7th instalment, File 78, p 58

page 171 *recruited children to drop off banned pamphlets; at public demonstrations, they sent cyclists to surveil police positions*: Nehru Memorial Museum and Library, Delhi Police Records, 1948–9

page 171 *the search for justice took seven young RSS workers*: Nehru Memorial Museum and Library, Delhi Police Special Branch, Non-Current Records, 7th instalment, File 78, pp 33–7

page 174 *join National Democratic Body*: Nehru Memorial Museum and Library, Delhi Police Records, c. 1949

page 174 *morally incumbent on Muslims to celebrate major RSS festivals; Wondering if Muslim citizenship could be revoked altogether*: Nehru Memorial Museum and Library, Delhi Police Special Branch, Non-Current Records, 5-54, pp 70–1

## 3. FAMILY MATTERS

### *Interviews*

Partha Banerjee, Dhaniram and Sachin, Harender Thakur, Nisar, member of Tripura State Rifles, Kitchenware store owner and son, Station House Officer, Rahul's mother and father, Bharadwaj, Mulayam Singh

### *References*

#### 1. The Family

page 183 *as an index of their self-conceited prestige*: Nehru Memorial Museum and Library, Delhi Police 7–68

page 183 *infuse sangh ideology in those parties*: Nehru Memorial Museum and Library, Delhi Police 7–76, p 4

page 183 *40,000 workers sign up for arrest*: Nehru Memorial Museum and Library, Delhi Police 7–76, p 93

page 183 *membership cost lowered*: Nehru Memorial Museum and Library, Delhi Police 5–54, p 15

page 184 *incumbent on us to keep a dynamic and vigorous mass of young men in check*: Nehru Memorial Museum and Library, Delhi Police 7–78, p 6

page 184 *number of Mahasabha branches*: Nehru Memorial Museum and Library, B. S. Moonje Papers, File 54, p 217

page 184 *keeping young men under effective check*: Nehru Memorial Museum and Library, Delhi Police Special Branch, Non-Current Records, 7th instalment, File 78, p 7

page 184 *Liaquat to Nehru: curb activities of orgs calling for reunification or separate Hindu homeland in Pakistan*: Nehru Memorial

Museum and Library, J.N. (S.G.), Vol 37, Part 1, 23 February 1950, pp 267–8

page 185 *Nehru to Liaquat: frequent killing, arson, looting*: Nehru Memorial Museum and Library, J.N. (S.G.), Vol 38, pp 234–7

page 185 *nearly half a million refugees arrived Nehru to B.C. Roy*: Nehru Memorial Museum and Library, J.N. (S.G.), Vol 40, p 67

page 185 *refugees arrive with shock in eyes and disaster on lips*: Nehru Memorial Museum and Library, J.N. (S.G.), Vol 38

page 185 *inciting people*: Nehru to chief ministers, Nehru Memorial Museum and Library J.N. (S.G.), Vol 37, Part 1, 27 February 1950

page 185 *exchange of population without considering consequences*: All India Radio address by Nehru a day before Holi, Nehru Memorial Museum and Library, J.N. (S.G.), Vol 38, 3 March 1950, pp 63–7

page 186 *poems on jute cultivators*: Ali, Tariq Omar, *The Envelope of Global Trade: The Political Economy and Intellectual History of Jute in the Bengal Delta, 1850s to 1950s*, Doctoral dissertation, Harvard University

page 186 *the Mahasabha has a remarkable way of always saying and doing the wrong thing Address to chief ministers*: Nehru Memorial Museum and Library, J.N. (S.G.), Vol 38, 1 March 1950

page 187 *suspension of fundamental rights*: Rajendra Prasad to Nehru, Nehru Memorial Museum and Library, J.N. (S.G.), Vol 41, Part 1, 2 April 1950

page 187 *blowing conches; weapons from 500 years ago; medieval state of mind*: Nehru's reply during debate on President's address, Nehru Memorial Museum and Library, J.N. (S.G.), Vol 36, Part 1, 3 February 1950, pp 96–7

page 187 *Aurangzebi tyrant*: Anonymous letter to Nehru, Nehru Memorial Museum and Library, J.N. (S.G.), Vol 42, Part 1, p 102

page 188 *if these people had their way, neither you nor I would have a tolerable existence*: Nehru to BC Roy, J.N. (S.G.), Vol 42, Part 2, pp 202–3

page 188 *Ashutosh Lahiri asks American consul general to fund Mahasabha UK*: National Archives DOI 33/1393, p 8

3. A Muder in East Delhi

page 219 *Karni Sena working with BJP/threaten to murder*: Citizens for Justice and Peace, https://cjp.org.in/bjp-haryana-leader-incites-violence-if-suresh-chavhankeis-arrested/

page 219 *Karni Sena vandalising property*: Scroll.in, https://scroll.in/article/866535/seven-states-35-cases-how-karni-sena-has-scaled-up-its-violentagitation-against-padmaava

page 219 *Karni Sena blames the constitution for corruption*: https://web.archive.org/ web/20230330095209/https://www.karnisena.org/about-us

page 220 *Parvesh Verma's demand of total boycott of Muslims*: https://www.ndtv.com/india-news/bjp-mp-parvesh-verma-faces-anti-muslim-speech-allegation-after-total-boycott-comment-3416031

page 220 *Aaj Tak news anchor's announcement*: https://www.youtube.com/watch?v=9okLYpdDjfQ

page 224 *on the United Hindu Front*: https://web.archive.org/web/20180812211159/https://unitedhindufront.org/

4. The Hindu Awakens at 6 a.m.

page 214 *on 'land jihad'*: https://www.youtube.com/watch?v=CimbTGN7w2Q

4. TECHNICAL DIFFICULTIES

*Interviews*

Alok Prasanna Kumar, Kumar Anand, Siraj Dutta, Reetika Khera, Aruna Chandrasekhar, Karan Saini, Srinivas Kodali, Angad Choudhury, Rony Das, Kiran Jonnalagadda, Vickram Crishna, Meenakshi Balasubramanian, Prof R. Ramakumar, Rahul Narayan, Vidya Krishnan, Pranesh Prakash, Raghu/Godavar, Siddharth Narrain, Tridip Suhrud, Pallavi Pratap, Praavita, Vasuman Khandelwal, Apar Gupta, Santosh Desai, Anivar Aravind, Rajiv Kane, hostel manager, Dr Gopal Krishna, O. P. Srivastava, Udhay Shankar, Jyoti Panday, M. S. Sriram, Nilesh Trivedi, Col. Mathew Thomas, Zainab Bawa, Pukhraj Singh, S. Prasanna, Usha Ramanathan, Jean Drèze, Viraj Chopra, Prof Vivek Borkar, Natasha Badhwar, Jude Terrence D'Souza, Prof Subhashis Banerjee, Prof Sandeep Shukla, Prof J. Nagarjuna, Prof Manoj Prabhakaran, Rachna Khaira, Harish Khare, Gopal Sankaranarayanan, Anuradha R.V., Shubhodeep Shome, Srikanth Lakshmanan, Nikhil Pahwa, Sanjay Palshikar, Anand Patwardhan, Ajay Khanna, Shivam Shankar Singh, Vashistha Iyer, Jawhar Sircar, Vijay Shukla, Kushan Mitra

1. The Visionary's Toys

page 260 *the rath yatra's toll*: see https://nagarikmancha.org/images/1242-Documents-Communal_Riots_in_India.pdf, and also news reports such as https://www.deccanherald.com/india/advanis-ram-rath-yatra-the-chariot-of-chaos-on-the-road-to-disorder-2858918

page 260 *Narasimha Rao's pseudonymous piece*: http://www.mainstreamweekly.net/article5438.html & https://www.orfonline.org/research/rao-singh-and-the-great-suicide

page 261 *Advani's youth*: Atmaram Kulkarni, *The Advent of Advani: An Authentic Critical Biography*, South Asia Book.

page 263 *Article by twenty-five prominent historians*: 'The Political Abuse of History: Babri Masjid-Rama Janmabhumi Dispute', *Social Scientist*, Vol. 18, No. 1/2 (Jan–Feb, 1990), pp. 76–81

page 267 *'The flames catch on' & a survey of residents*: Shri Krishna Commission report on 1993 Bombay riots

page 268 *hardline Hindutva as opportunistic*: 'BJP leader reaffirms US-India commitment', Wikileaks cable, Canonical ID: 05NEWDELHI3505_a, 10 May 2005

page 272 *Ram Madhav to diplomat*: 'RSS flexes political muscles, demands Advani's removal', Wikileaks cable, Canonical ID: 05NEWDELHI5320_a, 11 July 2005

page 272 *Advani on his eighty-fourth birthday*: https://www.rediff.com/news/report/party-has-given-me-much-more-than-pms-post-says-advani/20121108.htm

page 272 *does India need a younger leader*: https://m.rediff.com/news/2009/jan/22slid1-advani-chat-transcrip.htm

page 276 *the toll of Advani's rath yatra*: https://nagarikmancha.org/images/1242-Documents-Communal_Riots_in_India.pdf

page 279 *Advani on illegal infiltration in Assam*: https://www.deccanherald.com/india/advani-blames-illegal-immigration-assam-2350578

page 280 *Sanjib Barua's piece*: 'Immigration, Ethnic Conflict, and Political Turmoil--Assam, 1979-1985', *Asian Survey*, Vol. 26, No. 11 (Nov. 1986), pp. 1184–1206

page 280 *Hindus and Muslims together killed Bengali Muslims*: Arun Shourie, 'Assam Elections: Can Democracy Survive Them?' India Today, 31 May, 1983, p. 57

page 280 *Moonje on Assamese Hindus*: Moonje papers, folder 65, p. 109

page 280 *Advani on Assamese Hindus*: 'Advani blames UPA for influx of migrants in Assam', https://economictimes.indiatimes.com/news/politics-and-nation/advani-blames-upa-for-influx-of-migrants-in-assam/articleshow/3537986.cms

page 281 *refugees important base*: Malini Bhattacharjee, 'Tracing the emergence and consolidation of Hindutva in Assam', *Economic and Political Weekly*, Vol. 51, No. 16, 16 April 2016

page 282 *Advani against dialogue with hijackers*: Praveen Swami, 'Bowing to terrorism', *Frontline*, 8 January 2000

2. The Architect

page 285 *Sanjay Gandhi forcibly sterilised*: https://www.bbc.com/news/world-asia-india-30040790

page 288 *paper about unauthorised migrants*: Lt. General (Retd) S.K. Sinha, 'Report on Illegal Migration to Assam' (submitted to President of India), 8 November 1998

page 294 *'smart card technology' to reduce 'leakages'*: 'Excess food stocks, PDS and procurement policy' Arvind Virmani and P.V. Rajeev, Planning Commission, Working paper No 5/2002-PC, December 2001

page 294 *'valid document to fortify claim of Indian citizenship'*: 'Multi-purpose national identification card—instruction manual for filling up verification', Ministry of Home Affairs, 2003, p. 1

3. Towering Visions

page 310 *Professor R. Ramakumar's critique*: 'High-cost, high risk', Frontline, https://frontline.thehindu.com/the-nation/article30187957.ece

page 320 *Gujarat government five-year plan*: 'e-Governance policy for the state of Gujarat (2014-2019)', Department of Science and Technology, Government of Gujarat, November 2014

page 320 *Nandan Nilekani on tact*: 'Nandan Nilekani on what it takes to build the world's biggest social inclusion program', Knowledge at Wharton, 4 November 2010, https://knowledge.wharton.upenn.edu/article/nandan-nilekani-on-what-it-takes-to-build-the-worlds-biggest-social-inclusion-program/

4. Viscera

page 329 *on Premani's autopsy*: https://indianexpress.com/article/india/jharkhand-officials-rule-out-starvation-death-say-autopsy-reveals-foodgrains-in-stomach-4966586/

page 329 *on starvation deaths due to not having Aadhaar*: https://www.thehindu.com/news/national/other-states/jharkhand-where-not-having-aadhaar-could-starve-you-to-death/article61827611.ece

page 330 *beneficiary of Premani's money dead for twenty-five years*: https://timesofindia.indiatimes.com/city/ranchi/report-bank-fraud-behind-hunger-death-in-garhwa/articleshow/62277905.cms

page 333 *PDS needs 'IT-enabled reform'*: 'Report of the Technology Advisory Group for Unique Projects', Ministry of Finance, 31 January 2011

5. So Much Power

page 344 *the specifics of Nandan Nilekani's fortune*: election affidavit; also see: https://www.forbes.com/sites/saritharai/2014/03/21/tech-tycoon-nilekanis-asset-declaration-noteworthy-in-indian-politics/

page 345 *crocodiles and Modi's scars*: https://www.indiatoday.in/india/north/story/narendra-modi-the-game-changer-biography-sudesh-k-verma-192071-2014-05-06

page 345 *on Modi's wife*: Haima Deshpande, 'I am Narendra Modi's Wife', Open, 30 May 2009

page 347 *Ehsan Jafri's call to Modi*: https://www.catchnews.com/india-news/ehsan-jafri-called-modi-for-help-i-heard-modi-abuse-him-gulberg-survivor-1464888144.html

page 347 *HRW report on Gujarat*: https://www.hrw.org/report/2003/06/30/compounding-injustice/governments-failure-redress-massacres-gujarat

page 347 *sting investigation on Babu Bajrangi*: https://caravanmagazine.in/conflict/had-good-police-support-because-of-modi-babu-bajrangi-in-ashish-khetan-undercover

page 348 *HRW report on Gujarat*: https://www.hrw.org/report/2003/06/30/compounding-injustice/governments-failure-redress-massacres-gujarat

page 348 *advertising agency that worked on Modi's campaign*: https://www.adgully.com/exclusive-the-man-who-got-us-achche-din-anuraag-khandelwal-57794.html

page 349 *Baba Ramdev and Modi*: https://www.reuters.com/investigates/special-report/india-modi-ramdev/

page 354 *BJP opposing Aadhaar*: https://www.business-standard.com/article/elections-2014/we-ll-throw-aadhaar-into-the-dustbin-h-n-ananth-kumar-114032800298_1.html

page 354 *Modi opposing Aadhaa*r: https://x.com/narendramodi/status/453543852175925248?lang=en

6. The Case for Identity

page 364 *why the Supreme Court judges revolted*: https://www.thehindubusinessline.com/news/supreme-court-crisis-all-not-okay-democracy-at-stake-say-four-senior-most-judges/article64312451.ece; also see: https://www.thehindu.com/news/national/modi-a-versatile-genius-who-thinks-globally-and-acts-locally-justice-arun-mishra/article30887665.ece page 372 *false allegations against Teesta Setalvad*: https://timesofindia.indiatimes.com/india/teesta-setalvad-spent-ngo-funds-on-liquor-gujarat-government-in-sc/articleshow/59464870.cms

page 387 *science and technology and the politics of suspicion*: https://ielrc.org/content/a1003.pdf

5. AN EDUCATION

## *Interviews*

Rakshpal Singh, Nisar, Asma

1. Real History

page 405 *UCC is nationalist*: 'RSS Muslim wing pushes for Uniform Civil Code, to run awareness campaigns across country', *India Today*, 19 June 2023

## Acknowledgements

This book is the result of good fortune, favours, generosity, patience and kindnesses shown by strangers and friends over many years.

Osama Manzar, Kiran Jonnalagadda, Reetika Khera, Srinivas Kodali and Karan Saini let me follow them around for days while I figured out the book. Conversations and interviews with them spanned dozens of hours over entire days. The book changed as we spoke and after we spoke, as new connections emerged, and the experiences they shared with me have shaped this book. I'm in their debt.

Vinod Jose, Basharat Peer and Jonathan Shainin have been guardians. Aside from showing me how to write, they've always been around to give me advice, or write a letter that opened doors, and somehow say the right thing at the exact moment I needed to hear it.

Md Meharban showed me north east Delhi, and helped me understand what had happened there. He brought it all to life as we walked around Jamia and Okhla a year after the violence, and I saw during these conversations the toll it had taken on him. It was during one of these tours that I met Nisar, this book's protagonist. Without Meharban's advice and help, this would have been a very different book.

Many of the narratives in this book are based on hundreds of interviews done over seven years. People shared their experiences and perspectives, and patiently answered my questions. If doubts remained, or I learned something new a few years later, we had further conversations. The details here exist only because the following people were generous with their time: Aashiq, Col. Ali Ahmed, Ali, Kumar Anand, Anuradha R V, Dr Anwar, Apoorvanand, Anivar Aravind, Chinmayi Arun, Natasha Badhwar, Hartosh Singh Bal, Meenakshi Balasubramanian, Partha Banerjee, Professor Subhashis Banerjee, Anshuman Bapna, Zainab Bawa, Gautam Bhatia, Professor Vivek Borkar, Marzia Casolari, Soumen Chakraborty, Sambuddho Chakravarty, Aruna Chandrasekhar, Viraj Chopra, Vickram Crishna, Jude Terrance D'Souza, Rony Das, Deepak ji, Santosh Desai, Dhaniram *ji*, Vikas Dhoot, Vikram Doctor, Praveen Donthi, Jean Drèze, AS Dulat, Siraj Dutta, Abdul Gaffar, Jayanta Ghosal, Durba Ghosh, Raghu/ Godavar, Apurva Godbole, Apar Gupta, Rahul Gupta, Sonya Surabhi Gupta, Ilyas, Vashistha Iyer, J—, Ganesh Kanate, Rajiv Kane, Dilip Karambelkar, Pavan Kumar Kasera, Krishn Kaushik, Rachna Khaira, Vasuman Khandelwal, Ajay Khanna, Harish Khare, Sowmya Kidambi, Tanima Kishore, Gopal Krishna, Vidya Krishnan, Alok Prasanna Kumar, Srikanth Lakshmanan, SC Majumdar, Mukul Manglik, Minhajuddin, Kushan Mitra, Aasif Mujtaba, Aditya Mukherjee, Mitali Mukherjee, Mridula Mukherjee, Munni *ji*, Padmini Ray Murray, Professor J Nagarjuna, Rahul Narayan, Siddharth Narrain, Nikhil Pahwa, Joyojeet Pal, Sanjay Palshikar, Jyoti Panday, Tamanna Pankaj, Anand Patwardhan, Rohan Paul, Yogesh Pawar, Praavita, Manoj Prabhakaran, Pranesh Prakash, S Prasanna, Pallavi Pratap, Prashastika, Jyoti Punwani, Avinash Raghava, Alok Rai, Gulshan Rai, Professor R Ramakumar, Usha Ramanathan, Somak Raychaudhury, Debayan Roy, Raj S, Gaurav Sabnis, Amba Salekar, Gopal Sankaranarayanan, Tanika Sarkar, Meeta Sengupta, Shamsuddin, Taylor Sherman, Shubhodeep Shome, Vijay Shukla, Gurjeet Singh, Kapil Sibal, Rakshpal Singh, Shivam Shankar Singh, Sushant Singh, Chitranshul

Sinha, Pratik Sinha, Jawhar Sircar, Udhay Shankar, Professor Sandeep Shukla, Vijay Shukla, Pukhraj Singh, Pavan Srinath, MS Sriram, OP Srivastava, Tridip Suhrud, Anas Tanwir, Harendar Thakur, Col. Mathew Thomas, Salil Tripathi, Nilesh Trivedi, Audrey Truschke, Thejaswi Udupa, Ashutosh Varshney, Arvind Virmani, Neena Vyas, Aman Wadud and Waqaar.

There were unnamed sources who helped me understand Infosys, Aadhaar and Nandan Nilekani's political campaign from the inside. Their accounts were invaluable, and helped shed light on closed worlds. They know who they are.

I'm deeply grateful to Ameet Dutta, Monica Datta, Roopa Purushothaman, Rishi Majumdar and Abhishek Choudhary for their advice and help. Gabin Kuttikaran and Gaurav Sabnis understood what I was seeing and encouraged me to keep going. Nikhil Pahwa and Kiran Jonnalagadda too.

This book was supported by the Harvard Radcliffe Institute, where I was a fellow in 2022–3. The year I spent there was extraordinary. Claudia Rizzini, Sharon Bromberg-Lim, Elizabeth Antonellis, Alison Ney, Maria Pachon and Hyun Jin Yoo created a warm and inviting space that I will forever remember. The university's tremendous archives were invaluable, and I spent many days at Widener Library wishing I had a few more years to do research. The best thing about the year at Radcliffe, though, were the new acquaintances who felt immediately like old friends: Brodwyn Fischer, Omar Dewachi, Asifa Majid, Paz Encina, Joe Roman and Christopher Muller. I miss bumping into them.

It was a pleasure to work with the incredible Muskaan Arshad, who came through the Radcliffe Research Partner program. Her work made it easier to process some of the massive mounds of information I had gathered.

Sometimes all you need is a little affirmation, especially when you've been deep in the weeds for a few years. Brian Hatcher's enthusiasm for the project kept my spirits up. David Wolf, my editor at the *Guardian*, commissioned a story that forced me to make narrative connections I'd been avoiding.

Toby Mundy, my agent, saw what the book could be, and he encouraged me to take risks. His support made a huge difference. Richard Beswick's belief in the book was priceless, for it gave me the confidence to experiment with form and structure. Anu Roy-Chaudhury's crisp edit tightened this book, and Karthika VK was a saviour in ways I cannot reveal.

I'm certain James Crabtree has hidden wings and a halo. He has made life-altering introductions and opened doors to opportunities that I did not know existed. My debt to him is enormous. Dhirendra Jha, whose investigations of the RSS have already become part of the historical record, was unfailingly generous with sources and research tips. Akshaya Mukul showed me how to navigate the archives, took me out for meals in Delhi and kept telling me that I was on the right track. He has been a huge cheerleader for this book.

The manuscript was seen, in whole or in part, by journalists, editors, writers and historians who I admire. Nilanjana Roy, Prem Panicker, Ramachandra Guha, Sonia Faleiro, Akshaya Mukul, M Rajshekhar, Swati Narayan, Sana Aiyar, Andy Mukherjee and Brodwyn Fischer. They caught mistakes, found awkward sentences, interpreted my incoherence and generally saved my skin.

The writer Nilanjana Roy and editor/columnist/chess player/seaman Devangshu Datta made so much of this book possible. Without their support, it would just not have happened, not in this form. They opened their home in Delhi to me, and let me stay there for as long as the reporting took. I cannot even begin to assess how much I owe them for their support, their generosity, their friendship, their ability to keep a straight face while I worked through my anxieties about the book. Sonia Faleiro and Ulrik McKnight listened to various versions of *everything is so hard* and *why is this so hard* and *who does this willingly for a living* and just nodded sympathetically, knowing fully that being mildly unbearable is also part of the writing process. M Rajshekhar did support a little differently: the sadist went to town with my worries, showing me after ten or fifteen unbearable minutes how ridiculous they were.

They had lost almost everything, but Asma and Nisar Ahmed opened their home to me, and took the time to explain what had occurred in Bhagirathi Vihar. Their insistence on doing the right thing by going to court, even if their choices inconvenienced them, came from the belief that courage is contagious, and that building a just society is possible if enough people want it to be so. These are two of the bravest people I've known, and their desire for justice is driven not by a need for retribution or punishment, but to reassert the rights they have been assured by the Constitution. Unlike me, and many others I know, they do not take their rights for granted. This book is for him, Asma and the children.

I got lucky with my parents. My mother, who is no longer here but ever present, found an English teacher who changed my life. (Mr Khan of Deira in Dubai, I hope the name on the cover rings a bell and you find yourself here.) She figured I was going to be a writer, but died six months before I started writing for a living. I wished several times while writing this book that she was here to see it. A lesson: talk to your parents and write down their stories, or else you find their handwriting in notebooks filled with recipes and glass painting instructions, and you wonder about the person behind them. People's traits, voices and smells slip out of memory.

My father. What to say? This book was possible because of him. His encouragement and support are the bedrock of his children's life. He did what I thought all fathers do: worried for me when I took unwise risks, helped me imagine better times when life was difficult, and kept checking in. He sent entire meals while I wrote. He showed me what it means to work hard, and to have faith even when the future isn't clear. (I also promised him a car many years ago, so please buy a few copies of this book.) This book, an accounting of a country we love, is for him.

Ever since talk of the acknowledgements began, two sets of eyes have been watching me write this. Rhea and Aanya Bhatia have waited with uncommon patience for the end of this book, and asked for nothing but that we pick up *Haroun and the Sea of Stories* where we left off seven years ago (and that I credit them appropriately for their superhuman patience). They live and breathe stories, and will one day write their own. This book, an album of a time they will one day barely recall, is for them. So much of this book is because of Richa, my wife and partner in scepticism and alarm, who grappled with this book as much as I did. She read each word of the book, and knew every person inside it and in discarded drafts, and remembered lines I had forgotten years ago. She is among the best editors I know. She showed me sometimes that the book wasn't everything and at other times that the book was the only thing. She has had more faith than I've had, and encouraged me to apply for fellowships that ended up changing this book for the better. This record of who we were, who we are, who we strive to be, is for her. *We did it, Rich.*

# Index